Craig Claiborne's Favorites

Books by Craig Claiborne

The New York Times Cook Book
The New York Times International Cook Book
Cooking with Herbs and Spices
Craig Claiborne's Kitchen Primer
The New York Times Menu Cook Book

Craig Claiborne's Favorites from The New York Times

Quadrangle / The New York Times Book Co.

We are indebted to a number of photographers and artists whose work is reproduced in this book:

Bill Aller, pages 6, 7, 19, 31, 56, 65, 70, 71, 111, 117, 126, 155, 167, 214, 222, 239, 268. David Scott Brown, page 293. Jane Clark, page 288. Bill Clough, page 351. Enos, page 220. Enrico Ferorelli, pages 40, 115, 348. Jack Graves, page 194. James Hamilton, pages 13, 35, 47, 86, 107, 145, 225, 226, 227, 243, 295. Paul Hanson, page 215. J. Hnizdovsky, page 122. William Hudson, page 284. KOES, page 318. Landini Landino, page 196. Ron Lieberman, page 162. Mike Lien, pages 81, 82. Gene Maggio, pages 26, 94, 234, 257, 262. Esteban Martin, pages 39, 102. The New York Times, pages 302, 329. Bradley Olman, pages 179, 207. Gosta Peterson, page 313. Richard Samperi, pages 275, 276. Deborah Shipler, page 340. Michel Tcherevkoff, pages 256, 323. Bill Wingell, page 90. Dan Wynn, pages 199, 200, 201, 202, 203, 251.

Published simultaneously in Canada by Optimum Publishing Company Limited, 245 rue St-Jacques, Montreal, Quebec, H2Y 1M6.

Design by Paul Hanson

Library of Congress Cataloging in Publication Data

Claiborne, Craig.
  Craig Claiborne's Favorites from the New York times.

  Includes index.
  1. Cookery.   I. Title: Favorites from the New York times.
TX715.C5743   641.5   75-10599
ISBN 0-8129-0584-9

Second printing, November 1975

To Pleasure
the greatest muse
of them all

Contents

Foreword

I joined *The New York Times* almost 20 years ago—September 1957, to be specific. That surely must be yesterday for I recall in clear and careful detail the moment a telephone call arrived to inform me that I had been chosen to serve as *The Times* food editor.

Until 1957 I had been enormously discontent with almost all the professional aspects of my life. I had worked in public relations both in Chicago and in New York, and to say that I despised that line of work is to phrase the matter as delicately as possible. At the time, my major mission—an awful confession—was to "peddle" recipes using a national brand product generically termed "the yellow shortening." I would develop the recipes in my firm's test kitchen and offer them to food editors with the awful pretense that the shortening was all but the equal of the more expensive spread. Shameless. The conscience reels.

My predecessor at *The Times* was a vastly talented, knowledgeable lady named Jane Nickerson, and it was common knowledge in the so-called New York food establishment that Miss Nickerson, early in 1957, had decided to retire with her husband and children to Florida.

It was rumored that scores of applicants had filed through the employment offices of *The Times* with the goal of scrambling their eggs, so to speak, in Miss Nickerson's soon to be vacated omelet pan. Although I had known of her impending departure for months, it had never occurred to me—for one reason of ego or another—to apply for her job. Among other things, food editing was almost exclusively female territory. It was also a field dominated by home economists, and a home economist I wasn't—in spirit or training.

Although I had never worked as a reporter, I did hold a degree in journalism from Missouri University. More important I had spent a year at what was reputedly the finest hotel school in Europe, the Ecole Hôtelière, the professional school of the Swiss Hotelkeeper's Association in Lausanne. I had even finished eighth out of sixty (and most were Europeans) in the course in cuisine.

It was either in July or August of 1957, during a lunch with Jane at Manhattan's "21," that the thought entered my brain for the first time. I returned to my office with unaccustomed haste and, door closed, I wrote a feverish note to Jane asking if she felt there was even a remote possibility that *The Times* might consider an application from me. Not a word in reply.

A week or so later I was spending a few days on Fire Island

and was walking the beach in a prevailing dispirited humor when an acquaintance yelled from a pier that I was wanted on the telephone. It was *The New York Times*. Jane's voice on the other end of the line told me that I mustn't be too optimistic, but the editors wanted to talk to me. She had used my letter as a sort of application. I took a boat to the nearest town with a train and before sundown was interviewed by Elizabeth Penrose Howkins, the editor of what was then known as The Women's Page. It was love or an all embracing kind of respect at first sight. I raced back to Fire Island with what I am not ashamed to call a near delirious joy. Somehow, after 37 years full of doubt and discomfort, I had landed, safely, smack in the middle of the goddam target. I remember walking the beach the next morning, one moment elated, the next moment possessed with demons of wonder: What would one fill columns with day by day, year by year? I passed a man surface-casting. He hauled in a bluefish. They were running well that summer. That, at least, was the first column I ever wrote in my mind: Twenty Ways of Cooking Bluefish. And through some miracle (I am by no means above believing in extraterrestrial forces), new subjects came about week after week. Even year after year.

A few days ago, while riffling through an accumulation of old articles and clippings yellowed with time, I came across an article written about me by Gael Greene, a good friend and much admired colleague, for the now defunct *Look* magazine. In that article I stated that I would not leave *The New York Times* for $100,000 or some other exorbitant and arbitrary figure. I felt very strongly on that point; it was a quote not to be taken lightly. And yet, 15 years later, through some puzzling arrangement of circumstances, I did leave *The Times*.

It was in the spring of 1972. I have learned over the years that there's never a single reason for a major move in anyone's life, but if I were to give just one, I'd say I was tired. A decade and a half of writing three columns a week, plus the daily grind of visiting restaurants on the average of twice a day, and eating and writing about all those meals. (There were periods when I literally visited eight and more restaurants a day.) I had just returned from a long and exhausting trip halfway around the world, reporting from Hong Kong, Japan, Ethiopia, and Kenya. I badly needed a rest, and with considerable reluctance, I "retired" to the sand and seagulls on East Hampton.

It took me two years to discover there can be a surfeit not only of milk and honey but sand and seagulls, and thus I came back to *The Times* at the outset of 1974. I now have the best of both worlds. I have been absolved of local restaurant reporting and can finally face New York's dining establishment with a certain equanimity if not to say pleasure. And I still have my sand and seagulls as my visits to Manhattan, frantic place that it is, are kept at a minimum and most of my time is spent at a typewriter and stove in my home in East Hampton.

On my return to *The Times* I decided to come to grips with a problem that has given me genuine concern over the years. I have been asked hundreds of times by readers to devise some painless and failsafe method of keeping newspaper recipes intact. They are impossible to file. They crumble with age. They get lost (we get scores of requests for copies). They are outsized and often printed back to back. The frustration is certainly understandable. I have combed newspapers throughout the world to see if someone somewhere has come up with a solution. To the best of my knowledge, no one has. This book, conceived on my return to *The Times,* is the sole answer I can propose.

This book is not altogether a cookbook in the conventional sense although it does include more than 250 recipes, international in scope and running the gamut from appetizers to desserts. This volume is a collection of nearly all the columns that appeared under my by-line during the year 1974. It is projected as the first of an annual collection of such columns. In ways, it is a journal of my first year back at *The Times.*

Putting together this book, there were, of necessity, certain deletions made, but they are minor and are far outweighed by numerous emendations. These include certain personal and anecdotal reflections, some of which touch on my private life and all of which reflect a highly personal approach to cooking. There are also answers to readers' inquiries and other information I thought might be helpful.

In writing my columns, it has been my privilege and pleasure to interview some of the greatest amateur cooks, professional chefs, and "food philosophers" in this country and throughout the world. I am especially indebted to my great colleague and friend Pierre Franey, one of the greatest French chefs in America. His contributions over the years have been immeasurable, and since my return to *The Times,* to my great pleasure, we have shared a by-line on Sunday pieces.

As I see it, cooking is like music. It's comforting when you are alone. It can reach heights when shared with others, one or more. Either way it's to be enjoyed. So please enjoy. If the recipes in this volume give you pleasure, it will be gratification of a higher order.

Craig Claiborne's Favorites

January 1974

ALTHOUGH WE PAY our taxes to the town of East Hampton, the precise location of our home and kitchen is a tiny place called Springs about seven miles from the heart of East Hampton village on Long Island, New York. Springs is a small community of artists, the most famous of whom is without question Willem de Kooning. It is also a community of writers, the best known of whom is Jean Stafford, the Pulitzer Prize-winning short story writer and novelist. Although tiny, Springs is an enormously civic-minded place that each year has a number of fund-raising affairs to which Pierre Franey and I contribute various dishes, the sale of which benefits scholarship funds, community landscaping, and so on.

One of the most memorable fund raisings we participated in was a "gastronomic gala" for an annual celebration known as the Artists Festival. With two great chefs to assist us—Jean Vergnes, now the chef-proprietor of Le Cirque restaurant in New York, and Albert Kumin, one of the great pastry chefs of America and an instructor at the Culinary Institute of America in Hyde Park, New York—we prepared a meal for fifty people which was cooked and served in the local community hall called Ashawagh. The meal began with Striped Bass Tout Paris and the main course was Stuffed Squabs Derby. Years later an almost identical menu served for a Sunday Magazine feature titled "A Last Meal." The article concerned what we would ask for if we were allowed one last great meal on earth. This, incidentally, is a game we have played with many chefs throughout the world. It is astonishing how many chefs say for their last great feast they would like things on the order of tripe à la mode de Caen, cassoulet, and breaded pig's feet—real peasant fare. The recipes for "A Last Meal" come up on page 12.

P.S. To tell you the truth, we would willingly settle for a pound of fresh caviar and fresh buttered toast.

The Succulent Scallop

Lex McClosky, a tall, blond, handsome Bonacker with a fine tooth-paste grin, lifted a freshly harvested bay scallop from a yard-long dredge, opened it with his pen knife and threw the top shell over the side. He discarded the gooey dark mass that surrounded the scallop's coveted white muscle and popped that morsel into his mouth. No lemon juice, no salt, no nothing.

"Sweet," he averred and added, "I like scallops, but I can't afford to eat 'em that often."

Mr. McClosky—28 years old last week—was pursuing the profession that he has followed almost all his life, scalloping all winter, fishing all summer.

"When I was a kid," he said, "I scalloped with an old man named Harvey Fields. He paid me $10 a day. I went on my own when I was 14."

"How on earth could you afford a boat?" a passenger asked.

"Well, it wasn't much of a boat."

The scallop season in Bonacker waters (the name derives from the people who live around Accabonac Lake in East Hampton, but it has come to be applied to people who have lived on the eastern tip of Long Island for several generations as well as to places there that are land-marks) lasts from about the middle of September to the end of March.

"During the first two weeks of the season when the weather's good and the whole lake is loaded with scallops, I take my wife along," the fisherman continued. "With two people in a boat you can legally take 20 bushels of scallops in state waters; if you're alone, you're only allowed 10." The McCloskys are the parents of a girl and a boy, aged 4½ and 1½ years respectively.

Mr. McClosky's work day, summer and winter, is from before dawn to after dusk. These days, clad in double and triple weather gear, he gets into his boat just before sun-up and, short minutes later, his boat arrives in the middle of Montauk Lake. Over the hum of a motor he explained that he rarely misses a day of harvest.

"The only time I miss is when the harbor's frozen or when it's too rough or too cold. The wind's the worst that can happen to you. It *really* takes the fun out of it when it's under 20 degrees."

The scalloping procedure is backbreaking, but it is relatively simple. Mr. McClosky's 18-foot boat (scallop boats hereabouts are called "shar-pies") has six dredges, metal frames with seinelike, interlinking metal

Lex McClosky, one of the best-known scallopers and fisherman on eastern Long Island, tosses a metal frame dredge over the side. Each dredging takes about two minutes after dredge is overboard.

rings or woven line. Either four or six of the dredges are thrown over the side into the six-foot deep waters for each haul. The front dredges are primarily for clearing away sea grass, generally a mixture of eel grass and "sputnik" grass. A visitor asked how the latter achieved such a recently coined name.

"These waters didn't always have that kind of grass," he said. "It showed up in the lake at about the same time the Russians put up their first sky launch so everybody called it "sputnik-grass."

The skipper hauled up the second dredges, and mingled with a few dozen scallops were strands of sea grass, empty shells, and rocks. The scallops in the shell were quickly sorted and tossed into a half-bushel basket.

Scallops, the gentleman explained, have an 18-month life-span. Like an oyster, when a scallop is spawned it is so minute it is not visible to the naked eye. A full-grown scallop is possessed of a "growth" ring that occurs at the end of the first cycle of its life. The ring, which occurs halfway up the scallop shell, is curved and parallel to the upper perimeter of the scallop. The scallop at its maturity measures about two and one-quarter inches in width, and the scallop must have either the growth ring or that measurement to be taken legally.

At the end of the day the young man had harvested slightly more than five bushels of scallops, which he considers not a bad haul for an average season such as this. Last year was an excellent year, and next year, according to omens he did not explain, promises to be exceptional.

At the end of each day's harvest the scallops in the shell are taken to local shucking sheds where professional openers, generally women, wield their knives to extract a pure white muscle. A team of good workers, Mr. McClosky stated, can clean a bushel of scallops in slightly more than 10 minutes. Eventually each day's harvest is trucked to a local fish market, and the scallops are then packaged for Manhattan and points West.

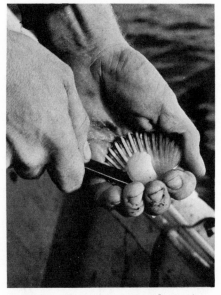

Once the technique is mastered, opening a scallop in the shell is a split-second operation. The knife is inserted between the shells near the base of the scallop. The top shell is tossed away and the dark mass that surrounds the coveted white "muscle" is removed. The muscle itself is then carved out.

Scallops with Tomato and Paprika Sauce

1 *pound scallops*
4 *tablespoons butter*
  Salt and freshly ground
  pepper to taste
¼ *cup cognac*
1 *cup tomato sauce (see note)*
1 *teaspoon paprika*
1 *teaspoon finely chopped*
  garlic
3 *tablespoons finely chopped*
  parsley
6 *teaspoons grated Gruyère*
  or Parmesan cheese

1. Preheat the oven to 450 degrees.

2. If the scallops are very large, cut them into 3 or 4 crosswise slices. If they are medium, cut them in half. If they are very small, leave them whole.

3. Heat 2 tablespoons of butter and add the scallops and salt and pepper to taste. Cook, shaking the skillet, about 2 minutes. Add the cognac and ignite it. Cook about 1 minute and add the tomato sauce, paprika, garlic, parsley, salt and pepper. Cook about 2 minutes.

4. Spoon equal amounts of the mixture into 6 scallop shells or individual ramekins. Sprinkle each with 1 teaspoon of cheese and 1 teaspoon of butter. Arrange on a baking dish and bake 10 minutes.

Yield: 6 servings.

Note: To make a quick tomato sauce, empty 2 cups of peeled, chopped, fresh or canned tomatoes into a saucepan. Cook to reduce to 1 cup. Add salt and pepper to taste.

Scallops in the Shell with Snail Butter

1½   *pints (3 cups) fresh bay scallops*
  2   *cups (approximately) milk*
      Salt and freshly ground pepper to taste
  3   *shallots, coarsely chopped*
  2   *cloves garlic, finely minced*
  5   *sprigs parsley*
  1   *cup fine fresh bread crumbs*
      Flour for dredging
      Oil for deep frying
  8   *tablespoons butter*
      Finely chopped parsley for garnish

1. Place the scallops in a mixing bowl and add the milk, salt and pepper.

2. Place the shallots, garlic, and parsley sprigs in the container of an electric blender and blend, stirring down as necessary. Empty the mixture into a mixing bowl and add the bread crumbs. Blend with the fingers. Set aside.

3. Drain the scallops and dredge them lightly in flour. Toss to coat and shake off excess flour.

4. In a heavy skillet, heat the oil for deep frying and add the scallops. Cook over high heat, stirring and shaking the skillet, about 3 minutes. Do not overcook. Remove the scallops with a slotted spoon and drain on absorbent peper towels.

5. Drain the skillet and wipe it out. Add the butter and when the foam subsides and the butter starts to turn hazelnut brown, return the scallops to the skillet, shaking the skillet briskly.

6. Sprinkle the scallops with the bread crumb mixture and cook, stirring, until piping hot, about 1 minute. Spoon them into 6 decorative clam shells or individual ramekins. Serve piping hot sprinkled with chopped parsley.

Yield: 6 servings.

Scallops and Shrimp Mayonnaise

¾   *cup dry white wine*
10   *peppercorns*
  3   *sprigs parsley*

2 sprigs fresh thyme or ½
   teaspoon dried
½ bay leaf
1 tablespoon sliced shallots
   or onion
1 clove garlic, sliced
   Salt to taste
1½ pounds fresh bay scallops
   (or sea scallops, quartered)
1½ pounds raw shrimp (about
   36), peeled and deveined
1 cup mayonnaise (see
   recipe)
2 tablespoons finely chopped
   shallots

1. Combine the wine, pepper-corns, parsley, thyme, bay leaf, sliced shallots, garlic, and salt in a saucepan. Simmer 5 minutes and add the scallops. Cover and sim-mer 3 minutes. Let cool.

2. Scoop out the scallops and let them chill in the refrigerator. Bring the liquid in which the scal-lops cooked to the boil. Add the shrimp. Simmer 3 minutes and let cool. Remove the shrimp and let them chill in the refrigerator.

3. Blend the scallops and shrimp with the mayonnaise and chopped shallots. Spoon the mix-ture into a serving dish and serve.

Yield: 6 to 10 servings.

Mayonnaise

1 egg yolk
1 teaspoon wine vinegar
1 to 3 teaspoons prepared
   mustard, preferably Dijon
   or Düsseldorf
   A few drops of Tabasco
   Salt and freshly ground
   pepper to taste

1 cup oil, preferably a light
   olive oil or a combination
   of olive oil and peanut,
   vegetable, or corn oil
   Lemon juice to taste,
   optional

1. Place the yolk in a mixing bowl and add the vinegar, mus-tard, Tabasco, salt and pepper to taste. Beat vigorously for a second or two with a wire whisk or elec-tric beater.

2. Start adding the oil gradu-ally, beating continuously with the whisk or electric beater. Con-tinue beating and adding oil until all of it is used. Taste the mayon-naise and add more salt to taste and the lemon juice if desired. If all the mayonnaise is not to be used immediately, beat in a table-spoon of water. This will help sta-bilize the mayonnaise and retard its turning when stored in the re-frigerator.

Yield: About 1 cup.

Breaded Scallops

1 pound scallops
1 egg
1 teaspoon peanut,
   vegetable, or corn oil
   Salt to taste
1 tablespoon water
   Flour for dredging
1 cup fine bread crumbs
   Oil for deep frying
   Lemon wedges

1. If the scallops are freshly opened, rinse and drain them.

2. Combine the egg, 1 tea-spoon oil, salt, and water in a dish such as a pie plate.

3. Dredge the scallops lightly on all sides in flour. Turn them in the egg mixture until coated. Dredge them on all sides in the bread crumbs. Arrange them on a rack so that they do not touch. The scallops may be prepared to this point about an hour in advance or they may be cooked immediately.

4. Heat the oil for deep frying and add the scallops. Cook them quickly, stirring with a slotted spoon, until golden brown. Drain on absorbent toweling. Serve with cucumber mayonnaise (see recipe), tartar sauce, or if you desire, a cocktail sauce. Serve garnished with lemon wedges.

Yield: 4 to 6 servings.

Cucumber mayonnaise

1   *cup mayonnaise,*
    preferably freshly made
    (see recipe, page 9)
1   *cup finely diced cucumber*
2   *tablespoons finely chopped*
    parsley

1. To cube the cucumber, peel it and scrape out the seeds with a small spoon or melon ball scoop. Finely dice the flesh.

2. Spoon the mayonnaise into a mixing bowl and add the cucumber and parsley. Blend well and serve.

Yield: About 2 cups.

Subsequent to this column, numerous letters arrived from readers about the extraordinary non-use of the reddish, arc-shaped coral that is part and parcel of scores of scallop dishes served in other countries. The editor of the *Sydney Morning Herald Limited,* Derryn Hinch, wrote: "I read your piece on scallops today and it raised a question that has puzzled me ever since I left my native Australia. Back there, where scallops are pronounced 'skollops,' the meat is always served with the bright orange roe attached. It doubles the size of the scallop, improves the taste, and is esthetically pleasing. Have you any idea why the best part of the shellfish is never served in this country?"

Mrs. G. Warren French of Upper Montclair, New Jersey, stated that she had hoped to learn "why we can't buy that beautiful roe that comes with the scallops in other countries. My fish market," she wrote, "says 'they throw it away.' Why should that be so when that morsel is even more delectable than the scallops! Two weeks ago at the Hermitage Hotel at Mt. Cook, New Zealand, I ordered coquille St. Jacques twice in a row because it had the roe in it and was utterly delicious. Please tell me if you know any place in this area that sells the roe with the scallops. If not, why not?"

We telephoned our friend, the redoubtable John vonGlahn of the Fishery Council, a trade association for the fishing industry, and he seemed to confirm that reply by Mrs. French's fish dealer. He stated that the roe is undoubtedly discarded because of the nature of things in "this land of plenty."

Scallops, as the article noted, are invariably shucked by hand immediately after the harvest, and it is an act that goes so fast as to resemble prestidigitation. A knife is quickly, almost surgically, entered into the shell and whisked around the white muscle which is reserved; all the other parts, including the roe, are jettisoned.

We recently did our own on-the-spot research into the question of the availability and edibility of the roe in American waters. We purchased six or so scallops, unopened in the shell, from our local fish market, Stuart's in Amagansett. We opened the scallops and reserved the roe and cooked it briefly with the muscles.

The roe from local scallops is smaller than that found in European waters. It is not particularly appealing to the eye, having a rather insipid beige color and a too-soft texture. In short, we found it had little going for it. The color of roe does vary from water to water and Mr. vonGlahn agreed with us that the scallop roe from local waters undoubtedly differs to a considerable degree from that of European, and doubtlessly, Australian and New Zealand waters.

Retracing our steps, we would like to add that the cucumber mayonnaise served with the breaded scallops a page back is also quite good with poached fish, smoked fish fillets, tinned fish, such as tuna or salmon, and hard-cooked eggs. It can be used as a base for something akin to salade russe with the addition of other cold vegetables like boiled potatoes, string beans, and carrots.

A Last Meal

WITH PIERRE FRANEY

Menu

Fresh caviar
Striped bass with
champagne sauce
Stuffed squabs Derby
Braised endive
Watercress and
Boston lettuce salad
Brie
Grapefruit sherbet

Vodka, Stolichnaya
Montrachet, Marquis de
Laguiche, 1970
Château Ausone, 1947

Romanée-Conti, 1959
Champagne,
Dom Pérignon, 1966

What would you command if you were allowed one last great meal on this earth? We have our answer. The menu would move blissfully from caviar with vodka (Stolichnaya, by choice) to, in due course, a fine fat squab stuffed with truffles and foie gras. It would end with an elegant ice. Now, preferences in food are highly subjective and there may be those who would question our choice of squab. But to our minds squab is one of the most sumptuous of birds and for that last go-round at table, we would not willingly accept a substitute. Except, just possibly, quail. We did not choose filet mignon as a principal dish, a fact that may astonish beef lovers, but as we have noted many times, we find it monotonous. We prefer hamburger. And what kind of cheese would there be for one's last meal? We choose Brie because ot us it is the king of French cheeses.

And that last meal would not be a solitary one. Not by any means. We would wish to share it with our closest friends—seven of them. The cost? Well, the price of caviar being what it is (about $90 a pound at this writing) and the price of Romanée-Conti 1959 being what *it* is ($200 a bottle), this coveted menu of ours—unstinting in any area—would hover around $900. Without the caviar and the wines, it might deflate to around $90.

Craig Claiborne selects the wines for a once-in-a-lifetime meal.

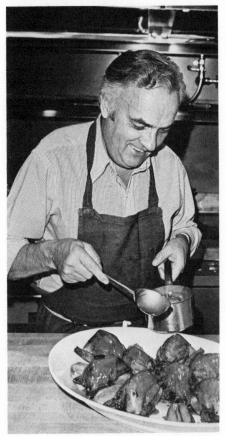

Pierre Franey spoons the sauce over stuffed squabs Derby.

Striped Bass with Champagne Sauce

2 cups fish velouté (see recipe)
4 pounds striped bass fillets
2 tablespoons butter
4 tablespoons finely chopped shallots
Salt and freshly ground pepper to taste
½ pound mushrooms, thinly sliced (about 4 cups)
1 cup brut champagne
1 cup heavy cream
Juice of ½ lemon

1. Prepare the velouté.

2. Preheat oven to 450 degrees.

3. While the velouté simmers, cut the fish into 8 equal portions.

4. Select a baking dish large enough to hold the fish in one layer. Grease the dish with half the butter. Sprinkle the shallots and salt and pepper to taste over the bottom of the dish. Arrange the fish pieces over all and scatter the sliced mushrooms over the fish. Sprinkle lightly with salt and pepper. Sprinkle with champagne.

5. Cut a square or round of wax paper to fit over the fish. Cover the fish with the wax paper and bring to the boil on top of the stove. Place the dish in the oven. Bake 20 minutes.

6. Remove the wax paper and carefully pour the cooking liquid into a saucepan. With a spoon, remove most of the mushroom slices and add them to the liquid. Cook over high heat until the cooking liquid is reduced to about 1 cup, about 12 minutes. Add the velouté and stir briskly with a wire whisk until blended and smooth. Add the cream and lemon juice. Swirl in the remaining tablespoon of butter. Serve the hot sauce over the fish.

Yield: 8 servings.

Fish velouté

4 *tablespoons butter*
8 *tablespoons flour*
2 *cups fish stock (see recipe, page 67, omit tomato)*

1. Melt the butter in a saucepan and add the flour, stirring with a wire whisk.

2. Add the stock, stirring rapidly with the whisk until the mixture is thickened and smooth. Continue cooking over low heat, stirring frequently, about 45 minutes.

Yield: About 2 cups.

Stuffed Squabs Derby

8 *squabs, each about ¾ pound cleaned weight (see note)*
2 *cups (approximately) baked rice (see recipe)*
5 *tablespoons butter*
8 *squab livers, each cut in half*
1¼ *ounces pure foie gras, available in tins in fine specialty food markets*

1 *tablespoon chopped truffles*
   Salt and freshly ground pepper to taste
3 *tablespoons cognac*
1½ *cups brown sauce for squab (see recipe)*
8 *truffle slices*

1. The squabs should be cleaned and ready for roasting, but reserve the necks, feet, and gizzard for the brown sauce. Reserve the livers for the stuffing.

2. Preheat oven to 425 degrees.

3. Prepare the rice and set it aside.

4. Heat 1 tablespoon butter in a small skillet and add the livers. Cook over high heat, shaking the skillet and stirring, about 1 minute. The livers must cook quickly or they will be tough. Add the livers to the rice.

5. Cube the foie gras. Add the foie gras and chopped truffles to the rice and stir to blend well.

6. Sprinkle the inside of the squabs with salt and pepper to taste and stuff them with the rice mixture. Truss the squabs. Sprinkle with salt and pepper.

7. Melt 3 tablespoons of butter in a heavy roasting pan large enough to hold the squabs. Turn the squabs in the butter until coated on all sides. Place squabs on their sides and bake 15 minutes. Baste often. Turn onto other side and bake 15 minutes, basting frequently. Place squabs on their backs and continue roasting and basting for another 10 to 15 minutes.

8. Remove squabs to a warm platter and cover with foil.

9. Skim off all fat from the roasting pan, leaving the squab drippings. Add 2 tablespoons cognac and ignite it. Pour in the brown sauce and stir to blend. Put the sauce through a fine sieve and bring it to the boil. Swirl in the remaining tablespoon of butter. Add the remaining cognac and serve piping hot with the squab. Garnish each squab with a truffle slice before serving.

Yield: 8 servings.

Note: The squabs may be boned before stuffing and roasting. Squabs are available in fine poultry and meat markets. Grocery stores and supermarkets in Chinese communities also sell fresh squabs.

Baked rice

2½ *tablespoons butter*
2 *tablespoons minced onion*
¼ *teaspoon minced garlic*
1 *cup raw rice*
1½ *cups chicken stock*
2 *sprigs parsley*
1 *sprig fresh thyme or ¼ teaspoon dried*
½ *bay leaf*
⅛ *teaspoon cayenne or Tabasco to taste*

1. Preheat oven to 400 degrees.

2. Melt 1 tablespoon of the butter in a heavy saucepan and cook the onion and garlic, stirring with a wooden spoon, until the onion is translucent. Add the rice and stir briefly over low heat until all the grains are coated with butter.

3. Stir in the stock, making sure there are no lumps in the rice. Add the parsley, thyme, bay leaf, and cayenne. Cover with a close-fitting lid and place in the oven.

4. Bake the rice exactly 17 minutes. Remove the cover and discard the parsley and thyme sprigs and the bay leaf. Using a two-pronged fork, stir in the remaining butter.

Yield: About 2½ cups.

Brown sauce for squab

1 *tablespoon oil*
  Necks, feet, and gizzards from 8 squabs (see note)
  Salt and freshly ground pepper to taste
¼ *cup chopped celery*
½ *cup chopped onion*
½ *cup chopped carrot*
3 *sprigs fresh thyme or ½ teaspoon dried*
3 *sprigs parsley*
½ *bay leaf*
2 *tablespoons flour*
½ *cup dry white wine*
1 *cup chicken broth*
1 *cup water*
1 *tablespoon tomato paste*

1. Heat the oil in a small, heavy saucepan and add the necks, feet, and gizzards. Sprinkle with salt and pepper. Cook, stirring frequently, until parts are nicely browned all over. Drain.

2. Return the squab pieces to the saucepan and add the celery, onion, carrot, thyme, parsley, and bay leaf. Continue cooking, stirring occasionally, about 5 minutes.

3. Sprinkle with flour and stir until all pieces are well coated. Cook, stirring occasionally, about 5 minutes. Add the remaining ingredients and stir rapidly until blended. Bring to the boil and simmer, uncovered, 1½ hours. Put the sauce through a fine sieve, pressing the solids with the back of a wooden spoon to extract as much of the liquid as possible. Discard the solids. Put the sauce in a small saucepan and simmer, uncovered, about 30 minutes longer.

Yield: 1½ cups.

Note: If the squabs have been trimmed of their necks, feet, and so on, bony chicken pieces such as necks may be substituted.

Braised Endive

16 *heads Belgian endive*
    Juice of 1 lemon
4   *tablespoons butter*
    Salt to taste
½   *cup water*
1   *tablespoon sugar*

1. Preheat oven to 450 degrees.

2. Trim off and discard any discolored leaves from the endive. Place the endive in a kettle and add the lemon juice, 2 tablespoons of butter, salt, water, and sugar. Cover and bring to the boil on top of the stove.

3. Place the kettle in the oven and bake 30 to 40 minutes. Drain well.

4. Melt remaining 2 tablespoons of butter in a skillet large enough to hold the drained endive in one layer. Add endive and brown on one side. Turn and brown on the other side. Serve hot.

Yield: 8 servings.

Grapefruit Ice

2 *cups sugar*
4 *cups water*
2 *cups freshly squeezed*
   grapefruit juice
   Crème de cassis, optional
   Vodka, optional

1. Combine the sugar and water in a saucepan and bring to the boil. Add the grapefruit juice and cool. Chill thoroughly.

2. Pour the mixture into the container of an electric or hand-cranked ice cream freezer and freeze according to the manufacturer's instructions. Serve individual portions, if desired, with crème de cassis and a touch of cold vodka poured over.

Yield: 2 quarts or 12 to 14 servings. Any extra may be stored in the freezer.

We had an interesting response to this piece. Numerous readers wrote to tell us what they would choose for their last meal. Ellen Burr of

New Paltz, New York, put the question to her 10-year-old daughter and the following menu was proposed: "Pickled baby corn, fried fillets of fresh sunfish, fried mashed potato cakes, wild asparagus tips with lemon butter, cucumber salad, Brie, and Pastel petits fours."

Mrs. Sylvia Rosenthal of Manhattan stated that we had invented a new game, "the last meal game." "Three people called me today," she writes, "to ask what mine would be. At this moment, it would be a turkey sandwich with cole slaw and Russian dressing on very thin, very fresh, very sour rye bread, lots of strong fresh coffee, and marron glacé with chocolate ice cream."

Watercress

Superficially there isn't much to distinguish Oviedo (pronounced O-VEE-DO) from any other small town in the central sector of Florida. It's a sleepy village with lots of Spanish moss and palmetto, and most people in nearby Orlando never heard of it. In fact, there are probably a lot of people in the town itself who do not know that Oviedo is what might be called the watercress capital of the world.

Watercress is—with its deep green color and roughly heart-shaped leaves—one of the most eye-appealing greens known to man, and its peppery flavor gives a desirable fillip to salad bowls. Watercress is by no means "typically" American. It is grown all over the world including China, France, Italy, Switzerland, Cuba, and England. Britain, in fact, may be the nation that prizes it most highly. There are approximately 30 watercress producers in America—Ohio, California, Tennessee, Texas, Colorado, and so on; more than twice that number thrive in Britain.

When we arrived at the B & W watercress farm here—the technical name is B & W Quality Growers, Inc.—the management was intrigued to know how we'd ever heard of the enterprise. We admitted in truth it was almost by accident. We'd stumbled over a box of watercress in our local grocery store, Gristede's in East Hampton, a few days earlier and, as a watercress fancier of long standing, we noted the name and address of the shipper on the box.

The B & W farm has two owners, Don Weaver, 43 years old, and Richard Burgoon, 36. "My wife's family," Mr. Burgoon explained, "started the business here about 100 years ago.") Today, the firm distributes its product, generally by refrigerator truck, sometimes by air, from Texas to Canada and throughout the East Coast. New York City consumes almost 65 percent of its output.

Watercress, as the name implies, depends on water—lots of it—for its sustenance. The 150-acre B & W farm is divided up into enormous, rectangular sunken tracts or beds—each about a sixth of an acre. These are constantly moistened by artesian well water that gushes onto the beds at the rate of 20 gallons a minute. Only the roots of the greens are covered with water. The sprigs are airborne.

No one has ever devised a method to harvest watercress mechanically, and thus it is all done by hand labor. There are workers in the field who have been at their occupation for 25 or more years. Each cutter has his own equipment, principally a hand-honed eight-inch butcher knife, which is used for the harvest. The cutters, in hip boots, bend to their

task, grabbing a good-sized bundle of watercress in one hand, slashing it off at the stem with the other. The bundles are either tied with string or bound with rubber bands and deposited in wire baskets that are later carted to the packing warehouse.

We have always been impressed with the cleanliness of most of the bunches of watercress that have come our way, and one of the things we have long wondered about is whether the processors of watercress recommended washing their product in the home before using. The answer is "Yes."

"It isn't a question of impurities," Mr. Burgoon explained. "The fields are pure and the water is pure, but there are times when you may get a random piece of string or wood inside a bunch. So, why not wash it?"

After the watercress is gathered and bundled, it is carted to the packing house, where the bundles are chilled immediately in cold water and run on an "endless" conveyor belt until it's time to box them. The boxes are iced and eventually relayed to refrigerator trucks for the journey to wherever. Watercress gathered on Tuesday, to choose a random day, is delivered to New York grocery stores on Thursday morning.

"We'd like to convert to packing watercress in plastic bags, and it's a tough decision," Mr. Burgoon said. "The American public is used to recipes that call for one 'bunch' of watercress, and they'd be confused, in the beginning at least, if it came loose in plastic bags. A bag of cress would simply be a loose 'bunch.'

"But then we remind ourselves of the story of the man who first thought of packaging spinach in plastic bags. You know what happened. He went broke because the public couldn't adjust to it immediately. Today, of course, it's different. Nobody—well, almost nobody—buys spinach in bulk."

Watercress is excellent in salads, either alone or tossed with other greens such as Boston lettuce or Belgian endive. It also makes excellent soups and is the classic garnish for roast chicken—poulet roti au cresson.

Watercress and Mushroom Soup

1 *pound mushrooms*
5 *tablespoons butter*
   Salt and freshly ground
   pepper to taste
1 *teaspoon lemon juice*
1 *bunch watercress (about ¾*
   pound)
¼ *cup coarsely chopped*
   onion
3 *tablespoons flour*
3 *cups rich chicken broth*

1. Cut off the stems of the mushrooms and chop.

2. If the mushrooms are very small, leave the caps whole. If they are medium size, cut them in half. If they are large, quarter them.

3. Melt 3 tablespoons of butter in a saucepan and add the chopped mushroom stems and the caps. Sprinkle with salt, pepper, and lemon juice. Cover closely and cook about 10 minutes, stirring occasionally. Drain but reserve the liquid. There should be about ¾ cup. Set the drained mushrooms aside.

4. Cut off and reserve the tender leaves of the watercress. There should be about 4 cups loosely packed. Chop the watercress stems coarsely and set aside.

5. In a heavy kettle, heat 2 tablespoons of butter and add the onion. Add the chopped watercress stems and stir to wilt. Cook about 2 minutes and sprinkle with flour.

6. Measure out 1 cup of mushrooms and set aside. Add the remainder to the kettle. Add the mushroom liquid and the chicken broth, stirring. Simmer 10 minutes. Add the mixture to the container of an electric blender—it may be necessary to do this in several steps—and blend coarsely.

7. Return the soup to the kettle. Add the cup of reserved mushrooms and the watercress leaves. Bring to the boil and serve hot.

Yield: 6 servings.

Poulet Roti au Cresson

(Roast chicken with watercress)

1   3-pound chicken
    Salt and freshly ground
    pepper to taste
1   bunch watercress
4   tablespoons butter

1. Preheat oven to 45 degrees.

2. Sprinkle the inside of the chicken with salt and pepper.

3. Cut off the bottom stems of the watercress, about halfway up the stalks. Stuff the chicken with the stems and reserve the leaves in a plastic bag to keep them fresh.

4. Truss the chicken. Sprinkle the outside of the chicken with salt and pepper.

5. Lay the chicken on one side in a small baking dish and dot the top side with half the butter.

6. Place the chicken in the oven and bake, basting occasionally, about 15 minutes. When golden, turn the chicken onto the other side. Bake 15 minutes, basting often.

7. Turn the chicken onto its back and bake 15 minutes longer, basting.

8. Tip the chicken so that the inside juices run out into the baking dish.

9. Untruss the chicken. Carve the chicken and arrange on a warm platter. Pour the pan juices over.

10. Heat the remaining butter in a skillet until it is hazelnut brown. Pour over the chicken. Garnish one end of the platter with the reserved watercress leaves. As the chicken and watercress are served, spoon a little of the natural sauce over both chicken and watercress.

Yield: 4 servings.

Potage de Cresson

(Watercress soup)

2   firm, bright green bunches
    of watercress
6   cups chicken broth
12 tablespoons butter
6   tablespoons flour
3   cups freshly cubed white
    bread
3   egg yolks
⅛   teaspoon grated nutmeg

1. Cut the watercress bunches in half and rinse well under cold running water. Drain well.

2. Bring a large quantity of water to the boil and add the watercress. Stir and bring to the boil. Simmer about 3 minutes and drain in a colander. Run under cold water. Drain and squeeze between the hands to extract most of the moisture.

3. Put the watercress in the container of an electric blender and add ½ cup of broth. Blend, stirring down as necessary.

4. Melt 4 tablespoons of butter in a saucepan and add the flour, stirring with a wire whisk. When blended, add the remaining broth and simmer 30 minutes.

5. Heat 4 tablespoons of butter in a skillet and add the bread cubes. Toss the cubes until golden brown all over. Set aside.

6. In a mixing bowl, blend the puréed watercress with the egg yolks and nutmeg. Add about ¼ cup of the boiling soup to the mixture, stirring. Add this to the soup, stirring constantly. Bring to the boil. Do not cook or the soup will curdle. Beat in the remaining 4 tablespoons of butter.

7. Serve the hot soup in bowls, garnishing each serving with the bread croutons.

Yield: 6 to 8 servings.

Frequently the subject of a food article in *The New York Times* will be quite astonished when you walk in for an interview, but no one could have been more surprised than the people who grow watercress in Oviedo, Florida. "Do you mean," one of the owners asked when we walked in with a photographer, "you flew all the way from New York just to watch watercress growing?" We stayed with them for about two hours and had, in fact, a fine time just watching the watercress grow.

A Stewpot on Every Hearth

WITH PIERRE FRANEY

In this age of energy consciousness, fireplace cookery is suddenly a better idea than ever. It is an interesting challenge, and a watched pot (one has to watch the pot and tend the fire) can create an exceptional appetite.

Potée Bourguignonne
(A main course Burgundian soup)

1   *2-pound chicken*
1   *cup finely chopped onion*
½ *teaspoon dried thyme*
1   *teaspoon chopped garlic*
2   *sweet Italian sausages*
    (about ¼ pound)
1   *chicken liver*
½ *cup fine bread crumbs*
1   *egg*
    Salt and freshly ground
    pepper to taste
1½ *pounds boneless shoulder*
    of pork, tied
7   *cups water*
1   *large onion*
5   *carrots, trimmed and*
    scraped
½ *bay leaf*
4   *cups closely packed*
    cabbage wedges
    Sea salt or kosher salt

1. Remove the fat from the wide cavity of the chicken and chop it. Put it in a saucepan and add the chopped onion. Cook on top of the stove until the onion is wilted. Add the thyme and garlic.

2. Remove the sausage meat from the casings and add it to the saucepan. Chop the chicken liver and add it. Add the bread crumbs, egg, salt and pepper to taste. Blend well. Stuff the chicken with the mixture and truss the chicken. Set aside.

3. Place the pork in a fireproof earthenware casserole or Dutch oven and add the 7 cups of water, salt and pepper. Add the onion, peeled and cut into eighths.

4. Cut carrots into thirds, add to casserole. Add bay leaf and cover. Place the casserole on the front bricks in the fireplace. Place hot coals beneath and around the casserole in the fireplace according to instructions below.

5. When it begins to boil, cook 1 hour and add cabbage. Cook 30 minutes and add chicken. Cook covered, always maintaining fiery hot coals and wood beneath and around the casserole. Cook 45 minutes to 1 hour or until the chicken is tender. Serve the soup with the vegetables along with the sliced pork, carved chicken, and chicken stuffing. Serve with sea salt or kosher salt on the side.

Yield: 6 to 8 servings.

How to Prepare a Fireplace

Clean out the fireplace, removing the grate if there is one. Place 4 fire or flue bricks toward the rear of the fireplace flat-side down, domino fashion. (Do not use ordinary red bricks for this. Fire bricks can be bought at builders' supply companies for about 40 cents each.) Place them parallel left to right with 5 or 6 inches of space between each brick.

Arrange 2 or 3 more bricks in front of these on which a fireproof casserole can be placed. Leave space between the bricks for hot coals. Construct the fire on and behind the rear bricks. Use long-burning hardwood such as oak or apple. Do not use an oily wood (like pine) that may impart flavor. Use as little paper as possible in lighting the fire.

Let the wood fire burn until most of the flames subside and the wood is fiery hot. Shovel some of the hot natural charcoal beneath the casserole and keep the hot wood situated closely around the casserole. Replenish wood as necessary to insure constant cooking.

One of the first requests on our return to *The New York Times* was that Pierre Franey and I create a dish to be cooked in the fireplace. (Remember that awful energy crisis or at least what seemed the beginnings of one?) When I told Pierre Franey, who is from a very small town in Burgundy, he said, "I was 12 years old before I knew people cooked any other way."

Dishes from a Small Kitchen

"This is my 57th dwelling place or whatever it is you call home," Barbara McGinniss recalled as she flattened a clove of garlic for a dish of zucchini provençale. "If that seems like a precise number, it is. I took a course in psychology a few years back, and my term paper had to do with shifting patterns in personal living.

"My father was in the Foreign Service, and we lived all over the country and a lot of the world. Oddly enough, I still recall most of the places where I've lived in terms of the food I ate. Italy is always basically a pastry shop on the Adriatic that sold incredible meringues. Argentina consisted of small and marvelous meat-filled pastries. We ate them on the cook's day off. And London was lovely, light spongecakes smeared with currant jelly and powdered sugar on top.

"London was also something else. We had a new Irish cook named Martha who informed us she made the best suet pudding in the world, and we thought that sounded interesting, indeed. She made one and it was dreadful, absolutely inedible, more suet than pudding.

"When it was served, she left the room and everyone took a bite. We all glanced at each other and father stood up. He picked up all of our portions and threw them into the dining room fireplace. A thicket of smoke billowed out, so we opened the windows and fanned it away, horrified that the cook might catch us in that charade. When she returned, we all told her how delicious the pudding was and she said, 'Oh, I'll make you another.'

"'Listen, Martha,' my mother said, 'I think we'd better discuss that.'"

Miss McGinniss lives in a standard-size "bachelor" apartment in Manhattan that consists of a living room, roughly L-shaped, a nice-sized bath, and a kitchen that is approximately the size of a double telephone booth. Thus she seems eminently qualified as the author of a just-completed manuscript tentatively titled *Claustrophobic Cooking* for people—like half of Manhattan maybe?—who must tailor their talents to kindred circumstances.

The book has numerous interesting recipes as well as advice for cooks who must work in closely circumscribed quarters. It includes such dicta as "Avoid a flotilla of small dishes" and "It's best to avoid broiling steak in small apartments because it smells up the place at the last minute." Miss McGinniss is no armchair oracle. She has been known to entertain 40 or more guests at a single soiree or matinee; she frequently offers a variety of dinners three evenings running; and she puts up preserves and pickles such as watermelon rind pickle, chutney, and apple butter made with cider. These are made, in season, within the confines of her kitchen and she sells them, without advertising, to friends and acquaintances.

"I started cooking when I was an infant," she confided. "As a child I hated dolls and on my eighth birthday my gifts included a candy thermometer, a meat thermometer, and two butcher aprons. Even at that age I couldn't stand those 'cute' hostess aprons since I always got splattered when I wore them."

One of her first gifts was also a remarkably sophisticated and still valid cookbook for children. It may or may not still be in print, but it should be. It was written by Florence La Ganke, who was food editor of the *Cleveland Plain Dealer* at the time the book was published by Little, Brown & Company in 1929. It is titled *Patty Pans,* and it offers such diverse fare as a chapter on how to set a table, the importance of keeping a kitchen clean and neat, and why you should eat your potato before you eat your dessert. There are also recipes for admirable foods like clear tomato soup, chocolate blanc mange, beef birds, and drop cookies.

Miss McGinniss's birth name is Barbara Mace (she has been married twice but became known professionally as McGinniss during her first

Barbara McGinniss finds her minuscule kitchen no obstacle.

marriage and afterwards retained the name). Her enthusiasm for cooking may have stemmed from her father, who was an agricultural economist. Among his other absorbing achievements, he was the co-inventor during World War I with Armours of canned meat. "I'm certain," Miss McGinniss said, "there are generations of soldiers who would willingly have killed him."

Miss McGinniss, who writes films for television and is involved in public relations work, states that her mother hated food preparation in all forms but was a fascinating hostess. "She always made certain there was a potted palm in the house for people to throw their olive pits. And, when she entertained over cocktails, if she became bored with her guests or thought they'd stayed too long, she'd serve demitasse cups of very hot black bean soup with a lemon slice. After you've been drinking, it gives you a killing appetite and everyone leaves for home or a restaurant."

Two of the dishes served at a memorable meal in Barbara McGinniss's "claustrophobic" quarters recently included an excellent leg of lamb with flageolets (pea beans may be substituted) and zucchini provençale. The following recipes embrace these dishes, as well as one for a three-day marmalade that she has adapted from her childhood cookbook, *Patty Pans*.

Leg of Lamb with Flageolets

1 *pound dried flageolets (available in delicacy and specialty food shops of major department stores) or pea beans*
2 *pounds onions, thinly sliced*
¼ *cup butter*
2 *pounds potatoes, unpeeled and thinly sliced*
2 *tablespoons salt*
¼ *teaspoon pepper*
1 *cup rich fresh or canned beef bouillon*
1 *bay leaf*
1 *6-to-7-pound leg of lamb*
1 *teaspoon rosemary*

1. Cover beans with cold water. Refrigerate, covered, overnight.

2. Drain the beans. Into a 6-quart saucepan pour 2 quarts water. Bring to a boil and add beans. Cover and simmer 45 minutes or until tender. Drain.

3. Preheat oven to 325 degrees.

4. Sauté onions in hot butter until golden.

5. In a 5-quart saucepan (see note) or Dutch oven, layer half of the potatoes, onions, beans, salt and pepper.

6. Repeat layering. Heat bouillon with bay leaf to boiling. Pour over vegetables.

7. Rub lamb with rosemary. Place on top of vegetables. Bake uncovered 2 to 2½ hours or until rare or medium well done.

Yield: 8 servings.

Note: The utensil Miss McGinniss uses for this dish measures 13 by 10 by 4 inches.

Zucchini Provençale

2 *large onions, peeled and thinly sliced, about 4 cups*
¼ *cup butter*
1 *1-pound eggplant, peeled and cut into 1-inch cubes*
1 *clove garlic, peeled and finely minced*
1½ *pounds zucchini, cut into ¼-inch slices*
2 *teaspoons tomato paste blended with ⅓ cup water*
2 *green peppers, cored, seeded, and chopped*
1 *2-pound-3-ounce can Italian peeled tomatoes*
1 *teaspoon crumbled basil*
½ *teaspoon crumbled oregano*
   Salt and freshly ground pepper to taste

1. Sauté the onions in butter in a kettle until translucent.

2. Add remaining ingredients. Simmer 1 hour or until mixture is thickened yet vegetables retain their identity.

Yield: 6 servings.

Florence La Ganke's Three-Day Marmalade

1 *grapefruit*
1 *orange*
1 *lemon*
   Sugar

1. On the first day, cut fruit in half and remove seeds. Cut away and discard the ends. Slice the fruit as thinly as possible. Barely cover with cold water in a china or enamel bowl. Leave overnight at room temperature, covered.

2. On the second day, put the mixture in an enamel or aluminum pan and boil 30 minutes. Cover and leave at room temperature.

3. On the third day, measure fruit mixture. Add an equal amount of sugar (you may decrease the amount by ½ cup if you prefer a tart marmalade). Cook over a slow fire, stirring frequently to prevent burning. One hour later test in a cold saucer for thickness. If still runny, cook a little longer. Pour into sterilized glasses and seal.

Yield: About 1 pint.

February 1974

WE HAVE A very fond February memory of watching a spectacularly colorful young Italian chef standing on a step stool in our kitchen preparing a fantasy of spun sugar to be served on a dessert called Zuccotto alla Michelangelo (page 49). Spun sugar looks like angel hair, and it is made by tossing a hot sugar syrup into the air. By the time Mr. Mariano Vizzotto had finished bandying about his forked whisk, our kitchen indeed resembled the remains of a dismantled Christmas tree.

This is one of those recipes that one prints without the least hope or suspicion that any reader will make it, but because it was such a pleasure to describe, we found it irresistible. Unfortunately, there was not enough space in the article to include a recipe for a spectacular meringue dessert created by the chef that same day. It is called Torta Cavour, and if you turn to June, you will find the recipe for it there.

For a Winter's Night: Pork and Lentils

WITH PIERRE FRANEY

Like juniper berries and sauerkraut or nutmeg and spinach, one of the great food pairings is a fine roast pork with puréed lentils. We offer here two roasts of pork and a recipe for the lentils. The first pork recipe—a soaringly good dish cooked with mustard—requires a specialty item called caul or lace fat that is rarely found in supermarkets. It is available in fine butcher shops, however, particularly those that specialize in pork products.

Roast Loin of Pork with Mustard

1   *4-pound loin of pork with bone*
    Salt and freshly ground pepper to taste
¼   *pound caul fat (sometimes called lace fat)*
½   *cup imported mustard such as Dijon or Düsseldorf (see note)*
6   *sprigs fresh thyme or 1 teaspoon dried*
1   *onion, about ½ pound*
24 *very small white onions, peeled*
¼   *cup water*

1. Preheat oven to 400 degrees.

2. Using a sharp knife, carefully trim away most but not all of the fat from the loin of pork. Sprinkle the pork with salt and pepper to taste.

3. Open up the sheet of caul fat on a flat surface. Place the pork, bone side down, in the center of the caul fat. Smear the mustard all over the pork. Arrange the thyme sprigs at various points over the pork. Or sprinkle with thyme if dried thyme is used. Bring up the edges of the caul fat to enclose the roast completely.

4. Place the roast, bone side down, in a roasting pan and bake, uncovered, 30 minutes.

5. Split the onion in half and thinly slice it. Scatter the slices around the pork. Arrange the small white onions around the roast.

6. Reduce the oven heat to 375 degrees and bake 45 minutes. Cover loosely with foil and cook 15 minutes longer.

7. Remove the foil and cover the roast with a heavy lid. Reduce the oven heat to 350 degrees and bake 30 minutes.

8. Remove the roast, leaving the juices in the pan. Remove the caul fat from the pork and transfer the roast to a serving dish. Use a slotted spoon and remove the small white onions. Spoon them around the roast as garnish.

9. Put the pan juices through a food mill or sieve into a saucepan. Skim off the fat. Bring the juices to the boil and add the water. Bring to the boil again. Slice the roast and spoon a little of the sauce over each slice.

Yield: 6 to 8 servings.

Note: If imported mustard is not available, blend your own mustard following the instructions on page 45.

Lentil Purée

1   *pound lentils*
¾   *pound potatoes, peeled and cut into eighths*
1   *small onion, stuck with 2 cloves*
1   *clove garlic, peeled*
1   *bay leaf*
6   *cups water*
    Salt and freshly ground pepper to taste
1   *cup heavy cream*
4   *tablespoons butter*

1. Combine the lentils, potatoes, onion, garlic, bay leaf, water, salt and pepper to taste in a saucepan. Bring to the boil and simmer 30 minutes or until the lentils are tender. Drain.

2. Pour the lentil mixture into a food press and pass it through into a saucepan. Discard any solids left in food press.

3. Add ¾ cup heavy cream, butter, and salt to taste. Beat well to blend. Smooth the surface and pour the remaining ¼ cup of cream on top to prevent a skin from forming. When ready to serve, heat thoroughly and stir to blend.

Yield: 8 to 10 servings.

Roast Pork with Garlic

3 *large cloves garlic*
1 *5-to-6-pound center cut pork roast*
  Salt and freshly ground pepper to taste
1 *tablespoon peanut, vegetable, or corn oil*
1 *small onion, peeled and quartered*
1 *teaspoon thyme*
1 *cup water*

1. Preheat oven to 400 degrees.

2. Cut each clove of garlic into 8 slivers. Make little holes near the bone end of the meat and in the fat. Insert the garlic slivers in the holes. Sprinkle the roast with salt and pepper to taste and rub all over with oil. Arrange the roast, fat side down, in a roasting pan.

3. Add the onion and sprinkle with thyme. Bake 30 minutes and turn the roast fat side up. Bake 45 minutes.

4. Pour off the fat from the roasting pan and add the water, stirring to dissolve the brown particles that cling to the bottom and sides of the pan.

5. Return the roast to the oven and reduce the oven heat to 375 degrees. Continue roasting about 45 minutes longer.

Yield: 6 to 8 servings.

Not only does lentil purée make an astonishingly compatible accompaniment to roast pork and baked fresh ham, it goes well with almost any kind of sausage served as a main course. Try it with cotechini (page 135) in place of lentils Côte d'Azur or with the Easter ham (page 106).

The Oyster: Indolent, Tender, and Fabled

There is probably more literature on great bouts of oyster-eating than any other food on earth. In a recently printed essay we recounted a few paragraphs on oyster-eating taken from M. F. K. Fisher's inimitable translation of Brillat Savarin:

"I remember that in the old days any banquet of importance began with oysters, and that there were always a good number of the guests who did not hesitate to down *one gross* apiece [12 dozen, 144]. I always wondered what the weight of this little appetizer would be, and finally I confirmed the fact that one dozen oysters (including their juice) weigh *four ounces,* which makes the gross amount of weight *three pounds.*"

One year in Versailles, Brillat Savarin met a gentleman named Laperte, who complained constantly that he never had enough oysters, "a real bellyful" as he told him he should put it. Brillat Savarin "resolved to give him this satisfaction for once, and invited him to dine the next day.

"He came," Brillat Savarin recalled. "I kept him company through the third dozen, and then let him go on alone. He managed very well without me, and by the end of the next hour was in his 32d dozen, eating slowly because the maid who opened them for him was none too skillful. All this time I was unoccupied, and since it is at table that this is especially painful, I finally interrupted my companion at the moment when he seemed going at his best speed, by saying, 'My dear fellow, it's your fate today not to have that bellyful: Let us begin our dinner.' We did so, and he enjoyed it with the vigor and polish of a man finishing a long fast."

There is a brilliant account of oyster-eating in Robert Courtine's *The Hundred Glories of French Cooking* (Farrar, Straus and Giroux, 1973, $15), one of the nobler recently published works of gastronomy. He speaks of Theodore, King of Corsica, who on finally returning to England consoled himself with the thought that now he could dine on as many oysters as he liked. "My three passions," he declared, "are love, military glory, and the oyster!" Only the third, the author declares, was not denied the king.

Mirabeau, the author continues, once dined on 360 oysters, and he confessed that the feast almost did him in. And on another occasion, when a publisher offered to buy Balzac dinner, the author downed a round 100 "just for starters."

We have been told that oysters are just about the laziest and most indolent of sea creatures, which contributes to their tenderness and delicate nature. They are also incomparable consumers of liquid, putting through their gullets more than 40 gallons of sea water a day.

(Wild stories have been told about the cunning of oysters in trapping their prey. They are said to have trapped mice in English cellars and, on at least one occasion, to have decapitated a mouse who had the misfortune to stick his neck too far into an open shell.)

The kinds of oysters available in the world today are literally without number (100 years ago it was put at around 360), and 300 years ago they were an important source of food for the poor who lived on America's coastal waters. Some of them were reputedly 12 inches from one edge of the shell to the other.

We very well recall when the Four Seasons Restaurant opened in Manhattan more than a decade ago, they prided themselves on "knife and fork oysters" and in the shell they were literally the size of a good-size salad plate. To our minds, using a knife and fork on an oyster seemed downright uncivilized, and we tried to down the creature whole. It took a good deal of exercise, spiritual as much as anything else, to recover.

Oysters are among the most versatile of what Europeans generally call "fruits of the sea." The ones pictured here were taken from the waters off Long Island, New York. On the half shell they make a marvelous base for oysters Rockefeller. Out of the shell they are especially toothsome stuffed into artichoke bottoms or baked potatoes.

Oysters are at their most blissful, or our most blissful, eaten raw. On the other hand, they lend themselves commendably to the cooked state. The recipe for oysters Rockefeller is, to our minds, the essence of what the New Orleans dish should be.

The recently conceived artichoke bottoms with oyster stuffing is quite French, although it, too, smacks of the Crescent City.

The recipe for baked potato stuffed with creamed oysters is one answer to the caviar and baked potato dish.

As far as our extended research is concerned there is no such thing as a "classic" or definitive recipe for oysters Rockefeller. The following is our version.

Oysters Rockefeller

36 oysters
1 pound or 2 10-ounce packages fresh spinach
1 cup finely chopped scallions
½ cup finely chopped celery
½ cup finely chopped parsley
1 clove garlic, finely minced
1 2-ounce can anchovies, drained
8 tablespoons butter
1 tablespoon flour
½ cup heavy cream
   Tabasco to taste
1 or 2 tablespoons Pernod, Ricard, or other anise-flavored liqueur
⅓ cup grated Parmesan cheese

1. Preheat oven to 450 degrees.

2. Open the oysters, leaving them on the half shell and reserving the oyster liquor.

3. Pick over the spinach and remove any tough stems and blemished leaves. Rinse well and put in a saucepan. Cover and cook, stirring, until spinach is wilted. Cook briefly and drain well. Squeeze to remove excess moisture. Blend or put through a food grinder. There should be about 2 cups.

4. Put the scallions, celery and parsley into the container of an electric blender and blend. There should be about 1 cup finely blended.

5. Chop the garlic and anchovies together finely.

6. Heat 4 tablespoons of butter in a skillet and add the scallion and celery mixture. Stir about 1 minute and add the anchovy mixture. Cook, stirring, about 1 minute, and add the spinach. Stir to blend.

7. Heat the remaining 4 tablespoons of butter in a saucepan and add the flour. Blend, stirring with a wire whisk, and add the oyster liquor, stirring vigorously with the whisk. Stir in the cream. Season with Tabasco. Do not add salt. Add the spinach mixture and Pernod. Let cool.

8. Spoon equal portions of the mixture on top of the oysters and smooth over the tops. Sprinkle with Parmesan cheese. Bake about 25 minutes or until piping hot.

Yield: 6 or more servings.

Note: The same spinach topping is equally as good (some think it is better) with clams on the half shell (Clams Rockefeller).

Oyster-Stuffed Potatoes

6 *baking potatoes weighing about ½ pound each*
½ *pint (1 cup) shucked oysters*
6 *tablespoons butter*
1 *tablespoon finely chopped shallots*
Salt and freshly ground pepper to taste
¼ *cup dry white wine*
⅛ *teaspoon grated nutmeg, or more or less to taste*
⅓ *cup heavy cream*
2 *tablespoons finely chopped parsley*

1. Preheat oven to 425 degrees.

2. Wash the potatoes and pat them dry. Place them on a rack in the oven and let them bake 45 minutes.

3. Meanwhile, fit a sieve over a mixing bowl or measuring cup and add the oysters. Let them drain.

4. Melt half the butter in a saucepan and add the shallots. Cook briefly, stirring, and add the drained oysters, salt and pepper.

Cook the oysters, shaking the skillet. Cook very briefly just until the oysters plump and curl, about 1 minute. Add the wine and bring to a boil. Remove the oysters with a slotted spoon, leaving the cooking liquid in the saucepan.

5. Prepare the potatoes for stuffing. Cut off a ½-inch thick slice from the top of each. Using a spoon, scoop out most of the inside of each potato, leaving them hollow for stuffing. Spoon half the flesh into a mixing bowl. Reserve the remaining flesh for another use such as pancakes or discard it.

6. To the flesh in the bowl, add the remaining butter, salt, pepper, and nutmeg. Mash together with a fork until well blended. Add equal parts of the mixture to each of the hollowed-out potatoes and smooth it over the bottom and up the insides. Arrange the potatoes on a baking dish and return briefly to the oven to keep warm.

7. Bring the oyster liquid in the saucepan to the boil and cook over high heat until it is reduced to about 3 tablespoons. At this point it will be thick and syrupy. Add the heavy cream and cook, stirring, about 1 minute. If any liquid has accumulated around the oysters, drain it into the sauce. Add the oysters but do not cook, merely heat thoroughly. Stir in half the parsley.

8. Spoon equal amounts of the oysters and sauce into each potato shell. Serve sprinkled with remaining chopped parsley. Serve with a well-chilled Chablis or a nice dry Muscadet.

Yield: 6 servings.

Fonds d'Artichauts Vieux Carré

(Artichoke bottoms with oyster stuffing)

This dish is of French origin, but in that it is reminiscent of certain dishes found in New Orleans, it has been christened Vieux Carré.

6   artichokes, about ¾ pound each
½   lemon
    Salt to taste
3   tablespoons flour
    Juice of 1½ lemons
3   tablespoons butter
3   tablespoons finely chopped shallots
½   pint (1 cup) shucked oysters
¼   cup heavy cream
    Freshly ground pepper to taste
½   cup fresh bread crumbs
1   egg yolk
1   teaspoon imported mustard such as Dijon or Düsseldorf
    Tabasco to taste
½   teaspoon worcestershire sauce
¼   cup finely chopped parsley
¼   cup grated Parmesan cheese

1. Preheat oven to 400 degrees.

2. Using a sharp knife, neatly trim off the stems of each artichoke. Run the knife neatly around the bottom of the artichoke to trim away and discard the leaves and green parts. As the bottoms are prepared, rub the cut portions with the lemon half.

3. Place the bottoms in a kettle and add cold water to cover and salt to taste. Make a paste of flour and cold water, stirring constantly and adding more water until it is quite thin. Add this to the kettle, putting it through a sieve if there are any lumps. Add the juice of 1 lemon. Bring to the boil and simmer until the bottoms are tender, 20 to 30 minutes. They must not become mushy. Drain. When cool enough to handle, use a spoon to scoop out and discard the fibrous "chokes."

4. Heat 1 tablespoon of butter in a saucepan and add the shallots. Cook, stirring, about 2 minutes and add the shucked oysters with their liquor. Poach 2 minutes, no longer, and drain, reserving both the oysters and their liquid. Return the liquid to the saucepan and reduce it by half.

5. Add the cream and reduce about 5 minutes. The liquid should be about as thick as a medium cream sauce. Add the ground pepper.

6. Chop the oysters finely and add them to the cream sauce. Stir in the bread crumbs and egg yolk. Bring just to the boil, stirring. Add the mustard, Tabasco, worcestershire sauce, and parsley.

7. Fill artichoke bottoms with the oyster mixture and arrange them on a buttered baking dish. Sprinkle with Parmesan cheese and bake 12 to 20 minutes until piping hot. Sprinkle with remaining lemon juice.

8. Heat remaining 2 tablespoons of butter until it is hazelnut brown. Pour it over the bottoms and serve immediately.

Yield: 6 servings.

Oysters Chauveron

12 plump oysters
 1 large clove garlic, finely chopped
¼ cup finely chopped parsley
 1 tablespoon finely chopped shallots
 8 tablespoons butter at room temperature
 1 tablespoon bread crumbs
    Salt and freshly ground pepper to taste

1. Preheat the oven to 400 degrees.

2. Open the oysters or have them opened and leave them on the half shell. Place them on a baking dish (on a bed of rock salt if you prefer).

3. Combine the chopped garlic and parsley and chop them together. Add them to a mixing bowl. Add the remaining ingredients and blend well.

4. Spoon equal amounts of the garlic butter onto the oysters and place them in the oven. Bake 10 minutes.

Yield: 2 to 4 servings.

Roger Chauveron among the grapefruit trees in his backyard.

Since the Café Chauveron closed its doors in Manhattan some years ago, we have often been asked about the health and whereabouts of Roger Chauveron, the owner, whose oyster recipe appears above. On a chance visit to Miami Beach, Florida, we met him again, and we are happy to report that the gentleman at 74 is healthy, tanned, and as garrulous as ever. And the Café Chauveron here, over which he presides, is a fountain of joy in this gastronomic desert. We dined sumptuously and well on a pâté of game, oysters Chauveron, contrefilet of beef with a masterful sauce périgourdine, and roast quail. If you happen to have a yacht, you can cast your lines over at the restaurant's terrace which is located Venicelike on the banks of a canal at 9561 East Bay Harbor Drive on Bar Harbor Island.

Endive and Veal

WITH PIERRE FRANEY

Belgian endive deserves better of the home cook than being relegated to the salad bowl. It makes, for instance, a ravishingly elegant accompaniment to veal chops in the first dish outlined below. Both are cooked gently, then bathed in an aromatic cream and cognac sauce and baked.

Veal Chops with Belgian Endive

4   *loin veal chops, about ½ pound each*
    Salt and freshly ground pepper to taste
¼   *cup flour*
4   *tablespoons butter*
4   *firm, white, unblemished heads of Belgian endive*
2   *tablespoons water*
2   *tablespoons finely chopped shallots*
3   *tablespoons cognac*
1½ *cups heavy cream*
¼   *cup grated Parmesan cheese*

1. Sprinkle the chops on both sides with salt and pepper. Dredge lightly on both sides in flour.

2. Heat 3 tablespoons butter in a heavy skillet large enough to place the chops in one layer. Cook chops over moderately low heat 8 to 10 minutes and turn. Cook, uncovered, 15 minutes longer.

3. While the chops are cooking, place the endive in a heavy sacuepan. Add the remaining tablespoon of butter, salt and pepper, and the water. Cover closely and simmer 25 minutes. Take care that they do not burn. If necessary, add a bit more water.

4. When the chops are done,

transfer them to a warm platter and cover with foil.

5. Add the shallots to the skillet and cook, stirring with a wooden spoon, for 30 seconds. Add the cognac and flame it. Stir with the spoon to dissolve the brown particles that cling to the bottom and sides of the skillet. Add the cream and cook, stirring, over high heat. Cook about 5 minutes or until the cream is thick and smooth. Strain the sauce into a saucepan and add salt and pepper to taste.

6. Preheat oven to 400 degrees.

7. Arrange the chops in one layer in an oval gratin or baking dish. Press the endive gently to remove any excess liquid. Arrange them around the chops. Spoon the sauce over all and sprinkle with the cheese. Bake, uncovered, 15 minutes.

Yield: 4 servings.

Veal Sauté
in Tomato Sauce

4 *pounds veal shoulder and/or breast, boned and cut into 2-inch cubes*
Salt and freshly ground pepper to taste
4 *tablespoons oil*

2 *cups finely chopped onions*
1 *tablespoon finely chopped garlic*
1 *teaspoon stem saffron, optional*
¼ *cup flour*
¼ *cup dry white wine*
3½ *cups peeled, chopped tomatoes or the contents of a 1-pound-12-ounce can whole peeled tomatoes*
1 *cup chicken broth*
2 *teaspoons rosemary*

1. Preheat oven to 375 degrees.

2. Sprinkle the veal with salt and pepper.

3. Heat the oil in a heavy, large casserole or Dutch oven and add the meat. Cook, stirring frequently, about 20 minutes. In the beginning the meat will give up liquid. This will evaporate as the meat cooks. Continue until the meat is browned all over.

4. Add the onions, garlic, and saffron and cook, stirring occasionally, about 5 minutes. Sprinkle with flour and stir until the pieces of meat are evenly coated. Add the wine, tomatoes, and chicken broth. Sprinkle with salt and pepper to taste.

5. Chop the dried rosemary. There should be about 1 teaspoon. Add it. Cover and bake 1 hour. Serve with buttered noodles or rice.

Yield: 6 to 8 servings.

Pasta Perfect Casseroles

WITH PIERRE FRANEY

While there is something excruciatingly mundane about dishes made with ground meat and noodles or macaroni (could it have something to do with their low-budget connotation?), they can also be outrageously good. To achieve this, the meat must be fresh and not too burdened with fat, the pasta must not be boiled to a mush before it is baked—and the whole must be put together with care and respect.

Beef with Noodles Casserole

5 tablespoons butter
2 cups finely chopped onion
1 cup chopped celery
¾ cup chopped green pepper
½ pound ground round steak
2 cloves garlic, finely chopped
2 cups chopped tomatoes
   Salt and freshly ground pepper to taste
½ teaspoon crumbled marjoram
1 tablespoon flour
¾ cup heavy cream
¼ teaspoon grated nutmeg
½ pound medium-width egg noodles, approximately
1 cup grated sharp Cheddar cheese

1. Preheat oven to 400 degrees.

2. Melt 3 tablespoons of butter in a skillet and add the onion, celery, and green pepper. Cook, stirring, until vegetables are crisp-tender. Remove from the heat.

3. Heat 1 tablespoon of butter in another skillet and add the ground meat. Cook, stirring and chopping down with the sharp side of a heavy kitchen spoon to break up the meat. Add the garlic and stir to blend. Add the cooked vegetables, tomatoes, salt and pepper to taste, and marjoram. Stir to blend and simmer 10 minutes.

4. In a saucepan, heat the remaining tablespoon of butter and when it is melted, add the flour, stirring with a wire whisk. When blended, add the cream, stirring rapidly with the whisk. When thickened and smooth, add salt and pepper to taste and nutmeg. Stir this sauce into the meat mixture and blend. Remove from the heat.

5. Drop the noodles into boiling salted water to cover and cook about 4 minutes. Do not overcook. They will cook again in the oven. Drain the noodles and run them under cold water to prevent sticking. Drain well.

6. In a rectangular dish measuring about 11¾ by 7½ by 1¾ inches, make a thin layer of sauce, a layer of noodles, a sprinkling of cheese, more sauce, noodles, sauce, and cheese. There may be noodles left over which may be reserved for other uses such as a soup ingredient. Place the casserole in the oven.

7. Reduce the oven heat to 375 degrees and bake 25 minutes. To give a nice glaze to the dish, run it under the broiler until golden brown on top.

Yield: 4 to 8 servings.

Macaroni and Beef Casserole

1½   cups elbow macaroni
3½   tablespoons butter
¾   cup chopped onion
¼   cup finely chopped green
     pepper
1   pound chopped ground
     chuck or round steak
1   teaspoon basil
1   teaspoon oregano
½   cup drained tomatoes
3   tablespoons flour
2   cups milk
2   cups (about 10 ounces)
     cubed Cheddar cheese
     Salt and freshly ground
     pepper to taste
¼   teaspoon grated nutmeg
     Cayenne to taste
     Grated Parmesan cheese

1. Preheat oven to 450 degrees.

2. Drop the macaroni into boiling salted water and simmer until macaroni is barely tender. Do not overcook because the dish will bake later in the oven. Drain in a colander and place under cold running water.

3. In a skillet, heat 1½ tablespoons butter and add the onion and green pepper. Cook, stirring, until onion is wilted. Add meat. Cook, stirring, until meat loses its red color. If there is an accumulation of liquid fat in the skillet, drain well in a large sieve. Return the meat mixture to the skillet. Add the basil, oregano, and tomatoes. Cook 3 minutes.

4. In a saucepan, heat the remaining 2 tablespoons of butter and stir in the flour, using a wire whisk. Add the milk, stirring rapidly with the whisk. Cook, stirring, about 5 minutes. Remove the sauce from the heat and stir in the Cheddar cheese. Stir until it melts. Add salt and pepper to taste, nutmeg, and cayenne.

5. Spoon the macaroni into a baking dish. Ours measured 7 by 10 by 2½ inches. Spoon the meat mixture over the macaroni and pour the cheese sauce over all. Sprinkle with Parmesan cheese and bake 30 minutes or until hot and bubbling throughout. Run under the broiler briefly to glaze.

Yield: 4 to 6 servings.

French Mustard

Over the years we have railed against "ball-park mustard" for fine cookery and rallied for "imported mustard, preferably Dijon or Düsseldorf."

The ball-park variety, as we have noted before, is great for open-air eating, particularly on hot dogs, but positively ruinous in fine sauces such as those made with shallots, white wine, and butter. We have only recently made the acquaintance of an absolutely splendid imported mustard, on a par with the best we have found anywhere. It is called Pommery mustard and also, in French, moutarde de Meaux.

Among its other virtues, it has exceptional flavor and a fine texture containing, as it does, coarsely cracked mustard seeds. The label states that "It was in the year of 1760 that a superior of the ancient religious order of Meaux transmitted to the Pommery family the 'secret recipe' of their marvelous specialty, 'Moutarde de Chanoines,' the Abbott's Mustard. This mustard has been served at the tables of the kings of France since 1632."

A neighbor of ours, a good friend and first-rate cook named Annie Damaz, brought us a 17½-ounce jar with the cordial good wish that we would enjoy it. The jar, incidentally, is sealed with sealing wax and is the devil's handiwork for cracking and getting into. But once into it you are apt to be addicted. It is great on sandwiches and superior in this recently conceived recipe for shrimp baked in ramekins or scallop shells.

Shrimp à la Moutarde de Meaux

2 pounds raw shrimp
5 tablespoons butter
4 tablespoons flour
2 cups milk
　Salt and freshly ground
　pepper to taste
⅛ teaspoon cayenne
3 tablespoons finely chopped
　shallots

½ cup dry white wine
¼ cup finely chopped parsley
1 egg yolk
4 tablespoons moutarde de
　Meaux or use another
　imported mustard such as
　Dijon or Düsseldorf
¼ cup freshly grated
　Parmesan cheese

1. Preheat oven to 450 degrees.

2. Shell the shrimp and split them down the back. Rinse away

the black vein. Drain and cut each shrimp in half crosswise. Set aside.

3. In a saucepan, melt 3 tablespoons butter and stir in the flour, using a wire whisk. Add the milk, stirring rapidly with the whisk. Season with salt, pepper, and cayenne. Simmer, stirring occasionally, 15 minutes.

4. In another saucepan, combine the shallots, wine, and chopped parsley. Cook over high heat until the wine is almost totally reduced. Add the white sauce and cook, stirring occasionally, about 10 minutes.

5. Beat the egg yolk lightly and add it to the sauce, stirring rapidly. Remove the sauce from the heat and add 3 tablespoons mustard.

6. Melt remaining 2 tablespoons butter in a skillet and add the shrimp. Cook just until the shrimp turn red. Add remaining tablespoon mustard and stir to coat well. Add a third of the sauce to the shrimp and stir to coat.

7. Spoon the shrimp into 8 individual ramekins or large scallop shells. Spoon an equal amount of the sauce over each serving. Sprinkle with an equal amount of Parmesan cheese and bake 10 to 15 minutes until piping hot.

Yield: 8 servings.

There are innumerable brands of good mustards available today. The best known Dijon mustard is Grey Poupon. The best known Düsseldorf is Lion brand. Should neither of these be available, prepare your own by blending ⅓ cup powdered mustard, preferably Colman brand, with 2 tablespoons cold water, white wine, milk, or beer and a touch of salt. The mustard should stand at least 15 minutes to develop flavor before you use it.

La Grande Bouffe

What started out as a simple reflection on a dish we always hunger for when we think of Rome, ended in an absolute orgy of eating or, as one guest dubbed it, l'abbuffata. La grande bouffe—Italian style.

The dish in question is carciofi alla Giudea, those incomparable artichokes turned and shaped in hot oil to resemble a large-petaled and eminently edible flower. Artichokes cooked in the style of Giudea are famous mostly in the restaurants—including da Piperno—in the old ghetto section of the Eternal City.

The remark was made casually one evening to Gino Innocenti, the tall, amiable, and distinguished owner of the La Pace hotel and restaurant in Montecatini, the watering spa 20 miles outside Florence.

"No matter how we've tried the dish," we confided, "we've never come out with even passable results."

Mr. Innocenti volunteered to visit our kitchen in East Hampton, Long Island and to bring along a few master chefs from his establishment. On the day agreed upon, the gentleman arrived with hampers brimfilled not only with a score or more of artichokes but half a calf's head, a calf's tongue, a large hen, mustard fruit, and zampone for bollito misto; anchovies and capers and oil for a marvelous cold appetizer called carpaccio alla Harry; chicken livers and bread for a delectable spread on rounds of toast, crostini dello chef; ham and pickles and chicken for a superior pasta dish with fusilli; and endless quantities of cream and eggs and assorted candied fruit for a wildly rich assortment of Italian desserts.

And an exceptional collection of talent in the persons of Marco Nesi, chef of La Pace; Mariano Vizzotto, pastry chef of La Pace; and Quinto Piana, chef and translator at the Rainbow Room.

They arrived at 10 o'clock in the morning and if you've ever wondered how long it takes for three professionals to turn out a veritable regale of 10 dishes in a foreign and unaccustomed kitchen, the answer is approximately four and one-half hours.

The menu included an extraordinary spiced pork roast literally boiled in oil until tender; a soup with pasta, cappeletti en brodo; and two singularly good desserts, a meringue confection filled with whipped cream and a rich golden yellow Italian spongecake filled with more of the same plus the candied fruits. And the latter was crowned with a gossamer, made-on-the-moment cotton-candylike crown of spun sugar.

And when the chefs and guests sat down to dine (with assorted California wines from the resident cellar), the talk turned, naturally, to what else? Food, pasta mostly, a lengthy exploration of the aesthetics of using pastas with soups and sauces.

It was noted that the current rage on the pasta scene, paglia e fieno—straw and hay—made by tossing white and green noodles together and served in a variety of cream sauces, is relatively new, a contrivance of the last decade.

Italian cooking in America, the chefs agreed, is largely a compromise.

And those artichokes. Fantastico.

There follows a sampling of a few of the dishes from our own Italian festival, chez nous.

Marco Nesi brought his own Italian herbs with him.

Mariano Vizzoto is convinced the best way to fold flour into eggs is with the hands.

Artichokes alla Giudea

6 *or more small artichokes,*
   about ½ pound each
½ *lemon*
4 *or more cups oil for frying*
4 *cloves garlic, peeled*
   Salt to taste

1. Using a sharp, heavy knife, cut off the top of each artichoke about 1 inch down and parallel to the base of the artichoke.

2. Pull off the tough outer leaves of each artichoke. Using a sharp knife, trim around the rim of each artichoke, making the sides uniform and neat.

3. Insert a melon ball cutter into the center of each artichoke and twirl it around the inside, scooping out the fiberlike "choke" of each vegetable. Leave all the inside leaves with the exception of the very center leaves intact. Using a paring knife, trim off the outside of each stem, leaving the stems intact.

4. Rub all cut surfaces of the artichokes with half a lemon to prevent discoloration. Place the artichokes, one at a time, top side down on a flat surface. Push down on the stem of each artichoke to open it slightly without breaking or damaging the artichokes.

5. Heat the oil in a heavy skillet to a depth of about 1 inch. Add the garlic. When the oil is very hot, add the artichokes top side down. As they cook they will soften. Press down on the stems to "flatten" the tops of the ar-

tichokes. When slightly flattened and brown, turn the artichokes on their sides. Continue cooking and turning in the hot oil until the artichokes are thoroughly tender, 8 to 10 minutes.

6. Drain on absorbent toweling and sprinkle with salt. Serve hot or very warm.

Yield: 1 artichoke per serving.

Confit de Porc
(Pork loin cooked with spices)

5 *pounds fat back*
1 *5-pound center cut of pork,*
   boned (about 3 pounds
   boned weight)
¼ *cup rosemary*
1 *tablespoon sage*
1 *large clove garlic*
   Salt and freshly ground
   pepper to taste

1. If there is a rind on the fat back, slice it off and discard. Grind the fat back, using the fine blade of a meat grinder. You can also grind the fat back in a food processor.

2. Put the ground fat back in a deep, heavy kettle and cook it, stirring with a wooden spoon as it melts. Continue cooking until it is completely rendered of fat. Strain the fat.

3. Using a long, sharp, thin knife, make an incision dead center inside the pork loin. This is for stuffing the loin with spices. A sharpening steel of the sort used for sharpening knives is excellent for this.

4. Make small incisions on the outside of the loin.

5. Put the rosemary, sage, and garlic on a flat surface and chop finely. Add salt and pepper.

6. Rub the outside of the loin with the spice and garlic mixture. Push as much of it as possible inside the center incision, using the sharpening steel or another instrument.

7. Fit the loin of pork into a baking dish in which it fits snugly without crowding. Pour the melted fat over it. The fat should cover or barely cover the loin.

8. Put the loin on the top of the stove and bring the fat to the boil. Let it simmer, uncovered, for 50 to 60 minutes, taking proper precautions that the fat does not catch fire.

9. Let cool. The pork is now ready to be removed from the liquid fat and served sliced. Or it may be kept in the fat which will harden as it cools. It will keep for months or even a year if it is properly stored in a very cool spot or refrigerated. Preserved pork is also excellent if stored in olive oil. It improves on aging. Before serving, of course, the fat must be melted and the meat removed. The original cooking fat, by the way, is excellent for sautéeing broccoli or broccoli rape, a fine leafy Italian vegetable sometimes available in supermarkets and Italian grocery stores.

Yield: 16 to 20 servings.

Zuccotto alla Michelangelo

1 *Italian spongecake (see recipe)*
⅔ *cup water*
1¼ *cups sugar*
1 *cup orange-flavored liqueur such as aurum (an Italian liqueur), Grand Marnier, or maraschino liqueur (available in wine and spirits shops)*
7 *cups heavy cream*
¾ *cup chopped candied fruit*
⅔ *cup coarsely chopped pecans*
1¼ *cups coarsely grated dark sweet chocolate*
⅔ *cup powdered cocoa Spun sugar, optional (see recipe)*

1. Prepare the spongecake and let cool.

2. Cut the spongecake into 16 or so sandwichlike slices, each about ¾ inch thick. Line completely a round-bottom mixing bowl (with a minimum 5-quart capacity) with the slices, arranging them so that they touch without overlapping. Cut the slices as necessary to fit snugly.

3. Blend the water and ½ cup sugar and stir until sugar dissolves. Add 1 cup of orange-flavored liqueur or maraschino. Brush the spongecake slices generously with some of the syrup.

4. Whip the heavy cream until almost stiff and add the remaining sugar gradually, beating constantly. When stiff, add the candied fruit, pecans, and 1 cup of the sweet chocolate.

5. Spoon half the whipped cream mixture into the sponge-cake-lined mold. Arrange another close-fitting layer of spongecake slices on top. Brush liberally with more of the orange liqueur syrup.

6. Stir the powdered cocoa into the remaining whipped cream mixture. Spoon the mixture into the bowl until it is almost filled. Cover with a final layer of spongecake slices. Brush with the remaining orange syrup. Place the bowl in the freezer and let stand at least 1 hour or until frozen. Meanwhile, reserve and refrigerate the remaining whipped cream.

7. When the cake is frozen, unmold it onto a round serving dish. Spread the remaining whipped cream over all and sprinkle with the remaining chopped sweet chocolate. Lift up spun sugar and arrange on top of cake. Serve immediately cut into wedges.

Yield: 12 or more servings.

Italian spongecake

15 *egg yolks*
7 *whole eggs, approximately*
1½ *cups sugar*
¼ *teaspoon vanilla*
   Salt to taste
2 *cups flour*
¾ *teaspoon baking powder*

1. Preheat the oven to 375 degrees.

2. Lightly but thoroughly butter a large cake pan (ours mea-

sured 10 by 3 inches) and sprinkle the inside with flour. Shake it around to coat the bottom and sides, then shake out and discard the excess flour.

3. Combine the yolks and eggs in a 2-cup measuring cup. There should be exactly 2 cups. If there is less, add another yolk or another egg.

4. Pour the eggs into a heavy saucepan and add the sugar, vanilla, and salt. Place the saucepan over an asbestos pad or, preferably, a metal Flame-Tamer. Cook over low heat, stirring constantly with a wire whisk, and without boiling for about 10 to 15 minutes. The eggs should thicken slightly. Do not boil at any point or the eggs will curdle.

5. Pour the mixture into the bowl of an electric mixer and beat about 10 to 15 minutes until it has the consistency of soft but thickened whipped cream.

6. Sift together the flour and baking powder. Add it to the egg mixture and fold it in, preferably with one hand.

7. Pour the batter into the prepared cake pan and bake 30 to 40 minutes. Turn the cake out onto a rack and let cool thoroughly.

Yield: 10 or more servings.

Spun sugar

⅔ *cup glucose*
1 *pound superfine sugar*
1 *cup water*
   Red food coloring
   Green food coloring

1. Take note in the beginning that the making of spun sugar requires a high degree of specialized skill and training. It should be done only by skilled professionals or amateurs with a high sense of daring if not to say derring-do. It involves cooking sugar with glucose to a high temperature, dipping a whisk into it and "throwing" the syrup into the air where it descends in fine "angel hair" strands onto a pair of rigged parallel tubes (and the floor).

2. To begin, take a multi-looped, sturdy, professional wire whisk and, using a wire cutter, cut off the tips of the loops about ½ inch from the top of the whisk. Properly done, this will produce a dangerous-looking broomlike device. Open up the strands of the whisk slightly by bending them gently outwards.

3. Install a couple of thin metal or wooden tubes on a table-top or other flat surface and secure them with weights to hold them in place. If worse comes to worst, the handles of very long salad forks and spoons may be used and held in place with a marble slab. The tubes or whatever should protrude at least 18 inches from the edge of the table. By all means do not attempt this recipe in a kitchen with wall-to-wall carpeting. It gets sticky.

4. If you are short, you may want to haul out a small stepladder to stand on.

5. When ready to perform, combine the glucose, sugar, and water in a saucepan and bring to the brisk boil. Cook over high heat to the hard-boil stage (the syrup when dropped in cold water will immediately become firm and brittle). The temperature should read 250 degrees on a candy thermometer.

6. Immediately stand on the stepladder if it is to be used. Dip the tips of the whisk into the syrup and fling it with agility and vigor to and fro using mostly wrist action. As the syrup spins through the air it will harden and land (hopefully) on the improvised, protruding handles. Much of it will also land on the floor, to the distress mostly of whoever has to clean up later.

7. Descend from the ladder, if used, and lift the spun sugar off and onto any given dessert (hollowed-out pineapple filled with pineapple ice; a compote of solidly frozen ice cream balls; cakes and so on). Were it not for the problems posed by our rather warm body temperature, spun sugar could be styled into a very nice bouffant hairdo à la Joan Sutherland.

8. Quickly get up on the ladder, if used, and start again. Up, down, and so on until all the syrup is used. If you really want to do this Italian-style, you can tint the syrup as you progress (and using 2 saucepans) red, white, and green, the colors of the national flag.

9. Dismantle the table and sweep the floor.

Yield: Enough spun sugar for 1 zuccotto alla Michelangelo.

Over the years we get hundreds of "referrals" from out-of-towners who have been told, "If you're in New York and want to find a source for something, simply call the food department of *The New York Times.*" Usually we can help them out. We mention this now because you may have trouble locating a source for glucose—which you need if you plan to involve yourself in the risky business of making spun sugar. We suggest you inquire of the food department of your local newspaper. (We have not verified this, but we have been told that light corn syrup can be used in place of glucose.)

Incidentally, we paid Mr. Innocenti and his hotel/restaurant a visit later in the year. We had a riotous time which we wrote about on pages 195–198.

Pears: For Poaching, Baking, and Eating Out of Hand

WITH PIERRE FRANEY

There is an ancient Italian saying that translates roughly as "Don't tell the peasant how good pears are with cheese. He'll steal both of them from you." But this has never been our way. Here we present two capital pear desserts—a handsome tart flavored with ginger, and pears poached in a coffee-liqueur-flavored syrup.

Pear and Ginger Tart

Sweet tart pastry (see recipe), chilled
8 *ripe but firm Comice or Anjou pears, about 3 pounds*
⅔ *cup sugar*
¾ *teaspoon powdered ginger*
½ *cup water*
6 *tablespoons apricot preserves*
Whipped cream, optional

1. Preheat oven to 425 degrees.

2. Roll chilled pastry about ⅛-inch thick to fit a 9-inch metal layer cake pan. Line pan with pastry and prick the bottom. Bake the crust 10 minutes and remove from the oven. Let cool thoroughly.

3. Meanwhile, peel 6 of the pears and cut each of them into eighths. Cut away and discard the cores.

4. Place the pear wedges in a saucepan and add the sugar, ginger, and water. Cover and cook until tender but still firm, 8 to 10 minutes. They must not be mushy. Turn the pear wedges as they cook so that the pieces cook evenly. Chill thoroughly. Drain but reserve 4 tablespoons of the pear liquid.

5. Arrange the pear wedges close together in the pastry shell.

6. Peel and quarter the remaining 2 pears. Scoop out and discard the cores. Cut the quarters into thin slices. Arrange the slices symmetrically over the cooked pears.

7. Combine the apricot preserves with the reserved pear liquid. Bring to the boil and strain.

8. Brush tart with half of the apricot mixture. Bake 30 minutes.

9. Remove from oven and brush with remaining sauce. Let

stand until warm. Serve with whipped cream.

Yield: 8 to 10 servings.

Tart pastry

2   *cups flour*
2   *tablespoons sugar*
¼   *teaspoon salt*
11 *tablespoons very cold butter*
2   *egg yolks*
2   *tablespoons ice water*

1. In a mixing bowl, combine the flour, sugar, and salt. Cut the butter into pieces and add it. Cut in the butter until the mixture has the texture of coarse cornmeal.

2. Beat the yolks and water together and add, stirring quickly with a fork. Gather the dough into a ball, wrap in wax paper, and chill 1 hour or longer.

Yield: Enough for a 9-inch tart.

Pears in Caramel Syrup

8   *firm, unblemished, ripe Comice or Anjou pears*
    Juice of 1 lemon

2   *cups sugar*
⅓   *cup coffee liqueur*
    Whipped cream, optional

1. Peel the pears, leaving the stem on. As each pear is peeled drop it into water with lemon juice added to prevent discoloration.

2. Measure 3 cups of water into a saucepan and add half the sugar. Bring to the boil and add the pears. Cook the pears in the liquid, turning them gently on occasion, until they are tender but firm, about 20 minutes. Carefully remove the pears and reserve the syrup. Arrange the pears neatly on a serving dish.

3. Pour 1 cup of the reserved syrup into a saucepan and add the remaining sugar. Bring to the boil. Cook 5 to 10 minutes until the syrup starts to caramelize, shaking the skillet in a circular fashion. When quite brown but not burned, quickly remove the saucepan from the heat and add the remaining syrup. Take care that you do not burn yourself. Bring to the boil again and add the coffee liqueur. Pour the sauce over the pears and chill. Serve cold with whipped cream if desired.

Yield: 8 servings.

The Spicy Dishes of Bahia

Dorotea Elman is a tall, reed-slender, and handsome Cariocan, a Yale graduate, mother, and graphic designer. She is also a spectacularly good cook, famous for her feijoada, the intricately contrived national dish of Brazil, as well as for roast suckling pig dinners. When she turns her talents to the cooking of Bahia, it is nothing short of a Latin American revel.

Over a glass of fiery elixir called caipirinha, she explained that Bahian cooking is perhaps the outstanding cuisine of her native country, because Bahia (the name means bay or harbor) has the oldest blending of European and native cultures in Brazil. It was founded in 1549 by Thome de Souza, the first Portuguese governor of Brazil. The Portuguese, of course, also brought along their slaves, and the cooking is actually a blend of South American plus Portuguese heavily accented with African flavors. The latter influence is most notably evident in the spicy hot nature of the cooking, in the massive use of dried shrimp, and in the prominence of dende or palm nut oil.

"Dende oil," she explains, "is essentially *the* characteristic flavor of Bahian cooking."

Mrs. Elman's repertoire of Brazilian dishes seems to be exceptional. A native of Rio, her knowledge of Bahian cookery is all the more phenomenal because she never has been a long-term resident of Bahia, either the city or the state.

"My first visit there came about when I was a student at Yale," she said. "I took a ship home, and the first stop in South America was Bahia. I was fascinated by the native fishing boats in the harbor, and I persuaded one of the fishermen to take me ashore. I stayed a few days on my first visit, and later I lived there for two weeks at a time. I grew up on Rio cooking, which is continental or European mostly, but I've collected recipes from many Bahian natives including my sister's mother-in-law."

Mrs. Elman is the wife of Lee M. Elman, the New York investment banker. Their country home is the Aston Magna 50-acre estate of the late violinist, Albert Spalding, in Great Barrington, Massachusetts. The estate was the center last year of a heated controversy between the owner and the town's Board of Selectmen. Mr. Elman, a distinguished, handsome man in his late 30s, is a baroque music enthusiast. He purchased the Aston Magna property in 1971 and established the Aston Magna Foundation for Music, as well as a center for baroque-music scholars and students on his home site. Six concerts were scheduled on the estate last

June and were banned by the board, in large part, it appeared, because of the "Tanglewood-type traffic" the concerts would create.

Mrs. Elman is a partner in the firm of Propper/Elman, graphic design consultants. The couple, who have a daughter, Alexandra, 5, entertain a great deal, and Mrs. Elman's customary routine is to shop two days in advance of an evening when guests are expected. She prepares much of the food on the evening before a sit-down dinner, adding that "a lot of Brazilian food tastes best if it is made a day in advance."

Any dinner she makes generally means trips both to Chinatown and to Greenwich Village. Greenwich Village is the site of what is undoubtedly the best-known source for Brazilian staples in Manhattan— a grocery store called the Portuguese-American Delicatessen at 323 Bleecker Street. It is frequented by Brazilian diplomats and their cooks and by lesser functionaries who want such authentic fare as the carne seca, dende or palm nut oil, Portuguese sausages, salted pork oddments such as pig's ears, and so on.

Chinatown is the source of the dried peeled shrimp essential to much Bahian cooking, including two enormously impressive dishes we

One of the best Brazilian cooks in Manhattan is Rio-born Dorotea Elman. One of her specialties is the food of Bahia.

dined on at the Elmans. One of them is vatapá, a marvelous hodgepodge or stew of coconut and cashew nuts, peppers and dried shrimp cooked and pounded to a paste. It is then further cooked with either fresh shrimp or raw chicken. The other, xin xin (pronounced sheen sheen), is an elaborately good chicken stew with coriander and peppers and more dried shrimp.

We hasten to add that the two dishes were prepared at our request, and that two dishes with such similar ingredients would not be served in the course of a normal Brazilian menu. The dinner also included the haussa rice made with carne seca and a blanc mange of coconut served with a prune compote.

Most of the Brazilian feasts in the Elman home are preceded with caipirinha, the drink that Mrs. Elman had offered us. It is made by blending cachaca, which Mrs. Elman describes as "a highly inexpensive rum," with sugar and lemon juice. It is not demeaned by diluting with ice or even by chilling, and it does indeed put an edge on the appetite.

Both the rum and another dish on which we dined that evening are part of Brazil's voodoo culture, Mr. Elman explained. The other dish is haussa rice made with coconut and carne seca, or "jerked beef," a common ingredient in Brazilian cooking. "Brazil is still a land of voodoo and the rum and rice are placed—along with candles—at a crossroad," he noted. "They are used to appease and ward off evil spirits."

Vatapá Jodo

1 pound dried peeled shrimp (see note)
1½ loaves French bread, approximately
1½ cups milk
⅓ cup olive oil
1 cup chopped onion
1 clove garlic, finely minced
Salt to taste
1 cup chopped green pepper
2¾ cups tomatoes
2 cups fresh or canned, unsweetened coconut cream or milk (see recipe)
1 cup water
1½ pounds fresh shrimp, peeled and deveined
1 cup dende oil (see note)

6 ounces unsalted cashew nuts
1 teaspoon ground coriander or 1 tablespoon finely chopped fresh coriander leaves
Freshly ground pepper to taste
¾ cup finely chopped loosely packed parsley
¾ cup chopped scallions
1 or more very hot small peppers (see note), or according to taste

1. Place the dried shrimp in a mixing bowl and add water to cover. Let stand several hours or overnight. Drain but reserve the soaking liquid. There should be about 6 cups drained shrimp.

2. Remove the crusts from the bread and slice the bread. Add it to a mixing bowl and add the milk. Let stand for an hour or so.

3. In a large casserole, heat the oil and add the onion. Crush the garlic with 1 teaspoon salt with mortar and pestle. Add it. Cook, stirring, until onion starts to brown.

4. Add the soaked dried shrimp, green pepper and cook, stirring, about 4 minutes. Add the tomatoes and cook over high heat about 5 minutes.

5. Add about 2½ cups of the reserved liquid in which shrimp soaked. Cover and cook about 10 minutes, stirring occasionally. Cook about 30 minutes longer.

6. Use a potato masher or other vegetable masher and pound and mash the ingredients.

7. Mash the soaked bread (about 5 cups in all) with a spoon to make a mush. Add it to the shrimp mixture and continue stirring and mashing about 20 minutes. Beat, if desired, with a wire whisk. The consistency should be pastelike.

8. Add the coconut milk, water, and fresh shrimp and stir to blend the shrimp without crushing into the pastelike mixture.

9. Gradually stir in the dende oil, stirring constantly.

10. If the cashew nuts are salted, rinse them off and pat dry. In any event, put them into the container of an electric blender and blend. Add them to the casserole. Add the coriander, salt, pepper, parsley, scallions, and peppers. Bring to the boil and turn off

the heat. Do not boil. If the casserole must be reheated, stir constantly.

Yield: 8 to 12 servings.

Note: Dried peeled shrimp are available in plastic bags in almost all Chinese groceries and supermarkets.

Mrs. Elman states that olive oil plus about one tablespoon of paprika would be a vague but acceptable substitute for the dende oil.

The traditional peppers used in this recipe are malagueta peppers which are very small, fiery hot chilies from Brazil. Substitute fresh hot green or red peppers or canned Mexican chilies such as pickled serrano peppers. Use them according to taste.

Coconut milk

1. Crack a coconut and remove the meat. Using a swivel-bladed potato peeler, cut off the thin brown coating on the outer surface of the meat. Cut the meat into cubes.

2. Line a mixing bowl with cheesecloth.

3. Add about ½ cup of the coconut meat at a time to the container of an electric blender. Add about ¼ cup of hot water and blend. Pour the mixture into the cheesecloth-lined bowl.

4. Continue blending cubes of coconut and hot water and add this to the bowl. Gather up the ends of the cheesecloth and squeeze the bag to extract as much coconut cream as possible.

5. If more coconut cream or milk is needed, measure out the coconut and add half the quantity of hot water. Squeeze again.

Yield: The yield will depend on the amount of liquid used.

Xin Xin

2 cups dried peeled shrimp (see note)
2 2½-to-3-pound chickens, cut into serving pieces
Salt and freshly ground pepper to taste
2 cloves garlic, finely chopped or mashed to a pulp with mortar and pestle
2 teaspoons ground coriander seeds
1 cup dende oil (see note)
2 cups thinly sliced, loosely packed onions
2 Tabasco peppers, fresh or bottled, chopped
½ cup finely chopped, tightly packed parsley
3 cups water

1. Place the shrimp in a mixing bowl and add cold water to cover. Let stand overnight until softened.

2. Sprinkle the chickens with salt and pepper and rub the pieces with garlic. Put the seasoned chicken pieces in a heavy kettle or Dutch oven.

3. Drain the shrimp well and put them into the container of an electric blender. Blend well, stir-

ring down with a plastic spatula as necessary. You may prefer to do this in two steps.

4. Add the shrimp to the chicken. Add the coriander seeds, dende oil (shake the bottle well before adding), onions, chopped Tabasco peppers, and parsley.

5. Add the water and cover. Bring to the boil and cook, stirring gently once in a while, about 1 hour or until chicken is thoroughly tender.

Yield: 8 or more servings.

Note: Dried peeled shrimp are available in plastic bags in almost all Chinese groceries and supermarkets. Olive oil plus about 1 tablespoon of paprika would be a vague but acceptable substitute for the dende oil.

Haussa Rice
(Rice from Aussa)

1 pound carne seca (dried beef known as "jerked" beef, see note)
3½ cups raw rice
½ cup peanut, vegetable, or corn oil
1 tablespoon garlic, finely chopped or crushed with mortar and pestle
Salt to taste
7 cups very hot water

¼   *cup dried, shredded,*
     unsweetened coconut,
     available at health food
     stores
2   *tablespoons butter*
1½ *cups thinly sliced onions*

1. Put the carne seca in a mixing bowl and add cold water to cover. Let stand several hours or overnight, changing the water occasionally. Drain. Carefully scrape off the thick coating from the beef.

2. Place the beef in a saucepan and add cold water to cover. Bring to the boil and drain. Add more cold water and bring to the boil. Drain once more. Let the beef cool, then pull it into small, bite-size shreds or cube it.

3. Rinse the rice in several changes of cold water and drain well.

4. Heat the oil in a deep saucepan and when very hot, add the garlic. Cook to brown and add the rice. Stir about 2 minutes and add the salt. Cook, stirring, about 5 minutes and add the water and coconut. Cover and cook about 20 to 25 minutes. Spoon the rice into a lightly oiled mold. Press down to make rice hold together.

5. Melt the butter in a saucepan and add the onions. Cook until wilted and brown and add the beef. Cook, stirring, until the meat is thoroughly hot.

6. Unmold the rice into a round platter and surround it with the sautéed onions and beef.

Yield: 8 or more servings.

Note: Carne seca or "jerked" beef is available in Manhattan at the Portuguese-American Delicatessen.

Acaraje Sauce

(A hot Brazilian condiment)

1   *to 8 fresh hot peppers (see*
     note), according to taste
½   *cup unsoaked dried ground*
     peeled shrimp (see note)
¾   *cup coarsely chopped*
     onions
½   *cup shredded unsweetened*
     coconut (see note)
¾   *cup hot, almost boiling*
     water
     Salt to taste
1   *teaspoon chopped fresh*
     ginger (see note)
¼   *cup dende oil*

1. Place the hot peppers, shrimp, onions, coconut, water, salt, and ginger in the container of an electric blender. Blend well.

2. Pour the sauce into a mixing bowl. Heat the oil and stir it in. Serve as a side dish with xin xin.

Yield: About 2 cups.

Note: Fresh hot peppers, dried shrimp, and fresh ginger are available in Chinatown. Unsweetened coconut is available at health food stores. Canned Mexican chilies such as pickled serrano peppers can be used in preparing acaraje sauce.

Coconut Blanc Mange

4   *cups milk*
¼ *cup rum*

1½ tablespoons (1½ envelopes)
  unflavored gelatin
4 tablespoons cornstarch
6 tablespoons sugar
3 cups unsweetened grated
  coconut
1 teaspoon vanilla extract
  Prune compote (see recipe)

1. Lightly oil a 5-cup or 6-cup mold and set aside.

2. Bring the milk just to the boil.

3. Combine the rum and gelatin and let stand until gelatin is softened.

4. Spoon and scrape the gelatin mixture into the container of an electric blender. Add half the hot milk and half the remaining ingredients except prune compote. Blend. Pour the mixture into a saucepan.

5. Blend the remaining ingredients except prune compote and combine with the first batch. Bring just to the boil, stirring, and remove from the heat. Let cool.

6. Pour the blanc mange into the prepared mold. Chill until set.

7. Unmold the blanc mange onto a serving dish. Surround it with the prune compote.

Yield: 8 servings.

Prune compote

1 pound prunes
  Water to cover

1. Soak the prunes in water to cover overnight.

2. Do not drain. Bring to the boil and simmer 15 to 25 minutes or until sauce thickens.

Yield: 8 servings.

Caipirinha
(A rum drink)

2½ cups inexpensive rum
¾ cup lemon or lime juice
¾ cup sugar

1. Combine all the ingredients in the container of an electric blender. Blend and serve without ice.

Yield: 6 to 12 servings.

The pepper problem—which pepper is which—is one of the most confusing problems you encounter in international cookery. Not only are there so many kinds of pepper, but so many are available only at specific times of the year. And frequently the greengrocer himself can't identify one from another. We find that the long skinny fresh green and red peppers can substitute for any pepper in almost all recipes. These, fortunately, are widely available throughout the year in international markets, principally Chinese and Mexican. There is no way to tell whether a pepper is hot or mild by looking at it; often both hot and mild peppers are sold in the same batch. You can only tell by taste.

March 1974

I N WRITING about food over the years, it is inevitable that certain phrases and/or quotations stick in the memory like a hook in the mouth of a fish. It was nearly 20 years ago one March while dining at Le Pavillon restaurant, then the most celebrated French restaurant in America, that Frank Schoonmaker, the most knowledgeable of American wine experts, quoted us a poem about shad. Not a March in our lives has passed, nor an occasion when we have dined on shad (see page 85), that we do not recollect the following:

> Oh, the spring is in his bones
> (And the shad has bones to spare)
> As he steers himself and moans
> For the warm bright Delaware . . .
> Don't wish him any less bones
> He'd be too good if he had
> But cry it in tempest tones,
> The fish of fish is shad!
> Brown and white to the heart's delight
> The broiled and beautiful shad.

There is one further thing we recall from that luncheon: Ludwig Bemelmans, the artist, essayist, and gourmand, was sitting at the table next to ours, and he was eating a hamburger.

Four Hearty Fish Soups

WITH PIERRE FRANEY

For those who fancy fish and seafood (and pity those who don't), there is nothing more gratifying to the senses of taste and well-being than a piping-hot fish soup.

Fish Soup with Shrimp and Lobster

¼ cup olive oil
2 cups finely chopped leeks
2 cups chopped onions
3 tablespoons flour
3 cloves garlic, minced
2 cups canned tomatoes, preferably imported Italian peeled tomatoes
3 cups fish stock (see recipe, page 67)
2 cups dry white wine
3 1-pound or 2 1½-pound live lobsters
    Salt and freshly ground pepper to taste
1 cup water
¾ pound shrimp, shelled and deveined
2½ pounds skinless fish fillets such as striped bass, cod, rock fish, flounder, cut into 2-inch pieces.
¼ pound thin pasta such as vermicelli or spaghettini, broken into 3- or 4-inch lengths

1. Heat the oil in a kettle and add the leeks and onions. Cook, stirring, until onions are wilted. Sprinkle with flour and add the garlic, stirring.

2. Add the tomatoes, fish stock, and wine and cook 15 minutes, stirring occasionally.

3. Plunge a knife into the center section of each lobster and sever the tail. Cut each tail crosswise into 3 pieces.

4. Crack the lobster claws. Split the carcass in half and remove and discard the tough small sac near the eyes. Save all the juices that come out of the lobsters.

5. Add the lobster pieces and the juices to the soup. Add the remaining ingredients. Stir, bring to the boil and cook 15 minutes.

6. When ready to serve, discard the pieces of lobster carcass.

Yield: 6 to 8 servings.

Fish Soup with Potatoes

2   *tablespoons butter*
1   *cup finely chopped onions*
½   *cup finely chopped celery*
2   *tablespoons flour*
1   *cup finely diced carrots*
1   *cup dry white wine*
1   *tomato, about ½ pound,*
     peeled, seeded, and diced
6   *cups water*
     Salt and freshly ground
     pepper to taste
½   *teaspoon saffron*
½   *teaspoon thyme*
1   *pound potatoes, peeled and*
     cut into ½-inch cubes
1   *pound fish fillets such as*
     striped bass, sea bass, sole,
     flounder, and so on, cut
     into ½-inch cubes
⅓   *cup heavy cream*

1. Melt the butter in a kettle or deep saucepan and add the onions and celery. Cook 5 minutes. Sprinkle with flour and stir to coat the vegetable pieces.

2. Add the carrots and wine, stirring. Add the tomato, water, salt and pepper to taste, saffron, and thyme. Cook 20 minutes and add the cubed potatoes. Cook 20 minutes and add the cubed fish. Simmer 10 minutes and stir in cream. Bring to boil and serve.

Yield: 6 to 8 servings.

Onion Soup Le Pirate

2   *large Bermuda onions,*
     about 1½ pounds
4   *tablespoons butter*
1½   *teaspoons chopped garlic*
2   *tablespoons flour*
1   *cup dry white wine*
1   *cup canned tomatoes,*
     preferably imported
     Italian peeled tomatoes
4   *cups fresh fish stock (see*
     recipe)
1   *cup heavy cream*
2   *teaspoons Pernod, Ricard,*
     or other anise-flavored
     liqueur
⅓   *cup crushed capellini or*
     vermicelli, optional

1. Cut the onions in half. Cut each half into thin crescent-shaped slices. Chop coarsely. There should be about 6 cups.

2. In a deep, heavy saucepan heat the butter and add the onions and garlic. Cook until wilted. Continue cooking, stirring frequently, until the onion is nicely golden, about 30 minutes.

3. Sprinkle with flour and stir to coat the onions. Add the wine, tomatoes, and fish stock and cook 30 minutes, stirring occasionally.

4. Add the cream and bring to the boil. Add the Pernod.

5. If the capellini or vermicelli is to be used, place the strands in a clean towel and break the strands with the hands. Add the pasta and cook about 3 to 5 minutes. Do not overcook.

Yield: 6 to 10 servings.

Curried Fish Soup

6   cups freshly made fish
    stock (see recipe)
4   tablespoons butter
¾   cup finely chopped onion
1   clove garlic
2   tablespoons curry powder
4   tablespoons flour
1   cup canned tomatoes,
    preferably imported
    Italian peeled tomatoes
½   cup raw rice
1¼ pounds white-fleshed, non-
    oily fish, skinned and boned
    (boned weight)
1   cup heavy cream

1. Prepare the fish stock while making the soup.

2. Melt the butter in a deep saucepan and add the onion and garlic. Cook, stirring, until onion is translucent.

3. Sprinkle with curry powder and flour and stir to blend. Add the tomatoes, fish stock, and rice and bring to the boil, stirring. Cook about 15 minutes.

4. Cut the fish fillets into 1-inch cubes and add them. Simmer about 5 minutes longer. Add the cream and bring to the boil. Serve the soup piping hot in deep bowls.

Yield: 6 to 10 servings.

Fish Stock

2   pounds bones from a
    white-fleshed, non-oily
    fish, including heads if
    possible
6   cups water
1   cup dry white wine
1   cup coarsely chopped
    celery
1   cup coarsely chopped
    onions
3   sprigs fresh thyme or 1
    teaspoon dried
1   bay leaf
10 peppercorns
    Salt to taste
1   medium-size tomato, cored,
    optional

1. If the fish heads are used, the gills must be removed. Run the bones under cold running water.

2. Place the bones in a kettle or deep saucepan and add the remaining ingredients. Bring to the boil and simmer 20 minutes. Strain.

Yield: About 6 cups.

Note: Leftover stock can be frozen for use in other dishes.

If there appears to be a predominance of fish and shellfish soups in this book it's because we live in a fishing community on the water where fresh fish and shellfish are found in abundance. Blessed are those who live on the water.

Anise Creole

As a child of the South, a goodly portion of our early diet consisted of creole dishes of one sort or another. We grew up during Prohibition, and wines and spirits were all but unheard of ingredients in most of the dishes cooked in the kitchen. We were, therefore, fascinated to receive a letter from an acquaintance in New Orleans who asked if we had ever heard of using an anise-flavored spirit such as Pernod or Ricard in shrimp creole. It struck us as a corking good idea. We made it and the result, to our taste, is felicitous.

Shrimp Creole au Pernod

1½   pounds uncooked shrimp
4   tablespoons plus 1 teaspoon butter
1½   cups coarsely chopped onions
1   cup coarsely chopped celery
1   green pepper, cored, seeded and cut into 1-inch cubes
3   cloves garlic, finely minced
3   cups peeled, red, ripe tomatoes, preferably the Italian peeled tomatoes if canned ones are used
2   tablespoons chopped fresh basil or 1 teaspoon dried
2   teaspoons thyme
1   bay leaf
     Tabasco to taste
1   teaspoon grated lemon rind
     Salt and freshly ground pepper to taste
1   teaspoon flour
3   tablespoons finely chopped parsley
     Juice of ½ lemon
1½   tablespoons Pernod or Ricard

1. Peel the shrimp and split them down the back. Rinse away the black vein. Set aside.

2. Melt 4 tablespoons of butter in a saucepan and add the onions. Cook, stirring, until they are wilted and add the celery, green pepper, and garlic. Cook, stirring briefly, about 3 minutes. Do not overcook, for the vegetables should remain crisp.

3. Add the tomatoes, basil, thyme, bay leaf, Tabasco, lemon rind, salt and pepper. Cook uncovered about 15 minutes.

4. Add the shrimp and cover. Cook about 3 minutes, no longer.

5. Blend the remaining teaspoon of butter and the flour and add it bit by bit to the simmering sauce, stirring constantly. Cook about 1 minute and add the parsley and lemon juice. Add the Pernod, heat and serve.

Yield: 4 servings.

The Right Equipment

Niccolo Paganini (1782–1840) was a legendary show-off. During the course of a concert he would, in the middle of a concerto, sonata, or whatever, snip one of the strings of his violin and continue unabated on three strings. Such trickery is great for the box office and dazzling to behold. But we know of a score of good cooks, most of them moderately well off and with something less than Paganini's virtuosity, who thrash about higgledy-piggledy, year after year, in three-string kitchens. It is a constant source of puzzlement. For most of them, cooking is only one of several hobbies, but whereas they will spend outrageous sums for clothes and equipment for skiing and après ski, in the kitchen they hobble along, as the saying goes, on one burner.

It is said that a genuinely accomplished chef, given the proper ingredients, could produce a meal of distinction given a skillet, wood, and a match. You can also make mayonnaise stirring with a wooden spoon. But who needs such odds and obstacles? We are suckers for creature comforts, and to our minds they include proper pots and pans of assorted shapes and sizes, wire whisks of solid make, and solidly constructed saucepans. And in addition to such basics as these and nests of mixing bowls, they also include a few niceties that might be outlined in detail.

First and foremost is a relatively new acquisition called the Cuisinart Food Processor, which has become the cooking gadget we would least prefer to do without. It is a handsome contrivance made in France, where it is aptly called Magi-Mix. It will do anything a blender can, but twice as well and more. It has a nice capacity, and it grinds, grates, and purées. It gives a marvelous texture to cream soups. It is a veritable Merlin at making mousses of fish for things like French mousses and Chinese shrimp balls (see recipe).

It is available at better department stores across the country, and is expensive—$175. Further information about the food processor and about sources of supply may be obtained by writing the importer, Cuisinarts, Inc., P.O. Box 352, Greenwich, Connecticut 06830.

Another all but indispensable item for a well-equipped kitchen is a standard food press consisting of a cone-shaped metal cylinder with a metal stand and wooden pestle. It has hundreds of uses and is the ultimate gadget for mashed or puréed potatoes, carrots, turnips, and the like. It also gives a silken smoothness to bean and split pea soups (recipe given) before they are puréed in the blender. The food press eliminates the tough "hulls" of cooked beans.

Another relatively new instrument that we would be loath to part with is a plastic spin-drier for salads. It is called a Rotor and is made in Switzerland by the Stockli Company.

Remember those old-fashioned French salad baskets in which wet greens are swung around and around by hand to eliminate the rinsing water? They were okay provided you had a great outdoors and a strong right arm. The spin-drier we have in mind consists of two parts, a removable inner basket for the greens and an outer stationary holder. There is

The Cuisinart Food Processor is one of the most versatile tools.

Professional-weight copper stock pot is from The Bridge Kitchenware Corp., $185.

A food press and pestle are ideal for puréeing soups. This model is available at The Bridge Kitchenware Corp., in New York, and costs $7.95.

For making any salad, spin-drier is a boon.

The Cuisinart line includes a stainless-steel kettle with strainer for steaming vegetables.

A coffee grinder can be used for grinding herbs and spices.

A meat pounder is an indispensable kitchen item.

a ring attached to a belt which, when pulled, causes the inner basket to rotate at high speed and the water from the rinsed greens to flow out by centrifugal force into the outside holder.

The spin-drier can be ordered from Bailey & Huebner, 92 Main Street in Southampton, New York. It is also available at many department stores. The cost of the drier at these outlets is about $15.

There is one small and invaluable item in the kitchen for which we have a few hundred uses, and it is a heavy, flat meat pounder. Among other things we find it indispensable for pounding such things as scaloppine and boneless chicken breasts. It comes in handy for flattening shrimp in order to "butterfly" them. It can be used for coarsely cracking peppercorns and for cracking nuts, too, but that is a minor use. Meat pounders come in various metals, but the best is made of solid brass. At The Bridge Kitchenware Corp., the cost of the least expensive meat pounder, stainless steel with a plastic handle, is $6.95. The cost of the solid brass is $16.95.

There is one gadget we prize which we rarely use for the express purpose for which it is made. It is a small grinder whose primary use, according to the manufacturer, is to grind coffee for espresso or filter pots. We, on the other hand, use it for grinding herbs and spices, a trick we adopted from our friend Diana Kennedy, author of the esteemed *The Cuisines of Mexico*. She uses it for grinding dried hot peppers. We use it for grinding a large range of things from peppercorns to cumin and bay leaves. Our grinder happens to be made by Braun and costs about $20.

One of the handiest pieces of equipment in our domain is a hand-operated meat grinder, also of German make. It is manufactured by Alexanderwerk and among the scores of things for which it is handy are grinding meats and stuffing sausages. During the cold months we prepare many pounds of fresh sausages (recipe given) and stash away the ones uneaten or unsmoked in the freezer. The grinder comes in three sizes, 5, 8, and 10 (small, medium, and large). We recommend the large size grinder which costs $39.95 at Bridge Kitchenware.

So much has been made over the Cuisinart Food Processor—that mechanical marvel imported from France—it has gone almost unnoticed that the same importer is responsible for a complete line of outstanding and widely available cookware ranging from small one-and-a-half-cup saucepans to an eight-quart stock pot with cover. We have used Cuisinart cookware with pleasure and continuing satisfaction for the last two years and can testify in depth to its merits. The cookware, made in France, is in stainless steel with a steel-covered aluminum reinforced bottom. Such a bottom is an even heat conductor, and the over-all advantages of the Cuisinart products are many.

We've held a theory for a long time that home broilers are by no means ideal for cooking steaks or chops. We prefer the pan broiling method, which involves adding the slab of meat or a chop to a very hot skillet, searing on one side, turning and searing on the other. The Cuisinart sauté pan is ideal for this because of the bottom's heat retention.

Cuisnart cookware is expensive and well worth the cost. Prices range from about $7 for the smallest saucepan to $79 for a seven-quart steamer. Covers for many utensils cost separately. The products are available around the country.

Traditionally, of course, there is one ultimate kind of cookware, and it is made of copper which is becoming one of the rarer metals of the world. There is an enormous difference, however, in cooking pieces made of copper. There is the thin sort, which is of dubious value where good cooking is concerned. We've always considered one of the big ripoffs of our generation all that stainless steel merchandise with the copper-clad bottoms that was sold some years ago from coast to coast. And perhaps still is.

In any event, the real treasure is solid professional-weight copper lined with tin. It is becoming scarcer and scarcer, but a new shipment of such merchandise recently arrived at The Bridge Kitchenware Corp. Mr. Fred Bridge has the finest heavy copper merchandise in town. The new shipment includes a stunning solid copper stock pot with tin lining; pounds-heavy saucepans of various volumes; and charlotte molds of lighter manufacture.

The cost is a king's ransom, but this is Tiffany-value stuff and will last well beyond the present lifetime of anyone reading this. The prices range from $20 for the charlotte molds to $185 for the stock pot, which includes an au gratin cover. The values will increase with time and in our books copper is a sound investment.

Dansk Design in Mount Kisco, New York, has just imported an impressive new line labeled (for better or for worse) Dansk Gourmet. The new line has first-quality paring and chef's knives, and we are particularly impressed with the latter. The knives, made in France, have admirable balance—weight and shape—that contributes to precision in cutting. Although made of carbon steel with plastic handles, they are dishwasher proof. They are priced from about $11.95 for an 8-inch chef's knife to $14.95 for the 9½-inch size. Like most good knives, these will require sharpening at intervals, and a sharpening steel in the same line is available at $11.95. Dansk Gourmet is available in leading department stores around the country.

Saucisses Chablisienne

(Sausages in the style of Chablis)

4   *pounds lean pork, cut into*
    2-inch cubes
2   *pounds solid pork fat, cut*
    into 2-inch cubes
    Salt to taste
1   *teaspoon finely ground or*
    cracked black pepper
5   *dried hot red pepper pods,*
    or about 1 teaspoon ground
1   *clove garlic, finely minced*
½   *cup dry white wine*
½   *teaspoon saltpeter,*
    available in drug stores
10 *to 12 prepared sausage*
    casings (see instructions
    for preparing below)

1. Put the pork and pork fat into a large mixing bowl and add the salt.

2. If pre-ground pepper is used, add it. Otherwise, grind the pepper using a peppermill. Or grind it in a small, clean coffee grinder. Grind and add.

3. If pre-ground hot red pepper is used, add it. Otherwise, add the pepper pods (without the stems) to the container of a small, clean coffee grinder. Grind and add.

4. Add the garlic, wine, and saltpeter. Mix well with the hands and cover. Let stand in the refrigerator overnight.

5. Put the mixture through a meat grinder fitted with the largest blade. Remove all the meat left in the grinder and clean the grinder blade.

6. Return the blade to the grinder and fit it, along with the special sausage attachment, to the mouth of the grinder.

7. Slide one prepared sausage casing onto the attachment and tie the end. Grind the meat, holding the casing to permit free entry of the filling into the casing. When about 16 inches of casing has been filled, pinch the casing at the end of the sausage attachment. Pull it out to leave about 5 inches of empty casing at that end. Tie that end. Tie both ends of the sausage together. Set aside. Continue making sausage in this manner until all the stuffing has been used.

8. The sausages will keep for several days in the refrigerator. Or they may be wrapped tightly and frozen. To cook them, place a sausage ring in a heavy skillet and add 2 or 3 tablespoons of water to prevent sticking. Cook over moderate heat, turning to brown evenly on all sides. Serve with mashed potatoes, lentils, and so on.

Yield: 6 to 10 sausage rings weighing ¾ to 1 pound each.

Note: Sausage casings are available in pork stores in metropolitan areas. There are a number of places in Manhattan, among them G. Esposito, 500 Ninth Avenue (at 38th Street).

How to prepare sausage casings

1. Sausage casings are normally preserved in salt. When ready to use, put them in a basin of cold water and let stand.

2. Drain and return to a basin of cold water.

3. Lift up one end of a casing and blow into it. They will expand, balloonlike. This is how you determine if the casings have a hole in them. Discard casings with holes or cut the casing at the hole and use the partial casing.

Purée Mongole

(Purée of split pea soup)

1½ pounds tomatoes
5 tablespoons butter
1 cup coarsely chopped onion
1 2-pound ham hock
1 pound yellow split peas
4 cups chicken broth
4 cups water
  Salt and freshly ground pepper to taste
1 white turnip, about ¼ pound, optional
1 carrot
1 cup heavy cream

1. Core the tomatoes and cut them into 1-inch cubes. There should be about 2 cups. Set aside.

2. Heat 2 tablespoons of butter in a kettle and add the onion. Cook until wilted, stirring, and add the tomatoes. Cook about 5 minutes and add the ham hock, split peas, chicken broth, water, salt and pepper. Cook about 2 hours.

3. Meanwhile, peel the turnip and carrot. Slice each very thinly. Cut the slices into very thin strips to resemble match sticks about 1 inch long. There should be about ⅔ cup each.

4. Drop the carrot sticks into boiling salted water and cook about five minutes. Add the turnip and cook 5 to 10 minutes until crisp-tender. Drain well.

5. Remove the ham hock from the soup and put the soup through a food press. Blend the soup, one portion at a time, and return it to a kettle. Add the cream and bring to the boil. Add the strips of carrot and turnip and swirl in the remaining 3 tablespoons of butter.

Yield: 10 to 14 servings.

Deep-Fried Shrimp Balls

2 cups shrimp paste, approximately (see recipe)
1 cup fresh bread crumbs (see note)
  Oil for deep frying

1. Prepare the shrimp paste and set it aside. Using fingers moistened in cold water, shape the mixture into balls about 1½ inches thick or slightly smaller.

2. Roll the balls in bread crumbs to coat them liberally.

3. Heat the oil for deep frying to 360 degrees. Drop the balls, a few at a time, into the hot fat and cook, turning carefully, until golden brown all over and cooked through.

Yield: 4 to 6 servings.

Note: One of the simplest methods of making bread crumbs is to trim a good grade of bread of its crust, break the white part into pieces and add to the container of a food processor or blender. Blend thoroughly. This may have to be done in several small batches, emptying the container after each batch.

Chinese fresh shrimp paste

4 to 6 *dried black mushrooms*
1 *pound raw shrimp*
Salt to taste
½ *cup finely diced water chestnuts*
1 *scallion, finely chopped*
1 *egg white*
½ *teaspoon sugar*
¼ *teaspoon monosodium glutamate, optional*
1 *tablespoon shao hsing or dry sherry*
2 *teaspoons chicken fat or finely minced fresh pork fat*
1½ *teaspoons ginger juice (see note) or finely chopped fresh ginger*

1. Place the mushrooms in a mixing bowl and add boiling water to cover. Let stand 20 minutes.

2. Peel and devein the shrimp. Run them under cold running water and pat dry. Place them in the container of an electric food processor or blender and blend to a smooth paste. This may require two operations.

3. Drain the mushrooms and squeeze them between the fingers to extract most of the moisture. Chop them finely and add them to the shrimp paste. Stir the mixture

vigorously with a wooden spoon, always stirring in the same direction.

4. Add the remaining ingredients, stirring briskly after each addition.

Yield: Approximately 2 cups.

Note: To make fresh ginger juice, grate a small cube of ginger and squeeze it in cheesecloth.

Escalope de Veau à la Moutarde
(Veal scallops with mustard sauce)

8 *veal scaloppine, about ¾ pound*
⅓ *cup flour*
Salt and freshly ground pepper to taste
4 *tablespoons butter*
2 *tablespoons finely minced shallots*
¼ *cup dry white wine*
½ *cup heavy cream*
1 *tablespoon imported mustard, preferably Dijon or Düsseldorf (see note)*

1. Place the scaloppine on a flat surface and pound thin with a flat metal meat pounder or the bottom of a clean skillet.

2. Blend the flour with salt and pepper and dredge the scaloppine on all sides.

3. Heat the butter in a large heavy skillet until it is quite hot but not brown. Add the scaloppine (note that they shrink as they cook). Cook quickly until golden, about 2 minutes, on one side

and turn. Cook until golden on the other side. Remove the scaloppine to a warm dish and keep warm and covered with foil. Add the shallots to the skillet and cook briefly, stirring. Add the wine and cook, stirring, until it is almost totally evaporated. Add the cream and let it boil up, stirring. Cook about 30 seconds and turn off the heat. Stir in the mustard. Do not cook further. Pour sauce over veal and serve. Serve with fine buttered noodles.

Yield: 2 or 3 servings.

Note: If imported mustard is not available, prepare your own mustard, following the directions on page 45.

It was what we deserved, we suppose, introducing a violinist to the food page. We immediately heard from someone at the Juilliard School of Music who informed us that Signor Paganini was considerably more virtuostic than we'd described: He would not, as we stated, in the middle of a concert snip one of the strings of his violin and continue unabated on three strings, but he would snip three strings and continue unabated on one.

It so happens we were in possession of that intelligence when we wrote the article. The source of our information was a book by our friend, neighbor, and colleague, Harold Schonberg. It is called *The Lives of the Great Composers,* and in it Harold states quite clearly that Paganini would "break a string in the middle of a composition and continue to the end on three strings. Or he would produce a scissors, cut three of the strings and perform miracles on the G-string alone."

To tell you the truth, we meditated at length over using the latter comparison and discarded the idea because we did not want anybody to think we know people who cook in one-string kitchens.

A Healthy Loaf

WITH PIERRE FRANEY

It started out as something to do on a boring afternoon and escalated into a home industry, a part-time one to be sure, but enough to keep Peter Moore, 15, as busy as he wants to be. The business? Baking bread. Good solid loaves of whole wheat flour and blackstrap molasses. Peter has figured out that the ingredients cost 55 cents at his neighborhood health store in Manhattan for a loaf that he sells to the same store for 90 cents. He is unconcerned with such trivia as the right temperature for raising dough. His does quite nicely, he reports, in the living room, "whatever temperature that is." His parents are quite keen on his product, but Peter says, "I eat plain old white bread myself."

Whole Wheat Bread with Blackstrap Molasses

4½ *cups scalded milk*
4½ *tablespoons butter or margarine*
⅔ *cup blackstrap molasses*
2 *packages (2 tablespoons) dry active yeast*
½ *cup lukewarm water*
9 *cups whole wheat flour, approximately*

1. Blend the scalded milk with the butter or margarine and molasses. Stir to melt the fat. Set aside until lukewarm.

2. Dissolve the yeast in the warm water.

3. Blend the cooled molasses mixture and dissolved yeast together in a large bowl. Stir in the flour gradually until a soft-sticky dough is formed. Clean up the sides of the bowl, cover with a damp towel and set in a warm place until doubled in bulk, about 1½ hours.

4. Punch the dough down and knead in the bowl for 5 to 7 minutes or until the mixture is elastic. Add only enough extra flour to prevent sticking.

5. Divide the dough evenly into 4 carefully buttered 8½-by-4½-by-2½-inch loaf pans.

6. Cover the pans with a damp towel and set in a warm place until the dough has almost doubled in size.

7. Preheat oven to 400 degrees.

8. Bake loaves 20 minutes, reduce oven heat to 375 and bake 20 minutes longer or until the loaves sound hollow when tapped on the bottom. Remove loaves from pan and cool on rack.

Yield: 4 loaves.

Swordfish Steak Is Back

We have recently received a letter from a reader in Connecticut who expressed his unfeigned delight at finding swordfish in his local market for the first time in a couple of years. We, too, are among those who have rejoiced at the welcome, delectable sight of those large rounds of the fish that we have encountered at rare intervals in markets where we shop.

For fish fanciers, one of the great deprivations of the last decade came about when alarm was evidenced over the mercury content of swordfish. Fortunately, the scare is past (although there are doubtless scores of people who will never touch it again). After too long an absence, the fish is with us once more.

Swordfish steaks are a delight when simply grilled or broiled and served with lemon butter and a touch of parsley, perhaps. There are various butters that are highly agreeable on the fish including anchovy butter (chopped anchovies plus melted butter and lemon juice) and caper butter (chopped capers plus melted butter and lemon juice). If you really want to be fancy, however, you might try sautéed swordfish in a cream sauce.

Espadon à la Crème
(Sautéed swordfish in cream sauce)

2 *pounds swordfish, about 1
  inch thick
  Salt and freshly ground
  pepper to taste
  Flour for dredging*
6 *tablespoons butter*
2 *tablespoons finely chopped
  shallots*
3 *tablespoons cognac*
1 *cup heavy cream*

1. Cut the swordfish into 4 or 6 individual servings. Sprinkle the pieces with salt and pepper and dredge on all sides in flour.

2. Heat 4 tablespoons of the butter in a heavy skillet large enough to hold the fish in one layer. Brown on one side about 3 to 5 minutes and turn with a spatula. Cook on the second side about 7 minutes or until cooked through.

3. Push the fish pieces to one side of the skillet and add the shallots. Cover and cook about 3 minutes. Do not overcook or the fish will become dry.

4. Transfer the fish to a warm serving platter and add the cognac to the skillet. Ignite it and add the cream. Cook over high heat about 2 minutes. Add the remaining butter to the skillet and swirl it in. Return the fish to the skillet. Spoon the sauce over and serve hot.

Yield: 4 to 6 servings.

An Abiding Affection For French Bread

Clyde Brooks is probably the only man in the world who kneads dough (no pun intended) while a myna bird at his elbow asks almost without respite, "Are you a pussycat?"

Mr. Brooks is a tall, bespectacled, markedly handsome man, whose hunger for the breads of Paris, where he lived for several years, has led him into an interesting side line, a seller of bread molds of his own design.

"My wife and I lived only a block away from a fantastic boulangerie, which we'd visit at least once and sometimes twice a day. Real French bread, once you're hooked on it, is something." He spoke and paused as if in reverie.

"I'd done some baking a long time ago in 1945 or 1946 when there was a great bread shortage after the war. I baked eight or ten loaves, nothing serious. When we came back from Paris, I started all over again and had the usual problems. We'd shape the loaves and instead of coming out round they came out flat. I took the predictable aluminum foil route, trying to mold them with that, but it didn't work. I finally hit on shaping pieces of thin solid aluminum. By golly it worked."

His molds do, indeed, work and admirably so. The "pans" that he devised consist of a single sheet of lightweight aluminum, bent in half at the center. Each half is then shaped into half-circular trays for greasing and holding the bread. The bread, when baked, comes out round, golden, and eminently edible, to use our favorite phrase. Light years from ordinary store-bought bread.

For his original home-use, Mr. Brooks bent the aluminum over a gas pipe in his basement, but now that he produces in modest volume he buys the aluminum in 50-foot rolls and has the molds shaped professionally at a shop near his home. The molds are 18 inches long.

He receives numerous love letters each month from people who have purchased or otherwise come by his bread-making utensil. One letter he showed us came from a lady down South. It started out, "Dear Mr. Brooks, Blessings a thousandfold. Over the years the jugs of wine have been quite accessible. There have always been plenty of 'thou's' around but until we heard of you we'd been seriously deprived of a respectable loaf . . ."

He also has correspondence from a woman in southern Maryland who came across a set of molds and explained she is now providing genuine French bread "to the children on our school feeding program."

Mr. Brooks states that the audience for his molds includes both men and women, and he is convinced that doctors more than any other professionals have the keenest interest in cooking in general and breadmaking specifically. He has also had numerous orders over the years from retired persons. He notes with some pride that he has shipped pans all over the world including Singapore and Africa "but," he adds ruefully, "no requests from France."

When shipped, the Brooks pans are accompanied by what may conceivably be the longest recipe ever written—six pages, triple spaced—plus a one-page condensed version.

"I wrote that recipe—instructions, actually—with some of the technical Air Force manuals in mind. They were always written on the theory that whoever reads them knows nothing about the subject."

The gentleman's molds are sold in sets of eight, and the accompanying recipe is for eight loaves. The recipe is easily halved or quartered for fewer loaves. The molds may be obtained by sending $9.90, which includes postage and handling, to Paris-C, 500 Independence Avenue, S.E., Washington, D.C. 20003.

Hallie Brooks, 6, of Summit, New Jersey, waits anxiously for her grandfather, Clyde Brooks of Washington, an aircraft company executive, to give her some of the French bread he bakes in self-designed molds.

At approximately the same time we learned of Mr. Brooks's bread pans, we received—quite coincidentally—a small typewritten, hand-bound booklet titled "Sourdough Rye and Other Good Breads." It is written by Sue Gross of Cortland, Illinois, and details the preparation of a sourdough starter plus, among other breads, one for sourdough French bread. We used her recipe with the Brooks pans and the results were thoroughly impressive. In addition to the recipes borrowed from her booklet and printed here, the slender work also includes recipes for sourdough rye with variation, pumpernickel, and pancakes. The booklet is available for $1.50 including postage and may be obtained by writing Sue Gross, Gross' Kitchen Harvest, Box 30, Cortland, Illinois 60112.

Clyde Brooks's French Bread

2½ *cups water (105 to 115 degrees for dry yeast; 80 to 85 degrees for fresh yeast cake)*
1 *package dry active yeast (or crumble 1 fresh yeast cake)*
1 *tablespoon salt*
1 *tablespoon sugar, optional*
7 *or more cups unbleached flour*

1. Combine the water and yeast in a warm mixing bowl and stir to dissolve. Add the salt, sugar, and 4 cups of the flour and stir and beat with the hands until well blended. Add more flour, about ½ cup at a time, mixing and stirring with the hands. The dough will be sticky.

2. Continue adding flour until dough leaves the side of the bowl almost clean. The dough at the proper point will be lumpy and sticky. Use only as much flour as necessary to achieve this.

3. Turn the dough out onto a well-floured board. Knead about

10 minutes. Quickly fold the dough towards you. Quickly push it away with the heels of the hand and give the dough a quarter turn. As you knead, spoon a little more flour onto the board so the dough does not stick. Continue kneading, pushing the dough away and giving it a quarter turn and flour-

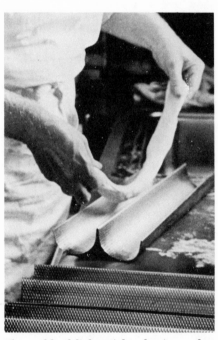

The mold of lightweight aluminum that Mr. Brooks designed.

ing the board lightly until the dough is smooth and pliable. Shape into a ball.

4. Place the ball of dough in a greased warm bowl and turn it in the bowl to cover lightly with the grease. Cover the bowl with a clean towel and set the bowl in a warm place. The temperature should be about 85 to 90 degrees. Let stand until double in bulk. The rising time will take from about 1 to 1½ hours (or longer if the temperature is too low). To bake, see instructions for shaping and baking bread dough, below.

Yield: 2 to 4 loaves.

Sourdough French Bread

(Sue Gross's version)

1 cup sourdough starter (see recipe)
2 cups warm water (the temperature should be about 80 degrees)
6 cups unbleached flour plus flour for kneading
1 package dry active yeast
1 tablespoon salt

1. Combine in a warm bowl the sourdough starter, 1 cup of warm water, and 2 cups of flour. Stir to blend and cover with plastic wrap. Let stand overnight in a warm but not hot place.

2. Dissolve the yeast in remaining cup of warm water. Add the yeast to the starter mixture. Add the salt and 4 cups of flour and stir to blend well.

3. Turn the mixture out onto a lightly floured board and knead patiently, adding more flour to the kneading surface as necessary. Knead for about 10 to 15 minutes or until the dough is smooth and elastic. Shape the dough into a ball.

4. Rub a mixing bowl lightly with oil or lard and add the ball of dough. Flop it around in the bowl 2 or 3 times until it is coated with grease.

5. Cover with a cloth and let stand in a warm place. The temperature should be about 85 or 90 degrees. Let stand until double in bulk. The rising time will take from 1 to 1½ hours (or longer if the temperature is too low). To bake, grease 3 French bread tins and follow instructions for shaping and baking bread dough.

Yield: 3 loaves.

Sourdough starter

1 package dry active yeast
2 cups warm water (the temperature should be between 110 and 115 degrees)
2 cups unbleached flour

1. Empty the yeast into a warm mixing bowl and stir in the water. Stir until yeast is dissolved.

2. Add the flour and stir well until it is blended. Cover with plastic wrap and let stand at room temperature for about 48 hours. When ready, the starter will be bubbly with a somewhat yellowish liquid on top.

3. When part of the starter is removed to make bread, the remainder must be fed with more flour and water. Add 1 cup of flour and 1 cup of water to replace 1 cup removed. Stir and cover with more plastic wrap. Let stand in a warm place for an hour or more or until bubbling action is renewed. The starter may be used and replenished for years and it improves with age. Store starter in the refrigerator in a mixing bowl covered with plastic wrap or in a jar with a loose-fitting lid.

Yield: About 3 cups of starter.

To Shape and Bake Bread Dough

1. Preheat the oven to 450 degrees.

2. If Mr. Brooks's bread molds are to be used, grease enough molds for 2 or 3 or more loaves with oil or lard.

3. If the molds are not to be used, grease a baking sheet with oil or lard and sprinkle lightly with cornmeal.

4. Punch the dough down when it is double in bulk and turn it onto an unfloured surface. Slice the dough into 2 equal parts.

5. Using the hands, shape one portion of dough at a time on a flat surface. Roll the dough into a long ropelike shape. Roll the dough back and forth under the palms until it is more or less uniform in diameter from one end to the other. Each "rope" should be about 1 inch shorter than the molds or the baking sheet.

6. Place the dough in the molds or on baking sheet. Place the molds uncovered in a warm place (85 to 90 degrees) and let stand until double in bulk.

7. Holding a razor blade on the bias, slash each loaf 3 or 4 times lightly on the top. The slashes should be about ⅛ inch or slightly deeper. If desired, the dough may be brushed lightly with water, milk, or lightly beaten egg or egg whites. This is to give color.

8. Place the loaves in the oven and bake 15 minutes. Reduce the oven heat to 350 degrees and continue baking 30 minutes or longer. If the loaves should expand and join each other at the sides, pull them apart and reverse their positions in the molds.

9. Remove the loaves from the oven and remove them from the molds or baking sheet. Place them on racks so that air can circulate freely.

Mr. Brooks has recently reported to us the findings of a cost study in which it was found that homemade French bread is about 40 percent cheaper than the spongy store-bought variety. The cost study is sent along with the rest of the literature that accompanies the molds.

The Inimitable Shad

WITH PIERRE FRANEY

Today, there is, for better or worse, almost no food on earth that isn't available out of season. One rare and notable exception is fresh shad, as much a sign of spring as the first jonquil or the robin on the lawn. On America's East Coast the first shad comes from southern waters. The fish then makes its way into all the river systems up the coast, including the "bright blue Delaware," the Hudson, and the Connecticut Rivers. An elegant way to celebrate the first shad of the season is to prepare it in the traditional French manner called Doria, which is served with cucumber ovals.

Shad Fillets Doria

2   *small shad fillets or 1 large fillet, about 1 pound*
¼   *cup peanut, vegetable, or corn oil*
1½ *tablespoons lemon juice*
2   *tablespoons finely chopped parsley*
½   *bay leaf, finely minced*
½   *teaspoon chopped fresh thyme or ¼ teaspoon dried Salt and freshly ground pepper to taste*
5   *tablespoons butter*
1   *cup small, fresh bread cubes*
½   *cup flour*
1   *egg, well beaten*
1   *cup heavy cream Parsleyed cucumber ovals (see recipe)*

1. If the fillets are small, cut each one in half. If there is one large fillet, cut into 4 equal-size pieces. Place the pieces in a flat dish. Blend the oil, lemon juice,

parsley, bay leaf, and thyme. Add salt and pepper to taste. Spoon this evenly over the shad pieces and turn them in it. Let stand an hour or so.

2. Meanwhile, heat 3 tablespoons of butter in a skillet and add the bread cubes. Cook, stirring and tossing so that the cubes are evenly coated with butter. Cook until golden brown on all sides. Drain well and reserve the butter.

3. Preheat oven to 400 degrees.

4. Season the flour with salt and pepper. Remove the shad pieces one at a time and dredge on all sides with flour. Dip in egg to coat on all sides.

5. Meanwhile, heat the butter reserved from browning the bread cubes and the remaining 2 tablespoons of butter in a skillet large enough to hold the fish in one layer. As each piece is dipped in egg add it to the skillet. Cook about 5 minutes until golden on one side. Carefully turn the pieces and cook on the other side about 7 minutes.

6. Arrange the fish on a heatproof dish and place in the oven.

7. Meanwhile, add the cream to a saucepan or small skillet and cook over high heat until it is reduced to ½ cup. Spoon this evenly over the fillets, sprinkle with the croutons and serve hot. Accompany the fish with the cucumbers.

Yield: 4 servings.

Parsleyed cucumber ovals

2 *large, firm, fresh*
   cucumbers
   Salt to taste
1 *tablespoon butter*
   Freshly ground pepper to
   taste
2 *tablespoons finely chopped*
   parsley

1. Trim off the ends of the cucumbers. Cut the cucumbers into 2-inch lengths. Quarter each section lengthwise. Using a paring knife, carefully trim the pieces, cutting away the green skin and the seeds and leaving only the firm flesh. The pieces are now ready to cook, although if you want to "turn" them, as French chefs do, neatly round the ends of each piece with a knife.

2. Place the pieces in a saucepan and add boiling water to cover and salt. Cook 1 minute and drain.

3. Return the cucumbers to the saucepan and add butter, salt and pepper to taste. Toss until butter melts. Sprinkle with parsley. Serve hot.

Yield: 4 servings.

Une Merveille!

Provincial to the core, we tended for years to dismiss Philadelphia as a decent place to visit but a negligible place to dine. And then, about 18 months ago, we discovered to our enormous pleasure what we observed in a personal journal to be "one of the finest restaurants in America." As our ardor mounted, we added, "there is not a restaurant in Manhattan with such elegance in its surroundings. The flatware is Christofle, the 'soda' is Perrier, the table water is Evian. The wine glasses are balloon-shaped, and there are fresh roses on each table. Le Bec Fin," for such is its name, "is a small restaurant (there are only 10 tables), and the walls are hung with crystal mirrors and tapestries. And now the dilemma of what to praise first. The quenelles, of course. . . ." We continued to heap praise on the chicken with cucumbers, kidneys bohemienne, and so on.

After our meal we met the owner and chef, Georges Perrier, and we were as much taken with his modest manner and good-natured charm as with his talent. Thus, when we were invited last week to visit a cooking class over which M. Perrier would preside, we accepted with enthusiastic dispatch. The class, the first of four sessions, was to be held at 10:30 in the morning in the home of Mrs. Jerome Kursman in this suburb about a 15-minute drive from the heart of Philadelphia.

We arrived about 10 and our hostess explained that she and her partner, Mrs. Arthur Keyser, had started their small "school," called La Bonne Cuisine, about a year ago, that M. Perrier's sessions would be the last of the current season, and that they were about to take off—in May—with their husbands for a wine and gastronomic tour of Provence, Périgord, Bordeaux, and the Riviera, picking up new ideas for the fall. Mrs. Kursman escorted us into the kitchen where we were greeted by the chef, a pencil-thin, smiling young man who stands five feet four inches tall when he is not wearing his toque blanche.

M. Perrier is a man of grand enthusiasm and an endearing lack of false modesty. He explained that he would be making three dishes that morning: poached striped bass with a beurre blanc sauce; poulet Albuféra, a dish made with chicken stuffed with foie gras and truffles and supposedly created by Carême; plus a raspberry sherbet. Our host, Mr. Kursman, poured us each a glass of well-chilled Mosel, and between sips the chef explained that he was 30 years old and is a native of Lyon. He started cooking when he was 15 and trained both at La Pyramide, one of the citadels of fine cookery, in Vienne, and at the equally celebrated Baumanière in Baux-de-Provence.

He turned to the task of preparing the chicken and between bouts of studied silence he described his procedure—in a highly comprehensible blend of French and English—to the assembled women students on the opposite side of the chopping block and stove.

"To make Albuféra, you must run your hands beneath the skin and the flesh like this," he explained as he ran his hands skillfully beneath the chicken's skin and the flesh. "Now we add slices of truffles between the skin and flesh. It is les truffes that give the chicken its perfume. This is the same technique as for chicken demi-deuil or chicken in half mourning, the truffles under the skin. French chefs can truffle anything: turkeys, chickens, any kind of white volaille."

M. Perrier directed his attention to a platter of cooked rice, tossing it with more truffles and foie gras. "The foie gras," he explained, "makes the Albuféra very nice. It is like a liaison, combining the ingredients and blending them together." He deftly stuffed and trussed three chickens, daubed them with butter, and placed them in a hot oven.

Seconds later he was at the stove making a court-bouillon or cooking broth for the fish—water, onion, carrot, a touch of white vinegar and wine, thyme, and bay leaf. As it simmered he glanced at the chickens and gave out a hearty and delighted appraisal. "You can smell the chickens, you can see the truffles. It smells beautiful," he noted contentedly.

Shortly the court-bouillon was ready for the fish and he added it. "Striped bass," he stated, echoing the sentiment of most French chefs on America's East Coast, "is the finest fish in American waters." As the fish cooked at a bare simmer, he turned his attention to what would be obviously for him the triumph of the day, his beurre blanc, or classic white butter sauce made with dry white wine, shallots, heavy cream, and butter.

"You combine the wine and shallots and boil it down. Quickly! The wine must be almost gone. The shallots should be wet but almost dry. You see," he said, passing saucepan first under his own nose and then to those of the assembled students. He then added cream and cooked that down and stuck in a ladle which he withdrew. Proudly. The sauce coated the spoon nicely. Then the butter, which he had massaged briefly to give it the proper consistency. He removed the saucepan from the stove and swirled in the butter, a little at a time, almost reverentially. He beamed. The sauce, like a thin, velvety custard, was a masterpiece. "Une merveille!" he added without pause or unnecessary thought.

His prestidigitations of the day had also included the making of a burgundy-red raspberry sherbet that churned away in an anteroom. Preparations completed, the food was carved, spooned, and ladled to the guests. It was eaten with justifiable gusto and adulation plus fine white and red wines from Burgundy and the session was over.

M. Perrier awarded us with his new menu, which offers a complete five-course dinner. It lists such appetizers as terrine of turbot, and foie gras of chicken livers, fish courses such as quenelles of pike with Nantua sauce and coquilles St. Jacques with beurre blanc; main courses such as salmis of guinea hen and fillet of beef Chambertin. The cost is $22. The restaurant is at 1312 Spruce Street, Philadelphia, and the telephone number is (215) 732-3000.

Mrs. Kursman told us that La Bonne Cuisine offers two classes in the fall and two in the spring. The five-lesson course costs $100. Information about the school may be obtained by writing La Bonne Cuisine, Golf House Road, Haverford, Pennsylvania 19041.

Poached Striped Bass

The court-bouillon

6 to 8 cups water
1 cup thinly sliced onion
1 cup thinly sliced carrots
1 leek, trimmed, split in half and well rinsed
½ cup dry white wine
¼ cup white vinegar
   Salt to taste
1 tablespoon peppercorns, crushed
3 sprigs fresh thyme or 1 teaspoon dried
2 bay leaves
2 cloves garlic, peeled and cut in half

The fish

1 3½- to 5-pound striped bass, cleaned, gills removed, and preferably with the head and tail left on.
   Beurre blanc or white butter sauce (see recipe)

1. Combine all the ingredients for the court-bouillon and bring to the boil. Simmer 10 minutes. Let cool.

2. Add the fish and cover. Bring to the boil and simmer 10 to 15 minutes. Let the fish stand in the cooking liquid for 10 minutes or longer.

3. Remove the fish and carefully pare away the skin. Serve lukewarm with white butter sauce.

Yield: 6 to 10 servings.

Beurre blanc
(White butter sauce)

1 cup dry white wine
¼ cup white vinegar
⅓ cup finely chopped shallots
2¼ cups heavy cream
   Salt and freshly ground pepper to taste
1 cup butter at room temperature

1. Combine the wine, vinegar, and shallots in a saucepan.

Cook over high heat until the liquid is almost totally evaporated. When ready, the shallots will still be wet-moist.

2. Add the heavy cream and cook at full boil about 10 minutes. When ready, the sauce will coat a spoon.

3. Remove the sauce from the heat.

4. Massage the butter lightly with the fingers and add it gradually to the sauce, stirring constantly with a wire whisk. Serve hot with poached fish.

Yield: About 2 cups

Chicken Albuféra

1   *3-pound chicken*
2   *to 4 black truffles*
    Salt and freshly ground
    pepper to taste
` 3   *tablespoons plus 1*
    teaspoon madeira
1   *teaspoon cognac*
4   *chicken livers*
3   *tablespoons plus 2*
    teaspoons butter
1   *tablespoon plus 2*
    teaspoons peanut,
    vegetable, or corn oil
1½ *cups baked rice (see recipe,*
    page 10)
1   *cup foie gras or pâté de*
    foie cut into ½-inch cubes
    (see note)
½   *cup brown chicken base*
    (see recipe)
⅓   *cup heavy cream*

1. Preheat oven to 500 degrees.

2. Separate the skin from the flesh of the breast and thighs of the chicken. To do this, start at the neck opening and run the fingers gradually between the skin and flesh, working the fingers first over the breast and then about halfway down the thighs. This is not difficult to do.

3. Cut half the truffles into thin slices and insert these at intervals between the skin and the flesh of the breast and thighs. Sprinkle the inside of the chicken with salt, pepper, and 1 teaspoon each madeira and cognac. Set aside.

4. Slice the chicken livers and cut the slices into thin strips Cut the strips into cubes. Sprinkle with salt and pepper.

5. Heat 2 teaspoons each butter and oil in a small saucepan and when quite hot, add the livers. Cook, stirring and tossing, about 3 minutes or until done. Drain.

6. Spoon the rice into a mixing bowl and add the drained livers.

Georges Perrier demonstrates to the class how to cut slices of chicken livers into thin strips, then into cubes, for chicken Albuféra.

7. Cut the remaining truffles into small cubes and add them to the rice. Sprinkle with 1 tablespoon of madeira and add salt and pepper to taste. Add the foie gras and toss to blend well.

8. Spoon the rice mixture into the chicken. Truss the chicken. Place the chicken on one side in a small baking dish and smear with the remaining 3 tablespoons of butter. Sprinkle with remaining tablespoon of oil and bake 10 minutes. Do not cover. Reduce the oven heat to 450 degrees.

9. Bake 10 minutes and turn the chicken onto its other side. Bake 20 minutes and turn the chicken on its back. Bake about 5 minutes or until golden brown. Sprinkle with remaining 2 tablespoons of madeira and add the chicken base.

10. Remove the chicken and bring the pan sauce to the boil. Tilt the pan and skim off any excess fat from the top. Add the cream and bring to the boil, stirring. Put the sauce through a fine sieve, preferably the French sieve called chinois. Press with a wooden spoon to extract any liquid from any solids in the sauce. Bring to the boil and serve hot.

11. Untruss the chicken and serve it carved with the rice stuffing and sauce.

Yield: 4 servings.

Note: Pure foie gras is the ultimate ingredient for this dish, but the tinned, far less expensive pâté de foie is acceptable as a substitute. Both are available in fine food stores and in most well-stocked supermarkets. Leftover rice can be served or used later for other dishes.

Brown chicken base

4 *pounds bony chicken parts such as wings, backs, necks, and so on*
Salt and freshly ground pepper to taste
¾ *cup coarsely chopped carrots*
¾ *cup coarsely chopped celery*
1 *cup coarsely chopped onion*
1 *clove garlic, finely minced*
1 *cup dry white wine*
4 *cups chicken broth*
6 *sprigs parsley*
1 *bay leaf*
1 *teaspoon thyme*
½ *cup chopped tomato*

1. Cut the chicken pieces into 2-inch lengths. Place them in a kettle and cook, stirring frequently, about 10 minutes. It is not necessary to add additional fat. The chicken will cook in its natural fat.

2. Add the carrots, celery, onion, and garlic. Cook, stirring frequently, 10 to 15 minutes longer or until chicken parts are nicely browned. Add the wine, broth, salt and pepper to taste. Add the parsley, bay leaf, thyme, and tomato. Cook, uncovered, about 1 hour, stirring frequently. Strain, using a wooden spoon to extract as much liquid from the solids as possible. Discard the solids. Leftover chicken base may be frozen.

Yield: About 3 cups.

The Versatile Chicken

WITH PIERRE FRANEY

Chicken is indeed a food for all feasts, a food for all seasons. Almost universally available, it is common in the kitchens of rich and poor alike. The methods for cooking it are literally without end. Not the least of its virtues is its cost. In any supermarket or grocery store it will stand fair comparison with other meats. Three recipes are given here. One is for chicken with lemon sauce. Another is a variation on the Italian classic, chicken cacciatore. This one has sausage. The third is for chicken in a tarragon sauce.

Note: More chicken recipes and a few comments on the virtues of chicken in parlous times can be found on pages 262–266.

Chicken with Lemon

2 *1¾-pound chickens, cut into serving pieces (see note)*
 Salt and freshly ground pepper to taste
3 *tablespoons butter*
¼ *cup finely chopped shallots*
10 *thin lemon slices*
½ *cup dry white wine,*

1. Sprinkle the chicken pieces with salt and pepper to taste.

2. Melt the butter in a skillet and brown the chicken skin side down. When golden, turn the pieces and brown on the other side.

3. Sprinkle with shallots and arrange the lemon slices over the chicken. Cover and cook 5 minutes. Pour off the fat and add the wine.

4. Cover and cook 15 minutes or until tender. Serve with the pan gravy and fluffy rice.

Yield: 4 to 6 servings.

Note: The preferred method for cutting the chicken is as follows: Separate the legs from the thighs. Split the whole breast in half. Bone the breast halves but leave the main wing bone attached.

Chicken and Sausage Casserole

4 *cups canned tomatoes, preferably imported Italian peeled plum*
1 *teaspoon sugar, optional*
1 *2½-pound chicken, cut into serving pieces*
 Salt and freshly ground pepper to taste
1 *tablespoon olive oil*

6 *sweet or hot Italian sausages, about 1 pound*
1 *cup coarsely chopped onions*
1 *cup sliced mushrooms*
1 *large green pepper, cored, seeded, and cut into 1-inch cubes*
1 *clove garlic, finely minced*
1 *teaspoon oregano*
½ *cup chicken broth*
½ *cup dry white wine*

1. Place the tomatoes in a saucepan and cook them down until reduced to 2 cups. Taste and if they seem acid, stir in the sugar.

2. Sprinkle the chicken with salt and pepper. Heat the oil in a skillet and add the chicken pieces skin side down. Prick the sausages with a fork and add them. Cook, turning the ingredients until browned on all sides, about 15 minutes. Carefully pour off all fat.

3. Scatter the onions, mushrooms, green pepper, and garlic between the pieces of chicken and sausages. Sprinkle with oregano.

4. Add the tomatoes, chicken broth, and wine and stir to dissolve any brown particles on the bottom of the skillet. Cover closely and cook 20 minutes. Serve with hot rice.

Yield: 4 to 6 servings.

Chicken in Tarragon Cream Sauce

2 *3-pound chickens, cut into serving pieces*
2 *cups dry white wine*
2 *cups chicken broth*
1 *tablespoon finely chopped fresh tarragon or ½ teaspoon dried*
  Salt and freshly ground pepper to taste
1 *cup heavy cream*
1 *tablespoon butter*
1 *tablespoon flour*

1. When the chickens are cut, it is best if the breasts are boned but the main wing bone should be left intact.

2. Arrange the pieces skin side down in one layer in a heavy casserole. Add the wine, broth, tarragon, salt and pepper to taste and cover. Bring to the boil and cook 15 to 20 minutes.

3. Remove the chicken pieces and cover with foil to keep warm.

4. Cook the sauce over high heat until it is reduced by half. Add the heavy cream and cook 8 to 10 minutes longer over high heat. Add salt and pepper to taste.

5. Blend the butter and flour and add it to the sauce, stirring. Do not boil. Pour hot sauce over the chicken and serve with buttered noodles.

Yield: 6 to 8 servings.

"Let All Who Are Hungry Come And Eat"

WITH PIERRE FRANEY

The youngest son of the family is the star at the Jewish feast of Seder as he opens this basic celebration of Passover by asking the centuries-old question: "Why is this night different from all other nights?" Mrs. Baruch Zeger says, "For me it is the time of an ingathering of my family and I love it. It's one of the few times I get all my sons together." This coming Saturday evening, there will be, as there have been in the past, 30 or more guests in Mrs. Zeger's home. Among the most honored will be her sons, Eric Segal, best known as the author of *Love Story;* David Segal, a stage and electrical designer, and Thomas Segal, a business executive. Below is a sampling of dishes that Mrs. Zeger will set forth.

Cynthia Zeger's table is set for that most symbolic of feasts, the Seder.

Matzoh Balls

½ cup matzoh meal
2 eggs, lightly beaten
¼ cup water
⅛ teaspoon chicken fat
1 teaspoon salt
1 tablespoon chopped
parsley

1. Stir the matzoh meal into the eggs. Gradually blend in the water, fat, salt, and parsley. Cover and set in the refrigerator for 20 minutes.

2. Form the mixture into 12 balls. Drop into simmering soup or boiling salted water and simmer gently 15 minutes. Drain if cooked in water.

Yield: 12 matzoh balls.

Gefilte Fish

2 pounds each
(approximately) of carp,
pike, and white fish,
filleted to give about 3½
pounds skinned fish;
reserve heads, bones and
skins
3 onions
3 carrots
Sprig of parsley
Salt and freshly ground
black pepper to taste
2 cloves garlic, optional
3 apricot kernels (see note),
optional
4 eggs, lightly beaten
½ cup water

1. Rinse the fish heads, bones, and skins and place in a saucepan with 1 onion, 2 carrots cut in quarters, parsley, salt and pepper to taste, 1 clove garlic, and 2 apricot kernels. Cover with about 2 quarts water.

2. Bring to a boil, cover and simmer 1 hour or longer. Strain broth, discard bones.

3. Grind the fish fillets and remaining onions and remaining garlic clove, if used, through the finest blade of a meat chopper. Grind a second time and then chop with the remaining apricot kernel if used, in a bowl or on a board, until the mixture is very fine. Transfer to a bowl if on a board.

4. Beat in the eggs, water, salt and pepper to taste to give a fine, smooth mixture.

5. Shape the fish mixture into about 20 medium-size balls. Heat the reserved, strained broth in a large skillet or sauté pan. Gently drop the balls of fish into the simmering, but not boiling, liquid. Partially cover and simmer very gently 1½ to 2 hours. Slice the remaining carrot thickly and add during the last 30 minutes of cooking time.

6. Drain and place the fish balls on a platter, cool slightly, cover and refrigerate. Remove carrot pieces and reserve for a garnish. Strain the broth into a bowl, cool, and chill overnight.

7. Serve the gefilte fish garnished with carrot pieces and with jellied broth or aspic.

Yield: 20 medium-size gefilte fish.

Note: Mrs. Zeger uses bitter almonds she has had for years. These cannot be bought on the retail market, but apricot (bitter) kernels are a substitute. In Manhattan, they can be bought at Lekvar by the Barrel, 1577 First Avenue and 968 Second Avenue; and Paprikas Weiss, 1546 Second Avenue.

Charosis

1   *large apple or 2 small apples, peeled, cored, and finely chopped*
1   *tablespoon ground cinnamon, or to taste*
1   *tablespoon ground ginger, or to taste*
½   *cup ground walnuts*
¼   *cup, approximately, sweet red Passover wine*

Mix ingredients together, adding enough wine to moisten.

Yield: 2 to 3 cups, depending on the size of the apples.

Carrot Ring

3   *cups ¼-inch-thick carrot slices*
1   *bay leaf*
1   *onion*
1   *teaspoon salt*
   Boiling water
3   *tablespoons ground cinnamon*
1   *tablespoon ground ginger*
   Freshly ground pepper
5   *eggs, separated*
1   *cup sugar*
½   *cup matzoh meal*
1   *cup ground walnuts*

1. Preheat oven to 350 degrees.

2. Place the carrots in a saucepan. Add bay leaf, onion, salt, and boiling water barely to cover. Bring to a boil, cover and simmer until carrots are very tender, about 20 minutes.

3. Remove onion and bay leaf, drain carrots and mash thoroughly. Stir in the cinnamon, ginger, 1 teaspoon salt, and pepper to taste.

4. Beat the egg yolks with the sugar until very thick and lemon colored. Stir in the carrot mixture.

5. Beat the egg whites until stiff but not dry and fold into the carrot mixture alternately with the matzoh meal and nuts.

6. Turn into a greased 2½- to 3-quart ring mold or cake pan and set in a pan of boiling water. Bake 40 minutes or until set. Alternately, a greased 10-inch spring form pan can be used and baked directly on the oven shelf with a pan of boiling water set on the bottom of the oven.

Yield: 12 servings.

Chocolate Cake

10   *eggs, separated and at room temperature or slightly warmer*
14   *tablespoons (about 1 cup) sugar*
6   *ounces bittersweet or semisweet chocolate, melted slowly over hot water and cooled*

2 *cups finely chopped (not ground)) walnuts*

1. Preheat oven to 350 degrees.

2. Beat the egg yolks and sugar until very thick and lemon colored. Stir in the chocolate. Fold in the nuts.

3. Beat the egg whites until stiff but not dry and fold into the chocolate-nut mixture. Turn into a greased 10-inch spring form pan and bake 1 hour or until the center springs back when lightly touched with the finger tips. Cool in the pan.

Yield: 8 to 12 servings.

Spongecake

12 *eggs, separated and at room temperature or a little warmer*

1¾ *cups sugar*
1 *cup cake meal*
⅓ *cup potato starch*
Juice and grated rind of 1 lemon and 1 orange

1. Preheat oven to 350 degrees.

2. Beat the yolks and sugar together until very thick and lemon colored.

3. Beat the egg whites until stiff but not dry. Fold into the yolk mixture. Fold in the cake meal and potato starch alternately with the juice. Fold in the rind. Turn into a lightly oiled 10-by-3-inch angel food cake pan which is lined on the bottom with wax paper.

4. Bake 1 hour or until a cake tester comes out dry. Cool upside down in the pan.

Yield: 8 to 12 servings.

One of the most popular Passover menu articles to appear in *The New York Times* over the last couple of decades was this one. Mrs. Zeger's chocolate cake is indeed exceptional.

April 1974

WE DINED on a lot of fine ethnic food in the month of April, including great Persian dishes with names like Fosenjohn, Abgushteh Limon, and Bareh Meveh. Just as impressive were some simply stuffed artichokes from the kitchen of a second generation Italian friend of ours, Joe Famularo. One of the things that intrigued us most about the interview with Mr. Famularo was learning that he and his family have shopped at the same Italian butcher for the past 40 years. We didn't think anything in Manhattan was that intransigent.

When the main column about Joe appeared (page 116), there was not enough room on the page for all the recipes we enjoyed in his home. It was not until one June Sunday that we got to describe an incredibly good meringue pie with a fantastic cream filling flavored with mirabelle. You will find the recipe on page 183.

Panamanian Paella

We had a communiqué recently from an acquaintance, a connoisseur of sorts (how much nicer to be labeled a "connoisseur of sorts" rather than a "gourmet") who told us he'd just eaten the best paella he'd ever had in the world.

"It was cooked by the wife of a former president of Panama," the friend said, "and I tell you it was special. I've eaten paella all over the world—in waterfront restaurants in Barcelona, in Valencia, and Madrid, and they're always made with too much rice. Last night the rice was only a pretext for calling the dish paella."

Like many another temptation, we found this too much to miss, so we hopped a plane for Miami and, in the company of our friend, visited the home of Marco A. Robles. Among Mr. Robles's claims to distinction, outside of his wife's paella, are not only that he was a president of Panama but that he stayed to finish a full term, which ended six years ago.

The Robleses live in a modest, comfortable home here with a living room dominated by signed photographs of such dignitaries as John F. Kennedy, Pope Paul VI, Lyndon B. Johnson, Prince Philip of England, and Makarios of Cyprus. They are warm, hospitable people and when we arrived, Mrs. Robles offered us an excellent dish of ceviche, the cold "raw" Latin American fish dish, delicately spiced and marinated in lime juice. It was made with corvinha, a Panamanian fish, which she had recently received frozen.

Mr. Robles poured us a fascinating apéritif made with the juices of pineapple, grapefruit, orange, and lemon. Plus Panamanian rum, Drambuie, Benedictine, and Chartreuse. The more we sampled that drink the better it became, and we asked Mr. Robles for his formula.

"It's al ojo," he informed us.

"Al what?" we asked.

"Al ojo," he answered. "The drink is made, as we say, 'by the eye.' You improvise."

We were led to another room where he opened a freezer bulging with good things from his native state—beef, fish, shrimp, and vegetables. "One of the nice things about being an ex-president, people keep stopping by to bring you things from home," said Mr. Robles, who only the week before had returned from a visit to Panama. "We have a steady flow of visitors."

Mrs. Robles fetched us to come into the kitchen where she was about to start her paella. We were fascinated with her demonstration for another reason than the quantity of rice she would use.

It amounts to a confession: The first time we encountered a paella pan we hadn't a clue as to whether it was a cooking utensil or a serving dish or both. We were blatantly young and too arrogant to ask. Some years later we went to a paella gathering outside San Juan and there, for the first time, we saw the pan in practical use with rice and chicken and seafood slowly simmering away in the pan which cooked over a rather expansive charcoal grill. Good enough, we thought, but what about using it on a gas or electric burner? Mrs. Robles, for 43 minutes precisely (we timed it), manipulated the paella pan with consummate skill back and forth over a heating unit so that all the ingredients cooked evenly.

And as she cooked she pampered us with a fascinating Panamanian appetizer called carimañolas. It's a very special shallow-fried turnover made with the Caribbean and Latin-American vegetable known as yucca. The vegetable is, incidentally, widely available at Spanish-speaking markets. The yucca, a root vegetable, is peeled and cored and cooked until tender like potatoes. It is then mashed and shaped into a turnover with a fine filling of ground pork seasoned with oregano and garlic. Crisp outside, tender within. The filling is excellent even if one doesn't want to bother with the yucca coating. We have had it on toast as well as with mashed potatoes on the side.

Mrs. Marco Robles serves a tray of paella.

Carimañolas

(Panamanian yucca turnovers)

The yucca

1½ *pounds fresh yucca*
    Salt to taste
2 *egg whites*
    Flour

The filling

½ *cup chopped onion*
1 *clove garlic, peeled*
⅓ *cup unpeeled, chopped*
    tomatoes
¼ *cup chopped celery*
1 *pound lean ground pork*

*Salt and freshly ground
pepper to taste*
½ *teaspoon oregano*
1 *tablespoon tomato paste*
1 *cup boiling water*
*Hot sauce such as Tabasco
to taste*

The oil

Oil for shallow frying

1. Cut off and discard about 1 or 2 inches from each end of the yuccas. Peel the yuccas and split them in half. Cut away and discard the fibrous core down the center line of each half.

2. Place the yucca halves in a saucepan and add water to cover with salt to taste. Bring to the boil and simmer until almost tender. It is better a bit undercooked than soft and overcooked. Drain but reserve the cooking liquid.

3. Put the yucca through the fine blade of a meat grinder while it is still hot, or blend it in a food processor. The yucca should have the consistency of mashed potatoes.

4. Put it in a mixing bowl and, beating, add salt to taste and the 2 egg whites. Do not beat the whites before adding. If the mashed yucca pulp seems too stiff, beat in 1 or 2 tablespoons of the reserved cooking liquid. Otherwise, discard the liquid. When ready, the yucca should be soft but not watery.

5. Meanwhile, put the onion, garlic, tomatoes, and celery into the container of an electric blender or food processor. Blend well.

6. Put the pork in a dry skillet and cook, using the sides of a kitchen spoon to break up any lumps. Cook until the pork loses its pink color. Add the puréed vegetables and stir to blend well. Add the salt, pepper, oregano, and tomato paste and cook, stirring almost constantly, for 10 minutes.

7. Add the boiling water. It should barely cover the meat. Cook, uncovered, over moderately high heat until water evaporates and the pork is almost dry. Stir frequently as it cooks. When we tested this recipe, the filling had a good deal of fat in the skillet, so we drained it in a sieve. In any event, let the filling cool.

8. When ready to assemble the turnovers, lightly flour a flat surface and pick up about ¼ cup of the yucca mixture and pat it out into a circle on the board. Add about 1½ tablespoons of filling. Dampen the edges of the circle and fold it over to enclose the filling. Press to seal and pinch the ends to make them pointed.

9. Heat the oil in a skillet to a depth of about ½ inch and add the turnovers, not too close together. Fry until golden brown on all sides, about 10 minutes. Drain on paper towels.

Yield: 12 to 18 turnovers.

Paella Robles

¼ *cup olive oil*
4 *cloves garlic, thinly sliced*
¾ *cup coarsely chopped
onion*

1½   cups unpeeled tomatoes,
      cored and cut into cubes
3   chorizos or Spanish
      sausages, cut into ¼-inch-
      slices
½   cup squid, cut into ½-inch
      thick strips
2   cups raw, shelled and
      deveined shrimp
¼   cup capers
⅓   cup tomato paste
12   cherrystone clams
1½   cups bay scallops
1   cup drained oysters
7   to 8 cups hot chicken broth
      (see recipe)
2   bay leaves
1   teaspoon oregano
2½   cups raw long-grain rice
      (see note)
      Hot sauce such as Tabasco
      to taste
6   cups cubed shredded
      chicken (see recipe)
      Garnish (see How to
      garnish paella)

1. Heat the oil in a paella pan (Mrs. Robles's paella pan has a 16-inch diameter) or a wide, shallow, heatproof casserole.

2. When it is very hot, add the garlic and cook, stirring, until it is golden brown. Remove the garlic with a slotted spoon and discard it.

3. To the paella pan, add the onion and cook, stirring, about 3 minutes. Depending on the source of heat, it will be necessary to shift the pan around so that the foods cook evenly.

4. Add the tomatoes and cook, stirring, about 5 minutes. Add the sausages and cook about 1 minute,

stirring. Add the squid and cook 1 minute, stirring.

5. Add the shrimp and cook until they turn bright red. Add the capers and tomato paste. Stir briefly and add the clams and scallops.

6. Add the oysters and cook, stirring, about 2 minutes. Add 5 cups of the chicken broth, bay leaves, and oregano.

7. Gradually sprinkle the rice into the pan so that it is evenly distributed. After the rice is added, the paella must be stirred constantly until the dish is finished. But do not stir the rice in a circular fashion. Instead, using a wooden spoon, dip it into the paella and stir gently back and forth in a small area. Move the spoon to another part of the pan and stir gently back and forth. Continue, taking care that all areas of the paella are stirred. Add the hot sauce.

8. After the rice has been cooking for about 8 or 10 minutes, add 2 more cups of hot chicken broth and continue stirring in the above-mentioned fashion. Cook about 5 minutes and distribute the chicken over the rice, pushing it into the stew.

9. The paella should be cooked in about 10 minutes. Continue cooking and stirring and if the dish seems to become dry, add more hot broth but gradually. The dish should not be soupy, however. The paella is ready when the rice is tender. Remove the bay leaves. Garnish the paella and serve.

Yield: 12 to 18 servings.

Note: Mrs. Robles uses a seasoned yellow rice available in Spanish markets. The brand she uses is Vigo and it comes in 10-ounce plastic bags.

Chicken and broth for paella

1   *3-pound chicken*
9   *cups unsalted chicken broth made from the bony parts of chicken, or use water*
½   *teaspoon freshly ground pepper to taste*
    Salt to taste
½   *teaspoon chopped Spanish saffron*
2   *large onions, cut into quarters*
2   *ribs celery with leaves*

1. Place the chicken in a kettle and add the remaining ingredients. Bring to the boil and simmer until the chicken is tender.

2. Strain and reserve the broth and the chicken.

3. Remove the meat from the chicken and discard the bones. Cut the meat into bite-size pieces and set aside.

Yield: About 8 cups of broth and 1 chicken.

How to garnish paella

The traditional garnishes for a paella include pimientos, generally cut into lozenges or strips; cooked green peas; Spanish olives stuffed with pimientos; and hard-cooked eggs, cut into wedges. The egg yolks may be put through a sieve and sprinkled over all. A piece of seafood such as a clam in the shell is centered in the pan. It is surrounded with wedges of egg white like the spokes of a wheel, with lozenges of pimiento in between. A cup of cooked peas generally serves as a border around the paella and the olives, approximately a cup, are scattered at random.

Cook's Choice for Easter

WITH PIERRE FRANEY

Easter—in America at least—is a holiday curiously lacking in ritual foods. Even the traditional hard-cooked eggs are more of a decorative artifice than a meaningful addition to Easter dinner. Our choice for the principal dish of an Easter feast is baked fresh ham.

Cream of Carrot and Tomato Soup

4 cups peeled, red, ripe
    tomatoes, fresh or canned
2 pounds carrots
6 tablespoons butter
    Salt and freshly ground
    pepper to taste
¼ cup water
3 tablespoons flour
1¾ cups chicken broth
3 cups milk
1 cup heavy cream
    Tabasco to taste
¼ cup chopped fresh dill
1 cup sour cream

1. Put the tomatoes in a saucepan and cook, uncovered, 30 minutes.

2. Trim the carrots and scrape them. Cut them into ¼-inch rounds.

3. Heat half the butter in a heavy saucepan and add the carrots. Cook briefly, stirring, and add salt and pepper to taste and water. Cover closely and cook 30 minutes.

4. Melt the remaining 3 tablespoons of butter in a saucepan and add the flour, stirring with a wire whisk. Add the chicken broth, stirring rapidly with the whisk. When thickened and smooth, continue cooking about 30 minutes.

5. Combine the carrots, tomatoes, and the sauce. Purée the mixture in an electric blender or a food processor. Pour it into a large saucepan and bring to the boil. Stir in the milk and cream. Add salt and pepper to taste. Add Tabasco and half the dill.

6. Beat the sour cream, adding a little salt to taste. Stir in the remaining dill. Serve the soup, hot or cold, with a dollop of sour cream on top.

Yield: 8 to 12 servings.

Baked Fresh Ham with Herbs

1 14-to-16-pound fresh,
    unsalted, uncured ham
4 cloves garlic
1 bay leaf

1 *tablespoon crumbled leaf sage*

½ *teaspoon thyme*
Salt and freshly ground pepper to taste

1. Preheat oven to 375 degrees.

2. It is preferable to have the butcher remove the small blade bone (opposite the butt end) of the ham. This is not imperative, however.

3. Cut garlic into 18 to 20 slivers.

4. With the tip of a sharp knife, make small incisions all over the ham and insert a sliver of garlic into each.

5. Using a very sharp knife, score the fat side of the ham rather deeply.

6. Place the bay leaf, sage, and thyme on a flat surface and chop them with a heavy knife. This may seem a little tricky, but it is easy to do. Chop as finely as possible.

7. Sprinkle the ham all over with the herb mixture, salt and pepper to taste. Rub the seasonings into the ham all over. Use a rather generous but reasonable amount of salt. Place the ham fat side up in a large baking dish (an ordinary roasting pan is too deep). We used a dish that measured 12 by 18 by 2½ inches.

8. Place the ham in the oven and bake, basting occasionally, for 2½ hours.

9. Reduce the oven heat to 350 degrees and cover the ham with aluminum foil. Continue baking about 2½ hours or until the ham is thoroughly cooked. When cooked, the ham should have an internal temperature of at least 170 degrees.

10. When the ham is cooked, remove it from the pan. Tilt the pan and skim off most of the fat from the natural gravy. A judicious amount of water may be added to the pan juices and brought to the boil for the sauce. Do not make the sauce too thin and flavorless, however. The cold leftover ham is delicious.

Yield: 24 to 30 servings.

Asparagus Milanaise

24 *to 32 asparagus spears*
    Salt
 4 *to 6 tablespoons melted*
    butter
½ *to ¾ cup Parmesan cheese,*
    preferably freshly grated
    Freshly ground pepper to
    taste

1. Preheat the broiler.

2. Using a swivel-bladed vegetable peeler, scrape the asparagus, starting about 2 inches from top of tips.

3. Line up the tips of the asparagus spears uniformly on a flat surface. Cut off the ends of the asparagus 3 or 4 inches from the bottom.

4. Place the asparagus in a skillet large enough to hold them and add cold water to cover. Add salt to taste. Bring to the boil and simmer from 1 to 5 minutes. Cooking time will depend on the size of the asparagus and how crisp you wish them to remain. Preferably they should be crisp-tender, not limp. Drain immediately.

5. Arrange the asparagus uniformly in a heatproof dish. Sprinkle with butter and cheese. Sprinkle with pepper to taste and glaze them until golden brown under the broiler.

Yield: 6 to 8 servings.

Potatoes Mont d'Or

 6 *baking potatoes, about 2*
    pounds
    Salt to taste
 1 *cup milk*
 6 *tablespoons butter*
    Freshly ground pepper to
    taste
⅛ *teaspoon nutmeg*
 2 *eggs, separated*
 3 *tablespoons freshly grated*
    Parmesan cheese

1. Preheat oven to 350 degrees.

2. Peel the potatoes and cut them into thirds. Drop them into a saucepan with cold water to cover and salt to taste. Bring to the boil and simmer about 20 minutes until tender.

3. Drain the potatoes well, leaving them in the saucepan. Place the potatoes in the oven to dry for about 3 to 5 minutes.

4. Meanwhile, bring the milk just to the boil.

5. Press the potatoes through a food mill into a saucepan and beat in the butter, salt and pepper, and nutmeg.

6. Add the egg yolks and beat them in. Beat in the hot milk.

7. Beat the whites until stiff and fold them into the potatoes. Spoon the mixture into a baking dish (we used an oval dish that measured 8 by 14 by 2 inches) and smooth the top. Or, if you want to be fancy, spoon half the mixture into a baking dish and pipe the remainder through a pastry tube. Sprinkle with cheese and bake 20 minutes. Brown under the broiler until glazed. Serve piping hot.

Yield: 8 or more servings.

Rum Ice Cream

10 egg yolks
1½ cups sugar
4 cups milk
4 cups heavy cream
¾ cup rum

1. Place the yolks in a large saucepan and add the sugar. Beat with whisk until thick and lemon colored.

2. Meanwhile, bring the milk and cream almost but not quite to the boil.

3. Gradually add the milk and cream to the yolk mixture, beating constantly. Use a wooden spoon and stir constantly, this way and that, making certain that the spoon touches all over the bottom of the saucepan. If a thermometer is available, use it. Cook to 180 degrees and remove the saucepan from the heat. If a thermometer is not available, cook the sauce until it becomes like a very thin custard. Continue stirring briefly after the sauce has been removed from the heat. Cool and chill.

4. Pour the sauce into the container of an electric or hand-cranked ice-cream freezer. Add the rum. Freeze according to the manufacturer's instruction. Serve, if desired, with a little additional spirit poured over each serving.

Yield: About 24 servings.

The term "ham" seems to be confusing in the minds of many readers. They have been conditioned all their lives to recognize only one sort of thing called ham—the pink-fleshed meat, always salted and frequently smoked, the all-American standby for picnics, buffets, and Easter feasting. A ham can also be a totally uncured item. It is purely and simply the thigh of a pig. To some minds, a fresh ham is more delectable than the cured version. Fresh hams do not come in cans and sacks, they are highly perishable like fresh pork chops and loins of pork and must be freshly butchered.

Robust Dishes by a Photographer–Cook

We've known for some years that Walter Chandoha is a pretty fair photographer. His photographs have appeared on more than 200 magazine covers and have illustrated advertisements and brochures for such various and prestigious companies as Eastman Kodak, Viceroys, Du Pont, and Ohrbach's. What we didn't know was that he is a cook of considerable talent.

We recently received a letter from a neighbor of his who said, "When Walter goes out to his garden and looks speculatively at a vineful of yellow squash, you can't know whether it will wind up on the cover of *Horticulture,* or a food publication, or in an elegant casserole—and quite likely it may be both."

We called the gentleman, who invited us to join him on the following day for a bowl of sauerkraut soup. When we arrived at Mr. Chandoha's 46-acre farm in the rolling and magnificent New Jersey countryside, now burgeoning with spring, he led us over the acre or so that would come alive as summer advanced with asparagus, eggplant, leeks, beets, Egyptian onions, raspberries, and currants.

We entered his 200-year-old home by way of the kitchen, a place full of good smells like sauerkraut and caraway and whose beams are hung with great sprays of last year's crop of basil, tarragon, sage, thyme, mint, and hot red pepper.

Actually, the host was preparing two soups for the day, a tortellini soup that had come from his wife's side of the family and the sauerkraut soup that derived from his mother.

"When I was growing up, my mother, who was born in the Ukraine, made soup almost every day," Mr. Chandoha recalled. "These things become part of your life. When I'm at home, I make one kind of soup or another almost every day." He offered us a bowl of an excellent, robust soup that contained not only sauerkraut and "country-style" spareribs but split peas as well.

He explained that the soup to follow was really their version of a soup his wife's father used to make. "Maria," he said, "is of Italian descent and her father made the greatest tortellini—small, stuffed dumplings—you could think of. My wife and I never made much pasta, so we decided to make his soup, using only the filling for the dumplings. To compensate for the dumplings, we add broad noddles."

The soup turned out to be a hearty, admirably seasoned chicken broth with feather-light meat balls and the noddles.

Mr. Chandoha has come by—in a serendipitous fashion—a few interesting writing assignments, food-related, for magazines. "Last summer," he said, "I took a random photograph of my raspberries, so I sent it off to *Modern Maturity*, a publication for retired people. The editor knew that gardening is my hobby, so he asked me to write him an article titled, 'Ah, Raspberries.' " A similar photograph taken around his English walnut tree is about to result in an article on nutting.

Both the Chandohas have a keen interest in cooking, and one of the dishes that their children admire most is something they choose to call squash pizza. To make it, yellow squash, fresh from the garden, are cut into quarter-inch slices, buttered, sprinkled with oregano and Parmesan cheese, baked, and broiled. Very good.

We complimented our hosts not only for a memorable meal but for their very deep, early spring tans, and they explained that they had just returned with one of their six children from a photography safari in Kenya.

"It was a fascinating trip in all respects," Mr. Chandoha told us, one of the most interesting things being a meal they'd dined on in Nairobi. The main course was boiled zebra. And how was it? "If we hadn't been told otherwise, we could have mistaken it for beef. Only a bit sweeter."

Walter Chandoha hangs sprays of last year's crop of herbs from the beams of the kitchen ceiling in his 200-year-old home.

Sauerkraut Soup

3 *pounds country-style spareribs*
10 *cups cold water*
2 *pounds sauerkraut*
1 *cup dried green split peas*
½ *pound bacon, preferably thick sliced*
1½ *cups finely chopped onions*
2 *tablespoons flour*

1. Trim off any excess fat from the spareribs.

2. Place the spareribs in a kettle and add 8 cups of the water. Do not drain the sauerkraut but add it.

3. Bring to the boil and simmer about 45 minutes.

4. Meanwhile, combine the split peas in a saucepan with remaining 2 cups of water and bring to the boil. Simmer about 30 minutes or until the peas are tender but not mushy. Add the peas with their liquid to the soup and continue cooking.

5. Cut the bacon into ¼-inch strips and cook it in a skillet until golden brown. Add the onions and continue cooking, stirring occasionally, over moderate heat about 15 minutes. Use a slotted spoon and transfer the bacon and onions to the soup.

6. Pour off and discard the fat from the skillet. Add the flour and stir it with a wooden spoon. Gradually add ½ a cup of the soup liquid to make a paste. Add this to the soup.

7. The soup may be served after 2 hours' cooking time. It may continue to cook, however, for 6 hours. The longer it cooks, the thicker it gets. Leftover soup is good reheated.

Yield: 12 or more servings.

Chicken Noodle Soup with Tortellini Balls

The soup

2   *quarts water*
1   *3-pound chicken*
1   *pound short ribs of beef*
2   *onions*
3   *carrots*
2   *ribs celery*
1   *bay leaf*

6   *fresh basil leaves or 1 teaspoon dried*
1   *sprig fresh tarragon or ½ teaspoon dried*
2   *sage leaves or ½ teaspoon dried*
2   *sprigs fresh thyme or ½ teaspoon dried*
    Salt to taste
10 *peppercorns*

The tortellini balls

10   *ounces Italian-style pork sausages*
2   *eggs*
½   *cup grated Parmesan cheese*
1½   *cups bread crumbs*
¼   *teaspoon grated nutmeg*
2   *teaspoons chopped chives*
2   *teaspoons chopped parsley*
1   *teaspoon oregano*
     Salt and freshly ground pepper to taste

The noodles

¼   *pound broad noddles*

1. Combine all the ingredients for the chicken soup and bring to the boil. Simmer 1½ hours.

2. Strain the soup but reserve the chicken for another use.

3. Bring the chicken broth to the boil and, if desired, add salt to taste.

4. Meanwhile, remove the meat from the sausage skins and add it to a mixing bowl. Add the remaining ingredients for the tortellini balls and blend well with the fingers. Shape the mixture into balls the size of marbles, ¾ to 1 inch in diameter. There will be from 60 to 80 balls.

5. Drop the balls into the simmering broth and cook about 10 minutes.

6. Add the noddles and cook until tender, about 7 minutes. Serve the soup piping hot.

Yield: 12 or more servings.

Squash Pizza

2 *yellow squash*
¼ *cup melted butter*
    Salt and freshly ground
    pepper to taste

2 *teaspoons or more oregano*
½ *cup grated Parmesan*
    cheese

1. Preheat oven to 350 degrees.

2. Trim off the ends of the squash but do not peel them. Line a baking sheet with aluminum foil and brush with butter.

3. Cut the squash lengthwise into ¼-inch slices. Arrange the slices on the foil. Brush the slices on one side with butter. Sprinkle with salt, pepper, and oregano.

4. Bake the squash about 10 minutes. Sprinkle with Parmesan cheese and run under the broiler to brown.

Yield: 4 to 6 servings.

Lamb's Poor Relatives

WITH PIERRE FRANEY

It has long been our aim in our columns to reflect the gamut from the wholly exotic to the simply good; from truffled pâtés to earthy meat loaves; from caviar to omelets. This column is devoted to two relatively inexpensive dishes made with breast of lamb. The Burgundy-style recipe is a peasant dish, great for buffets. The other is a sophisticated "rib" dish to eat with the fingers.

Breast of Lamb à la Francaise

2   to 2½ pounds breast of
     lamb with bones or lamb
     riblets
     Salt and freshly ground
     pepper to taste
1   cup fresh bread crumbs
1   tablespoon finely chopped
     shallots
1   tablespoon finely chopped
     parsley
1   clove garlic, minced
½   teaspoon chopped
     rosemary

1. Preheat oven to 450 degrees.

2. Have most of the fat trimmed from the top of the lamb breast. The breast should preferably be in one or two pieces and not cut into ribs.

3. Place the pieces of lamb meaty side down on a baking dish and sprinkle with salt and pepper.

4. Place the lamb in the oven and bake 30 minutes. Turn and bake about 15 or 20 minutes.

5. Turn once more and pour off the fat that has accumulated.

6. Combine the remaining ingredients and blend well. The lamb should be meaty side up. Sprinkle it with the bread crumb mixture and continue baking 15 to 20 minutes. The crumbs should be appetizingly brown. Cut into serving pieces.

Yield: 4 servings.

Burgundy-Style Lamb and Bean Stew

½   pound dried beans such as
     jumbo marrow, baby lima,
     pea, or navy beans
2   lamb shanks, about 1
     pound each
2   pounds breast of lamb with
     bones in
¼   pound salt pork
     Salt and freshly ground
     pepper to taste
1   cup coarsely chopped leeks

1 *cup coarsely chopped onions*
½ *cup coarsely chopped carrots*
2 *cups canned tomatoes, preferably imported Italian plum*
4 *cups water*
3 *sprigs fresh thyme or ½ teaspoon dried*
1 *bay leaf*

1. Soak the beans overnight in cold water to cover.

2. Have the butcher split the lamb shanks in half. Cut the breast of lamb with bones into 2- or 3-inch squares.

3. Cut the salt pork into small cubes and add it to a heavy metal or earthenware casserole or Dutch oven. Cook, stirring, until pork is rendered of its fat. Add the lamb shanks and breast of lamb, salt and pepper to taste. Cook, stirring frequently, until browned all over, about 10 minutes.

4. Add the leeks, onions, and carrots and stir.

5. Cook, stirring occasionally, about 5 minutes. Pour off the fat. Drain the beans and add to the casserole. Add the tomatoes, water, thyme, bay leaf, salt and pepper to taste. Cover and cook about 1 hour and 45 minutes until the meat and beans are tender. Uncover and cook 15 minutes longer. Transfer the casserole to a cooler place. Tilt the casserole and skim off the surface fat. Reheat and serve piping hot.

Yield: 6 to 8 servings.

When lamb riblets or shanks are a "special" in this West Side market, Milton Kaufman (left) and Joseph Amato are kept busy by budget-conserving customers.

The Bachelor Cook of Tara North

"When I was a kid on the West Side of Manhattan," Joseph Famularo said recently as he thumbed another blob of sausage meat into a hand stuffer, "my parents would never think of buying prepared sausages in a store. I remember reading about other communities having 'sewing circles.'" He laughed. "My mother had sausage-making circles.

"I remember coming home in wintertime from catechism classes. All her friends would be sitting around tables gabbing away and filling sausage skins, literally yard after yard. All the kids were given needles to puncture them as they were made. We took turns. We got so *bored*.

"As children, we couldn't imagine anybody doing that for the sheer pleasure of it," Mr. Famularo went on. "And I remember we were embarrassed to bring our friends home after school. After all, *their* families didn't do things like that.

"There were broomsticks all over the ceiling and fresh sausages hanging from them. And in the summer—if it wasn't sausages—it was homemade tomato paste. And homemade bread all year long. My grandmother would prepare the dough and take it to the neighborhood baker who would finish it in his ovens."

Mr. Famularo, a bachelor and senior vice-president of personnel and industrial relations at McGraw Hill, the publishers, was recounting scenes of his childhood in the splendid, herb-hung kitchen of his 100-year-old country home in Pawling, New York. The house sits at the end of a long drive and looks for all the world like Scarlett O'Hara's abode. So much so it was long ago christened Mr. Famularo's Tara North.

The gentleman, who has a well-deserved reputation as host and chef, reflects now that he relates many things in life to that warm childhood. He maintains an apartment in Manhatten, and although he now lives on the East Side, he still buys his meats from the family butcher from 50 years back, Tony's at 677 Ninth Avenue (at 46th Street).

Although his cooking is largely international, he frequently cooks Italian dishes because of his family background. His mother was born in Accettura, a town south of Naples, and his father, although born on Mott Street, New York, was raised in a small Italian town near Potenza.

Mr. Famularo notes that as a matter of convenience—and time—he frequently "cooks double," which is to say he frequently doubles the proportions of any dish he cooks for a single meal.

"In Manhattan," he adds, "there's just not that much time, and besides my kitchen is small." On the day of our visit, for example, the lunch would include among other dishes stuffed artichokes, manicotti, and braccioli plus a meringue pie. Of these, there would be enough manicotti to freeze six portions; the same amount of braccioli. The pieces would be frozen individually, to be defrosted according to future needs.

When he entertains, it is rarely for more than six to eight at table. Twice a year, however, he has two buffets, each for 18 people. Generally speaking his menu on those occasions consists of one sort of curry or another.

All of the dishes that came from the Famularo stove on the day we were there were of a high order. The braccioli or beef birds delicately flavored with orange peel and marsala; and the rich, excellent manicotti with almonds and cream. The artichokes were incredibly easy to prepare, with a sausage and bread crumb filling. And they were outrageously good.

Herbs hang from the wall in the kitchen of Joseph Famularo's country home.

Angela's Stuffed Artichokes

⅓ *pound sausage links,*
    pepperoni, ham, or
    prosciutto
1 *teaspoon olive oil*
1½ *cups fresh bread crumbs*
2 *tablespoons chopped fresh*
    parsley
2 *cloves garlic, finely minced*
3 *eggs*
¼ *cup milk*
6 *tablespoons olive oil*
    Salt and freshly ground
    pepper to taste
6 *large artichokes*
½ *cup peeled, drained*
    tomatoes, crushed
4 *cups water*
2 *whole garlic cloves, peeled*

1. Cut the meat into small pieces or slices. Heat the oil in a small skillet and cook the meat briefly, shaking the skillet and stirring. Drain and add to a mixing bowl. Add the bread crumbs, parsley, and minced garlic. Toss well.

2. Beat the eggs with the milk and 2 tablespoons of olive oil. Add the mixture to the bread crumb mixture. Add salt and pepper to taste. Stir to blend.

3. Using a sharp knife, cut off the stems of the artichokes to make a flat base. Pull off a few of the tough outer leaves. Cut off about ½ inch of the artichoke tops.

4. Open the tops of the artichokes with the fingers and invert the artichokes on a flat surface, one at a time, pressing down to open the leaves. Divide the bread crumb filling into 6 equal parts. Stuff the artichokes with the mixture, starting with the center of each artichoke, then stuffing between the leaves more or less at random. Push the stuffing down, as it is added, toward the bottom.

5. Select a casserole large enough to hold the artichokes snugly in one layer. Arrange them in the casserole and spoon equal amounts of tomatoes on the top of each. Pour the water around the artichokes and add the whole garlic cloves to the water. Sprinkle the artichokes with the remaining quarter cup of olive oil. Cover closely and bring to the boil. Reduce the heat and simmer until the artichoke bottoms are tender, 45 minutes to an hour. To test for doneness, pull off an outside leaf; if it comes off easily, the artichokes are done.

Yield: 6 servings.

Note: If the artichokes do not fit closely together, it is advisable to tie them around the center with string to help retain their shapes.

Braccioli in Brown Sauce

(Beef birds in brown sauce)

6 *thin slices of beef, each*
    measuring about 6 by 7
    inches and slightly less
    than a ¼ inch thick
2 *slices fresh orange peel*
3 *tablespoons butter*
¾ *cup finely chopped onion*
    or scallions

½ cup chopped heart of
   celery, including leaves
½ teaspoon oregano
   Freshly ground pepper to
   taste
½ cup fresh bread crumbs
4 tablespoons marsala wine
¼ cup pine nuts (pignoli)
   Salt to taste
6 thin slices prosciutto
2 tablespoons olive oil
4 cups brown sauce (see
   recipe)
1 tablespoon Escoffier sauce
   Robert (available
   commercially in bottles) or
   ⅓ cup madeira, optional

1. If the slices of beef are not thin enough, place them on a flat surface and pound them lightly with a flat mallet or the bottom of a clean skillet.

2. Cut the orange peel into very thin strips (julienne) and cut the strips into very thin dice.

3. Heat 1 tablespoon of butter and add the onion, celery, oregano, and pepper and cook, stirring, until pale yellow. Set aside.

4. Place the bread crumbs in a mixing bowl and add the onion mixture and orange peel. Add 2 tablespoons of marsala, pine nuts, and salt to taste. Blend well.

5. Spoon equal amounts of the mixture onto the slices of beef, pressing down with the fingers to help it adhere.

6. Spread a slice of prosciutto on top. Roll the meat jelly-roll fashion and skewer each serving or tie with string.

7. Melt 2 tablespoons each

butter and olive oil in a skillet and brown the beef on all sides, 10 to 15 minutes. Remove the braccioli and pour off the fat from the skillet. Add remaining 2 tablespoons of marsala and stir to dissolve the brown particles that cling to the bottom of the skillet.

8. Add the brown sauce to a casserole and add the braccioli. Cover closely and simmer 1 hour or longer until the beef is tender. Add the sauce Robert or madeira and serve piping hot with rice.

Yield: 6 servings.

Brown sauce

8 tablespoons butter
¾ pound ham, cut into small
   cubes
½ pound fresh mushrooms,
   finely chopped
2 carrots, scraped and cut
   into thin slices
2 onions, thinly sliced
⅓ cup flour
8 cups fresh beef broth,
   made according to any
   standard recipe
1 bay leaf
½ cup tomato purée
½ cup dry red wine
   Salt and freshly ground
   pepper to taste
1 tablespoon Escoffier sauce
   Diable (available
   commercially in bottles),
   optional

1. Melt the butter and add the ham, mushrooms, carrots, and onions. Cook, stirring frequently, until the ingredients are almost dry and starting to brown.

2. Sprinkle with flour and

cook, stirring, until flour starts to darken. Add the broth, stirring rapidly with a wire whisk. When thickened and smooth, add the bay leaf. Cover and cook, stirring occasionally, about 1 hour. Add the tomato purée, wine, salt, pepper, and Escoffier sauce. Continue to cook 45 minutes longer, stirring occasionally. Strain the sauce.

3. If the sauce is not thickened, you may blend 4 teaspoons of butter with 4 teaspoons flour and add it bit by bit, stirring with the whisk.

Yield: About 8 cups.

Note: Leftover brown sauce freezes well.

Manicotti with Creamed Chicken and Almonds

12 *manicotti pancakes (see recipe)*
2 *chicken breasts, skinned, boned, and cut in half*
½ *lemon*
3½ *tablespoons plus 1 teaspoon butter*
¼ *cup finely chopped onion*
2 *tablespoons flour*
1 *cup chicken broth*
½ *cup heavy cream*
½ *cup grated Gruyère or Swiss cheese*
 Salt and freshly ground pepper to taste
3 *tablespoons blanched almonds*
1 *tablespoon dry white vermouth*

1 *small egg*
1 *cup ricotta cheese*
6 *tablespoons grated Parmesan cheese*
3 *tablespoons chopped parsley*
½ *teaspoon grated lemon rind*

1. Prepare the pancakes and have them ready.

2. Preheat oven to 350 degrees.

3. Place the chicken breasts in a bowl and squeeze the lemon over it, adding the rind. Let stand.

4. Melt 1½ tablespoons of butter in a saucepan and add the onion. Cook, stirring, until onion is wilted. Sprinkle with flour and cook, stirring with a wire whisk.

5. Add the broth, stirring rapidly with the whisk. When thickened and smooth, add half the cream. Simmer about 10 minutes, stirring occasionally, and add the Gruyère cheese, salt and pepper to taste. Stir to blend and set aside.

6. Meanwhile, melt 1 teaspoon of butter in a small skillet and add the almonds in one layer. Place in the oven and bake, shaking the skillet and stirring the almonds until they are golden brown. Remove and let cool.

7. Drain the chicken pieces. Pat dry. Sprinkle with salt and pepper to taste. Melt 2 tablespoons of butter in a skillet and add the chicken. Brown on both sides quickly, about 3 or 4 minutes. Remove and add the vermouth. Cook about 30 seconds, stirring. Pour the drippings into a bowl.

8. Cut the chicken into ½-inch cubes and add it to the bowl. Add the almonds. Add the remaining heavy cream, egg (if the egg is large, use only half of it), ricotta cheese, 4 tablespoons Parmesan cheese, and chopped parsley. Blend well with a fork or whisk.

9. To assemble, spoon equal amounts of the chicken mixture down the center of the manicotti pancakes and roll them to enclose the filling.

10. Select a baking dish large enough to hold the rolled manicotti in one layer. Spoon enough sauce into the dish to cover the bottom. Arrange the filled manicotti over the sauce. Cover with a layer of sauce, reserving some sauce to be served separately.

11. Cover the dish with foil and bake 15 to 20 minutes until piping hot and bubbling. Sprinkle with remaining 2 tablespoons of Parmesan cheese and run briefly under the broiler to glaze. Sprinkle with lemon peel and serve hot with the remaining sauce brought to the boil on the side.

Yield: 12 servings.

Manicotti pancakes

3   *eggs*
1   *cup water*
1   *cup flour*
    Salt to taste
    Melted butter

1. Break the eggs into a bowl and beat with a whisk. Stir in the water. Add the flour gradually, stirring with the whisk. Add the salt and let stand ½ hour.

2. Heat a 7- or 8-inch crêpe pan or small Teflon skillet and brush lightly with butter. Add about 3 tablespoons of the batter and tilt the pan this way and that until the batter covers the bottom. The crepes should be quite thin but substantial enough to handle. Cook about 35 seconds on one side and turn, using a spatula or the hands. Cook on the other side briefly, 2 to 3 seconds. Slide out.

3. Continue making pancakes until all the batter is used, brushing the skillet lightly with butter if necessary before each pancake is made.

Yield: 12 manicotti pancakes.

The Marvelous Mushroom

WITH PIERRE FRANEY

The discovery of botulism in some batches of canned mushrooms during the past year not only sent sales of the canned variety plummeting, but those of fresh mushrooms as well. This is a shame. The F.D.A., in fact, has recommended that people buy fresh mushrooms. On this page, we rally to the support of the absolutely blameless fresh mushroom.

Mushrooms Stuffed with Crab Meat

1   pound mushrooms,
    preferably large ones
    (about 12 to a pound)
3   tablespoons butter
1   tablespoon flour
½   cup milk
    Salt and freshly ground
    pepper to taste
½   cup finely chopped
    scallions
⅓   pound crab meat
1   tablespoon cognac

1   egg yolk
    Tabasco to taste
3   tablespoons melted butter
¼   cup grated Parmesan
    cheese

1. Preheat oven to 400 degrees.

2. Remove stems and reserve the caps from the mushrooms. Chop the stems. There should be about 1 cup.

3. Melt 1 tablespoon butter in a saucepan and add the flour, stirring with a wire whisk. When blended, add the milk, stirring

rapidly with the whisk. When blended and smooth, add salt and pepper to taste.

4. In another saucepan, heat 2 tablespoons butter and add the scallions and mushroom stems. Cook, stirring, 4 minutes. Add the crab meat, stir to blend and add the cognac. Add the white sauce and salt and pepper to taste. Blend. Add the egg yolk and Tabasco to taste.

5. Place the mushrooms, hollow side down, in a buttered baking dish. Brush with half the melted butter and place in the oven for 10 minutes. Remove. Let cool.

6. Stuff the cavity of each mushroom with the crab mixture, heaping it up and smoothing it over. Arrange the mushrooms in the baking dish and sprinkle with Parmesan cheese and the remaining melted butter. Place in the oven and bake 20 minutes.

Yield: 6 servings.

Mushrooms Stuffed with Spinach and Anchovies

1   *pound mushrooms, preferably large ones (about 12 to a pound)*
1   *pound fresh spinach*
1   *2-ounce can anchovies*
½   *teaspoon chopped garlic*
½   *cup heavy cream*
3   *tablespoons melted butter*
¼   *cup grated Parmesan cheese*

1. Preheat oven to 400 degrees.

2. Remove stems and reserve the caps from the mushrooms. Chop the stems. There should be about 1 cup.

3. Pick over the spinach to remove any tough stems. Rinse the leaves well and drop them into boiling water to cover. Simmer about 1 minute and drain in a colander. Chill under cold running water and drain. Press the spinach between the hands to remove most of the moisture. Chop spinach. There should be about 1 cup.

4. Empty the oil from the anchovy can into a saucepan and add the chopped mushroom stems. Cook, stirring, about 5 minutes and add the spinach and garlic. Chop the anchovies and add them. Stir to blend thoroughly. Stir in the cream and bring just to the boil. Remove from the heat and let cool.

5. Meanwhile, place the mushrooms, hollow side down, in a buttered baking dish. Brush with half the melted butter and place in the oven for 10 minutes. Remove and let cool.

6. Stuff the cavity of each mushroom with the mixture, heaping it up and smoothing it over. Arrange the mushrooms in the baking dish and sprinkle with Parmesan cheese and the remaining melted butter. Place in the oven and bake 20 minutes.

Yield: 6 servings.

Mushroom and Noodle Casserole

1 *pound mushrooms, preferably very small button mushrooms*
8 *tablespoons butter*
3 *tablespoons finely chopped onion*
  Salt and freshly ground pepper to taste
½ *cup dry white wine*
1½ *cups heavy cream*
2 *tablespoons flour*
2 *eggs*
¼ *cup milk*
¾ *pound medium noodles*
¼ *cup grated Parmesan cheese*

1. Preheat oven to 475 degrees.

2. Rinse the mushrooms in cold water. Drain well. If they are button mushrooms, leave them whole. If they are medium, cut them into quarters or eighths or slice them.

3. Melt 2 tablespoons butter in a saucepan and add the onion. Cook until wilted. Add the mushrooms, salt and pepper to taste. Cook about 5 minutes and add the wine. Cover. Simmer about 5 minutes.

4. Add the cream, salt and pepper to taste. Cook about 5 minutes. Blend 2 tablespoons of butter with the flour. When well blended, gradually add it to the cream sauce, stirring rapidly.

5. Beat the eggs with the milk and add to the creamed mushrooms.

6. Cook the noodles in boiling salted water until almost done. Remember they will continue cooking in the cream sauce. Drain the noodles and stir in remaining 4 tablespoons of butter. Toss well.

7. Pour the noodles into a baking dish and spoon the mushrooms in cream sauce over all. Stir gently with a wooden spoon so that the ingredients blend lightly.

8. Sprinkle with grated cheese and bake 30 minutes.

Yield: 8 to 10 servings.

Persian Cookery

You should meet Cleopatra Birrenbach, our friendly feinshmecker told us recently. Her dining room is furnished with Persian antiques and you sit on floor pillows when you dine. She was born in Iran, he added, and she's a fantastic cook.

We telephoned the lady, who informed us that regrettably she was in the midst of dismantling her apartment in preparation for moving, but she had a friend who had a kitchen and if we didn't mind . . .

We didn't.

Mrs. Birrenbach, a handsome, black-haired damsel, greeted us in a small kitchen on Manhattan's West Side. It was scented with the tart and agreeable smell of pomegranate, rosewater, and lemon, and she explained that she would prepare traditional Persian dishes with such exotic names as fosenjohn, abgushteh limon, bareh neveh, chello, adas pollo, and niveh makhlout.

Fosenjohn, she explained, is a dish made with duck and meat balls cooked in a sauce made with a pomegranate syrup, raisins, and walnuts. The abgushteh limon would be a fine-brothed lemon soup made with dried lemons (which can be purchased) and the bareh meveh was a dish of her own contrivance, a leg of lamb cooked with dried mixed fruits available on any supermarket shelf.

Both the chello and adas pollo are rice dishes and the miveh makhlout a Persian-style mélange of fruits.

Mrs. Birrenbach was born in Teheran, one of six children. Her father was an enterprising antiques and jewelry shop owner who had lived in Russia long before she was born and made a fortune in oil before the Bolsheviks arrived.

She came to this country while still in her teens and attended the Fashion Institute of Technology in New York. When she was 21, she opened a shop as a designer and manufacturer of women's dresses under her maiden name, Cleopatra Bourmand. It was a solid success with 2,000 square feet of office space on 56th Street and with such clients as Neiman-Marcus, Saks Fifth Avenue, and Bonwit Teller.

She also got into coffee, merchandising her own spiced blend with a Persian coffee maker which sold at Bloomingdale's and Altman's.

"Like everyone else, I suppose, I learned about cooking from my mother, who was or is the greatest cook I know," Mrs. Birrenbach said. "She was northern and most of my cooking is north Persian."

Mrs. Birrenbach invariably speaks of Persia rather than Iran, and she explained that it is sentimental and romantic. Northern cooking, she added, is more refined than that of the south, and we reflected in how many cultures, including that of Italy and India, cooking of the north is more elevated and delicate.

The food of Persia, she told us, has many combinations of meat with fruit, and there are many combined meat flavors in numerous dishes, which she proceeded to demonstrate in the meal that followed. It included the quite outrageously good duck dish with meat balls that had been cooked with beef broth; the lemon soup with chicken cooked in beef broth; and the lamb cooked in both fruit and beef broth.

Rice is an ever present dish on Iranian tables, most usually in the form of chello, delicately flavored with butter and saffron and cooked on

Cleopatra Birrenbach: Cook, fashion designer.

a bed of sliced potatoes until the potatoes are browned, crisp, and hazelnut flavored. Or it may be pollo, in which the rice is cooked "with other things in it," such as lentils or cherries or lima beans.

Mrs. Birrenbach met her husband, Thomas, about a year and a half ago in the home of a friend and, she adds, it was love at first sight. He is an Argentine-born German who is a steel company executive, and he has recently been reassigned to Düsseldorf. In Germany, Mrs. Birrenbach hopes to open a Persian restaurant with backgammon as an entertainment. It is, she explained, her country's national game.

We were enchanted to learn that we share an enthusiasm of long standing with Mrs. Birrenbach. When nobody else is around, she likes to streak in the kitchen, except when she's deep frying. Then she wears an apron.

Note: Such ingredients as pomegranate molasses, chick pea powder, dried lemons, and Persian rice that appear in the following recipes are available at stores that specialize in Middle Eastern foods. Among them, in Manhattan, is Karnig Tashjian, 380 Third Avenue (between 27th and 28th Streets).

Fosenjohn

(Duck and meat balls
in walnut sauce)

The duck and sauce

½ pound walnut meats
1 15-ounce box dark raisins
   or 3 cups
   Salt and freshly ground
   pepper to taste
6 cups beef broth, fresh or
   canned
1 cup pomegranate molasses
   (see note above)
⅓ cup water
1 4-to-5-pound duck

The meat balls

2 pounds ground round steak
2½ cups coarsely chopped
   onion

6 tablespoons roasted chick
   pea powder (see note
   above) or fine dry bread
   crumbs
   Salt and freshly ground
   pepper to taste
½ cup milk

1. Using the fine blade of a meat grinder, grind the walnuts and raisins. Put them into a casserole large enough to hold the duck and sprinkle with salt and pepper. Add the beef broth and cook, stirring occasionally, about 10 minutes. Add a small clean piece of iron such as the grinder blade. This will give a dark color to the sauce.

2. Add the pomegranate molasses and water. Cook, stirring frequently, about 30 minutes.

3. Meanwhile, heat a heavy skillet and add the duck, breast side down. The duck will brown

in its own fat. When the duck is brown on one side, turn it. Continue turning the duck and cooking until it is well seared and brown on all sides. This should take about 20 minutes.

4. Remove the duck. Reserve the rendered duck fat, if desired, for another use. Add the duck, back side down, to the walnut and raisin sauce. Ladle the sauce over the duck and into the cavity. Add as much sauce as the cavity will hold. Continue cooking.

5. Put the ground meat into a mixing bowl.

6. Add the onions to the container of an electric blender and blend to a thin purée. Add them to the meat. Add the chick pea powder or bread crumbs. Add salt and pepper to taste. Blend well and add the milk. Work the mixture with the fingers until it is smooth and thoroughly blended. If you like spicy dishes, knead in more black pepper. Shape the mixture into meat balls about the size of golf balls. There should be 24 to 30 of them. Drop them around the duck into the walnut and raisin sauce. Cover and cook about 30 minutes.

7. Skim off most of the fat from the sauce and turn the meat balls in the sauce. Cover and cook 1 hour longer.

8. Remove the duck to a serving platter and surround it with the meat balls and sauce. Remove the piece of iron.

Abgushteh Limon
(Lemon soup)

5 cups water
1 3-pound chicken
12 sprigs parsley tied with a string
1 ¾-pound onion, peeled and quartered
4 carrots, about ¾ pound
1½ cups fresh or canned beef broth
   Salt and freshly ground pepper to taste
5 dried lemons (see note above)

1. Add the water to a casserole large enough to hold the chicken comfortably. Add the chicken, parsley, and onion.

2. Scrape the carrots and trim off the ends. Quarter the carrots, then cut each quarter in half. Add them to the casserole. Add the beef broth, salt and pepper to taste. Cook 1 hour and 45 minutes.

3. Prick 2 holes at opposite extremes of each lemon. Add them to the soup and cook 1 hour longer. Remove the parsley.

4. Remove the chicken and save it for a future meal.

5. Press the lemons with the back of a spoon to extract inside juices. The lemons may be served with the soup although they are quite sour and not for all tastes. Normally they are removed.

6. Serve the soup with the vegetables.

Yield: 6 to 8 servings.

Chello

(Plain rice)

4 cups Persian rice (see note, page 127)
16¼ cups lukewarm water
⅓ cup salt
8 tablespoons butter
½ tablespoon crushed stem saffron
1 large baking potato, about ½ pound

1. Pour the rice into a mixing bowl and rinse in several changes of cold water until the water comes clear. Drain.

2. Add 5 cups of lukewarm water and the salt and let stand 30 minutes or so.

3. Bring 10 cups of remaining water to the boil in a kettle and add the rice as well as the water in which it soaked. Bring to the boil and simmer 10 to 12 minutes or until the rice is about half cooked. Test a grain. It should have a bite to it. Drain in a colander and run cold water over the rice until it is chilled. Set aside.

4. Heat the butter in a heavy, deep casserole and when it is foaming, add 1 cup of water. When the mixture boils, remove from the heat.

5. Blend the saffron with the remaining ¼ cup of water and add it to the butter and water in the casserole. Pour off and reserve half this mixture.

6. Peel the potato and cut it into 6 lengthwise slices. Arrange these slices in one layer over the butter mixture remaining in the casserole. They should cover the bottom neatly.

7. Spoon in all of the rice. Use a spatula to shape the ingredients into a mound or cone. Insert the handle of a wooden spoon into the center of the mound to make a funnel. Spoon the reserved butter and saffron mixture around the edges to make a 2-inch butter circle. Cover as closely as possible and cook over very low heat for about 1½ hours. When ready the rice should be tender and the potatoes on the bottom crusty and brown. It may be necessary to loosen the potatoes with a spatula. Serve the rice on a large dish and garnish with the crusty potatoes.

Yield: 8 to 10 generous servings.

Bareh Meveh

(Lamb with fruit)

1 6-pound leg of lamb
5 tablespoons butter, duck fat, or chicken fat
2 cups thinly sliced onions
Salt and freshly ground pepper to taste
1½ cups fresh or canned beef broth
2 teaspoons ground cumin
1 11-ounce package dried mixed fruit

1. Place the lamb fat side down in a Dutch oven. Additional fat is not necessary. Brown the lamb well on all sides, turning as necessary. Remove the lamb.

2. Add the butter and onions. Cook, stirring often, until the onions are quite brown. Do not burn. Add the lamb, fat side up, and sprinkle with salt and pepper.

3. Add the broth and sprinkle with cumin. Cover and cook over low heat about 1½ hours.

4. Turn the lamb and cover. Cook about 10 minutes. Add the dried fruit and cover. Cook 1½ hours longer.

Yield: 8 or more servings.

After the appearance of this piece, a reader wrote to ask what rosewater is and what it is used for. It is a clear, highly aromatic flavoring. It smells strongly of roses and is much used in Middle Eastern and Far Eastern cookery, particularly desserts. This is the Persian dessert in which it is used.

Miveh Makhlout

(Persian fruit melange)

1 *honeydew melon*
1 *cantaloupe*
1 *pint strawberries, stemmed*
2 *tablespoons slivered almonds*
¼ *cup chopped, skinless pistachios*
1 *cup seedless grapes*
2 *tablespoons rosewater*
1½ *cups orange juice, sweetened to taste*
½ *cup Kirschwasser*

1. Split the honeydew melon and the cantaloupe in half and scoop out the seeds. Using a melon baller, scoop out the flesh of both melons into a serving bowl.

2. Stem the strawberries. Wash the berries under cold running water and pat dry. Add them to the bowl. Add the remaining ingredients and mix gently but thoroughly.

Yield: 8 servings.

May 1974

ONE OF THE major attractions in Manhattan during the month of May is a two-day celebration held each year on Ninth Avenue. We can recall many great markets throughout the world, the marvelous market in Bordeaux, the "floating" market of Bangkok, and the colorful in-depth farmer's market in Los Angeles. Somehow, because of our association with New York, Ninth Avenue has always seemed to us more personal. We admire it on many accounts, not the least of which is the great ethnic diversity of foods that can be purchased there. We also applaud and have a warm regard for anything in New York that can maintain its pure and authentic flavor for a fifty-year period. As far as we know, Ninth Avenue has flourished even longer. When we lived in Manhattan on a year-round basis we always found comfort and consolation in the thought that even on Sunday we could find fresh produce in those open air markets that line the street.

Ninth Avenue, New York

A few days ago we received a communication from the secretary of a library association. It contained a form letter directed to men and women in various professions asking what they would do on a busman's holiday in midtown if they had one day in New York. After some reflection, we answered that we would probably take a stroll in and out of the markets on Ninth Avenue. We meant it, for where variety is concerned, there is nothing in the heart of New York to equal it.

Ninth Avenue is a marvelous gastronomic melting pot of—we are told—22 ethnic groups. It is a vibrant, colorful, serious, knockabout, hodgepodge of good things to see and feast from 36th to 53d Streets.

We recently revisited a few of our favorite haunts, among them Giovanni Esposito's outstanding pork store at 500 Ninth Avenue (at 38th Street). This shop has an intriguing assortment of products on display including pig snouts, tripe, tongue, short sausages, and long sausages, some with cheese, some with vegetables, and if you take a peek through the glass window to the rear of the store when hands are busy, you can see the sausages being made, pumped into casings at the rate of about 100 feet a minute. They are furnishers of sausage to several score of outlets in the city. If you want to make your own sausage, you can buy your pork from them and they will furnish the empty casings.

Another specialty of the house is cotechini, what the French call saucissons à l'ail, the fabulously perfumed garlic-flavored sausage that is simply cooked by boiling for an hour to the pound.

Excellent cotechini are also to be found at, among other sources on the avenue, Molinari Brothers, 776 Ninth Avenue (near 52d Street), and at P. Carnevale & Son, 645 Ninth Avenue (at 45th Street). At the latter, where French and Italian are spoken fluently, you can also find a good country-style pâté made on the premises and some of the best Gorgonzola cheese to be found.

For the finest, whitest veal on the avenue go to Piccinini's, 633 Ninth Avenue (between 44th and 45th Streets), the market whose window is a garden of azaleas.

There is no finer source in midtown Manhattan for Greek groceries than at Kassos Brothers, 570 Ninth Avenue (between 41st and 42d Streets). There is excellent feta cheese in three strengths, mild, medium, and sharp; tarama in bottles for making that fantastic Greek appetizer, Taramosalata; and a great assortment of olives with such names as Alfonso, Victoria, Salonica, and Nafplion. The owner, John Kassos, a fine-looking giant of a man, also sells salted anchovies in bulk, as well as imported oils and honey.

The area's best Greek pastry shop is the Poseidon at 629 Ninth Avenue (between 44th and 45th Streets). It is chock full of freshly made pastries, most of them honey soaked and many stuffed with pistachios and almonds, things like kataifi and baklava. Also some dainty things called afali, which the management explains translates whimsically as "belly button."

There also is Casa Italian Bakery at 545 Ninth Avenue (between 40th and 41st Streets) with an impressive display of crusty round, long, and oval loaves both in the window and inside, where a wonderfully grumpy saleslady presides.

Manganaro's, of course, if almost without question the largest and most widely stocked retail Italian grocer in Manhattan. It is at 488 Ninth Avenue (between 37th and 38th Streets) and is a vast place with a horde of cheeses, like wonderfully perfumed stalactites, hanging from the ceiling.

The store is bountifully stocked with imported oils, truffles, pasta, and presumably every conceivable Italian delicacy that can be imported. To the rear of the store is a dining area where rather creditable hot foods and cold sandwiches can be purchased. There are hot soups, lasagne, spaghetti dishes, and the store's specialty, the arancini, or deep-fried rice balls stuffed with cheese and served with tomato sauce.

The last couple of years has seen the transformation of one block into a group of stores specializing in products and foods from the Philippines. One of them is the Mabuhay at 525 (at 39th Street). Not only does the shop have canned, fresh, and frozen Philippine merchandise, but there is a small restaurant to the rear that specializes in such foods as estufado (pig's knuckles with garlic, star anise, and sweet and sour seasonings), frittada (a chicken and pork dish with tomato sauce and chick peas), menudo (a pork with pepper dish), and lechon (fried pork with a sweet and sour sauce). The cost for a complete meal is less than $2.

The rundown here is the merest sample of the fascinating food stores, both open-air and enclosed, on Ninth Avenue. And perhaps the best restaurant in the entire area is Giordano's, 409 West 39th Street.

Many of the outlets on Ninth Avenue specialize in pork hocks. Here are recipes for some Ninth Avenue specialties: a ragout of pork hocks to be served with sauerkraut; another for cotechini or garlic sausages served with lentils; and taramosalata, a Greek appetizer.

Ragout of Pork Hocks

1 tablespoon lard or other
   fat
6 pork hocks (about 5
   pounds)
   Salt and freshly ground
   pepper to taste
1 cup finely chopped onion
1 cup finely diced carrot
3 whole cloves garlic, finely
   minced
3 tablespoons flour
2 cups chicken broth
1 cup water
2 sprigs fresh thyme or 1
   teaspoon dried
1 bay leaf

1. Heat the lard in a heavy casserole large enough to hold the pork hocks in one layer.

2. Sprinkle the pork hocks with salt and pepper and add them to the casserole. Brown well on all sides.

3. Add the onion, carrots, and garlic and sprinkle with flour. Cover and cook about 10 minutes.

4. Add the broth, water, thyme, and bay leaf. Cover and cook about 1¼ hours until the hocks are thoroughly tender. Serve, if desired, with sauerkraut.

Yield: 6 servings.

Sauerkraut with Caraway

2 pounds sauerkraut
2 tablespoons lard or other
   fat

1 cup finely chopped onion
1 clove garlic, finely minced
1 tablespoon sugar
2 teaspoons crushed caraway
   seeds
2 cups chicken broth
   Salt and freshly ground
   pepper to taste
1 small raw potato

1. Put the sauerkraut in a colander and squeeze or press to remove most of the liquid.

2. Melt the lard in a heavy casserole and add the onion and garlic. Cook, stirring, until onion is translucent.

3. Add the sauerkraut, sugar, caraway seeds, chicken broth, salt and pepper. Cover and cook 45 minutes.

4. Peel and grate the potato. There should be about ⅓ cup. Stir this into the sauerkraut. Cover and cook 15 minutes longer. Serve, if desired, with a ragout of pork hocks.

Yield: 6 servings.

How to Cook Cotechini or Garlic Sausages

2 1-pound cotechini (garlic
   sausages or saucissons à
   l'ail)
   Salt to taste
1 onion, sliced
3 sprigs fresh thyme or ½
   teaspoon dried
1 bay leaf
12 peppercorns

1. Prick the cotechini in several places. Place it in a kettle and add cold water to cover. Add the remaining ingredients and bring to the boil.

2. Simmer the sausages about 40 or 45 minutes. Let stand in the cooking liquid until ready to serve. Serve sliced, hot or cold. Served hot, these are very good with lentils or with hot potato salad.

Yield: 12 or more servings.

Lentils Côte d'Azur

3   *tablespoons butter*
¼   *pound smoked ham slice, fat left on, cut into quarters*
¼   *cup coarsely chopped onion*
½   *pound dried lentils*
2   *cups water*
4   *cups chicken broth, fresh or canned*
½   *bay leaf*
1   *sprig fresh thyme or ¼ teaspoon dried*
    Salt and freshly ground pepper to taste
⅔   *cup finely diced leek (1 leek)*
½   *cup finely chopped onion*
1   *clove garlic, finely minced*
1   *cup tomatoes, fresh or canned*
    Chopped parsley for garnish

1. Heat 1 tablespoon butter in a small kettle or deep saucepan and add the ham and coarsely chopped onion. Cook briefly until onion wilts.

2. Add the lentils, water, broth, bay leaf, thyme, salt, and pepper and simmer 30 to 40 minutes. Discard the bay leaf and ham.

3. Meanwhile, heat the remaining butter in a saucepan and add the leek and finely chopped onion. Add the garlic and cook, stirring, about 5 minutes. Add the tomatoes and cover. Simmer about 15 minutes.

4. Combine the lentils with the tomato sauce. Cover and cook about 15 minutes. Serve sprinkled with chopped parsley and sliced cotechini.

Yield: 6 to 8 servings.

Taramosalata

5   *level tablespoons tarama (carp roe, see note)*
1   *cup ½-inch bread cubes*
1½   *tablespoons cold water*
    Juice of 1 lemon, more or less to taste
1   *cup olive oil*
    Chopped parsley for garnish

1. Spoon the tarama into the bowl of an electric beater. If you use a portable beater, use a suitable mixing bowl.

2. Place the bread in another small bowl and sprinkle with water. Toss the bread to dampen the cubes. Add the cubes to the tarama.

3. Add the lemon juice.

4. Using an electric beater, start beating the mixture while

gradually adding the oil in a thin stream. Continue beating on high speed while adding the oil until it is all used. Serve cold sprinkled with chopped parsley. Serve with oriental bread, French bread, or buttered toast.

Yield: 6 to 8 servings.

Note: Tarama in bottles is available in Greek markets. If you wish, you may add grated onion to taste to the taramosalata.

Ninth Avenue has remained over the years, along with Chinatown, our favorite place for shopping or simply browsing. For anyone with a passing interest in fine food, it would be inconceivable to visit Manhattan without at least a brief sojourn to Ninth Avenue.

Zucchini: Bake, Boil, Stuff, Fry

WITH PIERRE FRANEY

Alphabetically, zucchini is at the bottom of the vegetable list, but this most versatile squash should be near the top of anyone's compendium of what's what out of a garden. Its potential is phenomenal. These recipes—for zucchini in a style of Provence, zucchini with tomatoes, fried green zucchini, zucchini stuffed with meat and pignoli, and Parmesan zucchini—simply hint at the possibilities of this little green squash.

Zucchini with Tomatoes

2 to 3 pounds zucchini
1½ pounds red, ripe tomatoes
3 tablespoons olive oil
1 cup finely chopped onion
1 tablespoon finely minced garlic
1 tablespoon chopped fresh basil or ½ teaspoon dried
   Salt and freshly ground pepper to taste

1. Trim off the ends of the zucchini and cut the vegetables into 1-inch-thick rounds. If the zucchini are very small, leave the rounds intact. If they are medium-size, cut the rounds in half. There should be about 8 cups.

2. Peel the tomatoes and cut them into 1-inch cubes. There should be about 4 cups.

3. In a heavy skillet, heat the oil and add the onion. Cook, stirring, until onion is wilted and add the garlic, tomatoes, basil, salt and pepper to taste and cook about 5 minutes. Add the zucchini and cover. Cook about 20 minutes. The zucchini should be tender yet crisp.

Yield: 8 or more servings.

Zucchini in a Style of Provence

½ pound onions
2 pounds zucchini
1 teaspoon loosely packed oregano
2 tablespoons olive oil
½ teaspoon finely minced garlic
3 eggs
   Salt and freshly ground pepper to taste
   Nutmeg

1. Peel the onions and cut them in half. Slice each half thinly. There should be about 2½ cups.

2. Trim off the ends and peel the zucchini. If they are small, cut

them in half lengthwise. Cut each quarter or half into 1-inch pieces. There should be about 6 cups.

3. Place the oregano in a small skillet and toast over moderate heat, shaking the skillet and stirring to prevent burning. Cook just until lightly toasted. Do not burn or the oregano will be bitter. Crush or grind the oregano and set it aside.

4. Heat the oil in a heavy saucepan and add the onions. Cover closely and cook without browning, stirring occasionally, about 20 minutes. Add the zucchini and the garlic. Cover and cook very gently, stirring often to prevent scorching, about 45 minutes. By that time the vegetables will be very tender. Stir vigorously with a spoon to make a purée.

5. Beat the eggs and add them. Cook about 2 minutes over moderate heat, stirring, and turn off the heat. Add salt, pepper, and nutmeg to taste. Stir in the toasted oregano and serve piping hot.

Yield: 6 to 8 servings.

Fried Green Zucchini

2 to 4 zucchini, about 1 pound
1 cup flour
 Salt and freshly ground pepper to taste
4 cups peanut, vegetable, or corn oil

1. Cut the zucchini into small "sticks." To do this, cut off the ends of each zucchini. Do not peel. Cut the zucchini into 2-inch lengths. Cut each length into lengthwise slices about ½ inch thick. Cut each slice into strips about ½ inch wide. There should be about 4 cups.

2. Blend the flour with salt and pepper to taste. Dredge the zucchini sticks in flour and shake off excess.

3. Heat the oil in a deep fryer to 360 to 380 degrees. Cook half the batch at a time, stirring, 3 to 4 minutes or until golden and crisp-tender. Remove and drain. Add the remaining batch and cook. Drain and serve piping hot sprinkled with salt and pepper.

Yield: 4 servings.

Zucchini Stuffed with Meat and Pignoli

2 or 3 medium or 5 or 6 small zucchini, about 1½ pounds
1 large tomato
1 tablespoon plus 1 teaspoon olive oil
½ cup finely chopped onion
½ teaspoon oregano
2 tablespoons raw rice
¼ pound ground lamb, beef, or pork
¼ cup pignoli (pine nuts)
⅛ teaspoon cinnamon
 Salt and freshly ground pepper to taste
1 cup chicken broth
2 teaspoons cornstarch
1 tablespoon water
2 egg yolks
 Juice of ½ lemon

1. Preheat oven to 350 degrees.

2. Trim off the ends of the zucchini and discard them. Cut the zucchini into 2½-inch lengths. Using a melon ball cutter, hollow out the centers of each length, leaving a wall about ⅓ inch thick. Chop enough of the zucchini pulp to make ½ cup.

3. Peel the tomato and chop it. There should be about 1¼ cups.

4. Heat 1 tablespoon of oil in a saucepan and add half the onion and the oregano. Cook about 1 minute and add ½ cup tomato. Cook about 1 minute and add the rice. Stir and set aside.

5. In a large skillet with a tight-fitting lid or a Dutch oven, heat the remaining teaspoon of oil. Add the remaining onion and tomatoes. Cook, stirring, about 1 minute and set aside.

6. Blend the meat with the pignoli, cinnamon, and salt and pepper to taste. Add the rice mixture and zucchini pulp and mix well.

7. Stuff the hollowed-out sections of zucchini with the meat and rice mixture, and as they are stuffed stand them on end in the skillet containing the tomato and onion base. Cover with the lid or foil and bake 45 minutes. Uncover and continue baking about 10 minutes.

8. Meanwhile, bring the chicken broth to the boil. Blend the cornstarch with the water and stir it in.

9. Beat the yolks in a mixing bowl and pour some of the hot sauce over them, beating vigorously. Pour the yolk mixture

into the hot sauce and heat, stirring, without boiling until the sauce is custardlike. If the sauce boils, it may curdle. Add the lemon juice.

10. Transfer the stuffed zucchini to a hot platter and pour the sauce over.

Yield: 6 to 8 servings.

Parmesan Zucchini

4 *or 5 small, firm zucchini,*
   about 1 pound
   Salt and freshly ground
   pepper to taste
¼ *cup grated Parmesan*
   cheese
2 *tablespoons melted butter*

1. Preheat the broiler.

2. Trim off and discard the ends of the unpeeled zucchini. Cut the zucchini into 2-inch lengths, then cut each length into quarters lengthwise.

3. Place the pieces in a saucepan and add water to cover and salt to taste. Bring to the boil and simmer 10 to 15 minutes or until crisp-tender. Do not overcook or the pieces will become mushy. Drain immediately and chill quickly under cold running water. Drain again in a colander.

4. Generously butter an 8- to 9-inch flameproof dish and arrange the zucchini pieces in one layer over the bottom. Sprinkle with salt, pepper, and cheese. Dribble the butter evenly over all. Run under the broiler until hot and golden.

Yield: 6 or more servings.

Born with a Ladle in His Hand

We can quote chapter and verse about the works and world of Georges Auguste Escoffier, the man who is to the Gallic table what games are to Hoyle. But somehow, in the course of our labors in the world of food, we had never heard of Edouard Nignon, another of the titans of French cooking.

We learned of him recently when Pierre Laverne, the distinguished chef of La Côte Basque in Manhattan, came to wield his knives in our kitchen. Over a regale of Mr. Laverne's devising—a superb fillet of bass fermière; brezolles, tender morsels of veal given greater glory with a succulent mushroom sauce; and an ultimately delectable apple tart—we learned that Edouard Nignon did, indeed, have a distinguished career. He worked in many of the most celebrated kitchens of Paris, at the Claridge in London, the Ermitage in Moscow. Toward the end of World War I he even served as chef to President Wilson.

Nignon wrote three books, printed apparently in limited editions of 2,000 each. They were the *Heptameron des Gourmets, Eloges de la Cuisine Française,* and *Plaisirs de la Table.*

Chef Laverne had in his possession the last two . . . splendid, serious, dedicated volumes, with hundreds of recipes written with almost poetic precision. They are written with remarkable clarity and with the unmistakable enthusiasm of a man in love with his subject.

We asked Mr. Laverne, who is 54 years old, how long he himself had worked at his profession, and he explained with some conviction that he was literally born a chef. He could scarcely remember when he wasn't.

"I was born in Montbard in Burgundy," he said. "My family was bourgeois in comfortable circumstances and, like everybody else in Burgundy, we ate well. The family tables in Burgundy were well furnished. They are to this day. My aunt was a fantastic pastry cook."

The chef added that he had worked in Paris, in London, and with various ships of the French line including the *De Grasse.* Before coming to America, Mr. Laverne remembers with greatest detail his years at the Hotel de la Côte d'Or in Chatillon-sur-Seine in France. It was there, under the influence of the owner-chef, that he discovered Nignon. Years before, the patron had worked under Nignon and, Mr. Laverne recalls, he was the one who had the greatest influence on his talents.

The chef is married, has two children and one grandchild. And even at home it is he who, on weekends, wears the toque blanche in the family. He rises early on Sundays, when La Côte Basque is closed, and has a cup of coffee with milk that he says is to him what a glass of white wine is "to the priest." At noon he contents himself with a thick ham sandwich larded with no small amount of sweet butter. And at dinner something simple. Perhaps an entrecôte or small steak sautéed with a little chopped shallot and parsley.

Those who dined with us recently lifted a glass to Edouard Nignon for whatever he contributed to the admirable talents of Pierre Laverne. His bass femière, his brezolles of veal, and apple tart were something to toast. With a fine white Burgundy, of course.

Striped Bass Fermière

2 *skinless and boneless striped bass fillets, about 5½ pounds*
2 *or 3 small carrots*
17 *tablespoons butter*
1 *cup thinly sliced shallots*
1½ *cups thinly sliced celery*
4 *mushrooms, thinly sliced*
1½ *cups dry white wine*
Salt and freshly ground pepper to taste
Juice of ½ lemon
Parsleyed cucumber ovals (see recipe, page 86)
1 *cup heavy cream*

1. Cut the fish fillets slightly on the bias into 8 "steaks." Refrigerate.

2. Trim and scrape the carrots and cut them into very thin rounds.

3. Select a heavy casserole large enough to hold all the pieces of fish in one layer. Add 8 tablespoons of butter. When it is hot, add the carrots, shallots, celery, and mushrooms. Add ⅓ cup of dry white wine. Cook until all the wine has been reduced, about 10 minutes. Add another ⅓ cup of wine and cook until it is reduced, about 10 minutes. Add another ⅓ cup of wine and cook until it is reduced, about 10 minutes. The total time for adding and reducing the wine is about 30 minutes.

4. Sprinkle the fish pieces with salt and pepper and arrange them in one layer over the vegetables. Pour the remaining ½ cup of wine over the fish and bring to the boil. Simmer about 6 minutes. Sprinkle with lemon juice.

5. Melt 2 tablespoons of butter in an oval serving dish large enough to hold the fish in one layer. Transfer the fish and cover to keep warm.

6. To the casserole add the cream and bring it to a boil over high heat, shaking the skillet so that it blends with the vegetable flavors, about 3 minutes. Add remaining 7 tablespoons of butter, bit by bit, while shaking the casserole. Pour this over the fish and serve immediately with parsleyed cucumbers.

Yield: 8 servings.

Brezolles
à la Maurette

3 pounds veal, preferably
    fillet (see note)
1 pound fresh mushrooms
6 tablespoons butter
    Juice of ½ lemon
1 shallot, peeled and split in
    half
    Salt and freshly ground
    pepper to taste
¾ cup brown veal sauce (see
    recipe)
½ cup plus 2 tablespoons dry
    white wine
1 peeled, seeded tomato,
    coarsely chopped
½ pound unsalted fat back,
    chilled thoroughly in the
    freezer
    Flour for dredging

1. Cut the veal into ½-inch "medallions." If another less tender cut of veal is used, it may be pounded lightly. Set aside.

2. Cut the mushrooms into very thin slices.

3. Heat 4 tablespoons of butter in a large skillet and add the mushrooms. Sprinkle with lemon juice. Add the shallot. Add salt and pepper. Cook, stirring occasionally, until the mushrooms are quite brown and dry, about 20 minutes. Add half the brown veal sauce and 2 tablespoons wine. Stir in the chopped tomato. Reduce slightly.

4. Place the fat back on a flat surface and cut it into ¼-inch slices. Cut the slices into ¼-inch strips. Place them in a bowl and add ice to keep the strips separate and firm. Use a larding needle and lard each veal medallion with 2 strips of fat back. If scaloppine is used, however, the larding will not be necessry.

5. Sprinkle the veal with salt and pepper and coat the pieces lightly all over with flour.

6. Heat remaining 2 tablespoons of butter in a large heavy skillet and when it starts to brown, add the veal pieces. Cook about 5 minutes on one side and turn. Cook about 5 minutes on the other. Transfer the meat to the center of a serving dish.

7. Add the remaining wine to the skillet and cook until reduced. Add the remaining veal sauce. Add the mushroom mixture. If the sauce is too thick, add a little water to thin it. Bring to the boil. Spoon the sauce over the meat. Serve with grilled tomatoes and rice pilaf.

Yield: 8 servings.

Note: Fillet of veal is very scarce and expensive. Scaloppine can be substituted.

Brown veal sauce

4 tablespoons butter
¾ pound veal bones, chopped
    into 2-inch pieces
    Salt and freshly ground
    pepper to taste
½ bay leaf
½ teaspoon thyme
¼ cup thinly sliced carrots
¼ cup chopped celery leaves
½ cup chopped onion
1 cup thinly sliced
    mushrooms

6 *sprigs fresh parsley*
⅓ *cup dry white wine*
4 *to 5 cups cold water*

1. Melt the butter in a heavy saucepan and add the veal bones, salt and pepper. Cook over moderate heat, stirring the bones around until they start to brown. Add the bay leaf and continue to cook, browning the bones, about 15 minutes longer. Add the thyme, carrots, celery, onion, mushrooms, and parsley. Cook about 5 minutes, stirring, and add ⅓ cup dry white wine. Bring to the boil and cover. Cook 5 minutes and add 2 cups of water. Cover and simmer 1 hour.

2. Add another cup of water and cook uncovered about 30 minutes, simmering slowly. When that liquid has almost reduced, add another cup of water and cook uncovered. Strain through a fine sieve, pushing the vegetables with a wooden spoon to extract as much of their flavors as possible.

Yield: There should be at least ¾ cup of sauce.

Tarte de Friande

(French apple tart)

Sweet pastry dough (see recipe)
3½ *pounds Golden Delicious apples, about 9*
12 *tablespoons butter*
1 *1-inch stick of vanilla bean, optional*
¼ *cup confectioners' sugar*
½ *cup marmalade*

2 *tablespoons water*
2 *tablespoons Grand Marnier*
¼ *cup toasted, slivered almonds*

1. Preheat oven to 400 degrees.

2. Roll out the pastry on a very cold board or surface (it will be hard to handle otherwise) and fit it into a 10-inch flan ring or pie plate. Refrigerate.

3. Peel the apples and cut them in half. Cut away and discard the cores. Select 12 choice apple halves to be used for the top of the tart. Cut off the small ends of each of these halves. Set the 12 apple halves aside.

4. Quarter the remaining apple halves. Cut them into very thin slices. There should be about 8 cups.

5. Heat 8 tablespoons of butter in a large heavy skillet and add the thinly sliced apples. Add the piece of vanilla bean and cook about 30 minutes, stirring, until the apples are quite dry and appetizingly browned. Stir in the remaining butter.

6. Spoon the browned apple mixture into the pastry-lined tart pan and smooth it over. Thinly slice the reserved apple halves and arrange them neatly—layer after layer—in an overlapping pattern over the cooked apples.

7. Spoon the confectioners' sugar into a small sieve and sieve it evenly over the tart.

8. Bake the tart about 1 hour.

9. Combine the marmalade and water in a saucepan and stir

Pierre Laverne sieves confectioners' sugar evenly over a French apple tart.

until thinned. Let cool and add the Grand Marnier. Spread it over the tart and sprinkle the toasted almonds over all.

Yield: 10 to 12 servings.

Sweet pastry dough

¼ *pound very cold butter*
½ *cup confectioners' sugar*
2 *egg yolks*
1¼ *cups flour*
    Salt to taste
½ *to 1 tablespoon ice water*

1. Cut the butter into small cubes and put it in a mixing bowl.

2. Add the sugar and egg yolks and mix thoroughly, using the hands or an electric beater.

3. Combine the flour and salt in a flour sifter. Sift them gradually and alternately with the water to the yolk mixture. Add just enough water so that the mixture holds together. Shape the dough into a flat cake and wrap it in wax paper. Refrigerate for ½ hour or so. Remember the pastry will work best if it is rolled out on a very cold surface, preferably marble.

Yield: Enough pastry for a 9- or 10-inch crust.

From Italy's Piedmont Region

The Italian bagna caôda is one of the most savory, delectable, and unlikely appetizers in the world. It is a sort of fondue (in the original and proper sense of the word, meaning melted) containing anchovies that melt in a bath of olive oil and butter and in keen liaison with 20 thinly sliced garlic cloves. Twenty is an arbitrary number. Frequently there are more. We had always assumed that bagna caôda meant "hot bath." But as we dipped an assortment of crisp vegetables into a bubbling pot of the aromatic and irresistible brew in the home of Teresa Candler in Closter, New Jersey, we were informed that it has another meaning entirely.

"Bagna," she told us, "is a dialectical Piedmont word for gravy or a thickened sauce. Today it is becoming more and more fashionable to dine on bagna caôda, but it started out as a peasant dish eaten by farmers during harvest time. The point was that it could be cooked at home in an earthenware casserole, then taken to the vineyard where it could be kept over an open fire. The best vegetable to eat with bagna caôda is the cardoon, but it's out of season now and hard to obtain." The vegetables with which we dipped were eminently serviceable—celery, sweet red peppers, and onions roasted in the skin.

It is such errors in thinking that "bagna" means bath that has persuaded Mrs. Candler to try her hand at a several-volume record of Italian cooking, starting with the Piedmont region, her homeland. "I know people who speak reasonably good Italian and know a reasonable amount about food who still think that antipasto means something you eat 'before the pasta.' It means, of course, 'before the meal.' Pasta means 'food' in Italian."

At the time of our meeting Mrs. Candler was in the midst of preparing several of the dishes to be included in her manuscript. They included another uncommon and quite exceptionally good appetizer, a kind of savory layered cake made with a dozen or so crespelle—the Italian word for crêpes. Each thin pancake of the dish had been smeared lightly with mayonnaise and layered with an assortment of fillings—thin slices of prosciutto, a bit of caviar mixed with sour cream, liver pâté, roasted peppers, wafer-thin slices of Fontina cheese, thinly sliced chicken breast, mashed tuna, and so on. A sort of drawing-room hero sandwich raised to the nth elegant degree. It was garnished with anchovy-wrapped olives and hard-cooked eggs and served cut into wedges.

Since we have a craving for almost all of the oddments of the animal, including sweetbreads, brains, and tripe, we were all but undone with the pleasure of dining on a Piedmontese pork and bean dish made with dried lima beans. It was a marvelous compendium of beans, pig's feet, and rolls of pork rind stuffed with touches of garlic and rosemary, long simmered in a clear soup flavored with sage and bay leaves. Mrs. Candler, born Teresa Gilardi, prefaced the dish by saying, "It will remind you of Boston baked beans." ("We could of died laughing," as a man once said in Back Bay.)

At one point the lady offered us a smashingly palatable wedge of Italian pastry, a marmalade tart with a crisp sweet crust and melting center.

Bagna Caôda
(Anchovy and garlic sauce for cold vegetables)

1 *cup olive oil*
½ *cup butter*
2 *2-ounce cans anchovy fillets*
20 *cloves garlic, peeled and · thinly sliced (about ½ cup)*
1 *small white truffle, available in Italian specialty food stores, optional*
¼ *cup heavy cream, optional Assorted raw vegetables*

1. Combine the oil, butter, anchovies, and garlic in a saucepan. Cook over very low heat for about 1 hour. The sauce must barely simmer as it cooks.

2. Slice the truffle thinly and add it to the saucepan. Add the cream and simmer about 5 minutes longer. Serve with assorted vegetables cut into bite-size cubes and lengths. Vegetables might include red or green sweet peppers, celery ribs, small new zucchini, carrots, and so on. Onions, baked in the skin, peeled and quartered, are good, too. To prepare them, bake medium-size onions in a 400-degree oven for 1 hour.

Yield: 4 servings.

Tofeja
(A pork and bean soup)

1 *pound dried lima beans*
4 *cloves garlic*
2 *teaspoons rosemary*
3 *teaspoons salt Freshly ground pepper to taste*
¼ *teaspoon nutmeg*
1 *pound fresh pork rind*
1 *carrot, trimmed and scraped*
2 *ribs celery, trimmed*
3 *pig's feet, cut into 2- or 3-inch pieces*
1 *medium onion, peeled*
4 *bay leaves*
4 *sage leaves or 1 teaspoon rubbed leaf sage or ½ teaspoon ground sage*

1. Place the beans in a large bowl and add warm water to cover. Let stand overnight.

2. Preheat the oven to 250 degrees.

3. Chop garlic cloves with the rosemary. Blend the mixture with

1 teaspoon of salt, pepper, and nutmeg. Blend well.

4. Rinse the pork rind and pat it dry. Cut it into 3-by-5-inch rectangles. Place the pieces skin side down and sprinkle each piece with equal amounts of the garlic and rosemary mixture. Roll up each piece and tie with string. Set aside.

5. Drain the beans and put them in an ovenproof bean pot.

6. Tie the carrot and celery ribs with string to facilitate later removal from the pot. Cut them in half if necessary to accommodate the size of the pot. Add the package to the beans.

7. Add the pork rolls, pig's feet, onion, bay leaves, sage leaves, the remaining clove of garlic, the remaining salt and pepper to taste. Add boiling water to cover. Cover the pot tightly with a lid and bake 4 or 5 hours or until the meat and beans are thoroughly tender. Serve piping hot.

Yield: 4 to 8 servings.

Crostata di Marmellata
(Italian marmalade pie)

    Italian sweet pie pastry (see recipe)
1 *pound marmalade*
1 *egg yolk*
1 *tablespoon cold water*
1 *tablespoon granulated sugar*

1. Preheat the oven to 400 degrees.

2. Prepare the dough and after chilling remove it from the refrigerator. Divide it in half. With a rolling pin roll out half the dough into a circle large enough to fit a 10-inch pie dish with a fluted edge. Fit the pastry in the pie dish, prick the bottom with a fork and bake 10 minutes.

3. Remove the pastry from the oven and add the marmalade. Spread the marmalade evenly with a spatula.

4. Roll out the second batch of dough and cut it into strips ¾ inch wide, using a pastry wheel. Arrange half the strips 1 inch apart over the pie. Repeat with remaining strips going in the opposite direction to make a diamond or square pattern.

5. Beat the yolk with the water and brush the strips with the mixture. Sprinkle with sugar and bake 15 to 20 minutes or until the pie strips are nicely golden.

Yield: 6 to 8 servings.

Italian sweet pie pastry

 2 *cups flour*
12 *tablespoons butter at room temperature*
½ *teaspoon salt*
½ *cup sugar*
 2 *eggs*
 1 *egg yolk*
 2 *teaspoons pure vanilla extract*
 2 *teaspoons freshly grated lemon rind*

1. Place the flour in a mixing bowl and add the remaining ingredients.

2. Work the ingredients with the fingers until well blended.

Shape into a smooth ball, cover with wax paper and refrigerate for 30 minutes or longer.

Yield: Enough pastry for 1-crust pie with lattice top.

Crespelle Belvedere
(Stuffed crêpes Belvedere)

The crêpes

3 *eggs*
1 *cup flour*
   Salt to taste
¼ *teaspoon white pepper*
1 *cup milk*
3 *tablespoons brandy*
2 *tablespoons peanut or vegetable oil*
1½ *cups mayonnaise (see recipe, page 9)*

The fillings

⅓ *cup tuna fish, mashed*
¼ *pound boiled ham or prosciutto, sliced as thinly as possible*
¼ *pound cooked chicken or turkey breast, sliced as thinly as possible*
⅓ *cup liver pâté*
¼ *pound roast beef, sliced as thinly as possible*
1 *or 2 roasted peppers (see note)*
¼ *pound thinly sliced Fontina, Swiss, or Gruyère cheese*
¼ *cup black caviar blended with 3 tablespoons sour cream*

The garnish

6 *flat anchovy fillets*

6 *stuffed green olives*
3 *hard-cooked eggs, cut into wedges*
2 *tomatoes, cut into wedges*

1. Break the eggs into a mixing bowl and beat until thoroughly blended. Sift in the flour, stirring. Add the salt and pepper and beat until smooth. Stir in the milk, brandy, and oil.

2. Heat a 10-inch Teflon pan or a large, well-seasoned crêpe or omelet pan and add enough of the batter to cover the bottom of the pan. Cook the crêpes, turning once. Transfer to a sheet of wax paper. Continue making crêpes until all the batter is used. There should be 10 to 12 crêpes. Let cool.

3. Place one crêpe on a flat surface and smear the top with a thin coating of mayonnaise. Neatly arrange one of the fillings over it. Cover with another crêpe, another thin coating of mayonnaise, another filling, and so on, ending with a crêpe. Cover the top and sides of the stack with mayonnaise. Chill.

4. When ready to serve, garnish the top of the stack with olives surrounded with anchovies, the egg and tomato wedges. Serve cut into thin wedges.

Yield: 12 or more appetizer servings.

Note: Roast in a very hot oven or over an open flame, turning frequently until the skin is wrinkled and charred. Drop into a paper bag and enclose tightly. When cool, remove and peel.

An Eggplant Sampler

WITH PIERRE FRANEY

Eggplant used to be called *mela insana,* mad apple, and it was thought to cause insanity. But that was a long time ago. We happen to be crazy about the vegetable ourselves, because it is earthy, yet elegant; meaty (think of eggplant parmigiana), but all vegetable; versatile and, yes, delectable.

Spaghetti with Eggplant

5 *tablespoons olive oil*
2 *cloves garlic, finely minced*
4 *cups peeled tomatoes, preferably imported if canned*
4 *tablespoons tomato paste*
¾ *cup water*
1 *teaspoon sugar*
   Salt and freshly ground pepper
½ *cup chopped parsley*
1 *tablespoon finely chopped fresh basil or ½ teaspoon dried*
1½ *pounds eggplant*
½ *pound or more spaghetti*
¾ *cup grated Parmesan cheese*

1. Heat 1 tablespoon of oil in a saucepan and add the garlic. Cook, stirring, without browning and add the tomatoes, tomato paste, water, sugar, salt and pepper to taste, parsley, and basil. Stir to blend. Partially cover and cook, stirring frequently, about 45 minutes.

2. Meanwhile, cut off the ends of the eggplant. Peel the eggplant. Cut it into ½-inch cubes.

3. Heat the remaining oil in a large skillet and when it is very hot, add the eggplant and salt to taste. Cook the eggplant, tossing, until it is nicely browned and tender. Add the eggplant to the tomato sauce and cover. Cook 30 to 40 minutes or until the eggplant blends with the sauce.

4. Cook the spaghetti to the desired degree of doneness and drain. Serve hot with the sauce. Serve grated Parmesan cheese on the side. This sauce is excellent when reheated.

Yield: 6 to 8 servings.

Deep-Fried Eggplant with Almonds

1¼ *pounds eggplant*
    Salt
1   *cup milk*
1   *cup flour*
    Oil for deep frying
4   *tablespoons butter*

½ cup slivered, blanched
    almonds

1. Cut off the ends of the egg-plant. Peel the eggplant. Cut the eggplant into slices about ⅛ inch thick.

2. Cut the eggplant slices into small rectangles, measuring about 1 by 1½ inches. Put the pieces into a mixing bowl and sprinkle with salt. Toss lightly. Let stand about 30 minutes.

3. Add the milk to the egg-plant and let stand about ½ hour. Drain well and discard milk.

4. Dredge the eggplant pieces in flour.

5. Heat the oil for deep frying to 375 degrees and add the egg-plant pieces. Cook, stirring con-stantly, until very crisp, about 3 to 5 minutes.

6. Remove the pieces with a slotted spoon and let drain on ab-sorbent paper toweling. Sprinkle lightly with salt and transfer to a hot serving dish.

7. Heat the butter in a skillet and when it is hot and starting to brown, add the almonds, stirring constantly. When the butter is ha-zelnut colored, pour the almonds and butter over the eggplant. Serve piping hot.

Yield: 4 to 6 servings.

Eggplant Rollatine

1 1½-pound eggplant
   Salt
2 cups olive oil

½ pound ground pork
½ cup chopped onion
1 clove garlic, finely minced
   Freshly ground pepper to
   taste
1½ teaspoons crushed oregano
2 tablespoons finely chopped
   parsley
2 cups tomato sauce (see
   recipe)
½ pound Mozzarella cheese
½ cup grated Parmesan
   cheese

1. Preheat oven to 400 de-grees.

2. Trim off the ends of the eggplant and cut the eggplant into ⅛-inch-thick slices. There should be about 20 slices. Sprinkle lightly on both sides with salt and place on a rack. Liquid will ac-cumulate on both surfaces of the slices. Let drain about 1 hour. Pat dry.

3. Heat 2 cups of oil in a large skillet and when it is piping hot and almost smoking, add the egg-plant slices, turning once and cooking quickly. Drain on absor-bent paper toweling.

4. Heat a saucepan and add the pork. Additional fat is not nec-essary. Add the onion, garlic, salt, pepper, and a teaspoon of oregano. Cover and cook about 5 minutes. Stir in the parsley.

5. Lay the slices of eggplant on a flat surface and spoon equal portions of filling in the center of each.

6. Spoon a thin layer of to-mato sauce over the bottom of a baking dish. Roll up the eggplant slices to enclose the filling and ar-range the rolls in one layer over

the bottom of the dish. Add a layer of sauce. Arrange slices of Mozzarella over the eggplant rolls and cover with remaining sauce. Sprinkle with remaining ½ teaspoon of oregano. Sprinkle with the Parmesan cheese. Bake 30 minutes or until the casserole is bubbling hot all over.

Yield: 4 to 6 servings.

Tomato sauce

2 *tablespoons butter*
1½ *teaspoons finely chopped garlic*
2 *cups peeled chopped tomatoes, preferably imported if canned*
   Salt and freshly ground pepper to taste
2 *tablespoons chopped fresh basil or 1½ teaspoons dried*

1. Melt the butter in a saucepan and add the garlic.

2. Add the tomatoes, salt and pepper to taste, and the basil. Cook, stirring occasionally about 20 minutes.

Yield: About 2 cups.

Eggplant au Gratin

1 *1-pound eggplant*
   Salt
½ *pound fresh mushrooms*
3½ *tablespoons butter*
   Juice of ½ lemon
1½ *tablespoons flour*
½ *cup milk*
¼ *cup heavy cream*

Freshly ground pepper
¼ *teaspoon nutmeg*
   Tabasco
1 *egg, lightly beaten*
2 *tablespoons bread crumbs*
2 *tablespoons grated Parmesan cheese*

1. Preheat oven to 425 degrees.

2. Peel the eggplant and cut the flesh into 1-inch cubes, more or less. Drop the cubes into boiling salted water and cook about 5 minutes just until cooked. Drain well.

3. Meanwhile, slice the mushrooms. There should be about 3 cups. Heat 1 tablespoon of butter in a skillet and add the mushroom slices. Sprinkle with salt and about 1 teaspoon lemon juice. Cook, stirring and tossing, until wilted and the juices come out. Continue cooking until the liquid evaporates. Set aside.

4. Melt 1½ tablespoons of butter in a saucepan and add the flour, stirring with a wire whisk. Add the milk and cream, stirring rapidly with the whisk. When blended and smooth, add salt to taste, pepper to taste, the remaining lemon juice, nutmeg, and Tabasco to taste. Stir in the mushrooms and eggplant. Stir in the egg. Spoon the mixture into a baking dish (we used an 8-by-1-inch pie plate). Sprinkle with a mixture of crumbs and cheese and dot with the remaining tablespoon of butter. Bake 30 to 40 minutes and then brown under the broiler.

Yield: 4 to 6 servings.

Curry Powder Is the Villain

We have been fascinated over the years by letters received after we have printed recipes for "curries" that do not contain curry powder. We have at hand what we consider the final word on the subject, and it appears in the work of a friend, Madhur Jaffrey. It is an explication found in the introduction to her book, *An Invitation to Indian Cooking* (Alfred A. Knopf, 1973, $7.95), perhaps the best Indian cookbook available in English.

"To me the word 'curry' is as degrading to India's great cuisine as the term 'chop suey' was to China's," she states. "But just as Americans have learned in the last few years to distinguish between the different sytles of Chinese cooking . . . I fervently hope they will soon do the same with Indian food instead of lumping it all under the dubious catch-all title of 'curry.' 'Curry' is just a vague, inaccurate word which the world has picked up from the British, who, in turn, got it mistakenly from us. It seems to mean different things to different people.

"Sometimes it is used synonymously with all Indian food. In America it can mean either Indian food or curry powder. To add to this confusion, Indians writing or speaking in English use the word themselves to distinguish dishes with a sauce, i.e., stewlike dishes. Of course, when Indians speak in their own languages, they never use the word at all, instead identifying each dish by its own name.

"If 'curry' is an oversimplified name for an ancient cuisine, then 'curry powder' attempts to oversimplify (and destroy) the cuisine itself. Curry powders are standard blends of several spices including cumin, coriander, fenugreek, red peppers, and turmeric—standard blends which Indians themselves never use. Here again I am sure the British are responsible for its creation. This is how I imagined it happened."

A British officer in full uniform (possibly a young David Niven) is standing under a palm tree looking fondly at his bungalow as Indian servants go back and forth carrying heavy trunks from the house into a waiting carriage. When the carriage is loaded, the servants line up on the veranda with tears in their eyes. The officer himself, overcome with emotion, turns to khansamah (cook):

OFFICER. How I shall miss your delicious cooking. My good man, why don't you mix me a box of those wonderful spices that you have been using. I will carry it back with me to Surrey, and there, whenever I feel nostalgic about India, I will take out this box and sprinkle some of your aromatic spice mixture into my bubbling pot.

KHANSAMAH. Yes, sa'ab, as you say, sa'ab. (*Runs off into kitchen.*)

Scene shifts to kitchen, where cook is seen hastily throwing spices into the box. He runs back with it to officer.

KHANSAMAH. Here is the box, sa'ab. Sa'ab, if your friends also like, for a sum of two rupees each, I can make more boxes for them as well. . . .

Several years later: Former cook is now successful exporter. He is seen filling boxes marked "Best curry powder." When boxes are filled, he puts them in a large crate and stamps it in black: "for export only."

Madhur Jaffrey, the wife of Sanford Allen, the violinist who is with the New York Philharmonic, would seem eminently qualified to write scripts about food. An established actress, who has recently returned from England where she appeared in a television script with James Mason to be shown in the fall on National Educational Television. It is an autobiography of an Indian princess and has to do with the end of royalty in India.

In an interview, she told us that she is currently engaged in writing a vegetarian cookbook, that she and her family (which includes three children ranging in age from 12 to 15 years) return to India each summer, and that the children in particular adore it.

"I'm related to half of Delhi," she said, "and for my children it is something like paradise. Here they're just ordinary people."

She added that Indian cooks did, indeed, combine spices according to their own taste. One blend is called garam masala (garam means hot and masala means spices). Rarely, if ever, would you find two cooks using the same conbination of flavors. She noted that despite the name, the mixtures contain a blend of what are known as "hot" and "cooling" spices.

"Hot tea," she said, "is considered cooling in India." It is one of those seemingly contradictory things, but empirically it is known to be true. "Similarly we know that cumin and coriander, for example are cooling spices, while cinnamon, cloves, and nutmeg are heating spices. By the way," she added, "we also know that asafoetida and ginger help indigestion."

Here is a recipe for an excellent lamb "barbecue" using a garam masala blend among other spices, plus a Bengalese cabbage dish. For what it's worth, Mrs. Allen cooks her lamb on a small electric portable "Open Hearth" made by Farberware. She offers a series of cooking classes at the James Beard Cooking School. For information you may telephone WA 4-6287.

Madhur Jaffrey, a cookbook writer, sets record straight on Indian cuisine.

Madhur Jaffrey's Grilled Boneless Leg of Lamb

1 8-to-9-pound leg of lamb, boned
2 medium-size onions
1 piece fresh ginger, about 3 inches long and 1 inch wide

5 to 7 cloves garlic, peeled and coarsely chopped
⅔ cup lemon juice
1 tablespoon ground coriander
1 teaspoon ground cumin
1 teaspoon garam masala (see recipe)
1 teaspoon ground turmeric
¼ teaspoon ground mace
¼ teaspoon ground nutmeg
¼ teaspoon ground cinnamon
¼ teaspoon ground cloves
1 cup olive oil
2½ teaspoons salt
¼ teaspoon freshly ground pepper
   Cayenne to taste, optional
   Coloring (see note)
12 radishes for garnish

1. Have the butcher "butterfly" the meat, or do it at home. Cut the meat, leaving it in one piece, so that it will lie flat on a grill.

2. Chop 1 onion and put it into the container of an electric blender. Add the ginger, garlic, and ¼ cup lemon juice. Blend to a smooth paste.

3. Pour the mixture into a stainless steel or enamel dish large enough to hold the meat. Add all the remaining ingredients except the lamb, the remaining onion, and radishes, and blend well.

4. Carefully cut off all fat and tissue from the lamb and use a sharp pointed knife to pierce the flesh at many spots on both sides. Add the meat to the dish and rub in the paste of herbs and spices. Cover and place in the refrigerator. Let stand 24 hours, turning it occasionally.

5. Grill the meat over charcoal, under the broiler, or on an electric grill. In India the meat is generally cooked until well done. Ideally, it should be quite dark on the outside and slightly pink within, with no juices flowing.

6. As the meat cooks, slice the remaining onion into very thin rounds and drop into ice water. Cover and refrigerate. Clean the radishes and make radish roses if desired. Drop into ice water and refrigerate.

7. When ready to serve, transfer the meat to a warm platter. Garnish with the drained onion slices and radishes.

Yield: 10 to 12 servings.

Note: Ideally, the coloring for this dish is an Indian food coloring in powdered form. Recently it was not available at shops contacted. A good substitute is about 12 drops of red food coloring, 15 drops of yellow food coloring, and 1 tablespoon of mild paprika added to the herb and spice mixture.

Garam masala

1   *tablespoon peeled cardamom seeds*
1   *2-inch stick cinnamon, crushed*
1   *teaspoon whole cloves*
1   *teaspoon whole black peppercorns*
⅓   *teaspoon grated nutmeg*
1   *teaspoon cumin seeds, optional*

1. Combine all the ingredients in a small coffee grinder

and blend thoroughly. The mixture may be kept for weeks if tightly sealed.

Yield: About 3 tablespoons.

Bengalese Cabbage with Mustard Seeds and Coconut

⅓   *cup (loosely packed) freshly grated coconut*
6   *tablespoons mustard oil (see note)*
1   *teaspoon whole black mustard seeds (see note)*
2   *bay leaves*
1   *medium-size cabbage (3 to 3½ pounds), cored and finely shredded*
¾   *teaspoon salt*
1   *hot green pepper, cut into fine, long strips resembling cabbage strips*

1. When buying a coconut, shake it and make sure it has liquid inside. This liquid is not needed in the recipe, but it insures a moist interior. Crack the coconut open with a hammer and pry away the meat by sliding a pointed knife between it and the hard shell. Cut off the brown skin of the meat and discard it. Wash the white meat and grate it finely.

2. Heat the oil in a wide, casserole-type pot over medium-high flame. When the oil is hot, add the mustard seeds and bay leaves. As soon as the bay leaves darken and the mustard seeds begin to pop (this takes just a few seconds), add the shredded cabbage.

3. Turn heat to medium. Stir and cook for about 5 minutes or until cabbage wilts. Add the salt and hot pepper strips. Stir and cook 3 to 5 minutes more. Turn off the heat.

4. Sprinkle with grated coconut, mix well and serve.

Yield: 4 to six servings.

Note: Mustard oil and black seeds are available at Indian food shops. Among them, in Manhattan, are Foods of India, 120 Lexington Avenue (at 28th Street); India Foods and Condiments, 811 Lexington Avenue (between 62d and 63d Streets); and Sahadi Importing Company, 187 Atlantic Avenue, Brooklyn.

It must seem that we're never bored with the discussion of Indian cookery. It's so, we never are. Some more favorites come up on pages 268–273.

Concerning chutney, which is so often served with Indian food, we got a request from a reader to print "the origin of Major Grey's chutney pickle and tell us who Major Grey was." We have done some casual research over the years and have not come any closer to the identity of the gentleman, if indeed he ever did exist, than when we first began our quest.

We asked one major producer of Major Grey's chutney for information, and an hour later they returned our call with a very dull script. Major Grey, we were informed, was a British army officer (what else?) stationed in India (but, of course), during the late 1800s (give or take a few years). He had a passion for curries (hear, hear!), and he liked to cook, so he concocted a chutney to go with his curry.

And he sold it to our script writer's firm, which did not have the good sense to go out and copyright the name. Since that time every cheating Tom, Dick, and Harry food producer within a thousand miles of Bombay has been stealing his firm's original recipe and calling their chutney Major Grey.

Before hanging up, our man told us that unfortunately in his research he had not unearthed the Major's first name.

I hasten to add a footnote to this. Chutney in India is not considered "a pickle," as Madhur Jaffrey points out in her estimable cookbook. Chutneys are relishes, although they are sometimes in India used as a sauce for hot and cold dishes. Some of them are also served in India as a vegetable.

Chutneys come in hundreds of varieties. They may be salty, sweet or sour, hot or cold, or a blend of several of these qualities. They are made with an endless list of ingredients including mangos, ginger, tamarind, bananas, fresh coriander leaves, mint, yogurt, onions, garlic, coconut, and raisins. Some are designed to be eaten immediately after they are made. Others can be put up like preserves and stored indefinitely.

We might point out that inasmuch as the name Major Grey is in the public domain and numerous firms produce a "Major Grey" chutney, they are more or less similar. The base is generally mango, with tamarind and raisin among other ingredients added.

June 1974

UNE IS A TIME we look forward to with particular pleasure for it is then that the fresh vegetable markets open in full splendor on Long Island where we live. It is also the season of fresh strawberries, perhaps the most versatile of foods to come out of a patch. One of the things we remember best about strawberries and the month of June is a bit of information we came upon a few years ago in the home of neighbors who had recently returned from Peru. They told us of a drink commonly served in that country. In Peru it is made with pisco, a very strong brandy, but vodka works admirably well. To make it for two, blend 1 pint of strawberries (this makes about a cup of juice). For each drink, put ½ cup of strawberry juice in a bar glass and add 1½ ounces of vodka, the juice of half an orange, 2 tablespoons of sugar, and 1 tablespoon of egg white. Add cracked ice and shake vigorously. Strain and serve. It is a drink so smooth, so soft and delicious going down, a word of caution is necessary. It is positively lethal and guests should be restricted to two.

The Geography of Chowder

WITH PIERRE FRANEY

Chowder sounds as American as Indian pudding, but the word actually is French in origin. It is derived from the French word chaudière, meaning cauldron. This was the vessel in which French immigrants cooked their fish stews when they settled in the coastal areas of America. The chowders here represent two of this nation's favorites—Manhattan clam chowder and Boston clam chowder.

Manhattan Clam Chowder

24   *chowder clams or razor clams*
4   *cups water*
¼   *cup bacon*
2   *cups carrots cut into fine dice*
1½   *cups celery cut into small cubes*
2   *cups chopped onions*
¾   *cup chopped green pepper*
1   *clove garlic, finely chopped*
1   *teaspoon thyme*
1   *bay leaf*
1   *cup fresh or canned tomatoes*
4   *cups potatoes cut into ½-inch or slightly smaller cubes*
     Salt and freshly ground pepper to taste

1. Wash the clams well. If razor clams are used, they may be placed in a basin of cold water to which about ½ cup of cornmeal is added. Let stand about 1 hour to disgorge excess sand. Drain well and rinse thoroughly. Drain again.

2. Place the clams in a kettle and add the water. Simmer until shells open.

3. Meanwhile, chop the bacon and add it to a kettle. Cook until bacon is rendered of its fat. Add the carrots, celery, onions, and green pepper. Cook about 5 minutes, stirring often.

4. Add the garlic, thyme, and bay leaf.

5. When the clams open, strain them but reserve both the clams and their liquid. Add 10 cups of liquid to the bacon mixture. (If there are not 10 cups, add enough water to make 10 cups.) Add the tomatoes. Cook 15 minutes.

6. Remove the clams from the shells and discard the shells. Chop the clams finely on a flat surface or put them through a meat grinder, using the small blade. Add them to the kettle and add the potatoes. Add salt and pepper to taste and cook about 1 hour.

Yield: 8 to 10 servings.

Boston Clam Chowder

24   *chowder clams or razor clams*
2   *cups water*
1½   *pounds potatoes*
3   *slices finely chopped bacon*
1   *cup chopped onions*
     Salt and freshly ground pepper to taste
3   *cups milk*
1   *cup heavy cream*

1. Rinse the clams well. If razor clams are used, they may be placed in a basin of cold water to which about ½ cup of cornmeal is added. Let stand about 1 hour to help disgorge excess sand. Drain well and rinse thoroughly. Drain.

2. Place the clams in a kettle and add the water. Cover closely and bring to the boil. Simmer until the clams open.

3. Drain the clams and reserve the liquid. There should be about 3½ cups. Remove the clams from the shells and discard the shells. Chop the clams finely on a flat surface or put them through a meat grinder using the small blade.

4. Peel the potatoes and cut them into ½-inch cubes or slightly smaller.

5. Put the bacon in a kettle and cook until it is rendered of fat. Do not brown. Add the onions and clam broth. Add the potatoes, chopped clams, salt and pepper to taste. Simmer 45 minutes. Add the milk and cream and salt and pepper to taste. Bring to the boil and serve piping hot.

Yield: 8 to 10 servings.

Strawberry Season

WITH PIERRE FRANEY

In the words of some poet, we are now knee-deep in June, and the sweetest of all June's bounties is the red-ripe strawberry. Out here on Long Island, the fields are awash with fat berries. Berries for eating out of hand or baking in fragrant tarts or churning into ice cream.

Strawberry Ice Cream

6 *egg yolks*
2 *cups plus 1 tablespoon sugar*
4 *cups milk*
1 *cup water*
2 *pints strawberries*
1 *cup heavy cream*

1. Place the yolks in a large saucepan and add 1 cup sugar. Beat with a wire whisk until light and lemon colored.

2. Meanwhile, bring the milk almost but not quite to the boil.

3. Gradually add the milk to the yolk mixture, beating constantly. Use a wooden spoon and stir constantly, this way and that, making certain that the spoon touches all over the bottom of the saucepan. If a thermometer is available, use it. Cook to 180 degrees and remove from the heat. If a thermometer is not available, cook the sauce until it becomes like a very thin custard. Immediately pour and scrape the sauce into a mixing bowl to prevent further cooking. Let cool.

4. Meanwhile, put the water in a saucepan and add 1 cup of sugar. Stir and bring to the boil. Simmer 10 minutes and remove from the heat. Let cool.

5. Put the strawberries into the container of a food processor or an electric blender and blend thoroughly. Combine the strawberries with the sugar syrup and the custard.

6. Whip the cream and before it is stiff beat in the remaining tablespoon of sugar. Fold the cream into the strawberry mixture. Pour the sauce into the container of an electric or hand-cranked ice cream freezer. Freeze according to the manufacturer's instructions.

Yield: 12 to 16 servings.

Strawberry Tart

Sweet pastry dough (see recipe, page 145)
Pastry cream (see recipe)
3 *pints firm, fresh, red, ripe strawberries hulled, rinsed, and drained*
1 *cup orange marmalade*
1 *tablespoon water*
⅓ *cup toasted almond slivers (see note)*

1. Preheat the oven to 375 degrees.

2. Roll out the dough on a cold surface. Line a 9- or 10-inch pie plate or, preferably, a flan ring, with the pastry. Prick the bottom. Line with wax paper. Add two layers of dried beans to the pastry to weigh the bottom down. Put in freezer for 30 minutes.

3. Bake 15 minutes. Remove beans in wax paper and reduce oven heat to 350 degrees. Bake 10 to 15 minutes longer or until center is dry and edges are lightly browned. Remove from the oven and let cool.

4. Spoon the pastry cream into the pie shell and smooth it over. Arrange the strawberries bottom side down, close together and symmetrically over the pastry cream.

5. Spoon the marmalade into a saucepan and add the water. Cook, stirring, until the marmalade is thinned. Put it through a strainer.

6. When the marmalade is cooled but still liquid brush the berries with it. Sprinkle the almonds over all. Cut into wedges to serve.

Yield: 8 to 10 servings.

Note: To toast the almond slivers put them in one layer in a heat-proof dish and bake at 350 degrees, stirring occasionally until nicely browned.

Pastry cream

3   *egg yolks*
½   *cup plus 1 teaspoon sugar*
½   *teaspoon pure vanilla extract*
½   *cup flour*
1   *cup milk*
¼   *cup heavy cream*

1. Put the yolks in a mixing bowl and add ½ cup of sugar and the vanilla. Beat until light and lemon colored with a wire whisk or portable mixer. Add the flour and beat it in thoroughly. Spoon and scrape the mixture into a saucepan.

2. Bring the milk to the boil and add it to the yolk mixture, beating vigorously with the whisk. Beat and cook over moderate heat until well thickened. Cook only briefly to prevent curdling. Remove from the heat and let cool.

3. Whip the cream until stiff, beating in the teaspoon of sugar.

4. Fold the cream into the pastry cream.

Yield: 1¾ cups.

We wish we had coined that old chestnut about strawberries (if you will forgive our metaphors) that belongs to Izaak Walton: "Doubtless God could have made a better berry, but doubtless God never did." Actually, the old angler was quoting a Dr. Boteler and acknowledges as much.

Lox: It's Not Smoked, It's Soaked

"You," David Sklar said, "are the 4,742d person to ask me that question."

We hastened to explain that after 20 years we still felt like newcomers to the New York scene, and if at this late date we still didn't know the difference between lox and "nova," it should be excused on the grounds of obviously arrested development.

Mr. Sklar is one of the owners of the Nova Scotia Food Products Corporation in Brooklyn. He is a man with gentle manners, an easy smile, and a patient air. He is considered by many to be perhaps the leading authority on smoked fish in this area.

"A long time ago," he began, "back in the early 1920s, universal refrigeration was a rarity. The only salmon shipped to New York back in those days came from Alaska in barrels, and salt was used as a preservative. It was very heavily salted, in fact, and to make it edible it was necessary to remove most of the salt. To do this the salmon had to be soaked for a long time in cold running water." That was the original lox.

"Back in those days," the gentleman continued, "we took it one step farther. We smoked the lox briefly." But mark it well, good reader, lox today is no longer smoked. It is simply soaked to the desired degree and sold over the counter. "We stopped smoking lox at approximately the end of World War II," Mr. Sklar noted. The name lox derives from the Scandinavian word for salmon, which is lax, and the German, which is Lachs.

And then he elaborated on Nova Scotia salmon, which is also spoken of as "nova" or simply "smoked salmon." "Smoked salmon has been a European tradition for many, many years, and in this country it is—relatively—a recent thing," Mr. Sklar pointed out. "There are still vast areas in America where it is largely unknown."

When the smoked salmon or Nova Scotia salmon industry had its origins in the United States, the salmon used for it was shipped from Nova Scotia. Eventually the market grew until it became necessary to seek other sources of supply. Now the name "nova" is applied to genuine smoked salmon (as opposed to lox) no matter where the fish itself is shipped from.

"Our smoked salmon arrives in a frozen state and we salt it ourselves," Mr. Sklar went on. "This salting or 'cure' takes about three to five days, but that is a rule of thumb. The amount of dry salt used and the time it takes depends on where the salmon came from. The fat content varies from source to source." Knowing the quantity of salt to use and the time of cure is, he indicated, where the expertise comes in.

There are great differences in the quality, flavor, and texture of salmon from source to source. It is generally agreed that the finest salmon is "Eastern" or "Atlantic" salmon from the East Coast. The salmon used to prepare lox comes only from Western waters. Smoked salmon or "nova" may come from Eastern or Western waters, and while the fish from the Western sources may be eminently edible, it is not in the same class with the Eastern variety. It is this differential, incidentally, that would account for the great variance in prices between a pound of "nova" at one outlet and another pound at another.

Mr. Sklar's firm, which produces smoked and marinated fish under the name of Novie, has his wares distributed throughout the country, but mostly in metropolitan areas.

One of the great outlets for smoked fish in Manhattan—and perhaps the finest in the city—is Murray's Sturgeon Shop at 2429 Broadway (between 89th and 90th Streets). It is to our minds a sort of paradigm of the city's smoked and marinated fish outlets on several counts.

The displays of herring—cream, schmaltz, matjes, and so on; salmon, including "nova" and lox; smoked whitefish, sable, and chubs—are marvelously appealing to the eye and the quality is beyond reproach.

Murray's, by the way, has some of the most modestly priced top quality caviar in the environs, $79 for a "pound" of malossol Beluga, private stock. Some people also claim that the shop's bagels are the best to be had both from the standpoint of flavor and size. The smoked fish platters are another of the store's delights and are priced according to the selection of foods. The average price is from about $30 to $40 a platter.

Murray's, named for the owner, Murray Bernstein, does not carry smoked salmon made from Western fish. Their lox is further processed in the shop to the taste of the owner. A pound of Nova Scotia salmon is priced at $12 a pound; lox costs $7.55 a pound.

We recently contrived a splendid sauce for smoked fish (whitefish, chubs, sable, and so on) made with horseradish, sour cream, and ground walnuts. It is to feast.

Horseradish Sauce with Walnuts

1 *cup sour cream*
¼ *cup heavy cream*
⅓ *cup grated horseradish,*
   preferably freshly grated
1 *4-ounce can walnuts*
1 *tablespoon sugar*
   Salt to taste

1. Combine the sour cream, heavy cream, and horseradish in a mixing bowl.

2. Blend the walnuts until fine but do not blend to a paste. Add them to the sauce along with the sugar and salt. Stir to blend well. Serve cold with smoked fish, cold or lukewarm poached fish, cold roast beef, boiled beef, and corned beef.

Yield: About 2 cups.

David Sklar takes a slab of lox— unsmoked, salted salmon—out of a barrel. The fish will be desalinated with cold running water and then sent to market.

To Accompany an Aperitif

WITH PIERRE FRANEY

Two marvelous appetizers were among the tasty results of a four-hour cooking session we spent with two of Italy's leading chefs, Marco Nesi and Mariano Vizzotto of La Pace hotel and restaurant in Montecatini. One is toast topped with chicken-liver paste; the other is thinly sliced raw beef served with a delectable sauce. Both are outlined below. In addition, we offer a shrimp appetizer. (Other recipes by these two talented chefs can be found on pages 48–52.)

Crostini dello Chef

¼ cup olive oil
¼ cup finely chopped onion
¼ cup coarsely chopped celery
¼ cup coarsely chopped carrot
¼ pound round of beef, cut into ½-inch cubes
¼ pound lean pork, cut into ½-inch cubes
    Salt and freshly ground pepper to taste
¼ cup dry white wine
¼ teaspoon nutmeg
½ pound chicken livers, cut into ½-inch cubes
3 tablespoons drained capers
3 flat anchovies, drained
2 teaspoons cognac
2 teaspoons dry sherry
2 tablespoons butter, at room temperature
½ cup hot beef broth, approximately 28 slices French bread, each about ½-inch thick (see note) Olive oil

1. Heat ¼ cup of oil in a saucepan and add the onion, celery, and carrot. Cook, stirring frequently, about 10 minutes until the onion is golden brown.

2. Add the beef, pork, salt and pepper and continue cooking about 15 minutes, stirring frequently.

3. Sprinkle with white wine and nutmeg and cook until wine is reduced, about 10 minutes, stirring frequently.

4. Add the chicken livers and cook, stirring occasionally, 15 minutes.

5. Add the capers and anchovies and cook about 10 minutes longer. Stir and add the cognac and sherry.

6. Remove the saucepan from the heat and add the butter. Stir over very low heat, gradually adding about ¼ cup of broth. Add salt and pepper to taste. Spoon the mixture into the container of a blender or food processor and blend until smooth.

7. Preheat the oven to 400 degrees.

8. Arrange the slices of bread on a baking sheet and sprinkle or brush each slice with a little olive oil. Bake until crusty, 10 to 15 minutes.

9. Brush each slice with a little of the remaining beef broth and spread each slice with the paste.

Yield: 8 to 12 servings.

Note: The number of slices depends on the size of the bread. The number indicated here is for a loaf about 2½ inches in diameter. If a large loaf is used, use half the number and cut each slice in half.

Shrimp with Mustard and Dill Sauce

2 *pounds shrimp in the shell*
1 *bay leaf*
12 *whole allspice*
6 *sprigs parsley*
1 *rib celery with leaves, quartered*
   Water to cover
   Salt to taste
10 *peppercorns, crushed*
1¼ *cups mustard and dill sauce (see recipe)*

1. Combine the shrimp, bay leaf, allspice, parsley, celery, water, salt, and peppercorns in a saucepan.

2. Bring to the boil and turn off the heat. Let the shrimp cool in the cooking liquid. Chill.

3. Shell and devein the shrimp and serve with the mustard and dill sauce.

Yield: 6 or more servings.

Mustard and dill sauce

1 *egg yolk*
1 *teaspoon wine vinegar*
3 *tablespoons prepared mustard, preferably Dijon or Düsseldorf*
   A few drops of Tabasco
   Salt and freshly ground pepper to taste
1 *cup oil, preferably a light olive oil, or a combination of olive oil and peanut, vegetable, or corn oil*
   Lemon juice, optional
¼ *cup finely chopped fresh dill*

1. Place the yolk in a mixing bowl and add the vinegar, 1 tablespoon mustard, Tabasco, salt and pepper to taste. Beat vigorously for a second or two with a wire whisk or electric beater.

2. Start adding the oil gradually, beating continuously with the whisk or electric beater. Continue beating and adding oil until all of it is used. Taste the mayonnaise and add more salt to taste and the lemon juice if desired. Beat in the remaining mustard and the dill. If all the mayonnaise is not to be used immediately, beat in a tablespoon of water. This will help stabilize the mayonnaise.

Yield: 1¼ cups.

Note: The mustard and dill sauce can be served with any kind of cold steamed shellfish or cold poached fish or hard-cooked eggs.

Carpaccio

1¼ *pounds raw lean beef, preferably top round*
½ *cup white vinegar*
12 *very small sour pickles, preferably imported French cornichons*
½ *cup finely chopped parsley*
2 *cloves garlic, finely minced*
3 *anchovy fillets*
½ *cup capers*
3 *tablespoons coarsely chopped onion*
⅓ *cup mustard, preferably imported mustard such as Dijon or Düsseldorf, or use domestic creole or spicy mustard (do not use ball-park mustard)*
¾ *cup olive oil*

1. Trim the meat carefully to remove all outside fat. Have the meat sliced as thinly as possible. If a good, sturdy electric slicer is not available, the meat may be partially frozen to facilitate slicing with a very sharp knife.

2. Arrange the meat neatly in one layer on one large or two medium-size serving dishes.

3. Put the remaining ingredients into the container of an electric blender or a food processor. Blend without overblending. The sauce should have a slight texture. Serve the sauce with the meat on the side to be dipped into it or spoon the sauce over the meat.

Yield: 6 servings.

Fine Dining in Paris

We first set foot in Paris 25 years ago this month. There were no quick-service restaurants, no pizza parlors, no high rise apartments blackening the landscape, and no whatcha-may-call-'em drugstores in any part of town. We lived in a 20-room hotel only a few blocks from where we now sit in a small and very good hotel, the Hotel de L'abbaye St-Germain on the Left Bank.

After dinner one recent evening we strolled down the Boulevard St-Germain for what must be the hundredth time of our lives. It was nearly midnight and the street was the same old marvelous carnival—young groups hastening nowhere or somewhere; couples blissfully linked arm in arm; solitary flaneurs; a few good-natured drunks lurching about; and every seat taken on the sidewalk terraces of the Café de Flore and Aux Deux Magots.

Over a coffee and cognac we could hear the static from those voices back home that tell us year after year that Paris will never be the same. Of course there is no more Les Halles, no more those male chauvinist comfort stations that so ignobly perfumed the city streets. But where restaurants are concerned, we doubt the food has ever been better or more conscientiously prepared. And at prices that can still be considered acceptable.

One of the places where we dined was the Au Quai d'Orsay, 49 Quai d'Orsay, and it was practically without fault. There was a surpassing beginning and now we sit wishing we could prettify the name of that dish for those who may be undone with the name unalloyed. It was stuffed duck neck.

We have dined on stuffed duck neck in years past, but this was special and inspired. The skin had been filled with a blend of chopped duck and pork, masterful seasonings, and pistachios. It was cooked in a well-flavored broth, served sliced and lukewarm with a creditable aspic and toast. It was laudable on all counts including taste and texture.

We also shared—a seductive dish of fresh pleurotes de peupliers, marvelous French mushrooms that grow wild under poplar trees. They were meaty and firm and served in a cream sauce.

We feel this way and that way about meat with fruit sauces or poultry and fruit dishes such as duck à l'orange. They can be overly sweet and detestable. One of the best dishes of the genre ever to come our way, however, was the Quai d'Orsay's veal chop à l'orange. It was far superior to most dishes made with duck, the veal admirably seared on both sides and served in a very dark, sweet and savory orange sauce.

The Quai d'Orsay menu has a host of bourgeois dishes (that is not a put down), and one of the best we sampled was the calf's head ravigote. It was commendably tasty, fork tender and excellent—equal to the best we recall from the old Les Halles' restaurants, where we dined on it frequently.

One disappointment of the evening was the restaurant's boiled beef made with plat de côte. It is one of the establishment's specialties, but we found it chewy and lukewarm and the portions unreasonably large.

The Quai d'Orsay, on the banks of the Seine, is a handsome restaurant with an old-fashioned elegance and bouquets of fresh flowers strategically placed throughout both dining rooms. The restaurant's tables are close together but somehow it did not seem a negative quality. With the meal, we drank two half-bottles of wine—one Muscadet, 1973; one Brouilly (Beaujolais), 1973.

The cost of the main courses at the restaurant is from about $3.70 to $6. Our meal cost about $15 per person with wines and service. The telephone number is 551 58-58. Reservations are essential. The restaurant is closed Saturday and Sunday.

Strange thing. In the United States we are uncomfortable and generally irritable in restaurants when tables are situated cloth to cloth. We more often than not attribute it to the greedy nature of the restaurateur. Yet here in Paris such proximity seems somehow cozy if not to say proper. And a moment after we are seated we are largely unaware of any discomfort or claustrophobic feelings. The tables at the Au Pactole, perhaps the most frequently discussed and generally praised restaurant in the city, has tables that touch or come within a centimeter of it. But the clientele is discreet and the food sufficiently transporting to obliterate anything negative.

One guidebook states that the Pactole's maître d'hôtel is malicious. He didn't know us from Adam's off ox and we found him kind, generous, and enthusiastic. The meal began with an outstanding platter of frogs' legs in a sorrel and cream sauce. Sorrel is in season now and another guest had an expertly made dish of salmon with sorrel. There were sweetbreads en tourte—the sweetbreads braised in a bordelaise sauce with olives and served with deep-fried egg.

One of the finest dishes, however, was the steamed calf's liver. It was of an uncommon tenderness and flavored and bordered on the sublime.

Negatively, as needs we must be at times, the sweetbreads had not been sufficiently weighted after cooking and—although their quality and the sauce in which they were bathed was superior—the flesh itself was "puffy." A minor point, for the Pactole deserves its high-flying reputation. It is a very small restaurant (17 tables) and stylish. Main courses are priced from about $4 to $10, with complete meals priced at $10. The Au Pactole is at 44 Boulevard St-Germain and the telephone is 326 92-28.

Unless we translated incorrectly, the waitress at La Falcatule near the Bastille told us that the name of the restaurant is old French for "a kind of tooth." Perhaps it has something to do with toothsome, for the chef has genius in several directions, including his cold mousses among the appetizers and a dish of duck liver with raisins that has rarely been equaled in our experience.

We dined on a mousse of duck in an orange aspic and a mousse of quail with raisins. A soaring beginning for a meal that proceeded into a fish course of crayfish tails en timbale then a cassolette of sweetbreads—these cooked to a notable turn—and the duck liver.

The crayfish tails were a marvel of tenderness and flavor—some whole, some converted into a coarse-textured and delectable mousse and all in a marvelously seasoned cream sauce.

We did in truth find the duck liver dish on the exalting side. We presume that the liver must have come from an especially fattened bird. It was of great size and inordinately tender, smothered in a distinguished and delicate unsweet sauce with raisins; sliced and served on a bed of finely sliced apples cooked in a gossamer, soufflé-like egg custard. We quickly add that this dish will not appeal to all comers. It rather floats in butter, but for those who can accommodate such a mass of richness it is a singularly gratifying experience. Another point: The dish should not be preceded by anything as rich as a game mousse but, preferably, by thinly sliced ham or a cold vegetable appetizer.

The meal ended with delicate crêpes soufflés au Grand Marnier—the crêpes baked with a soufflé mixture and a ring of baked meringue on top. One serving looks as though it would serve two but it is deceptive.

All dishes at La Falcatule are à la carte. Main courses are priced from about $3.60 to $7.60 (the cost of the duck liver). The restaurant is at 14 Charles V and tell the taxi driver it is near the Bastille. The telephone number is 277 98-97.

We know in depth the perils and pitfalls, pleasures and pratfalls of our unruly enthusiasms. We are acutely aware that the critique of a professional kitchen is a highly subjective exercise. But if Taillevent, 15 Rue Lammenais, isn't the greatest French restaurant in Paris, we will willingly give up Chinese restaurants forever. Rarely in a lifetime—including a quarter century of serious dining—have we found a restaurant with such a distinguished sum of virtues. There are three elementary planes on which any restaurant is judged: the kitchen, the service, the ambiance or physical appeal of the dining room. On each of these levels Taillevent soars.

Physically it has the aristocratic nature of an elegant and stylish hotel particulier, which indeed it was when built near the Etoile more than 100 years ago. The walls—from the entrance with its winding central staircase to the main dining room—are hung with carefully chosen art. The blue velvet banquettes admirably complement the natural wood walls of the main room. The kitchen is a diadem of excellence, and it can seriously be questioned if better cooking existed before, during, or after the age of Escoffier.

If ever the word "impeccable" could be applied to the table service of a restaurant the word is deserved at Taillevent. The waiters carve the roasts, bone the fish, or spoon up the purée of celery root with a dedication combined with appropriate dispatch that borders on the reverential.

In the last few months, we have dined three times at Taillevent and we have a catalogue of things to praise. Among the hors d'oeuvres, the silken smooth slab of fresh foie gras and delectable Roquefort cheese soufflé; among the soups, a splendid consommé germiny with a rich egg-thickened broth and fresh sorrel; among the fish dishes, a terrine of pike with a white wine and mushroom sauce and the fresh salmon in a court-bouillon.

Perhaps the most memorable dish was one sampled a day or so ago—a spectacularly good cervelas aux fruits de mer—a sausage-shaped affair in which a sauce made of fish and sea food is blended in a casing before being cooked in a court-bouillon. The "sausage" is sliced at table and served with a delicate beurre blanc made by whisking fresh butter into a reduced essence of shallots and dry white wine.

A salmis of squab with rare meat was an undisputed triumph. Kidneys in a light vinegar sauce was a testimonial to what is called "la nouvelle cuisine." We found a pear soufflé a bit too sweet and once we recall an artichoke vinaigrette that tasted too sour. Forgivable trivia. If you are ever at Taillevent and find on the menu a dish listed as fresh whole pear on a praline tart with pastry cream and candied orange shreds, don't miss it.

Taillevent's cellar is celebrated. On our most recent visit we drank what may be the most agreeable white wine we ever tasted—a white Nuits Saint Georges, 1973. It was liquid beauty and is available in the most limited quantities.

Taillevent is closed Sundays. Representative costs at the restaurant are the sea food cervelas for two, priced at $13, the squab and kidneys at $8. Reservations are imperative. The telephone number is 359 85-23.

Some time ago we wrote about the restaurant La Marée and observed that it might be the finest sea food restaurant in Paris. Another fine one is called Le Duc and is on the Left Bank near Montparnasse. The meal we recently dined on there began with an impressive high-piled platter of fresh and cooked sea food including large full-fleshed crabs, their plump bodies abundantly filled with delicious roe; fat, raw clams called clovis; steamed snails, periwinkles, raw mussels, oysters, and other delights of the sea.

Raw fish seems to be on the verge of becoming this year's rage in Paris. At Le Duc we dined on a distinctly different appetizer. A raw fish tartar made with chopped raw bass and scallops and some of the ingredients of steak tartar. Subsequently we sampled a thinly sliced raw salmon dish with nothing but olive oil and crushed fresh peppercorns. We also sampled a house specialty, deep-fried salted baby shrimp in the shell; excellent hot abalone strips quickly sautéed in olive oil with garlic; and clams in a sauce a bit too thick with flour and too strongly flavored with garlic. We also had an uncommonly good fish dish, loup de mer steamed on a bed of seaweed.

Le Duc, whose owners are said to be Corsican, is a simply decorated, unpretentious fish restaurant. The cost of the main courses is about $4 to $10. The restaurant is closed Sunday and Monday. It is at 243 Boulevard Raspail and the telephone number is 326 59-59.

When we first explored the great restaurants of Paris and France we willingly played Pantagruel morning, noon, and night, sampling any dish that issued forth from oven or saucepan. We seldom passed a pastry shop between meals without spending a few centimes for a barquette here, a sorbet there. Perhaps it is the ravages of age but more and more we've discovered in Paris the joys of alternating la grande cuisine or bourgeois cooking of France with the joys of other cultures. We will not argue the merits of international cooking in Paris as opposed to other cities, but we do find foreign tables here endowed with special virtues. Not the least of these are the restaurants in the Maison du Danemark at 142 Avenue des Champs Elysées, an establishment with a particularly uninventive if not to say uninviting facade. We have passed it many times in years past without a thought of entering, but at a recent dinner at Chez Paul Bocuse in Lyons we were told that the restaurants now have a new manager and new chef and that they are introducing what may be the finest herring and salmon dishes this side of Scandinavia.

We stopped for a brief but enormously agreeable lunch at the Restaurant Copenhagen on the Maison's second floor and the sampling of herrings and salmon with a glass or two of aquavit and Danish beer provided an admirable shifting of taste buds, so to speak. We tasted a new creation, thin slices of the most delicately seasoned, mildly salted salmon ever to come our way. It was served cold with potatoes in a hot cream and dill sauce that was absolute velvet.

The menu offers numerous main courses including stuffed crêpes, crayfish à la nage, roast pigeon, and so on, and it might be predicted with some confidence that they are prepared with high merit. The restaurant's chef worked for a long time in the kitchen of Roger Verge, celebrated as one of 12 or 13 of France's greatest toques blanches and chef-owner of the Moulin de Mougins near Cannes.

The ground-floor restaurant at the Maison du Danemark is known as the Flora Danica Grill. It has both grill and outside garden and the menus are comparable with à la carte main courses from about $4 for Danish meatballs with cabbage to $8 for reindeer fillets with juniper sauce. The telephone number is 359 20-41.

We have a long-standing passion for couscous, that staple, tender cereal of North Africa and we've never eaten better couscous than in Paris. And that would include Morocco and Algeria. Two admirable Paris sources for the dish include Abel at 15, Rue St. Vincent de Paul (878 41-88) and Le Petit Chevreau at 22 Rue de la Huchette (033 18-13). We recommend them in that order.

Abel is larger, more colorful and among the appetizers the merguez—spiced North African sausages—have more character than at the Chevreau. Abel also has fantastic first courses that include a cold brains and egg dish in tomato sauce and a wildly good brik Tunisienne—deep-fried pastries flavored with thyme and with a whole egg in the center.

Le Petit Chevreau is a very small, very good restaurant with 11 tables almost co-joined. It is neat as a whistle. The couscous in both establishments is comparable, both served with a rich broth and vegetables and hot condiment sauces on the side. They both offer either chicken, lamb or combination platters and the main courses at Abel are priced from about $1.40 to $1.80; at the Petit Chevreau from about $2.50 to $2.75.

As far as food in concerned, Le Petit Chevreau is in one of the most interesting quartiers of Paris. If you go there, wander about the streets after 11 in the evening for an international bazaar of colorful sights and smells. There are scores of oriental restaurants with skewered dishes, Greek tavernas, outdoor stands where Brittany pancakes are made on turntables, and so on.

Although the Vietnamese kitchen employs many of the same ingredients as that of the Chinese, there are many differences where nuance of flavor are concerned. In some ways the Vietnamese table is more delicate, in others it seems more primitive. That is, of course, the observation of an outsider.

We are much taken with the Vietnamese foods we have been privileged to sample and there are two restaurants in Paris that seem of special interest. One is La P'tite Tonkinoise, 56 Rue Faubourg-Poissonière (770 29-35), the other Luu Dinh, 6 Rue Thouin (326 91-01). Both are of modest décor, although the former is, relatively speaking, far more elegant and refined and a trifle larger.

We remember with the greatest pleasure dining at La P'tite Tonkinoise. We ate crab farci or stuffed crab and rouleaux impériales—deep-fried egg (or spring) rolls wrapped in fresh lettuce and made with fresh mint sprigs. They are dipped in a blend of pepper sauce and nuoc mam, a salty, fermented fish sauce. The main courses there include pigeonneau lacqué, or dark brown squab flavored with star anise and cinnamon, and hot, grilled, skewered chicken on a bed of cold noodles.

We enjoyed our visit to Luu Dinh but found the food far less sophisticated. We ordered the potage de Hanoi or "Pho" soup, the rouleaux du printemps (similar to the rouleaux impériales, but with the cooked filling wrapped in lettuce), and a cold thin pastry resembling strudel leaves. A chicken with ginger dish and another made with shrimps and green peppers were palatable.

The cost of main dishes at La P'tite Tonkinoise is from about $2 to $4; at the Luu Dinh from about $1.40 to $1.80. Complete meals at the latter are priced from about $2.60 to $8.

Until we took the train from Paris to Lyons a few months ago, we had forgotten that dining on a train in France can be pleasure enough to be an end in itself. On the Paris-Lyons express we found ourselves speeding along at 100 and more kilometers per hour in immaculate, bright, and airy surroundings that were, to quote ourselves, an invitation to the senses. The table was done up in dazzling napery, the silver was polished and the menu light-years removed from anything we had ever encountered. It included a first course of soupe des pecheurs (fish soup) or quenelles de brochet Dieppoise (poached forcemeat of fish with a white wine and seafood sauce). We chose the soup and found it uncommonly good, although a trifle salty.

We noted that had we been served the same soup on an American train, we would have become positively gluttonous and sent our compliments to the chef. Instead the waiter offered us the quenelles, which were excellent. We proceeded then to roast guinea hen (there had been a choice of the guinea hen or beef and lamb kidney en brochette), admirably cooked, and a fantastic Brazilian bombe with candy coffee beans and whipped cream.

On this present trip we found an occasion to take Le Mistral, which travels to the south of France. We boarded it in Paris at 1:40 P.M., a decent hour to begin a meal for a four-hour ride to Lyons. It is possible on the TEE, or Trans-European-Express, to reserve a seat in the dining car from which you need not move during the course of the trip. After a meal the dinner accouterments are simply removed and you are left to dawdle over coffee and cognac or whatever other amusements you may have at hand.

The setting was comfortably familiar. The same comparable starched white linen, polished silver, and crystal. And a menu to appeal to the senses. To one American it was impressive in its imagination. As a first course there was a choice of sweetbreads Dijonnaise in a puff pastry shell or snails en brochette. As a main course there was a choice of stuffed chicken or braised beef with a red wine sauce. There was salad, cheese, and a choice of sherbet or fresh strawberries in red wine.

The meal which we shared began auspiciously with the sweetbread course. Cubes of the braised delicacy were in a light, well-seasoned sauce along with sliced mushrooms and pieces of well-cooked salt pork. The snails were large and tender and served with a smooth, professionally made velouté of chicken.

The chicken was very well roasted and served with a flavorful pâtélike ground pork filling. The steak—coeur du Charolais—was rare, but we had the assurance of one of our dinner companions that while it was quite tender and edible, the flavor, even with a Burgundy wine sauce, was on the bland side. The salad was simple, the cheese well varied and at the proper stage of ripeness. The strawberries were a bit overripe, but the sherbet, made with cassis, the dark currant cordial of Dijon, was brought nearer perfection with spoonfuls of sweetened raspberries.

Negative notes: The coffee was as weak as you would find on American trains . . . and a half bottle of Beaujolais tasted just a bit of the cork, although a second was in sound and admirable condition.

Our first-class ticket from Paris to Lyons cost about $23. The cost of the reserved seat in the dining car cost about $5. The cost of the meal was about $7.60. Half bottles of white Burgundy cost about $2; red Beaujolais, $2.60. In France we applied for our tickets at the French Government Tourist office. They may also be purchased at train stations, and it is best to reserve in advance.

Summer Soups

WITH PIERRE FRANEY

Cold soups were a rarity in this country until the late Louis Diat came up with vichysoisse in the kitchen of the Ritz-Carlton Hotel about three decades ago. Today, cold soups of all persuasions help make sultry summers palatable. Three extraordinarily good ones are offered below.

Gazpacho with Corn and Zucchini

2   to 4 ears corn on the cob
2   pounds fresh, red, ripe
     tomatoes
1   onion, preferably a red
     onion, coarsely chopped
2   cloves garlic, finely minced
2   cups peeled, coarsely
     chopped cucumber
1½   cups tomato juice
     Salt and freshly ground
     pepper to taste
¼   cup olive oil
¼   cup red wine vinegar
½   small zucchini, peeled
1   cup finely diced cucumber
3   tablespoons finely minced
     fresh basil or 1 teaspoon
     dried

1. Drop the shucked corn into boiling water to cover. Cover and when the water returns to the boil, remove it immediately from the heat. Let stand 5 minutes, no longer. Drain. Let the corn cool. Cut off the kernels. There should be about 1 cup.

2. Drop the tomatoes into boiling water to cover. Let stand 12 seconds and drain immediately. Pull the peel from the tomatoes, using a paring knife. Cut away and discard the core. Coarsely chop the tomatoes. There should be about 4 cups.

3. Put the tomatoes into the container of an electric blender. It may be necessary to do this in two or three steps. Add the onion, garlic, the coarsely chopped cucumber, and tomato juice. Blend thoroughly in one or two steps, depending on the blender. Add salt and pepper to taste.

4. Pour the mixture into a bowl and add the olive oil and vinegar.

5. Cut the zucchini into fine dice and add it. Add the corn. Add the diced cucumber and basil. Add more salt and pepper to taste. Chill thoroughly.

Yield: 6 to 8 servings.

Cucumber, Tomato, and Avocado Soup

4   tablespoons butter
1   cup chopped onion
4   tablespoons flour
4   cups peeled, cubed
     tomatoes, preferably fresh
     although canned may be
     used
4   cups peeled, cubed
     cucumbers
     Salt and freshly ground
     pepper to taste
4   cups chicken broth
1   ripe, unblemished avocado
1   cup heavy cream

1. Melt the butter in a deep saucepan or kettle and add the onion. Cook, stirring, until wilted and sprinkle with flour. Add the tomatoes, stirring rapidly with a whisk. Add the cucumbers, salt and pepper to taste. When blended, stir in the broth.

2. Simmer 25 minutes. Pour the mixture, a few ladlesful at a time, into the container of an electric blender. Blend well. Strain the soup into a bowl if it is to be

served cold and chill. If it is to be served hot, return it to the stove and heat thoroughly.

3. Peel the avocado and remove the pulp. Chop the flesh finely and add it to the soup, stirring rapidly with a whisk. Stir in the cream. Serve very cold or piping hot.

Yield: 8 servings.

Cream of Carrot Soup

1 pound (8 to 10) carrots
1 pound (3 to 5) potatoes
2 tablespoons butter
½ cup coarsely chopped onion
6 cups rich chicken broth
2 sprigs fresh thyme or ½ teaspoon dried
1 bay leaf
1 cup heavy cream
⅛ teaspoon Tabasco, or more to taste
½ teaspoon worcestershire sauce
½ teaspoon sugar
Salt and freshly ground pepper to taste
1 cup cold milk

1. Trim off the ends of the carrots. Peel the carrots and potatoes with a swivel-bladed vegetable scraper. Cut the carrots into rounds. Cube the potatoes. Set aside.

2. Heat the butter in a kettle and add the onion. Cook briefly, stirring. Add the carrots, potatoes and broth and bring to the boil. Add the thyme and bay leaf. Bring to the boil and simmer 30 to 40 minutes until the carrots and potatoes are tender.

3. Put the mixture through a food mill and let it cool. Put it into the container of an electric blender and blend. This may have to be done in two stages. If the soup is to be served hot, bring it to the boil and add the remaining ingredients. When the soup returns to the boil, serve it piping hot. If it is to be served cold, add remaining ingredients to blended mixture, stir well and pour into a bowl and chill thoroughly. Serve very cold.

Yield: 6 to 8 servings.

Meringue
WITH PIERRE FRANEY

The most sophisticated meringues are those that are spread thin and baked in a slow oven until fragile and crisp, easily shattered with a fork. We have recently fallen heir to two marvelous recipes—a Torta Cavour and a spirited pie in a meringue shell. The first is from an Italian pastry chef and the other from a first-rate cook and friend, Joe Famularo.

Torta Cavour

The meringue

8   *egg whites (about 1 cup)*
½   *teaspoon cream of tartar*
¼   *teaspoon vanilla*
    A pinch of salt
2   *cups superfine sugar*

The filling and assembly

4   *cups chilled heavy cream*
1   *cup plus 2 tablespoons granulated sugar*
½   *cup toasted chopped almonds*
6   *tablespoons coarsely grated, dark sweet chocolate*

1. Preheat oven to 200 degrees or lowest setting.

2. Put the whites into the bowl of an electric mixer and beat until frothy. Add the cream of tartar and continue beating until the eggs are half stiff. Add the vanilla and salt. Gradually add ½ cup of the sugar and continue beating until the whites stand in stiff peaks when the beater is lifted.

Continue beating on high speed while gradually adding the remaining sugar. Continue beating until the whites become quite glossy and very, *very* thick.

3. Line two baking sheets with parchment paper or butter them and sprinkle them lightly with flour. Shake off the excess flour. Trace two 10-inch circles in the flour. To do this, place a 10-inch round utensil such as a pie plate on one of the baking sheets and run a small knife around the rim of the dish to trace its outline on the surface of the buttered and floured or lined baking sheets.

4. Fit a pastry bag with a No. 4 star tube.

5. Fill the pastry bag with the meringue and pipe the meringue into each of the outlined circles. To do this, place the tube on the perimeter of one of the outlined circles and start piping out meringue. Continue piping in ever decreasing circles to the center of the pattern. Fill both circles similarly. Pipe out the remaining meringue at random on the prepared baking sheets in any desired form—stars, ladyfinger shapes, or whatever. The shape is unimportant since these meringues will be chopped for garnish.

6. Place the baking sheets in the oven. The most important thing in making meringue is the baking temperature. It must be very, very low but still hot enough for baking. If the lowest temperature in your oven seems quite warm, leave the oven door slightly ajar. Let the meringues stay in the oven until they are totally crisp and firm. In our oven the baking time is about 2 hours, but the time will vary depending on the heat of the oven. If it is very low, the time might be 3 hours and so on. A perfect meringue is solidly crisp and snow white. If it browns slightly, do not be discouraged. In any event, allow plenty of time for the meringues to dry in the oven.

7. When the meringues are done, remove them from the oven and let stand until thoroughly cooled.

8. When ready to finish the torta, whip the cream, gradually beating in the 1 cup plus 2 tablespoons sugar.

9. Take up one of the meringue circles and spread it lavishly with about a third of the whipped cream. Smooth it over with a metal spatula. Sprinkle with 3 tablespoons each of almonds and chocolate. Cover with remaining meringue circle. Spoon another thick layer of whipped cream on top, leaving enough to coat the sides. Smooth over the top and coat the sides with remaining whipped cream, smoothing it around with a spatula.

10. Chop the random pieces of meringue remaining on the baking sheets. Coat the sides of the torta with chopped meringue.

11. Garnish the top of the torta with the remaining chopped almonds and grated chocolate. Carefully transfer the torta to a round serving dish and place in the freezer for several hours. It should be frozen. Serve cut into wedges.

Yield: 10 to 16 servings.

Mirabelle Meringue Pie

The meringue pie shell

4 *egg whites*
¼ *teaspoon cream of tartar*
⅛ *teaspoon vanilla*
   A pinch of salt
1 *cup superfine sugar*
   Vegetable oil for greasing a dish

The filling

4 *egg yolks*
½ *cup granulated sugar*
1 *tablespoon fresh lemon juice*
   Salt to taste
3 *tablespoons mirabelle or other liqueur such as kirsch or pruneau or Grand Marnier*
1 *cup heavy cream Confectioners' sugar, optional*

1. Preheat oven to 200 degrees or lowest setting.

2. Put the whites into the

bowl of an electric mixer and beat until frothy. Add the cream of tartar and continue beating until they are half stiff. Add the vanilla and salt. Gradually add ¼ cup of sugar and continue beating until the whites stand in stiff peaks when the beater is lifted. Continue beating on high speed, while gradually adding the remaining sugar. Continue beating until whites are very glossy and very, *very* thick.

3. Oil lightly a 9-inch Pyrex pie dish. Spoon part of the meringue into the dish and, using a rubber spatula, smooth the meringue out to the sides, making a layer over the bottom and sides about ¼ inch thick. The object is to create a pie shell with the meringue. Spoon the remaining meringue around the edge of the pie plate, building it up high, more or less evenly, and shaping it with the spatula all around the edge. It will have a rough look but that is proper.

4. Place the dish in the oven. The most important thing in making meringue is the baking temperature. It must be very, very low but still hot enough for baking. If the lowest temperature in your oven seems quite warm, leave the oven door slightly ajar. Let the meringue stay in the oven until it is totally crisp and firm. In our oven the baking time is about 2 hours, but the time will vary depending on the heat of the oven.

If it is very low, the time might be 3 hours and so on. A perfect meringue is solidly crisp and snow white. If it browns slightly, do not be discouraged. In any event, allow plenty of time for the meringue to dry in the oven.

5. When the meringue is done, remove it from the oven and let stand until thoroughly cooled.

6. Place the yolks in the top of a double boiler or improvise what is known as a bain marie. That is to say, place a saucepan inside a heat-proof dish such as a skillet and add water to the skillet, about an inch or so around the saucepan.

7. Add the sugar to the yolks and, using a wire whisk, beat the yolks over simmering or boiling water until they are quite thick. The moment they are thickened, however, remove the saucepan from the water or the yolks may curdle. Continue beating until the mixture starts to cool or it will continue to cook from retained heat.

8. Stir in the lemon juice, salt, and liqueur. Let cool to room temperature.

9. Whip the cream and fold it into the yolk mixture. Pour the filling into the shell and chill in the refrigerator at least 3 hours before serving. If desired, sprinkle the filling with confectioners' sugar before serving.

Yield: 6 to 10 servings.

July 1974

BACK A FEW months we had met the owner of a fantastic hotel restaurant called La Pace in Montecatini Terme, Italy, and it was in July that we paid him a visit. It was not so much the lure of an elegant hostelry that drew us to Montecatini. We had learned in the course of our conversation with Mr. Gino Innocenti that Montecatini is celebrated as the place to "take the cure." We had never "taken a cure," and we found the notion so appealing that we willingly submitted ourselves to a drastic cut in our food intake and went on the wagon for a week. (It came back to us, early on, that abstinence is something we recommend only for the very very young and the very very old.) We survived and wrote the account that appears a few pages onward.

We might add as a post script (a bit of information not in the original article) that on the last day of full temperance we sped to a great little bistro in Florence about 30 miles away and dined on an incredible spread of pasta, followed by veal, followed by salad and Gorgonzola, one of the greatest cheeses on earth. We downed this with an excellent bottle of Soave followed by Valpolicella, and ended the meal with an Italian ice and, as a digestif, very black coffee and a touch of anisette. We never felt better in our lives.

Fine Dining in Amsterdam

One of the European continent's most agreeable dining rooms and certainly one of Holland's finest kitchens is that of the Excelsior Restaurant in the Hotel de l'Europe. The surroundings are glittering and resplendent in the *ancien régime* tradition: the table service is smooth, precise, and classic, and the chef quite purposefully knows what he's about.

The kitchen excels, among other things, in fish preparations. The sole meunière, crisp on the outside, melting yet firm in the flesh, is a delight. The Scotch salmon steak, baked with butter and herbs en papillote—which is to say, in this day and age, in aluminum foil—and served with a golden-rich and hot hollandaise, is simple but splendid. The veal chop Esterhazy (the Count Esterhazy lent his Hungarian name to many paprika-seasoned dishes in French cooking) was of first caliber. Holland, we have noticed, seems to enjoy with Italy a corner on veal of exceptional whiteness and tenderness. The veal chop at the Excelsior was a paragon in those qualities and smothered in a piquant yet smooth mushroom and paprika sauce further flavored with strips of green pepper.

We mention an appetizer last because it is one of those dishes with tremendous national appeal that might be greeted with less than enthusiasm by an uninitiated American. These are the fresh herrings, widely available in June and shortly thereafter. The residents of Amsterdam, in their enthusiasm, swallow them whole—boned of course—on the first two days of the season. They are mildly salted and served with chopped onion, toast, and butter.

There was a time, a dozen or so years ago, when we labeled the Lutèce Restaurant in New York conspicuously expensive for charging $7 or $8 for a main course. Today throughout the world that would seem a bargain-basement price in any luxury establishment. The Excelsior Restaurant menu is all à la carte with the main courses priced from about $7 to $10.

The Hotel de l'Europe is at 2 Nieuwe Doelenstraat, and the telephone number is 23-48-36. It is open every day.

Some restaurants amuse us in the same way that we can be enchanted by wicked children, provided they're intelligent and sophisticated enough to know what the traffic will bear. That is the way we feel about the straight-faced but clownish Black Sheep ('t Swarte Schaep) Restaurant here. It doesn't play it for laughs, but it is subject to them unless you take it seriously. It may be the only restaurant where wines are stored over the head of the customers and the maître d'hôtel has to stand on the banquette to reach them.

The Black Sheep's menu is rather extensive, most of the dishes being French and along the lines of snails in the traditional Burgundian manner, sole amandine, duck à l'orange, pepper steak, and pêche Melba. Get the picture? On the other hand, the food seems conscientiously prepared and presented—haltingly at times—with a suitable flourish.

There are three fixed-price menus somewhat coyly dubbed as table du prince ($18), table du roi ($22), and table de l'empereur ($26). The menus vary in length, of course, greedy by nature (it would also give us the chance to sample a larger number of dishes), we chose the emperor's table. Not bad.

At first course, a generous two-ounce serving of fresh, large-grained caviar; an ample portion of turtle soup (darkened with burnt caramel and out of a can) with sherry wine; admirable fillet of sole Véronique (made with fresh grapes which is a tonic); tender, laudable veal sautéed and interred, unfortunately, beneath a curry sauce containing the equivalent of a fruit salad—pineapple, ginger, peaches, grapes, plus slivered almonds. What a waste of a notable veal chop. In any event, the meal ended with an acceptable crêpe dish with flaming, freshly poached cherries.

The Black Sheep has a comfortable, shabby-elegant decor—leaded glass windows, clear and stained-glass panes; rough-hewn wood beams, and so on. Our notes remind us that the toast for the caviar was moldy. There are only 12 tables at the Black Sheep and reservations are recommended. Main courses cost from about $7.50 to $12. It is at 29 Korte Leidesedwarstraat. The telephone number is 22-30-21.

There are times when one knows intuitively that a restaurant is better than it was in the course of a single visit. Besides which, we have a built-in mean streak that makes us order a single dish destined to be inferior to everything else on the menu. In any event, that visit to De Boerderij (The Farm, to you) began auspiciously with a crab meat cocktail in its traditional European sauce. That is to say, a sauce made with a fresh mayonnaise, just enough catchup to give it coloring, and cognac for flavoring. Europeans never, or hardly ever, drench a seafood with the usual American catchup-and-horseradish blend.

It was followed by a soup that is something of a trademark in Amsterdam. Lady Curzon's turtle consommé seems omnipresent in the first-rate restaurants of the city and properly made, it is a tour de force among soups. It consists of turtle soup (canned again) flavored with curry, enriched with egg yolk, and spirited with cognac and/or sherry. A joy.

Then the main course arrived, the complete disaster. We had a choice of specialties. Fillet of sole, veal chop with mushrooms, sweetbreads "grand duc," all sorts of good-sounding things. And we chose the veal knuckle farm-style. It was insanity and we knew it. In the first place, it would have to be cooked in advance; it is the kind of main course that chefs have small conscience about reheating. We know how culinary cards can be stacked, and the dish was miserable. So were we. At the end of the meal the chef came out and seemed genuinely contrite (although he wore a soiled apron and we prefer our contrition in a clean apron).

In any event, we do recommend De Boerderij. There is a cunning, chic-provincial decor and engaging service by fresh-faced and ambitious young waiters in black tie. Don't fail to sample Lady Curzon's contrivance. Forget the veal knuckle.

The prices, we hasten to add, are about average for a first-class Amsterdam restaurant. A la carte dishes from about $7 to $9.50. The restaurant is at 69 Korte Leidsedwarsstraat. Closed Sunday. The telephone number is 23-69-29.

We have now sampled the best rijsttafel we have ever found in Amsterdam, and we will outline it in detail with the prefatory thought that the number and kinds of dishes served at most rijsttafels in Amsterdam follow a similar pattern. Qualitatively they are something else again.

Rijsttafel literally means rice table. In local practice it consists of 16 to 24 foods, each served in separate dishes at private tables and ranging from meat on skewers to salted peanuts. Some of the dishes, such as toasted grated coconut and zesty cucumber pickles, are served cold. Some, by previous intent or not, are served lukewarm. About half the dishes are served on plates that are—theoretically, at least—kept piping hot on rechauds or candle warmers.

When the meal begins, each guest—and the meal is served to one or presumably any number—is furnished with a hot soup bowl. Rice is offered, and it is the focal point of the meal. The rice and other foods are added to the soup bowl, and one object of the exercise is to avoid making a mishmash of the various foods and flavors. There are side dishes of two or three enraged red pepper sauces to be added at will, according to palate and conscience.

The object of our affection where Amsterdam rijsttafel is concerned is a highly accessible two-room restaurant called the Sama Sebo at P. C. Hooftstraat 27. It is of neat design, colorful without quaintness, and has an enthusiastic staff. The tables are laid with cloths of native design and the walls and sills are furnished with Indonesian fabrics, carvings of gods and goddesses, and jewelry.

The rijsttafel there consisted, among several other things, of a thin, good soup with cauliflower "flowerettes" and bits of cabbage and carrot; a pork stew with a soy sauce base; a cubed beef stew in a rather sweet, dark, spicy sauce; braised chicken; a compelling dish of deep-fried sweet potato sticks; deep-fried whitebait (not listed among the menu's dishes); an intriguing and delicious combination of cucumbers, apple slices, and orange sections in a sweet sauce; sour pickles; a delicious and hitherto unknown dish of deep-fried soy beans which resembled and tasted like a shredded meat dish. And, of course, the inevitable krupuk or crisp, deep-fried shrimp bread served at room temperature.

Our favorite Indonesian dish in our bout of the rijsttafel is the satay or pork in peanut sauce. It is very, very good at the Sama Sebo. The meal over-all was a tantalizing experience. We stopped eating with a certain effort, and in all modesty that is high praise.

We were wounded to feel that after all the years of hearing about the celebrated Bali Restaurant, we found it dreary. On expressing our disappointment to friends the next day, they recommended the Indonesia, perhaps the second most famous Indonesian restaurant in town. It was, if you used a taste micrometer, preferable, but they're both very much in the same bag. Both are physically tremendous establishments, with high ceilings and a plethora of chandeliers. Both are like food factories, the chefs either too long removed from their homeland to recall what made their native dishes exciting or they've catered too long to tourist taste. The seasonings in their dishes are one-dimensional, conventional, and bland in a European way. In their desire to appeal to the masses, they have become debilitatingly second rate.

The cost of a complete rijsttafel in almost any of these restaurants is from about $4 to $12 (at the Sama Sebo it is $8). The menus almost always list complete meals such as nasi goreng (about six dishes) or bami goreng, and they cost in the vicinity of $4. Beer is the best drink with rijsttafel.

The Indonesia is located at 550 Singel, telephone 23-20-35; the Bali at 89-97 Leidsestraat, telephone 22-78-78. The telephone number of the Sama Sebo is 72-81-46.

We had twice been told that the finest Chinese restaurant in Europe could be found in Amsterdam. The name of the gem is the Fong Lie, 80 P. C. Hoofstraat, only a stone's throw from the Rijksmuseum. On the basis of a final meal in Amsterdam, we are willing to join in the general huzzahs. If it is not equal to our personal favorite, the Tong Yen, 1 bis rue Jean Mermoz in Paris, it is certainly a justifiable challenger.

The Fong Lie is a small, dignified restaurant as neat as new chopsticks. There is a simple decor with a minimum of what we take to be genuine Chinese objets d'art and a rear wall mural of swans in flight.

The food, Cantonese with a few Indonesian dishes scattered here and there, may be a trifle Westernized but it is wonderfully subtle. The wonton soup has pure, rich chicken broth as a base, and the dumplings have a fine meat filling enclosed in fragile wonton skins. The stewed prawns with vegetables are fresh and tender and served with something new to our purview—shrimp with shrimp roe. The pork with bean sprouts had a deliberate, desirable burnt flavor achieved by turning the heat up under the wok just as most of the food had been ladled out. The chicken with almonds was lofty.

All dishes are à la carte with main courses from about $2.50 to $3.75. The telephone number is 71-64-04. The restaurant is closed on Monday.

As far as we can determine there is only one restaurant in Amsterdam whose menu is dedicated solely to fish. It is the Oesterbar at 10 Leidseplein and it shares another distinction. For reasons we still can't fathom it must be the most popular restaurant in town. We have been told that there are four turnovers both noon and night, and there's many a restaurant throughout the world that would wish to boast half that number.

The Leidseplein is one of the liveliest squares in town. The Oesterbar actually consists of two dining rooms—one at floor level with tables and a counter; another upstairs with more elaborate and "formal" furnishings.

The best dishes, it seems to us, are those that require the least elaborate preparation—quick sautéed fish or seafood or poached fish. One order of sole meunière was downright burned, although the flesh of the fish was good. We had a fine crayfish soup with bits of rice and a decent platter of quickly cooked shrimp on toast. One involved dish, halibut in mustard sauce, was both overcooked and the sauce had curdled.

The kitchen is simply too ambitious and staffed no doubt by an overzealous chef. The foods are piled lamentably high on a plate. All main courses are à la carte and are priced from about $4 to $8. There are cocktails and wines, but don't expect to dawdle over your meal. The telephone number is 23-29-88.

Broodjes—small sandwiches on small buns with numberless fillings—are to Holland what the hamburger is to America or fish and chips to England. At their best they make a fine light snack. The fillings may and almost always do include such basics as sliced ham or cheese, but they may go on to the likes of tartar steak, raw herring (currently in season and dear to every Dutchman's palate), smoked herring (beautiful), small bay shrimp, smoked eel, and so on.

We have tried two broodjes shops, the Broodje van Kootje (which we believe to be a chain) at Leidseplein and the Dobbe in Rembrandt Square. The cost of a single broodje is from about 40 cents to $1.20.

If you have access to a private car, you might spend a highly agree-able summer evening dining on the terrace of the Kasteel "De Hooge Vuursche" in the town of Baarn about half an hour's drive outside Amsterdam. The castle gardens are, particularly by day and at dusk, a special delight, and the food is generally excellent. We remember with great pleasure scallops in a cream sauce with tiny shrimp served in a scallop shell with a border of potatoes. And a kind of coarse quenelle with a combination of chopped seafood (dartois de fruits de mer) in a white wine sauce. We dined on an excellent dish of veal Orloff, the veal in individual medallions rather than the whole saddle. It was preferable to a steak dish, tournedos Lucullus, with sautéed chicken livers and mushrooms.

Main courses cost from about $6 to $12. The castle maintains all the old appurtenances and its address in Baarn is 14 Hilversumsestraatweg. The telephone number is 54-25-41.

An Intimate Little Clambake

WITH PIERRE FRANEY

Blessed are those who live by the sea for theirs is the kingdom of shellfish and seaweed, the two principal ingredients of an old-fashioned clambake. Clambakes out here in East Hampton come in two sizes: the large traditional back-breaking affair with pits to dig and rocks to fire and sand to sweep, and the more recently evolved wash-boiler clambake for smaller gatherings. The latter, of course, may lack the color of the original, but we can state emphatically that the results are more or less equal. And there is one vast and important difference. The marvelous, old-fashioned clambake demands 600 pounds of seaweed. With the wash-boiler type you can settle for a child's portion—24 pounds. Bonackers—the natives who were born on the eastern tip of Long Island (and specifically in the vicinity of Accabonac)—have their own method for testing the doneness of a wash-boiler clambake. They put a raw potato in the center of the top layer of seaweed. When the potato is tender without being mushy, it is time to feast. The clambake described here is one recently staged by Ed Gorman, a Baltimore-born part-time Bonacker.

Wash-Boiler Clambake

24 pounds wet seaweed or enough to fill the wash boiler
2 3½- to 4-pound chickens, quartered
Peanut, vegetable, or corn oil
2 teaspoons paprika
Salt and freshly ground pepper to taste
24 or more cherrystone or littleneck clams
17 potatoes, preferably red-skinned, "new" potatoes, about 2½ pounds

3 or 4 quahog or chowder clams (for flavor only)
8 1¼-pound lobsters or 4 5-pound lobsters
16 ears fresh corn, unshucked
½ pound butter, melted
4 lemons, cut into wedges
Tabasco, optional
Worcestershire sauce, optional

1. Gather the seaweed and have it ready.

2. Make a large wood fire in a grill, improvised if need be, on which the wash boiler will sit.

3. Make a charcoal fire for grilling the chicken pieces.

4. Select a wash boiler or other kettle with an 18-gallon capacity.

5. Place the chicken in a large dish and add enough oil to coat the pieces. Sprinkle with paprika, salt and pepper and rub well.

6. Grill the chicken pieces quickly first on one side, then the other until they are golden brown but not cooked. Tie 2 pieces of chicken in each of 4 cheesecloth bags.

7. Make individual cheesecloth packages of cherrystone or littleneck clams, about 3 or more per serving.

8. Add about a sixth of the seaweed to the bottom of the wash boiler. Add the chicken in cheesecloth.

9. Cover with the same amount of seaweed and add all but one of the potatoes.

10. Add more seaweed and the packaged clams. Add the quahogs.

11. Add more seaweed and the lobsters.

12. Add more seaweed and the corn. Add a final layer of seaweed and place the reserved potato directly in the center. Cover closely with a lid. Weight the lid down with heavy stones. Cook over a good fire for about 1¼ to 1½ hours or until the potato on top is tender without being mushy.

13. Serve all the foods simultaneously with melted butter, lemon wedges, and the optional sauces. Cold beer, but of course. Plus ice cream or watermelon.

Yield: 8 servings.

A layer of seaweed . . . then the lobsters . . . then more seaweed. Ed Gorman presides over a backyard, wash-boiler clambake on Long Island.

The Cure in Italy

When we were very young (and very, very poor), we used to read the novels of authors such as Henry James and Edith Wharton, and it seemed to us that their characters were forever rushing off to Europe "to drink the waters" and "take the cure," and it sounded rousingly sophisticated, worldly, and romantic. We decided that spas were places for important people who were eternally engaged either in hopeless love affairs, international intrigue, or contemplating suicide. Thus, when we were invited to Montecatini Terme, Italy's best-known spa, we found the invitation irresistible on several counts. Although we had recently been assured that our livers were models of resilience, we thought this visit might provide the occasion to give them a respite of seven days without alcohol. After all, we reflected, not a day had passed in 20 years that it had not been dosed with a goodly supply. In the second place, by following a diet of our own devising, we would set as our goal the loss of a pound of flesh a day for each day of our stay. Our medicine man in Manhattan had in no sense been averse to that idea, either.

We planned to stay at La Pace in Montecatini Terme, and we had had a foretaste of the glories of that kitchen some months previous. Last winter two of the chefs had prepared a monumental meal, devastatingly good and devastatingly caloric in our home (see page 46). They had promised at the time that if we came to La Pace, they could be equally adept at low-calorie feasts.

We arrived at the hotel an hour before dinner so we changed clothes and went downstairs to discuss our plight with our universal friend, the bartender. Tomorrow, we told him, we're quartering the calories and giving up both wine and booze for seven days running. He was marvelously sympathetic. "Have a drink," he said.

We awakened the next morning with a hangover and the thought that after all those years of wistfully speaking of spas and watering places, we really hadn't a clue as to what the "cure" implied. We soon found out.

On arrival the hotel's general manager, a distinguished native, had told us he would have an English-speaking doctor come to the room early the next morning to prescribe a regime. We were to eat nothing before his arrival. Dr. Sirio Stefanelli, a well-tailored, smiling fair-skinned man in his late 40s, arrived and withdrew a neat, 16-page form from his attaché case. He felt the pulse, prodded the liver, listened to the heart and sampled the blood pressure. He wrote out a "prescription," to begin immediately. No breakfast before the waters.

There are several stabilimenti where the waters are taken in Montecatini, all of them open to the public for a $2 fee. We were assigned to the stabilimento Tettuccio, a multiform, theatrically designed place, which although built in the early 1900s, resembles a Roman forum.

It is estimated that more than 10,000 visitors of international origin visit the thermal sources each day and/or take the massages and mud baths which are also available. The hordes mill about the travertine marble columns and more than once the principal thermal sources, the Tettuccio establishment, has been compared to Rome's Circus Maximus without the horses.

There are six basic waters which are prescribed for whatever reasons you happen to be in Montecatini Terme; the four principal ones being Torretta, Regina, Tettuccio, and Tamerici. All of the waters have a not-unpleasant saltiness, tasting rather like something you'd gargle with on other occasions.

The principal thermal source at Montecatini Terme is at Tettuccio, which resembles a Roman forum.

On the first morning each guest is furnished by the hotel with a personal glass, graduated with cubic centimeter markings and with the maximum volume of 250 cubic centimeters or approximately one cup. We were instructed to drink four cups of water, to be taken at intervals, each morning. As we set out, cup in hand on the first day, the hotel manager said in passing, "Hurry back when you drink the last glass." It was, we learned, no idle farewell salute.

Much of Montecatini Terme (as opposed to Montecatini Alto, a charming old medieval city on top of the mountain and 10 minutes distant by funicular) was built at the turn of the century, and it revels in an admirable Victorian setting with Art Nouveau in abundance. Typical are the gilded and enameled spigots from which the medicinal waters flow into numerous marble basins, cold from the left, hot from the right.

Each morning we began with one and one-half cups of warm toretta water to be drunk in five minutes, followed by a five-minute pause. Then one and one half cups of warm regina water taken in 15 minutes, followed by a 10-minute pause. Finally a single glass of lukewarm Tettuccio water to be drunk in 10 minutes. The precise benefits of those various waters are still unknown to us.

The waters are drunk to the tune of a seven- or eight-piece ensemble playing music—mostly waltzes with a few light opera arias thrown in—in an adjoining bandstand. As we sipped our final glass of water en route back to the hotel we mused on how many visitors to the spa could have written an essay titled "A Funny Thing Happened on the Way *from* the Forum."

The prescription booklet that Dr. Stefanelli provided contains a page on diet, plus an extract from one Pietro Grocco, a clinical physician and health director at Montecatini Spa at the turn of the century. "The inefficiency of the cure," the good doctor wrote, "is often due to a wrong diet. Be, therefore, moderate at the table and watch out for excess in food and drinking even though the waters may increase your appetite."

By high noon we were engulfed by tempests of hunger and thirst. We were also having wild misgivings about such a precipitate leap into the world of moderation. Or deprivation as it seemed to us then. Strange aberrations started to set in. We remembered an editor who got a bad case of gout each time he went on the wagon. What, we tempted ourselves, if we had an attack of gout? We remembered a friend of ours, a bit on the chubby side, who swore that when she went on a diet she still gained weight just thinking about food. Somehow we felt heavier.

You decide to shake the fantasies and take a walk. And who do you see? Nobody taking the cure. Only the local types who seem to be rushing at you, gluttonizing on pizzas, pastries, and ice cream cones. You remember a line of poetry by Emily Dickinson: "Those little anodynes that deaden suffering." What did she have in mind? One extra dry martini, perhaps, straight up with a twist of lemon. Instead you settle for those Stygian-black and delicious cups of espresso coffee so certain to murder the following night's sleep.

We had learned on arrival at the hotel that there is no diet specifically formulated for the guests. The food in the dining rooms is first rate, however, and much of it easily assembled into a low-calorie pattern. The foods recommended in our prescription folder were spelled out as follows: nonfat and only lightly salted appetizers; vegetable soups; white meat either boiled, roasted, or grilled; non-oily fish, steamed or grilled; boiled or mashed vegetables; ripe and fresh or cooked fruits; fresh cheeses. Beverages included lightly charged mineral waters, coffee, and tea.

For seven days we rather steadfastly adhered to that diet, eating in limited quantities and avoiding fat foods, starchy foods—such as pasta, potatoes, and bread—and, of course alcohol. We eschewed all desserts except fruits.

The chief irony of our stay came about on the second day. It was a time when we were seeing temptation in every turn—nuts, olives, peanuts, potato chips, and pickles. We decided to take in a movie. The feature of the day was "La Grande Bouffe," the classic study in overindulgence and gluttony. After the movie (the third time we had seen it) we returned home and picked up Piers Paul Reid's *Alive*, the study of cannibalism in the Andes.

During a seven-day period we lost six pounds.

If anyone plans to suffer the agonies of a "cure" including complete abstinence from alcohol and a severely limited intake of food, there could scarcely be a pleasanter setting and accommodations than La Pace in Montecatini. It is one of Europe's most civilized hotels and at one time or another the residence of royalty from all over the world including King George V and Kings Vittorio Emanuele and Umberto I of Italy. Toscanini, Leoncavallo, and Giordano stayed there, as well as Verdi who stayed three months each year. Cole Porter, Spencer Tracy, Katharine Hepburn, Clark Gable, and Truman Capote have all signed the register.

It is a marvelously comfortable place with built-in comforts most modern hostelries couldn't afford, including great oversized linen sheets and pillows, fine art, and antique mirrors. There is a mammoth swimming pool. Although La Pace is situated in a spa, there are many guests who come each year for the pleasure of the hotel and the town itself, which is situated equidistant, about 45 minutes by car, from Florence and Pisa.

The menu is French and the kitchen excellent. The hotel has 170 rooms and 22 suites. The cost, with three meals a day included, is $35 for a single room; $65 a day for a suite with single occupancy, $110 a day for a suite with double occupancy.

Making Puff Pastry

One of the ironies of the world of food in America is the paucity of training facilities for young women who wish to become professional chefs. The finest facility that exists of which we have certain knowledge is the Culinary Institute of America in Hyde Park, New York. It boasts a host of chefs, many of them European born, who are teaching international cookery to young aspirants in the domain of institutional and haute cuisine.

One of the most distinguished members of the staff is Albert Kumin, an indefatigable and enormously talented chef pâtissier, a native of Wil, Switzerland. After several years in European hotels he came to this hemisphere and worked in Bermuda and Canada and later as pastry chef for the Four Seasons in New York.

In this column over the years, a rare, almost wholly unexplored area of cooking has been the art of making puff pastry—the basis for vol-au-vents or patty shells, Napoleons, and so on. Albert Kumin recently came to our kitchen in East Hampton to demonstrate his technique in the field.

It should be added that puff pastry is conceivably the most difficult of all pastries to make. If the technique for making it can be mastered, it is also one of the most gratifying.

Puff Pastry

5   *cups flour plus additional*
    as necessary
1½ *pounds sweet butter*
⅓   *teaspoon salt*
1½ *cups water*

1. Place the flour and butter in the freezer and let stand until very, very, cold.

2. Spoon ¾ cup of flour onto a flat, cold surface, preferably marble. Make a well in the center and add 1¼ pounds of butter. Using a pastry cutter or knife,

Wrap the square. Step 2.

chop the butter until it is coarse-fine. Knead it, incorporating the flour a little at a time. Knead the mixture well and shape it into a square measuring about 4½ by 2 inches. Wrap the square in a length of wax paper and place in the refrigerator to chill, 10 minutes or longer.

3. Clean the work surface and add remaining flour. Make a well in the center and add salt and the remaining ¼ pound of butter. Cut the butter into coarse-fine pieces. Pour 1 cup of cold water into the well. Add flour if neces-

out with the heel of the hand as you work. Have ready additional flour (other than the 5 cups) for flouring the board as you knead to keep the dough from sticking. The additional flour added in this step should be about 6 tablespoons.

4. Gather the dough into a ball and place it on a lightly floured board. Flatten it slightly. Using a knife or pastry cutter, make slashes about ½ inch deep in the top of the dough to make a cross.

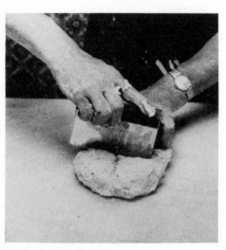

Make slashes. Step 4.

Pour water into well. Step 3.

sary to keep the water from overflowing. Start working the three elements together, gradually incorporating the flour and adding more water as necessary. The total amount of water used in preparing this recipe recently was 1 cup plus 6 tablespoons. Knead the mixture well, scraping the work surface as necessary with a spatula or pastry scraper. Push the dough

5. Using the fingers, open up the four edges of the dough formed by the slashes. Roll out the four edges, clover-leaf fashion as shown. The center of the "clover-leaf" should be slightly padded and large enough to hold the square of dough that is being chilled. The four "clovers" should be large enough to completely envelop the square of dough when it is added. Always sprinkle the dough with as little flour as necessary to prevent sticking.

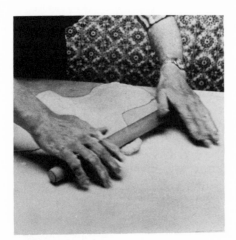

Roll out edges. Step 5.

6. Add the square of chilled dough and fold one "clover" over it, stretching the edges down and almost under the dough. Fold over another "clover," stretching the edges down and almost under the dough. Fold over the third and finally the fourth "clover." When the fourth "clover" is folded over, stretch the edges under the dough without tearing. Press the dough with the fingers to make a 10-inch square.

7. Roll out the dough into a 10-by-15-inch rectangle. Line a jelly roll pan with wax paper and place the rectangle of dough on it. Cover with a slightly damp cloth and refrigerate 20 minutes or longer.

Place dough in pan. Step 7.

8. Lightly flour a flat surface. Remove the damp cloth and tip the puff pastry out onto the surface.

Add square of dough. Step 6.

Tip pastry out of pan. Step 8.

9. Roll out the pastry. Sprinkle both the work surface and the dough lightly with flour as necessary to prevent sticking. Roll the dough into a rectangle measuring about 16 by 30 inches (about ¼ inch thick).

Roll out dough. Step 9.

10. Fold the dough into thirds. Fold the right (or left) side over and brush the flour from the surface of the dough.

Fold and brush. Step 10.

11. Neatly fold over the left (or right) side of the dough, brush off the surface and make a slight indentation with one finger to indicate the first folding step is concluded. Repeat the step lining a jelly roll pan with wax paper, covering the dough with a damp cloth, and chilling 20 minutes.

Finger indentation. Step 11.

12. Repeat steps 7 through 11. When the dough has been rolled out and properly folded, make two indentations in the center of the dough. Refrigerate at least 20 minutes and preferably overnight. (Note: In this step the dough may be made even flakier if it is rolled into a rectangle measuring about 15 by 29 inches. The dough may then be folded into quarters instead of thirds by folding both ends toward the center and folding both halves over each.)

13. Repeat the rolling and folding through a total of five procedures (and five finger indentations). The dough is now ready to be used for any desired purpose.

Yield: About 3½ pounds of puff pastry. One portion at a time can be used and the remainder frozen.

Vol-au-Vents
(Patty shells)

Puff pastry (see recipe)
1 *whole egg, beaten*

1. Prepare the puff pastry. There is sufficient pastry for 20 3-inch patty shells. Divide it in half to prepare 10. The remaining pastry may be closely wrapped in foil or plastic wrap and frozen.

2. To prepare patty shells for 10, roll out half the puff pastry into a rectangle measuring about 13 by 17 inches. With the fingers flick a little water over a cooky sheet.

3. Use a 3-inch biscuit cutter and cut out circles of puff pastry. Arrange half the circles uniformly over the cooky sheet. All scraps of leftover dough may be pressed together and used for dishes like Napoleon layers and palmiers.

4. Brush the tops of each circle with a little beaten egg.

5. Using a 1-inch biscuit cutter, cut out the centers of the remaining 10 rounds of pastry. Arrange these neatly placed on top of the rounds on the baking sheet.

6. Brush the tops of the circles with a little beaten egg. Refrigerate for several hours.

7. Preheat the oven to 425 degrees.

8. Bake shells 30 to 40 minutes. In the course of baking, note carefully that the shells do not tend to become lopsided. If they seem to go in that direction, cover lightly with a piece of cardboard.

9. When cooked, use a small paring knife and carefully lift out and reserve the centers of each patty shell. Serve the shells filled with creamed dishes such as chicken, shrimp, ham, or sweet-

Cut out circles. Step 3.

Completed shells.

breads. Or with an extravagantly good toulousaine filling (see recipe). Garnish each serving with the reserved small center removed from the baked patty shell.

Yield: 10 to 12 patty shells.

Vol-au-Vents Toulousaine

(Patty shells with creamed filling)

10 *to 12 patty shells (see recipe)*

The chicken quenelles

1 *pound skinless, boneless, raw breast of chicken*
1 *egg yolk*
1 *cup heavy cream*
   Salt and freshly ground pepper to taste
⅛ *teaspoon grated nutmeg*
   Boiling water

The sweetbreads, mushrooms, and chicken

2 *pair sweetbreads, about 1½ pounds*
1 *tablespoon butter*
3 *tablespoons finely chopped shallots*
½ *pound mushrooms, preferably button mushrooms*
   Salt and freshly ground pepper to taste
½ *cup dry white wine*
½ *cup rich chicken broth*
¾ *pound skinless, boneless, raw breast of chicken*

The sauce

   Chicken broth
3 *tablespoons butter*
3 *tablespoons flour*
2½ *cups heavy cream*
   Juice of ½ lemon
¼ *cup madeira or marsala*
¼ *teaspoon grated nutmeg*
2 *egg yolks*
   Pinch of cayenne

The garnish

10 *to 12 slices black truffles, optional*

1. Prepare the patty shells and have them ready.

2. To make the quenelles, cut the chicken into cubes and add half of it to the container of an electric blender or a food processor. Add the egg yolk, half the cream, salt and pepper, and nutmeg. Blend, stirring down as necessary. Spoon the mixture out and add the remaining chicken and cream. Blend thoroughly. Combine the two mixtures and stir to blend. If a good processor is used, this can be done in one step.

3. Use 2 teaspoons or small tablespoons and have a bowl of hot water standing by. Hold one spoon in the left hand and spoon out some of the mixture. Dip the other spoon into the water and turn the spoon over and inside the other spoon. This should shape the mixture like a miniature football. That is a quenelle. Spoon it onto a baking dish. Continue making quenelles until all the mixture is used. Cover the quenelles with a sheet of wax paper cut to fit the inside of the baking dish more or less precisely. Sprinkle the top of the paper with salt. Pour boiling water over the paper so that it flows off the paper and over the quenelles until they are covered.

4. Bring the water to boil and turn off the heat. The quenelles will cook from retained heat. Let stand.

5. Place sweetbreads in a bowl and add cold water to cover and salt to taste. Change the water occasionally. Bring to the boil and simmer about 5 minutes. Drain and chill quickly in cold running water. Drain.

6. Put the sweetbreads on a plate and cover with a cake rack. Add weights (glass jars filled with rocks, metal mallets, and so on). Let stand at least 1 hour.

7. Trim the sweetbreads well, removing and discarding connecting tissues. Cut the sweetbreads into bite-size cubes. Heat 1 tablespoon of butter and add the shallots. Cook, stirring, and add the sweetbreads. If the mushrooms are very small, leave them whole. If not, slice them. Add them to the sweetbreads. Sprinkle with salt and pepper.

8. Add the dry white wine. Cover and cook about 20 minutes. Add the ½ cup broth. Place the chicken breast on top and cover. Cook about 20 minutes.

9. Pour off the cooking liquid into a measuring cup. If necessary, add enough chicken broth to make 2 cups.

10. Melt the butter in a saucepan and add the flour, stirring

with a wire whisk. Add the cooking liquid, stirring rapidly with the whisk. Cook, stirring occasionally, about 20 minutes. Add 2 cups cream and continue cooking, stirring frequently, about 5 minutes. Add the lemon juice, madeira, and nutmeg.

11. Beat the yolks with a whisk and beat in the remaining cream. Season with cayenne. Add this to the sauce, stirring rapidly. Bring just to the boil and remove from the heat.

12. Remove the chicken breast and cut into bite-size pieces. Add the chicken breasts and drained quenelles to the sweetbread mixture. Strain the sauce over all and bring to the boil.

13. When ready to serve, heat the patty shells in a moderate oven without cooking. Place them on individual plates, spoon some of the filling into the center, some around the patty shells. Garnish each serving with a truffle slice and the reserved small round center that was removed from the baked patty shell.

Yield: 10 to 12 servings.

Napoleons

1½ *pounds puff pastry (see note)*
1¾ *cups pastry cream (see recipe, page 164 or use any standard recipe)*

1. Preheat the oven to 375 degrees.

2. Roll out the puff pastry into

a ¼-inch-thick rectangle. It may measure about 18 by 25 inches. Prick it liberally with a fork. Arrange it on a large baking sheet and brush with beaten egg. Let rest in the refrigerator for 1 hour.

3. Bake the pastry sheet for 30 minutes or until puffed and golden brown. Let cool.

4. Cut the pastry lengthwise into strips about 5 inches wide. Spread one strip with pastry cream. Cover with another strip, more pastry cream, and so on. Chop any scraps of baked pastry. Spread the top and sides of the Napoleon with whipped cream and garnish the top and sides with chopped pastry. Sprinkle with confectioners' sugar and serve.

Note: Scraps may be combined and rolled out for this.

Yield: 20 or more depending on size.

Almost any creamed dish—creamed chicken, creamed mushrooms, creamed sweetbreads, and so on—makes an excellent filling for vol-au-vents. For a fine first course, serve steamed asparagus covered with a hollandaise sauce in patty shells.

Three Ways with Veal Scaloppine for Two

WITH PIERRE FRANEY

Two's company—and never more so than when the cook plans to serve veal scaloppine. For unless this delectable cut of meat is to be braised, scaloppine is difficult to cook properly in large quantities (although expert chefs may disagree). The reason is that it should be cooked as quickly as possible on both sides. Otherwise, it will dry out and toughen. (It may be just as well that veal demands a certain intimacy, for the price of really good veal scaloppine ranges from about $4.50 to $7.50—and sometimes even higher.) Here are three ways to prepare veal scaloppine for two.

Veal Piccata with Lemon

½   pound veal scaloppine,
      cut into ¼-inch thick slices
      Flour for dredging
      Salt and freshly ground
      pepper to taste
2   tablespoons butter
2   tablespoons olive oil
2   tablespoons dry white wine
2   tablespoons lemon juice
2   slices thinly sliced lemon
2   teaspoons finely chopped
      parsley

1. Unless the scaloppine are very small, cut them into pieces measuring about 3 inches by 3 inches or slightly larger. Place them between sheets of wax paper and pound lightly to flatten, using the bottom of a heavy skillet or a flat mallet.

2. Blend the flour with salt and pepper. Dip the meat into the flour to coat lightly.

3. Using a large heavy skillet, heat the butter and oil and when it is very hot but not brown, add the meat in one layer. Cook over relatively high heat until golden brown on one side. Turn and cook until golden brown on the other. The cooking time should be from about 4 to 6 minutes.

4. Carefully pour off the fat from the skillet, holding the meat back with a spoon or lid.

5. Return the skillet to the heat and add the wine. Cook briefly until it starts evaporating, stirring to dissolve any brown particles in the skillet. Add the lemon juice and turn the meat in the thin sauce thus created. Transfer the meat to two plates and garnish each with a lemon slice and parsley.

Breaded Veal Milan-Style

½   pound veal scaloppine
      Flour for dredging
      Salt and freshly ground
      pepper to taste
1   egg
1   teaspoon water
2   tablespoons plus ½
      teaspoon peanut,
      vegetable, or olive oil
¼   teaspoon nutmeg
¾   cup fresh bread crumbs
¼   cup grated Parmesan
      cheese
2   tablespoons butter
2   to 4 lemon slices

1. Unless the scaloppine are very small, cut them into pieces measuring about 3 inches by 3 inches or slightly larger. Place them between sheets of wax paper and pound lightly to flatten, using the bottom of a heavy skillet or a flat mallet.

2. Season the flour with salt and pepper.

3. Beat the egg with the water, the ½ teaspoon of oil, and nutmeg.

4. Blend the bread crumbs with Parmesan.

5. Dip the scaloppine on both sides first in flour, then in egg, and finally in the bread crumb mixture. As the scaloppine are breaded place them on a flat surface and tap lightly to help the bread crumbs adhere.

6. Heat the butter and remaining oil in a heavy skillet and add the scaloppine. Cook until golden brown on one side, 2 to 4 minutes. Cook until golden brown on the other side. Serve hot with sliced lemon as a garnish.

Veal Scaloppine with Marsala

½ pound veal scaloppine, cut into ¼-inch thick slices
Flour for dredging
Salt and freshly ground pepper to taste
2 tablespoons butter
2 tablespoons olive oil
¼ cup marsala

1. Unless the scaloppine are very small, cut them into pieces measuring about 3 inches by 3 inches or larger. Place them between sheets of wax paper and pound lightly to flatten, using the bottom of a heavy skillet or a flat mallet.

2. Blend the flour with salt and pepper. Dip the meat into flour to coat lightly.

3. Using a large, heavy skillet, heat the butter and oil and when it is very hot but not brown, add the meat in one layer. Cook over relatively high heat until golden brown on one side. Turn and cook until golden brown on the other. The cooking time should be from about 4 to 6 minutes.

4. Transfer the meat to two plates and keep warm. To the skillet add the wine and stir to dissolve the particles in the pan. Reduce wine slightly and pour equal amounts over each serving.

August 1974

THERE FREQUENTLY comes a time in writing about food when editorial decisions must be made as to whether a dish should relate specifically to the season. Generally speaking, our feeling is that good food is good food, regardless of the season. Nonetheless we wouldn't write of shad roe in mid-December or fruitcakes in mid-July. We mention this here because among the pages that follow you will find an article for curing pastrami and corned beef that ran in August, one of the hottest months of the year. As far as our taste is concerned, pastrami and corned beef are dishes that know no season. We could hunger for them in the middle of a blizzard or in the middle of a desert, and a store-bought version isn't made that can compare with these meats cured in the home.

Mexican Cookery

A forthcoming volume on tortillas, tacos, enchiladas, and related esculents may be the only cookbook in the world ever spawned by a jogging accident. It will be the work of Diana Kennedy, who must set the best Mexican table in all of Manhattan.

"It happened in the spring," she related recently. "My plans were made to travel the provinces of Mexico for a few weeks. I do nothing but relax. Then one morning I went to Riverside Park for a morning jog when foolishly, clumsily, I fractured not one but both of my heels. Suddenly I found myself not in Zihuatanejo, but confined to my bed with my feet in the air.

"So I gathered together all my Mexican cookbooks and started to read. The more I thought about tortillas the more I thought of their infinite uses. They can be used like pasta in casseroles; like shovels for food; they are used to thicken soups; as edible plates—tostadas for example; as fillers; and so on. They can be used fresh, stale, or dried to a crisp; whole, broken up, or ground. It came to me that no one has ever done the complete tortilla cookbook, so I was launched on a new project."

We had the pleasure some time ago to write the foreword to Mrs. Kennedy's first book, *The Cuisines of Mexico* (Harper & Row, 1972, $12.50), in which we stated that we first met her on the Calle Puebla in Mexico City when she was married to the late Paul Kennedy, a newspaper correspondent who covered Central America, Mexico, and the Caribbean. We noted then that she was a friend of the late Agustin Aragon y Leiva, considered to be the greatest Mexican gastronome and authority of his country's cuisine, and spent many hours in research in his library.

She may have, we noted, the finest collection of Mexican cookbooks north of the border, including many antique volumes. Among the latter is her "bible," *Nuevo Cocinero Mejicano: Diccionario de Cocina*, published, oddly enough, in Paris, in 1878.

For her book, titled *The Tortilla Book* (Harper & Row, 1975, $10.00), she has garnered a mass of information about tortilla cookery, including quotations. For example, in *The Discovery and Conquest of Mexico* by Bernal Diaz del Castillo, it is stated that ". . . while Moctezuma was at table eating, as I have described, there were waiting on him two other graceful women to bring him tortillas, kneaded with eggs and other sustaining ingredients, and these tortillas were very white and they were brought on plates covered with clean napkins."

Diana Kennedy, author of a cookbook about tortilla cookery.

In Frances Calderon de la Barca's 1838 book, *Life in Mexico*, it is explained that tortillas are "particularly palatable with chili, to endure which, in the quantities it is eaten here, it seems to be necessary to have a throat lined with tin."

One of the anecdotes about Diana that has always amused us is her search in Manhattan for epazote, a much-used herb in Mexican cooking. For a long time she shopped all the local markets where Spanish and Mexican herbs are sold with no success. One day while strolling in Riverside Park, she found epazote growing wild and in abundance at her feet. Perhaps it is significant that she was jogging around a field of epazote in the same park when she fractured her heels.

Here are some recipes that appear in her new book.

Mushroom Tacos

3 tablespoons peanut oil
1 small onion, finely chopped
2 cloves garlic, peeled and chopped
2 medium-size fresh tomatoes, peeled and chopped, or 1½ cups canned peeled tomatoes, drained
3 fresh hot green peppers (serranos), finely chopped
1 pound fresh mushrooms, finely sliced
3 sprigs epazote (see note), optional, or parsley
1 teaspoon salt
12 tortillas (defrosted tortillas can be used)
Oil or melted lard for frying

1. Heat 3 tablespoons oil to smoking in a saucepan, lower flame and cook the onion and garlic gently until soft but not brown.

2. Add the remaining ingredients except tortillas and oil for frying and cook the mixture, uncovered, over a fairly high flame, stirring from time to time, until the mushrooms are soft, 15 to 20 minutes. The mixture should be fairly dry. Set aside to cool off a little.

3. Put a little of the mixture across one side of the tortilla—not in the center—and roll it up fairly tightly. Fasten with a toothpick. (If you are using defrosted tortillas and they are cracking, put them briefly into a steamer or colander over boiling water, or immerse them in hot fat for a few seconds only. This will make them softer and more flexible.)

4. Heat the oil or lard—there should be no more than ¼ inch in the frying pan or it will seep into the tacos—and fry them, turning them over and removing the toothpicks. They should be just crisp, but not hard. Drain on paper toweling and serve immediately. They become leathery if left heating through in the oven after you have made them. This is pan-to-mouth food and should be eaten as soon as your fingers can hold them. They can be served just as they are or with a little sour cream.

Yield: 12 tacos.

Note: There is no excuse not to use the real thing. Epazote is a tall, greenish plant with flat pointed leaves. It is growing riotously in city parks, hedgerows, and empty lots. It gives an exotic touch with its distinctive, pungent flavor.

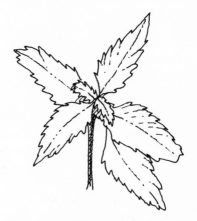

Epazote is a tall greenish plant with flat pointed leaves. It grows riotously in city parks, hedgerows, and empty lots. Pick your own.

Tostadas of Jellied Pig's Feet

>Peanut or safflower oil for frying
>12 tortillas, made 2 or 3 hours ahead or defrosted (they should not be warm and damp)
>Jellied pig's feet (see recipe)
>1½ cups finely shredded and lightly dressed lettuce (see note)
>1 small avocado, cut into thin slices
>1½ cups tomato sauce (see recipe), warm
>3 tablespoons finely grated Sardo (Argentinian Parmesan-type), Romano, or Parmesan cheese
>1 medium-size onion, thinly sliced

1. Heat ¼ inch oil in a frying pan until it smokes. Lower flame slightly and fry the tortillas, one by one, until they are crisp around the edge and slightly browned but not too hard in the center. Drain well on paper toweling.

2. Garnish tortillas liberally with the jellied pig's feet, lettuce, avocado, tomato sauce, grated cheese, and last of all the onion rings. Serve immediately. It is best eaten with two hands.

Yield: 12 tostadas.

Note: Lettuce should be tossed in a rather sharp oil and vinegar dressing.

Jellied pig's feet

2   *fresh pig's feet, split in half*
1   *small bay leaf*
⅛   *teaspoon thyme*
¼   *teaspoon oregano*
1   *tablespoon salt, or to taste*
2   *cloves garlic, peeled*
½   *medium-size onion, peeled*
6   *peppercorns*
    Freshly ground pepper to taste

1. Put all the ingredients, except ground pepper, into a saucepan and cover with cold water ½ inch above the level of the ingredients. Bring slowly to a boil. Lower the flame and simmer about 2½ hours. The meat should be tender but not too soft. Leave to cool in the broth.

2. When pig's feet are cool enough to handle, remove all bones carefully and chop the meat, gelatinous gristle, and rind into small pieces. Place meat in a shallow dish and season with pepper.

3. Strain the broth and measure 1⅓ cups. Pour this onto the chopped meat. Refrigerate the dish about 2 hours or until set firmly.

4. Cut the jelly into small squares and use as a topping for tostadas or sopes.

Yield: Sufficient for 12 normal-size tostadas.

Note: Leftover jelly can be served as an appetizer either dressed with a rather acidy vinaigrette or lemon juice and finely chopped parsley.

Tomato sauce

2   *medium-size tomatoes (12 ounces), broiled, or 1½ cups canned tomatoes, drained*
¼   *medium-size onion, peeled and roughly chopped*
1   *clove garlic, peeled and roughly chopped*
1   *or 2 fresh hot green peppers, optional*
1½ *tablespoons peanut or safflower oil*
¼   *teaspoon salt, or to taste*

1. Place the unskinned tomatoes with the onion, garlic, and hot pepper in the container of a blender and blend until smooth. Do not overblend.

2. Heat the oil in a saucepan until it smokes. Lower the flame and add the sauce and salt and cook over a fairly high flame, stirring it all the time, for about 3 minutes. Set aside and keep warm.

Yield: About 1¼ cups.

Green Chili Gordas

12 dried tortillas (see note)
 3 peeled green peppers
    (Anaheim), fresh or canned
    (one 4-ounce can)
⅔ cup hot milk plus ¼ cup
    cold milk
 1 tablespoon melted lard or
    oil
¾ teaspoon salt
    Lard or oil for frying
 1 medium-size onion, peeled
    and finely chopped
1½ cups sour cream, thinned
    with a little milk and
    salted

1. If the tortillas are not completely dry, spread them out onto a baking sheet and put them into a slow oven for about ½ hour. Remove and cool. When they are cool, break them into small pieces and blend until fine but not pulverized. Transfer to a bowl.

2. Remove and discard some of the seeds from the peppers and blend peppers with the milk until smooth. Add, together with melted lard and salt, to the ground tortillas and knead mixture well. Add more milk if dough is not pliable enough. Set dough aside for about 1 hour or longer, well covered.

3. Divide dough into 12 equal portions and roll into balls about 1½ inches in diameter. Flatten to form 2-inch cakes about ⅜ inch thick.

4. Heat ¼ inch oil or lard in a frying pan and fry the cakes gently about 3 to 5 minutes on both sides (take care that the fat is not too hot, or it will make a crust on the outside instantaneously and the inside of the dough will not be heated through properly).

5. Drain well on paper toweling. (They will hold in a 350-degree oven for about 20 minutes if necessary.) Garnish with the chopped onion and sour cream and serve immediately.

Yield: 12 gordas.

Note: Defrosted tortillas will do perfectly well for this recipe.

Homemade Pastrami

WITH PIERRE FRANEY

Robert Louis Stevenson once set down a haunting, poignant, and much quoted reflection on food. He has Ben Gunn say in *Treasure Island,* "Many's the long night I've dreamed of cheese—toasted, mostly." We recently thought of that line again in relation to displaced New Yorkers. In the Alaskan tundra or on the banks of the Ganges, New Yorkers yearn for the delis of Manhattan, particularly for their corned beef or pastrami. Over the years, we have had scores of requests from these displaced souls, asking for directions on how to cure one's own. If one can find the basics—a slab of beef flanken or brisket of beef and a smoker— the recipe, basically simple, is here. Pastrami? In summer? Indeed, yes. And in winter, spring, or fall as well.

Home-Cured Pastrami

1   *4½-pound slab of beef flanken (see note)*
½   *cup salt, preferably kosher*
2   *tablespoons sugar*
2   *teaspoons ground ginger*
1   *teaspoon saltpeter, available in drug stores*
1   *tablespoon coriander seeds*
¼   *cup peppercorns*
1   *clove finely chopped garlic*

1. Pat the meat dry.

2. Combine the salt, sugar, ginger, and saltpeter in a mixing bowl.

3. Coarsely crush the coriander seeds and peppercorns, using a mallet or the bottom of a clean, heavy skillet. Or grind coarsely. Add them to the bowl along with the garlic. Blend well. Rub the mixture into the meat.

4. Place the seasoned meat in a plastic bag and seal tightly. Place in a tray large enough to hold it. Refrigerate and turn the bag over once a day so that the meat seasons evenly. Let the meat cure for 7 or 8 days.

5. Remove the meat and drain the liquid that accumulated. Save the solid seasonings and discard the liquid. Rub the solid seasonings back into the meat. Use a needle to run a string through the meat. Tie the ends of the string together. Suspend the meat on the string and let it dry in a dry, cool, windy place or use an electric fan. Dry for about 24 hours.

6. Hang the meat in a smoker (see note) and smoke 2½ to 3 hours at about 150 to 160 degrees, or smoke according to the manufacturer's instructions.

7. To cook, cover with cold unsalted water and simmer 2 hours or until meat is tender.

Yield: 8 to 12 servings.

Note: Brisket of beef may be substituted for the flanken, but it will not be as juicy. Home smokers are available from L. L. Bean, Inc., Freeport, Maine 04032, for about $27.50 and from Luhr Jensen & Sons, P. O. Box 297, Hood River, Oregon 97031. Catalogues may be ordered.

Home-Cured Corned Beef

To cure

7 *quarts water*
3 *cups kosher salt, approximately*
1 *raw egg in the shell for testing brine*
1 *6-to-9-pound brisket of beef*
3 *cloves garlic, peeled*
20 *cloves*
20 *peppercorns*
1 *bay leaf*
6 *sprigs fresh thyme or 1 teaspoon dried*
½ *tablespoon saltpeter, available in drug stores*

To cook

Water to cover to the depth of 1 inch over top of meat
1 *bay leaf*
1 *onion, sliced*
6 *sprigs fresh thyme or 1 teaspoon dried*
16 *peppercorns*

1 *clove garlic, sliced*
1 *carrot, scraped and cut into 3-inch lengths*
2 *ribs celery, trimmed and cut into 3-inch lengths*

1. To cure the brisket, you will need a large earthenware, enamel, or stainless-steel crock. Do not add the meat to the crock at this time.

2. Pour the water into the crock and add the salt, stirring to dissolve it. Add the egg. The egg is used to test the salt content of the brine. If the egg floats in the solution, it is ready. If it does not float, continue adding salt a little at a time, stirring to dissolve, until the egg floats. Remove the egg.

3. Add the brisket to the brine. Add the garlic, cloves, peppercorns, bay leaf, thyme, and saltpeter. Stir well. Place a clean, heavy weight on the meat to make certain it is covered. Place a lid on the crock and refrigerate for from 8 to 12 days. Turn the brisket occasionally, but keep it weighted down.

4. When ready to cook the corned beef, remove it from the brine and rinse it well.

5. Combine all the cooking ingredients in a kettle. Do not add salt. Bring to the boil and simmer 2 to 3 hours or until tender.

6. Remove the corned beef and cut it into the thinnest possible slices. Serve with rye bread slices and mustard and/or butter. Serve with garlic pickles on the side.

Yield: 12 or more servings.

Unbeknownst to readers, a number of recipes printed in *The New York Times* have a rather special personal meaning, and such is the case with the foregoing. These recipes came about after a long trip through the Far East during which we hankered for corned beef or pastrami sandwiches. It is a hunger that can be profound. When we returned home we decided to gratify that hunger by making our own. A home-made pastrami or corned beef, by the way, is infinitely superior to the store-bought or deli-bought types. Pastrami is also incredibly easy to make provided you have a small smoker.

Small Craft Food

Over the years when we have explored the potentials of dining aboard small craft, we've found our interest lagging. Most of the people we've talked to say they would rather swab decks than cook, and almost all the recipe books instruct the cook to open a can of cream soup, beef stew, or corned beef hash.

We met William (Sy) Goode on the beach this summer when he was climbing over rocks at Gardiner's Bay foraging for periwinkles. When we asked what that was all about, he said he was going to cook them with a few seasonings and take them for a snack when he went sailing later that day. He invited us for a ride and we accepted with alacrity.

During the course of the day we discovered that Mr. Goode is a professor of sociology at Columbia University, that he is a former president of the American Sociological Association, and that he is an enthusiastic sailor, cook, and spinner of food lore. "Periwinkles," he told us, "were introduced into this country from England in the mid-1800s. Don't ask me why. I do know they grow different sizes in different locations. I spent many summers on Martha's Vineyard and they're much larger there than they are here."

A short while later, in Mr. Goode's tow, we found ourselves peering over the side of a dock where he, sporting fins and snorkeling gear, had dived for local oysters.

"It's a secret place," he had explained earlier. He had discovered the oysters while looking for fish and he had gloomy news about his bed. "They aren't spawning," he told us. "There aren't any small young oysters anywhere around."

Given the time, Mr. Goode could willingly have been pressed into a search for crabs off Louse Point. Instead, it was back to the kitchen for further preparations for the lunch aboard his 20-foot craft. The gentleman, who is 56 years old and the father of four, proceeded to prepare the periwinkles; to make a spectacularly good cold zucchini soup to be blended with yogurt; mussels alla Romana with a touch of garlic and white wine; and a ceviche made with local scallops and freshly caught striped bass fillets. A guest, Lenore Weitzman, arrived and went to work on a quickly made and interesting quiche Lorraine. She made it in store-bought frozen pie shells and without the usual cooking of the onions before they are added. It proved to be excellent.

Mr. Goode, who won the American Sociological Award for one of his 12 books, *World Revolution and Family Patterns*, has a fascinating collection of likes and dislikes in the field of taste. "I don't like beer," he told us. "Oh, I used to drink it in college because it seemed very macho, popular front, and all that. I like the looks of it, but I never touch it anymore. I also don't like arugula. In my early youth I thought I didn't like caviar until I tasted fresh caviar. That was a sad day."

The sociologist attributes his foraging instincts to his father, who was a disciple of the late Bernard MacFadden, the body-builder. "He preceded the current natural foods movement by decades and my father followed his advice. We did a lot of searching for the finest and freshest merchandise, both in the markets and in the fields."

After an hour or so in the kitchen, the foods were packed in baskets and taken aboard the small boat lying at anchor a few yards away. On hand for the sail were Betty Friedan, the leader of the women's movement; David Manning White, the journalist, author and pop-culture authority; and Miss Weitzman.

Zucchini Soup with Yogurt

4   large zucchini, about 3 pounds total weight
8   tablespoons butter
4   cups coarsely chopped onion
3   cups chicken broth
1   clove garlic, finely minced
    Salt and freshly ground pepper to taste
2   cups yogurt
½   cup chopped scallions

1. Trim off the ends of the zucchini. Do not peel the vegetable, but cut it into 1-inch cubes. Set aside.

2. Melt the butter in a deep kettle and add the 4 cups of coarsely chopped onion. Cook, stirring, until the onion is wilted and golden. Add the zucchini and cook, stirring, about 1 minute longer.

Sporting fins and snorkeling gear, William (Sy) Goode exits from "a secret place" in the Hamptons with a pail of oysters.

3. Add the chicken broth, garlic, salt and pepper and cover. Simmer about 5 minutes. The zucchini must remain crisp. If any of the pieces of zucchini seem too large, chop them inside the kettle.

4. Chill and stir in the yogurt. Serve sprinkled with chopped scallions.

Yield: 8 or more servings.

Ceviche of Scallops and Striped Bass

1   *pound bay scallops*
½   *pound boneless, skinless striped bass, cut into ¾-inch cubes*
1   *clove garlic, finely chopped*
2   *bay leaves, crumbled*
1   *teaspoon crushed red pepper flakes*
¾   *cup lime juice*
1   *squeezed lime, cut into fine dice*
⅓   *cup chopped scallions*

1. Combine all the ingredients in a bowl and refrigerate 12 hours or longer.

2. Serve as an appetizer with slices of French or Italian bread.

Yield: 6 to 8 servings.

Mussels alla Romana

36   *mussels, well scrubbed*
2   *tablespoons or more olive oil*
½   *cup dry white wine*

1   *clove garlic, finely minced*
¼   *cup finely chopped parsley Hot red pepper flakes*

1. Wash the mussels well under cold running water and set aside.

2. Select a skillet large enough to hold the mussels in one layer. Add enough oil to barely cover the bottom of the skillet. Add the mussels and cover.

3. Cook, shaking the skillet until the mussels open, 3 minutes or longer. Remove from the heat.

4. Pour the pan juices into a saucepan. Add the wine, garlic, and parsley and bring to the boil. Reduce by about half.

5. Meanwhile, remove and discard the top shell from each mussel. Place the mussels on the half shell in a bowl and pour the wine mixture over them. Sprinkle with red pepper flakes and chill.

Yield: 6 servings of 6 mussels each.

Periwinkles à la Goode

1   *pint freshly harvested periwinkles*
¼   *cup olive oil Water to barely cover Juice of 1 lemon*
12   *coriander seeds, crushed*
10   *peppercorns*
1   *whole clove*
1   *bay leaf*
3   *tarragon sprigs or 1 teaspoon dried Salt to taste*

1. Wash the periwinkles well in cold water and drain. Set aside.

2. Pour the oil into a saucepan and add enough water to barely cover the periwinkles when they are added. Add the remaining ingredients except periwinkles and bring to the boil. Simmer about 10 minutes; let cool.

3. Add the periwinkles and bring to the boil. Simmer 3 to 4 minutes and remove from the heat. Let stand to room temperature. Drain.

4. Let the guests serve themselves and offer small toothpicks or pins to extract the periwinkles.

Yield: 6 or more servings.

Quick Quiche Lorraine ·

1 *frozen 9-inch pie shell or enough pastry to line a 9-inch pie plate*
4 *strips bacon*
½ *cup chopped onion*
¾ *cup grated Swiss and Jack cheeses*
3 *eggs*
1 *cup heavy cream*
2 *tablespoons dry sherry Grated nutmeg to taste Salt and freshly ground pepper to taste*

1. If the frozen pie shell is to be used, defrost it. Otherwise line a 9-inch plate with pastry.

2. Preheat the oven to 375 degrees.

3. Cut the bacon into small pieces and cook until crisp, stirring often. Drain on absorbent toweling.

4. Sprinkle the bottom of the pie pastry with bacon, the chopped onion, and cheese. Beat the eggs until well blended. Beat in the cream and sherry and add nutmeg, salt and pepper. Pour the mixture over the cheese and bacon.

5. Bake 30 to 40 minutes or until the custard is set. Serve lukewarm or at room temperature.

Yield: 6 servings.

The "How To" of a Leg of Lamb

WITH PIERRE FRANEY

To prepare

1. Place meat fat side down. Cut off and discard the loose flap from the under side.

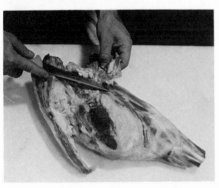

2. Using a boning or large paring knife, follow the outlines of the top leg bone known as the aitch bone. Bone it all around and sever it at the joint. Crack the bone and save it.

3. Turn the leg over and "French" the very end of the shank bone, cutting away about 1½ inches of meat surrounding the bone.

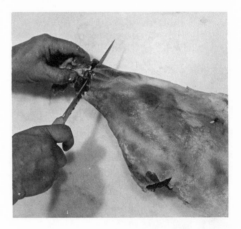

4. Tie the boned section of the leg with string as shown.

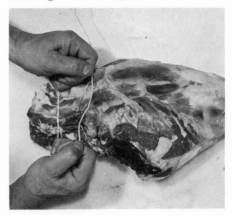

5. With the tip of a small knife, make 16 or so slits in the meat and insert slivers of garlic.

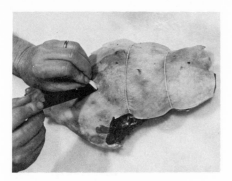

6. Place it fat side down in a baking dish. Sprinkle with salt and pepper. Add reserved bone.

To roast

1. Preheat oven to 450 degrees.

2. Place a 6-to-7-pound leg of lamb in oven and bake 30 minutes.

3. Turn the lamb and cook 15 minutes. Pour off all fat.

4. Bake 20 minutes longer and add 1 cup of water. Cover with foil. Reduce heat to 400 degrees. Total roasting time is 1½ hours.

5. Pour pan juices into a saucepan and reheat. Let lamb rest 20 minutes. Add juices that accumulate to saucepan.

Yield: 8 to 12 servings.

To carve

1. To carve the lamb, slice down about 2 inches from the end of the shank bone.

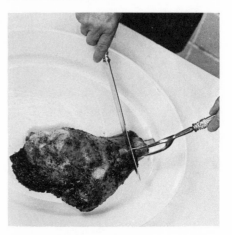

2. Hold the knife at a very slight angle and carve toward the initial slice.

3. Continue making very thin slices at an angle.

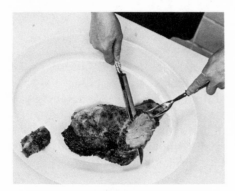

4. The lamb may be served on individual dishes as it is sliced or served on a platter as shown.

5. When the upper portion of the lamb has been carved and served, turn and carve from right.

6. Then turn and carve from the other side and finally the bottom side.

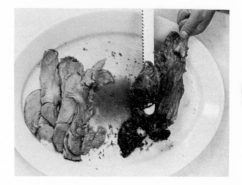

A Young Talented Cook

One of the nicest interviews we've had was one with Jane Berquist, a young woman who by some interesting twist of things thought we had been partially responsible for her training at the estimable Lycée Technique Hôtelier Jean Drouant in Paris. Miss Berquist has had a rather exceptional career in the world of French cuisine, particularly in view of the fact that she is only 26 years old and both technically and legally blind. Despite the handicap, Miss Berquist gads about the world with enviable purpose and enthusiasm.

She has spent weeks employed in the kitchen of Fauchon, the nonpareil market in the Place Madeleine in Paris, and two years ago she met Simone Beck who engaged her to teach English-speaking students enrolled in the Ecole des Trois Gourmandes, the school that spawned *Mastering the Art of French Cooking.*

Back in this country, Miss Berquist opened a cooking school in her home in Chatham, New Jersey. One of the recipes she demonstrates is for these Roquefort cheese timbales.

Timbales au Roquefort

¼ cup Roquefort cheese
2 tablespoons butter
¼ cup Philadelphia cream cheese
    Freshly ground pepper to taste
    Paprika to taste
3 eggs
2 to 3 tablespoons crème fraiche (see recipe)
1 tablespoon finely chopped chives
    Fried croutons
    Puréed spinach or braised spinach in butter, optional

1. Preheat oven to 350 degrees.

2. Break up the Roquefort cheese and cream it with the butter and cream cheese. Season with pepper and paprika.

3. Beat the eggs and crème fraiche together and add to the preceding mixture. The resulting mixture should not be lumpy; if so, strain through a sieve. Add the chopped chives.

4. Butter 4 baba timbale molds well. Add the mixture to each and place in a pan of hot water. Bake 15 to 20 minutes. The crème is done when it begins to pull away from the mold.

5. Unmold timbales on fried croutons and arrange on a plate

with a border of puréed spinach or on a bed of braised spinach in butter.

Yield: 4 servings.

Note: This first course dish is even better when it is served with a sauce made by reducing 1 cup of fresh cream perfumed with ½ tablespoon chopped chives.

Crème fraiche

1   *cup heavy cream*
1   *tablespoon buttermilk*

1. Put 1 cup heavy cream in a screw-top jar with 1 tablespoon buttermilk. Shake for 1 minute. Let stand at room temperature at least 24 hours, then refrigerate 24 hours before using.

We recently found out that Miss Berquist is now Mme. Jean Phellipon, and that she is no longer giving classes in New Jersey but is giving them in France. She is living with her husband in Asnières, a suburb of Paris. Information about her classes may be obtained by writing Mme. Jean Phellipon at 27 Rue d'Anjou, Asnières, 92600, France. We wish the young couple well.

Port-au-Prince Delights

One day recently we were thinking out loud about our last visit to Haiti. We hungered, we said, for that Haitian rice dish—stygian black—made with small dried mushrooms. Almost reflectively someone said, "Haitian? The best Haitian cook in all of America lives in Manhattan. She's Josephine Premice Fales, and we think she's in town." Sure enough she was. And sure enough she invited us over for djon-djon—the black mushrooms—with rice.

Mrs. Fales—or Josephine Premice as she is known on the stage and in nightclubs—is a classic beauty with a beguiling natural animation and a voice with deep vibrant tones. An orchestra leader once told her in Rome that he hoped she would will her voice to New York City.

"My voice," she asked, "for heaven's sake why?"

"They can break it up and use it for gravel!"

She offered us an insidiously good Haitian rum punch and a piping hot, salt cod fritter. She explained that she was born in New York of Haitian parents and had spent much of her childhood in Port-au-Prince and environs. She said her mother had never taught her to cook and that she learned instinctively. We can vouch that she is one of the great natural cooks of this generation.

She offered us another fritter, curiously known as a marinade in Haiti. It is a small, savory, hunger-making delicacy. The batter for making it, she explained, is always kept ready for use in the best Haitian homes. You simply add a solid food such as shredded or chopped fish or meat, she added, and deep fry it as guests arrive.

Miss Premice invited us into the kitchen, where she proceeded to chop and slice and make preparations for an assortment of toothsome specialties from Haiti. She noted that she was in the process of writing a very personal cookbook in the form of a memoir.

We asked what her father had done professionally in Haiti, and she replied that he was "a happy revolutionary," who had been deprived of his passport two years ago.

The Faleses, the parents of two children, Susan, 12 years old, and Enrico, 14, were last in Haiti about two years ago. "I was nervous," she stated. "After all, most of my relatives had been assassinated, but when we arrived, they rolled out the red carpet. We hope some day to build a home there."

Miss Premice, best known for her performances some years ago in "House of Flowers" and "Jamaica" (with Lena Horne), was last seen in the off-Broadway production of "The Cherry Orchard." Timothy Fales is an amateur sportsman and a retired Wall Street broker now writing a novel about Louis del Gres, one of the important revolutionary figures in Guadeloupe during the Napoleonic era.

On the way to the kitchen we had noted a fascinating display of paintings by her friend and neighbor, Geoffrey Holder, the multifaceted artist and dancer; by Benay Venuta, the actress and painter; and assorted Haitian artifacts. One of the most eye-arresting pieces in the home is a tall silver epergne, and it has an amusing history.

"I had an aunt," Miss Premice related, "who lived in Paris. She was a woman of some wealth, and she died when I was 18 years old. In her will she left money to everyone in the family except me. She left me the epergne, and in my innocence I cried for days. Today it's my favorite material possession, and I've been offered thousands for it." It stands almost four feet high and is marvelously ornate, with an upper basin for fruits or flowers and four bottom compartments for more of the same or food. She used it that evening for the components of the dinner that included Haitain-style chicken, a spicy, piquant dish resembling an escabeche; a delectable, long-simmered watercress soup; cornmeal with beans; the rice with black mushrooms; a splendid okra "pickle"; plus flamed native fruits.

During the course of the meal, our hostess stated that over the years much imagery had been used in "the media" to describe her. *The Times* man once said she looked as though she were constructed of pipe cleaners. Rex Reed claimed she had "the face of an evil angel." "My one regret," she added, "is no one has ever called me sexy."

We would like to correct that, Josephine Premice is the sexiest-looking and one of the most talented cooks we've ever known.

Rum Punch

1 6-ounce can (¾ cup) frozen pink lemonade, slightly defrosted
6 tablespoons (½ can) water
1 large-size pitted peach (see note)
¼ cup Triple Sec, Cointreau, Grenadine, or syrup of cassis
1¼ cups dark Haitian rum

Combine all the ingredients in the container of an electric blender. Blend thoroughly. Serve in individual glasses over ice cubes.

Yield: 6 to 8 servings.

Note: Almost any fruit may be used to replace the peach. Peeled, pitted mangoes (about ¼ mango per recipe) are excellent.

Marinade
(Haitian salt cod fritters)

¾   *pound boneless, very*
    white, dried salt cod
    Cold water to cover
    Fritter batter made with
    2 cups flour (see recipe)
    Oil for medium frying,
    about 2 cups

1. Add the cod to a saucepan and add cold water to cover. Bring to the boil. Drain. Taste the cod. If it remains too salty, add more water to cover. Bring to the boil and drain. Repeat if the cod remains too salty. Generally 1 or 2 boilings will be sufficient. Do not cook the salt cod until it becomes bland and tasteless.

2. Shred the cod. There should be about 1½ cups.

3. Add the cod to the fritter batter (where indicated in step 3 of the fritter batter recipe). Heat the oil in a skillet and spoon portions—2 or 3 tablespoonfuls at a time—into the fat. Cook until golden on one side. Turn and cook until golden on the other. As the fritters are cooked drain them on absorbent toweling. Serve hot.

Yield: 34 2- or 3-inch fritters.

Haitian fritter batter

2   *cups flour (see note)*
    Salt to taste
1⅓ *cups water*
¼   *cup finely chopped parsley*
    or 3 sprigs of parsley
    mashed to a paste in a
    mortar with 1 or 2 bottled

green Tabasco peppers in
vinegar (see note)
1   *large egg yolk*
    Freshly ground black
    pepper
¼   *teaspoon hot pepper flakes*
1   *teaspoon vinegar,*
    preferably hot pepper
    vinegar
1   *teaspoon baking powder*

1. Put the flour in a mixing bowl and add salt to taste. Add 1 cup of water, stirring rapidly with a whisk. When smooth, beat in the remaining water.

2. Add the parsley and egg yolk. Stir to blend and add the black pepper and pepper flakes.

3. When ready to use, add the vinegar, salt to taste, and 1½ cups of the solids to be used, such as shredded salt cod, seafood, and so on, and stir in the baking powder. Use immediately. Do not add the baking powder until ready to cook.

Yield: Enough batter for 34 2- or 3-inch fritters.

Note: Mrs. Fales uses Hecker's flour. She gets the bottled Tabasco peppers in vinegar in Spanish markets.

Chicken Haitian-Style
(A kind of escabeche)

3   *2½-pound chickens,*
    quartered
½   *lemon or lime*
¾   *cup tarragon vinegar*
2   *cloves garlic, finely*
    chopped

½ teaspoon freshly ground
black pepper
Salt to taste
½ long fresh hot red or green
pepper, or 1 bottled green
Tabasco pepper in vinegar,
chopped or cut into rings
2 onions, about ¾ pound
total weight
½ cup coarsely chopped,
loosely packed parsley
¼ cup peanut or corn oil
½ cup dry white wine
½ cup chicken broth
1 teaspoon tomato paste

1. Rinse and drain the chicken pieces well. Rub the pieces all over with half a cut lemon or lime. Place in a mixing bowl. Add the vinegar, garlic, black pepper, salt, and hot pepper.

2. Cut the onions into ¼-inch slices and break the slices into rings. Add them. Add the parsley and let stand an hour or so, turning the chicken in the marinade from time to time.

3. Heat the oil in a large, heavy skillet and cook the chicken, a few pieces at a time, until browned on all sides. As the pieces are cooked transfer them to a Dutch oven large enough to hold them all. When the pieces are transferred, add the marinade to the skillet and stir to dissolve all brown particles that cling to the bottom and sides of the skillet. Cook about 5 minutes. Add the wine, chicken broth, and tomato paste. Add salt to taste.

4. Pour this over the chicken and partially cover. Cook, moving the pieces of chicken around occasionally, about 45 minutes or until very tender. Serve the chicken with the sauce. Serve hot or cold.

Yield: 8 to 12 servings.

Riz au Djon-Djon
(Haitian rice with black
mushrooms)

2 cups dried black Haitian
mushrooms (see note)
2½ cups cold water
2 slices bacon, cut into ¼-
inch pieces
1 or 2 cloves garlic, finely
chopped
2 tablespoons peanut or corn
oil
Salt to taste
½ teaspoon red pepper flakes,
more or less to taste
2 whole cloves
2 sprigs fresh summer
savory, optional
½ small onion, thinly sliced
(about ½ cup)
1¾ cups rice (see note)

1. Pick over the mushrooms to remove any very tough and relatively large stems.

2. Put the water in a saucepan and add the mushrooms. Let soak 2 hours.

3. Add the bacon pieces, garlic, oil, salt, and pepper flakes. Bring to the boil and add the cloves, savory, and onion.

4. Stir in the rice and bring to the boil.

5. Cut out a round of paper, preferably from an ordinary brown paper bag, slightly larger than the circumference of the saucepan. Cover with the paper round, then with a lid. Cook 30 to 35 minutes or until rice is tender.

Yield: 6 or more servings.

Note: The mushrooms known as djon-djon in Haiti are available at the Spanish markets. Mrs. Fales uses Uncle Ben's converted rice for this dish.

Okra Guadeloupe-Style

2 *10-ounce packages frozen okra, defrosted*
1 *small onion, about ¼ pound*
   Salt to taste
½ *cup tarragon wine vinegar*
½ *cup water*
½ *teaspoon red pepper flakes, more or less to taste*

1. Place the okra in a skillet. Peel and cut the onion into thin strips. Add it.

2. Add the remaining ingredients and let stand, stirring occasionally, about 1 hour. Cover and bring to the boil. Cook 7 minutes. No longer. Serve at room temperature or chilled.

Yield: About 1 quart.

Unknown to her, we have had a crush on Josephine Premice since we first saw her (we prefer to forget how many years ago) on Broadway in Truman Capote's musical, "House of Flowers." We were thus overjoyed at a late night party when in the company of Lena Horne we were introduced to Miss Premice. Lena, who is no mean cook herself, told us that Josephine is one of the best cooks she knows. Subsequently, Josephine granted us this interview.

A Picnic of Distinction

WITH PIERRE FRANEY

We can recall in clearly etched detail some fairly fancy spreads we've been privileged to enjoy around the world—fresh caviar in Iran; fresh foie gras in Alsace; bouillabaisse and bourride in restaurants around the Vieux Port in Marseilles. But it literally is true that truffles and champagne are no more apt to aggravate and appease the appetite than humbler foods taken at a country outing. Five dishes for al fresco dining are offered here: an escabèche of fish; marinated beef to be grilled over charcoal; spareribs, vaguely Hawaiian; roasted peppers with anchovies; and sugared mango slices with champagne.

Skewered Beef with Herb Sauce

1   *pound fillet of beef or rib of beef, cut 1½ inches thick*
12 *raw shrimp, shelled and deveined*
    Salt and freshly ground pepper to taste
¼   *cup peanut, corn, or olive oil*
⅛   *teapsoon pulverized bay leaf*
⅛   *teaspoon thyme*
6   *tablespoons butter, melted Tabasco*
4   *lemon wedges Watercress for garnish, optional*

1. Prepare a hot charcoal fire or preheat the broiler.

2. Cut the beef into 12 1½-inch cubes.

3. Alternate 3 cubes of beef and 3 raw shrimp on each of 4 skewers. Sprinkle with salt and pepper.

4. Blend the oil with the bay leaf and thyme. Brush the oil on the skewered foods. Place on hot grill or under broiler. Grill about 5 minutes, turning once or twice.

5. Meanwhile, melt the butter and add a dash of Tabasco. Serve the skewers with the hot butter poured over. Serve with lemon wedges. Garnish with watercress if desired.

Yield: 4 servings.

Escabeche of Fish

1¾ *pounds (cleaned weight) fish, left whole but with head removed*
    Salt and freshly ground pepper to taste
½   *cup flour*
2   *cups oil, preferably olive oil*

10 *small cloves garlic, unpeeled but lightly crushed*
1 *cup thinly sliced carrot rounds*
1 *small onion, thinly sliced*
⅓ *cup wine vinegar*
3 *tablespoons water*
2 *sprigs fresh thyme or ½ teaspoon dried*
2 *hot dried red pepper pods*
1 *bay leaf*
6 *parsley sprigs*

1. Any firm-fleshed fresh fish such as porgy or sea bass can be used in this recipe. Score both sides of the fish with a sharp knife, making parallel and fairly deep gashes on both sides. Sprinkle inside and out with salt and pepper.

2. Put the flour in a bag and add the fish. Shake the bag until fish is well coated with flour.

3. Heat the oil and when it is very hot, add the fish. Cook about 5 minutes or until golden on one side. Turn and cook until golden brown all over, about 3 or 4 minutes. Transfer the fish to a deep dish.

4. Strain the oil and reserve 1 cup of it. Pour the cup of oil into a saucepan and add the garlic cloves and carrot. Cook about 1 minute and add the onion rings. Cook over high heat about 2 minutes and add the vinegar, water, thyme, pepper pods, bay leaf, parsley sprigs, and salt and pepper to tasts. Cover and simmer about 10 minutes.

5. Pour the mixture over the fish and cover with wax paper.

Cover with a lid and refrigerate about 24 hours.

Yield: 4 to 6 servings.

Peppers and Anchovies Italian-Style

1 *pound green or red sweet (bell) peppers*
3 *tablespoons olive oil*
1 *2-ounce can flat anchovies*
2 *tablespoons drained capers*
1 *teaspoon oregano*
 Salt and freshly ground pepper to taste
1 *teaspoon finely chopped garlic*
1 *tablespoon red wine vinegar*
1 *tablespoon finely chopped parsley*
 Lemon wedges

1. Core and seed the peppers and cut them lengthwise into ½-inch strips. There should be about 4 cups.

2. Heat the oil in a heavy skillet and add the peppers. Cook, stirring and shaking the skillet, about 2 minutes.

3. Drain and chop the anchovies and add them to the peppers. Add the capers, oregano, salt and pepper, and garlic. Cook, stirring and shaking the skillet, about 2 minutes. Sprinkle with wine vinegar and remove from the heat. Serve hot or cold sprinkled with parsley. Serve with lemon.

Yield: 6 to 8 servings.

Barbecued Ribs with Ginger Sauce

1   cup catchup
1   teaspoon freshly grated
    ginger
4   teaspoons butter
2   tablespoons worcestershire
    sauce
3   tablespoons lemon juice
½   teaspoon finely minced
    garlic
2   tablespoons honey
1   teaspoon ground coriander
1   rack of spareribs, the
    meatier and smaller the
    ribs the better
    Salt and freshly ground
    pepper to taste
¼   teaspoon monosodium
    glutamate, optional

1. Preheat the oven to 350 degrees.

2. In a saucepan combine the catchup, ginger, butter, worcestershire sauce, lemon juice, garlic, honey, and coriander. Bring to the boil and stir to blend.

3. Place the spareribs on a rack meaty side up and sprinkle with salt and pepper and monosodium glutamate. Place in the oven and bake 30 minutes or until nicely browned.

4. Brush the spareribs with a layer of sauce and bake 15 minutes longer.

5. Turn the spareribs and brush with sauce. Bake 15 minutes longer and turn. Brush with sauce. Continue baking 15 to 30 minutes longer, basting as necessary. Serve hot or cold.

Yield: 4 servings.

Mango Slices with Champagne

3   very ripe but firm mangoes
½   cup confectioners' sugar
¼   cup framboise (a raspberry
    eau de vie)
    Chilled champagne

1. Peel the mangoes. Run a knife around the perimeter of the mangoes all the way to the pit. Use a large kitchen spoon and, starting at one end, carefully push the spoon's blade around the large pit of the fruit. Repeat on the other half of the mangoes. Discard the pit.

2. Cut the mango flesh into strips.

3. Place the strips in a bowl and sprinkle with sugar. Add the framboise and chill. Spoon the fruit and liquid into 6 serving dishes and add champagne (or any good dry white wine) to taste.

Yield: 6 servings.

A French Restaurateur Examines the Seafood on These Shores

When we visited Paris a few months back we wrote with consider-able enthusiasm of a seafood restaurant which, we stated, may be one of the two finest in that city. It was called Le Duc, (page 175), and we dined there sumptuously and well on great platters of raw and cooked sea creatures, including one of the tenderest lobsters we'd eaten any-where. It had been steamed on a bed of seaweed. The entire experience smacked of Marseilles and Brittany.

Recently, Jean Mincielli, le patron and market-man of Le Duc, paid a visit to Manhattan to explore the possibilities of opening a restaurant in America. During the course of his stay, we joined him on a pre-dawn junket to the Fulton Fish Market to look at the local fish and seafood supplies. We were out of bed by 4 A.M., and in a taxi we yawned our way through darkened streets from 57th Street to Fulton. We descended, quite coincidentally, at the Paris Bar and Grill, 119 South Street, an un-ceremonious gathering place where numerous fish merchants were start-ing their day with coffee and danish. Mr. Mincielli asked for a coffee with cream and the manager extended the milk pitcher.

In the party were Paul Kovi and Tom Margittai, owners of both the Forum and The Four Seasons; Yanou Collart, a Frenchwoman on hand to translate for Mr. Mincielli; and John vonGlahn, head of the New York Fishery Council. Mr. Mincielli asked Mr. vonGlahn how many kinds of fish and shellfish are sold at the Fulton Street Market, and Mr. vonGlahn answered, "At the last count it was something like 195."

The party wandered among scores of open corrugated iron bins where tons of salmon, porgy, ocean scallops, crabs, pompany, red snap-per, striped bass, mussels, and so on were on display. We passed the lobster enclave and someone averred that you can tell the point of origin of a lobster by the color of the raw shell ("If it's red, it's from Canada; if it's blue, it's from Maine").

The color question was put to Harry Jorgensen, said to be the oldest lobster dealer in the market. He shrugged and said "Nah," with a gri-mace. "How can you tell? I can tell you the difference between a male and a female."

Jean Mincielli, center, checks some salmon with fellow restaurateurs, Tom Margittai, left, and Paul Kovi.

Mr. Mincielli, a tall, lean specimen, born in Corsica and raised in Marseilles, asked if there was any abalone around. We walked over to where the abalone had at one time been available. The owner there noted that it is rare in these parts. "The problem is shipping," he explained. "We can only handle 5,000 to 10,000 pounds at a time. They won't ship it from the West Coast, where it comes from, with less than a 30,000-pound order. To fly it in would be prohibitive."

Mr. Mincielli led the way to the docks where a boat, the *Felicia*, was unloading a fresh load of ocean scallops, some the size of a goose egg. Through his translator, Mr. Mincielli asked if he could buy scallops in the shell as he does in France. "Not normally," he was told by Harold Walsh, a ruddy-faced fisherman who said the boat had been out 11 days off the New England coast. Mr. Walsh, who noted among other things that he has a doctor's degree from the University of Illinois, stated that his boat's present haul weighed in at about 15,000 pounds.

As the early morning rambles came to an end we queried Mr. Mincielli about his findings and the differences between his home markets
and here. Many of the shellfish that he would like to introduce to an
American audience are not available, he told us. Coquillages with such
names as lavagnon, vernis, coque, venus, pousse-pied, petites crevettes
vivantes, praires, and amande de mer. These are assorted ocean wonders
in various shapes, colors, and sizes and all eminently edible. There are
also numerous fish including English sole, turbot, and loup de mer that
do not inhabit American waters.

"Also," Mr. Mincielli added, "here you don't have the small boats
that go out in the morning and come back at night. Each port in Brittany
has its local seafood specialty, and in Paris I can get these brought in
overnight."

Throughout his visit, Mr. Mincielli persisted that he was not a chef,
that his brother, Paul, was totally in charge of the kitchen. He insisted
that his one area was in shopping for the merchandise and supervising
the dining room of Le Duc. On the other hand, we persuaded him to
visit us in our kitchen in East Hampton, and he turned out to be a first-
rate cuisinier. He provided us with a duplicate of that lobster baked on
seaweed; with that excellent raw salmon dish that is now a rage in several European restaurants including Le Duc; with quickly-made and
succulent soft shell crabs, deep fried and served with no season but salt
and pepper; with freshly harvested periwinkles cooked in sea water; and
with moules Madras with a light curry sauce, one of the best creamed
mussels dishes we ever hope to try.

Lobster Cooked on Seaweed

The lobsters

6   1¼-to-1½-pound lobsters
6   to 8 quarts freshly
    harvested, wet seaweed

The sauce

½   pound sweet butter
    Salt to taste
2   cloves garlic, smashed

1. Preheat oven to 500 degrees.

2. Select a tray large enough
to hold the lobsters in one layer

3. Place half the seaweed on
the tray and place the lobsters
shell side up. Cover with the remaining seaweed and place the
tray in the oven. Bake 15 minutes.

4. Remove the tray and
quickly split in half the tail of
each lobster. Do not split the
carcass or main body portion at
this time. Return the lobsters to
the tray, shell side up, and bake
30 minutes longer.

5. Meanwhile, prepare the
sauce. Add the butter to a saucepan and let it melt. Add the salt

and garlic and heat until piping hot.

6. Remove the lobsters from the oven and use a sharp, heavy knife to split the main body portions in two. Serve half a lobster to each guest along with the hot sauce and nutcrackers for the claws.

Yield: 6 to 12 servings.

Moules Madras

2   cups heavy cream (see note)
2   quarts well-scrubbed mussels, the smaller the better
2   teaspoons curry powder
¼   teaspoon cayenne pepper, more or less to taste (see note)

1. Pour the cream into a small skillet and cook it about 20 minutes over fairly high heat until it is reduced to about 1½ cups. Set aside.

2. Heat the mussels equally divided in 2 large skillets. Cook, shaking the skillets briefly, and add ¾ cup cream to each skillet. Do not add salt.

3. Immediately blend the curry powder and cayenne and add equal amounts to each skillet. Cook, stirring, over high heat until mussels open. As they open transfer them to individual serving bowls. Let the sauce in each skillet reduce slightly, stirring, and pour equal amounts of sauce over each serving.

Yield: 6 servings.

Note: French cream is much thicker than that available in America. In France it is not necessary to reduce the cream before cooking. In this country it is advisable. The amount of cayenne pepper to use is a matter of taste. Ideally the dish should be a bit hot.

Poisson Cru Le Duc
(Raw fish with green peppercorns)

The fish

2   pounds raw fish or seafood such as salmon, striped bass, or very fresh bay scallops
¼   cup green peppercorns

The dressing

⅓   cup olive oil
2   small onions, peeled and thinly sliced
4   whole cloves
¼   teaspoon cognac

1. Bone the fish or have it boned at the fish market. If necessary, use eyebrow tweezers to pull out certain bones.

2. Place the fish on a flat surface and with a long, very sharp, flat knife, cut it into the thinnest possible slices, ⅛ inch thick approximately. As the slices are cut arrange them in a single layer on individual plates or, if they are to be served on small pieces of toast, on a chilled platter.

3. Combine the ingredients for the dressing and set aside.

4. When ready to serve, brush the salmon slices very lightly with the oil in the marinade. The best way to do this is to dip a large spoon into the oil and gently smear the fish with the back of the spoon.

5. After the salmon is brushed with oil, place 1 peppercorn in the center of each piece of salmon and flatten it with a knife. Or put the salmon on small toasts (see note) and add 1 peppercorn for each toast, crushing it. Serve without lemon wedges or other garnish.

Yield: 6 to 8 servings.

Note: To make small toasts or croutons, slice small rounds of French or Italian bread. Brush with melted butter and toast under the broiler, turning once or twice.

Deep-Fried Soft-Shell Crabs Le Duc

6 to 12 soft-shell crabs
1½ quarts peanut oil or more
    for deep frying
    Salt and freshly ground
    white pepper to taste

1. Clean the crabs or have them cleaned. Do not add salt and pepper.

2. Heat the oil until it is very hot but not quite smoking. Add the crabs a few at a time and cook quickly about 1 minute, turning once. Drain. Sprinkle with salt and pepper and serve hot without lemon or other garnish.

Yield: 6 servings.

Periwinkles Piquantes

2   quarts periwinkles
    Sea water
2   sprigs fresh thyme or 1
    teaspoon dried
2   fennel leaves or 1 teaspoon
    fennel seeds
1   bay leaf
4   sprigs fresh parsley
1   medium-size onion, sliced
1   clove garlic, peeled and
    lightly crushed
¼   teaspoon cayenne, or more
    or less to taste
1   teaspoon freshly ground
    black pepper, or more or
    less to taste
10 whole cloves

1. Rinse the periwinkles well and put them in a kettle. Add fresh sea water to cover to a depth of about 2 inches above the level of the shells.

2. If fresh thyme and fennel are available, tie them with the bay leaf and parsley sprigs in a bundle. Add them. Add the remaining ingredients. Bring to boil and simmer 2 hours. Drain and serve hot, lukewarm, or cold with toothpicks, letting guests help themselves. These are eaten without sauce.

Yield: 20 or more servings.

Cold Fish

WITH PIERRE FRANEY

Such dishes as cold salads and other savories made with seasonal fish and shellfish are eminently pleasing to summer appetites. Served lukewarm with a sauce ravigote or vinaigrette, they are a palatal delight. Recipes for poached striped bass as well as for three seafood salads—one for lobster, one for shrimp, and one for fish—are given here.

Poached Striped Bass

The court-bouillon

4 *quarts water*
2 *cups chopped onion*
1 *cup coarsely chopped carrots*
2 *cups coarsely chopped celery*
2 *cups coarsely chopped leeks*
  Salt to taste
10 *peppercorns*
2 *cups dry white wine*
1 *bay leaf*
6 *sprigs fresh parsley*
3 *sprigs fresh thyme or 1 teaspoon dried*
2 *cloves garlic, peeled and cut in half*

The fish

1   *3½-to-5-pound striped bass, cleaned, gills removed, and head and tail left on if possible*

1. Combine all the ingredients for the court-bouillon and bring to the boil. Simmer 10 minutes. Let cool.

2. Add the fish and cover. Bring to the boil and simmer 10 to 15 minutes. Let the fish stand in the cooking liquid 10 minutes or longer.

3. Remove the fish and carefully pare away the skin. Serve lukewarm or at room temperature with a sauce such as a vinaigrette with tomato or a sauce ravigote.

Yield: 8 to 12 servings.

Sauce vinaigrette with tomato

2   *tablespoons prepared mustard, preferably Dijon or Düsseldorf (do not use the ball-park variety)*
1   *tablespoon red wine vinegar*
¼   *cup olive oil*
¼   *cup peanut, vegetable, or corn oil*
1   *red, ripe tomato, peeled and cubed (about ⅔ cup)*
2   *tablespoons finely chopped shallots*
1   *tablespoon finely chopped basil*
1½ *tablespoons finely chopped parsley*
    Salt and freshly ground pepper to taste

1. Place the mustard and vinegar in a mixing bowl and whisk in the oils.

2. Stir in the remaining ingredients and serve at room temperature.

Yield: About 1½cups.

Sauce ravigote

3   *tablespoons finely chopped onion*
2   *tablespoons small, drained capers, chopped*
¼   *cup finely chopped parsley*
2   *tablespoons finely chopped tarragon*
2   *tablespoons finely chopped chives*
2   *tablespoons finely chopped chervil*
¼   *cup wine vinegar*
1   *cup olive oil*
    Salt and freshly ground pepper

1. Combine the onion, capers, parsley, tarragon, chives, chervil, and vinegar in a mixing bowl.

2. Gradually add the oil, stirring vigorously with a wire whisk. Add salt and pepper. Serve with boiled beef, calf's head, or poached fish.

Yield: About 1½ cups.

Cold Shrimp Salad à la Grecque

12 *thin slices red onion*
24 *cooked shrimp, shelled and deveined*
½   *cup crumbled feta cheese*

1 *bunch watercress,
   trimmed, rinsed, and
   shaken dry*
24 *cherry tomatoes or 16
   wedges of standard size,
   red, ripe tomatoes*
3 *tablespoons finely chopped
   fresh dill, or basil, optional*
3 *tablespoons fresh lemon
   juice*
3 *tablespoons olive oil
   trimmed, rinsed and
   shaken dry*
24 *cherry tomatoes or 16
   wedges of standard size,
   red, ripe tomatoes*
3 *tablespoons finely chopped
   fresh dill, or basil,
   optional*
3 *tablespoons fresh lemon
   juice*
3 *tablespoons olive oil
   Salt and freshly ground
   pepper to taste*
1 *clove garlic, finely minced
   Tabasco to taste*

1. Arrange the onion rings in the bottom of a salad bowl.

2. Arrange the shrimp over the onions.

3. Sprinkle with feta cheese and cover with watercress.

4. Drop the cherry tomatoes into boiling water to cover and let stand exactly 12 seconds. Drain quickly and run under cold water. Drain well. Use a small paring knife and pull away the skin of each tomato. Garnish the salad bowl with the tomatoes.

5. Combine the remaining ingredients in a bottle and shake well. Pour the dressing over the salad and toss well.

Yield: 4 servings.

Lobster and Tarragon Salad

1 *egg yolk*
1 *tablespoon prepared
   mustard, preferably Dijon
   or Düsseldorf*
1 *tablespoon tarragon wine
   vinegar
   Tabasco
   Salt and freshly ground
   pepper to taste*
½ *cup peanut, vegetable, or
   corn oil
   Juice of ½ lemon*
1½ *cups cubed cooked lobster
   meat (see note)*
3 *hard-cooked eggs, cut into
   ½-inch cubes*
1 *cup chopped celery*
2 *tablespoons capers*
1 *tablespoon finely chopped
   fresh tarragon or 1
   teaspoon dried*
1 *tablespoon finely chopped
   parsley*
3 *tablespoons finely diced
   green pepper*

1. Place the yolk in a mixing bowl and add the mustard, vinegar, Tabasco, and salt and pepper to taste. Blend well with a wire whisk. Add the oil gradually, beating vigorously with the whisk. Beat in the lemon juice.

2. When the mixture is thickened and smooth, add the lobster, eggs, celery, capers, tarragon, and parsley. Blend with a spatula and spoon the salad into a serving dish. Sprinkle with the green pepper and serve.

Yield: 6 servings.

Note: Cooked crab meat or cubed white fish such as cod or striped bass may be substituted for the lobster.

Fish Salad Espagnole

1½ cups carrots, sraped and
     cut into ½-inch cubes
1½ cups turnips, peeled and
     cut into 1-inch cubes (see
     note)
     Salt to taste
½   cup green pepper, cored,
     seeded, and cut into
     ¾-inch cubes
1   egg yolk
1   tablespoon prepared
     mustard, preferably Dijon
     or Düsseldorf
2   teaspoons vinegar
     Tabasco
     Freshly ground pepper to
     taste
1   cup olive oil
3   cups freshly cooked white-
     fleshed non-oily fish such
     as striped bass or weakfish
     (see recipe for poached
     striped bass, page 243)

1. Cook the carrot and turnips separately. Cover each with cold water to cover and salt to taste. Bring to the boil and simmer until just tender, about 10 minutes. Drain.

2. Add the cubed pepper to another saucepan and add water to cover and salt to taste. Bring to the boil and simmer about 1 minute. Drain immediately.

3. Put the yolk in a mixing bowl and add the mustard, vinegar, Tabasco, and salt and pepper to taste. Start beating with a wire whisk and gradually beat in the oil until thickened and smooth.

4. Combine the fish and vegetables. Add half the mayonnaise and stir gently to blend.

5. Arrange the fish salad in a mound on a serving dish and spoon the remaining mayonnaise over it. Serve at room temperature.

Yield: 6 to 8 servings.

Note: If turnips are not available, substitute an equal amount of new potatoes or green peas cooked until tender.

An Oriental Barbecue

The Vietnamese Version

For better or for worse (and we consider it our loss), we have never been in Vietnam. For a long time, however, we have been intrigued with the brief glimpses and flavors of Vietnamese cooking we have experienced on occasional visits to Paris, which boasts several very good Vietnamese restaurants. We are still haunted by the foods we have dined on there including the rouleaux du printemps, or spring rolls; the canard lacque, or lacquered duck; and the various and exotic vegetable dishes that frequently contain pousse-bambou, or bamboo shoots, and germes de soja, or bean sprouts.

We know by reputation that the Vietnamese admire spicy foods, and a staple of the table is the delightful nuoc mam, an insidiously good and somewhat salty sauce made with bottled fish essence (it is rather like a light amber colored soy with an intriguing fish flavor).

We have felt deprived over the years never to have had in our possession a really good book that details Vietnamese cooking. Other dishes that have captivated our palate include grilled pork patties, wrapped in fresh lettuce leaves, which provide a marked and delectable contrast to the hot grilled filling; and a marvelous grilled duck dish with a delicate lemon flavor. Both are served with nuoc mam sauce as a dip. We came across an admirable source for these dishes in a new book called *Oriental Barbecues* (Macmillan Publishing Co., 1974, $6.95) by May Wong Trent. It has recipes from China, Mongolia, Korea, Japan, and Indonesia as well as Vietnam.

Here are adaptations for the grilled pork and grilled duck dishes plus another for grilled shrimp patties. There is also the recipe for nuoc mam sauce. The basic fish sauce used in making the nuoc mam is widely available in Chinese food outlets in Manhattan and elsewhere.

Vietnamese Grilled Pork Patties in Lettuce Leaves

The pork

2 pounds ground pork

2 cloves garlic, finely chopped or mashed between wax paper
1 teaspoon grated fresh ginger
1 tablespoon dry sherry or Chinese shao-hsing wine (available in liquor stores in Chinatown)

2   *tablespoons light soy sauce*
    (preferably imported)
2   *tablespoons peanut,*
    vegetable, or corn oil
1   *teaspoon sugar*
    Salt to taste

The wrapping and garnishes

24 *large Boston lettuce leaves,*
    well rinsed and patted dry
1   *cup loosely packed fresh*
    coriander (also called
    Chinese parsley, cilantro,
    and culantro) leaves,
    available in Chinese and
    Spanish markets
1   *cup loosely packed fresh*
    mint leaves
1   *cup chopped scallion*
2   *cups raw rice cooked*
    without salt until tender
    and cooled to room
    temperature
    Nuoc mam sauce (see
    recipe)

1. Combine all the ingredients for the ground pork in a bowl and blend well with the fingers. Place the bowl briefly in the refrigerator. Do not freeze. The chilling will facilitate shaping the patties.

2. Meanwhile, prepare a charcoal fire.

3. With the fingers and palms, shape the pork into 2-inch balls. Make them all approximately the same size.

4. Maneuver each ball into a miniature football shape, approximately 3 inches long. Chill until ready to use.

5. Run a skewer lengthwise

(see note) through each patty and grill, turning frequently, until browned and cooked through. Serve immediately. The technique for eating the patties is as follows: Open a lettuce leaf and add a sprig of Chinese parsley, 1 or 2 mint leaves, chopped scallion, and a small spoonful of rice. Add the hot pork patty and wrap the leaf around. Using the fingers, dip the "package" into the nuoc mam sauce and eat with the fingers.

Yield: 4 to 8 servings.

Note: We cooked the patties prior to skewering. We skewered them after they were cooked to facilitate handling.

Grilled Shrimp Patties in Lettuce Leaves

2   *pounds raw, shelled*
    deveined shrimp
1   *egg, lightly beaten*
2   *scallions, finely chopped*
1   *or 2 cloves garlic, finely*
    chopped or mashed
    between wax paper
2   *tablespoons fish sauce*
    (see note in recipe for
    nuoc mam sauce)
3   *tablespoons peanut,*
    vegetable, or corn oil
1   *teaspoon cornstarch*
½   *teaspoon sugar*

1. Place the shrimp on a flat surface and chop finely with a knife or cleaver.

2. Put the shrimp in a bowl and add the remaining ingredients. Mix well with the hands.

To shape, cook, and serve, follow the instructions for cooking, wrapping and garnishing the grilled pork patties in lettuce leaves.

Yield: 4 to 8 servings.

Grilled Lemon Duck

1 4½-to-5½-pound duck, cut into quarters
4 scallions, trimmed and finely chopped
1 teaspoon grated fresh ginger
2 teaspoons powdered turmeric
2 tablespoons dark soy sauce (see note)
1 teaspoon sugar
   Salt and freshly ground pepper to taste
½ teaspoon grated lemon rind
   Lemon wedges
   Nuoc mam sauce

1. Quarter the duck or have it quartered. If the backbone is removed it will lie flatter on the grill. It will also cook more evenly if the wing tip and second wing bone are removed. Use a sharp knife and trim away all peripheral and excess fat.

2. Combine the scallions, ginger, turmeric, soy sauce, sugar, salt and pepper, and lemon rind. Rub the mixture into the duck. Let stand 4 hours or so, turning the duck pieces in the marinade.

3. Meanwhile, prepare a charcoal fire. When the fire is ready, place the duck fat side down.

Cook about 1 hour, turning the duck frequently and as necessary until it is evenly cooked and the skin crisp. Serve with lemon wedges. Serve individual small bowls of nuoc mam sauce on the side as a dip for the duck.

Yield: 4 servings.

Note: The usual soy sauce served in America is light soy sauce. Dark sauce, a basic ingredient for Chinese cookery, is somewhat heavier both in color and density. It is widely available in Chinese groceries including those listed for fish sauce (see note for nuoc mam sauce).

Nuoc Mam Sauce

1 cup fish sauce (see note)
1 tablespoon finely chopped, peeled fresh ginger
2 cloves garlic, finely chopped
1 teaspoon hot red pepper flakes or a little cayenne to taste
3 tablespoons lemon juice
2 tablespoons sugar
¼ cup water

1. Combine all the ingredients and stir to blend. Serve equal portions into individual bowls and serve with Vietnamese dishes. Leftover sauce may be kept refrigerated for a week or longer.

Yield: About 1½ cups.

Note: Fish sauce is widely available in Chinese groceries.

Among them, in Manhattan, are the United Supermarket, 84 Mulberry Street; Yuet Hing Market, 23 Pell Street; and the Wing Fat Company, 35 Mott Street. May Wong Trent suggests that a light soy sauce (preferably imported) such as that found on most American supermarket shelves may be substituted for the fish sauce.

The Mongolian Version

We have long nourished a keen appetite for a Genghis Khan or Mongolian "barbecue" in which foods were cooked at table over a curved grill that resembles a rather broad and shallow helmet.

The name is said to derive from the twelfth century when the hordes of the conqueror built fires under their rounded metal headpieces and cooked their lamb, or whatever else was at hand, on top. We found the upper portion of this grill recently at The Bridge Kitchenware Corp., 212 East 52d Street, in Manhattan. The cost of the grill is $10 and it does not come with a base.

The Mongolian grill is made with thinly sliced meat—lamb, beef, chicken, and so on—dipped in or brushed lightly with a soy sauce and ginger mixture. The meat is grilled quickly and dipped into more of the sauce before eating. After the meat is cooked, other items, such as watercress, mushrooms, bean curd, and spinach are added to the grill. This is a guest participation dish in which those assembled cook their own foods.

While there are some minor negative aspects to the Mongolian grill, these are far outweighed by positive virtues. It is almost imperative, for example, that the grill be used out of doors and guests dress accordingly. No silks and satins, for the oil tends to sputter into the air when the foods are cooked.

In the Orient, Korea, for example, there are special metal charcoal bases for the grills on which the grill sits precisely. Without such a base it is necessary to improvise with a round hibachi or small charcoal grill with the same circumference. The charcoal fire must be very hot.

In her book, *Oriental Barbecues,* May Wong Trent offers her version of the Mongolian fire grill and proposes that the foods may be cooked on a makeshift heavy metal cookie sheet placed over an electric grill or charcoal fired hibachi. Here is our version of the Mongolian dish prepared once in collaboration with Virginia Lee, the Chinese cooking instructor.

The Mongolian curved grill is prepared for thinly sliced sirloin.

Genghis Khan Grill

1½ pounds top sirloin or round
   steak or any well-marbled
   cut (boneless lamb or
   chicken, thinly sliced,
   could be substituted for
   the beef)
1 cup light soy sauce
   (preferably imported)
¼ cup finely minced fresh
   ginger
3 tablespoons finely minced
   garlic
2 tablespoons dry sherry or
   shao-hsing Chinese wine,
   (available in liquor stores
   in Chinatown)
3 scallions, finely chopped
¾ teaspoon sugar
   Salt to taste
½ teaspoon hot red pepper
   flakes, optional

½ cup peanut, vegetable, or
   corn oil
½ pound spinach, well
   washed and drained,
   optional
2 bunches watercress, tough
   stems removed, optional
1 pound zucchini, trimmed
   and cut into small "sticks"
   or batons about 2 inches
   long and ½ inch square
½ pound fresh bean sprouts,
   optional
2 pads fresh bean curd,
   available in Chinese
   markets, optional
½ pound mushrooms, thinly
   sliced, optional

1. Slice or have the meat sliced as thinly as possible against the grain. It should be sliced as for sukiyaki or shabu-shabu or a Chinese chrysanthemum pot. Arrange the meat in one layer, slightly overlapping, on a platter or on small, individual dishes. If desired and the slices seem too thick, they may be pounded lightly with a flat mallet to make them thinner.

2. In a small bowl combine the soy sauce, ginger, garlic, wine, scallions, sugar, salt, and red pepper flakes.

3. Brush or spoon a little of the sauce over the meat when it is ready to be cooked.

4. Place the vegetables on individual serving plates or in bowls. The kinds of vegetables do not matter but there should be several.

5. Start a fire with charcoal in a unit over which the Mongolian grill will sit securely. The circumference of the charcoal base should approximate that of the Mongolian grill. Use sufficient charcoal to create intense heat. Make certain that the charcoal unit is well-insulated so as not to burn the table on which it sits. We used a portable round concrete slab.

6. When the charcoal is ready, add the top part of the grill. Brush the top of the grill with oil and pour about ⅛ inch around the inside rim. Add a few teaspoons of sauce to the oil.

7. Using chopsticks or a fondue fork, let each guest prepare and cook his own food, first adding the beef to the grill and then alternately the remaining ingre-dients. Initially the meat will probably tend to stick to the grill, but we find that as the cooking progresses and the grill becomes "cured" through heat and oil, the foods will cook without sticking. As the oil and sauce disappear in cooking, add a little more of both. Continue adding oil and sauce as necessary. Serve with hot, freshly cooked rice.

Yield: 4 servings.

Note: The top grill sections for this dish are available, in Manhattan, at The Bridge Kitchenware Corp., 212 East 52d Street. The cost of the grill top is $10. It may be used over a round hibachi or charcoal burner with approximately the same circumference.

The foregoing column, which was written in August, began with the wistful thought that we had never, to our regret, been in Vietnam. As readers of this volume may find, we made it to Vietnam in December, and an account of our discoveries can be found on pages 339–343. There are several foods in the Vietnamese kitchen to which we became addicted during our stay in Saigon. One of them is Chinese parsley which is really fresh coriander leaves. It is a widely used herb in the cuisines of not only Vietnam, but Mexico, India, Puerto Rico, and, of course, China. In Spanish, the name is both culantro and cilantro. It has a strangely appealing pungent and, to some minds, musty flavor. It has thousands of uses both as a seasoning and as a garnish.

September 1974

W HEN WE WERE very young, we had a cook, a warm, kind and generous lady, who could never be persuaded to buy a jar of mayonnaise. When asked why she always made her own, she said, "Any food tastes better if you beat a little love into it." It's true, of course; with rare exception, any food tastes better if it is salted, smoked or "put up" by yourself. Inasmuch as we have access to great fresh produce, it comes as second nature to us to put up enough tomatoes each September to last at least six months. Not only is it a practical and economical thing to do, you simply cannot buy canned tomatoes of equal caliber. We have a passion for fresh tomatoes in any form, be it in salads, soups, or sauces, and nothing gives us more comfort or gratification than the sight of a long pantry shelf stocked front to back and wall to wall with a few score jars of red ripe tomatoes of our own processing. For how to put up tomatoes and process other end-of-summer delights, see page 257.

The Ultimate Cheesecake

WITH PIERRE FRANEY

It is at times mind-boggling to discover the extent to which one ingredient can alter, even glorify, the nature of a dish. Some years ago, we came into possession to a cheesecake recipe that seemed to be the essence of all great cheesecakes. It was delicate, rich, and subtly flavored. Moreover, it was ultimately refined in texture. Sometime later, we purchased a pound of toasted hazelnuts at the Maison Glass, New York's finest source for toasted nuts. These we ground and blended into the cake's batter. The result is to our minds a paradigm of cheesecakes. We hasten to add that hazelnuts are a luxury. Already toasted, a pound costs $5 at Maison Glass. Many supermarkets carry untoasted hazelnuts which may be roasted in home ovens before using.

Hazelnut Cheesecake

1½   cups shelled, toasted, hulled hazelnuts or blanched, toasted almonds
       Butter
⅓   cup graham-cracker crumbs, approximately
2   pounds cream cheese, at room temperature
½   cup heavy cream
4   eggs
1¾   cups sugar
1   teaspoon vanilla extract

1. Because of the importance of oven temperature, the nuts must be toasted well in advance of proceeding with the recipe. If your hazelnuts are untoasted, preheat the oven to 400 degrees. Place the nuts on a baking sheet or in a skillet and bake them, stirring them often so that they brown evenly. When nicely browned, remove them and let cool.

2. When ready to make the cheesecake, preheat the oven to 300 degrees.

3. Place the nuts in the container of an electric blender or food processor and blend. If you want a crunchy texture, blend them until coarse-fine. If you want a smooth texture, blend them until they are almost pastelike.

4. Butter the inside of a metal cake pan 8 inches wide and 3 inches deep. Do not use a springform pan.

5. Sprinkle the inside with graham-cracker crumbs and shake the crumbs around the bottom and sides until coated. Shake out the excess crumbs and set aside.

6. Place the cream cheese, cream, eggs, sugar, and vanilla into the bowl of an electric mixer. Start beating at low speed and, as the ingredients blend, increase the speed to high. Continue beating until thoroughly blended and

smooth. Add the nuts and continue beating until thoroughly blended.

7. Pour and scrape the batter into the prepared pan and shake gently to level the mixture.

8. Set the pan inside a slightly wider pan and pour boiling water into the larger pan to a depth of about ½ inch. Do not let the edge of the cheesecake pan touch the other larger pan. Set the pans thus arranged inside the oven and bake 2 hours. At the end of that time, turn off the oven heat and let the cake sit in the oven 1 hour longer.

9. Lift the cake out of its water bath and place it on a rack. Let the cake stand at least 2 hours.

10. Place a round cake plate over the cake and carefully turn both upside down to unmold the cake. Serve lukewarm or at room temperature.

Yield: 12 or more servings.

Note: The 8-inch-wide, 3-inch-deep metal pans are available, in Manhattan, at The Bridge Kitchenware Corp., 212 East 52d Street. The consistency of the cake is softer than most cheesecakes.

Putting Up Tomatoes (and While You're at It)

Random thoughts for the end of summer: Who steals my store-bought tomatoes steals trash; who steals my hand-processed tomatoes steals gold.

Although there has been some recent rain, rarely can we remember a time of such prolonged drought as we've endured the last few months. Despite the vagaries of the season, however, the local markets are coming into their own now with a bountiful supply of tomatoes, an abundance of new cabbages, and a score of other marvels to "put up" for the winter ahead.

For us, the "putting up" of foods offers the same sense of gratification as found in breadmaking. Last week we stopped at our favorite
market, The Green Thumb, in Water Mill, and loaded the back of the car
with a bushel of so-called canning tomatoes. These are the ones that sell
at a special price because of a minor blemish here and there. The going
rate, and apparently it will continue there, is $6 a bushel. Other markets
sell similar produce from about that price to $8 a bushel. Each bushel of
tomatoes yielded 18 quarts of processed tomatoes, an approximate cost of
35 cents per quart. The last time we bought tomatoes at our local supermarket the cost was about $1.11 a quart.

Herein we offer a potpourri of good things for the end of summer—
things to be processed. They include home-cured sauerkraut made from
fresh cabbage; an end-of-summer relish from a friend in New Jersey;
and, by special request, a recipe for pesto sauce plus instructions for
freezing it. Incidentally, the relish recipe calls for green tomatoes. These
are available on special order from tomato-producing markets in the
greater New York area.

One of the best and most comprehensive books on home canning is
The Blue Book of Canning, published by the Ball Corporation, manufac-
turers of mason jars. The book is available for $1 postpaid by writing the
Ball Corporation, Muncie, Indiana 47302. The recipe for sauerkraut,
printed here, is adapted from that book. A companion volume on freezing fresh produce is also available for 50 cents.

Processing Tomatoes

1. If the tomatoes still have traces of soil on them, rinse well and drain.

2. Bring enough water to the boil to cover the tomatoes when they are added. When the water is vigorously boiling, add a batch of tomatoes. Use extreme caution, taking care that the water does not splash on you. Let the tomatoes stand 30 seconds (a few seconds longer isn't critical, but don't overdo it).

3. Have an empty colander, a basic size or a large one, handy. Again with extreme caution drain the tomatoes and run under cold water. Let stand until cool enough to handle.

4. Cut out the cores from the tomatoes and peel them. After the boiling-water bath, the skin comes away easily.

5. Leave the tomatoes whole or quarter them. Pack them into quart, pint, or, ½-pint jars. Press the air spaces in the jars with a spatula to release the air. Add a few crushed tomato pieces to the jar to bring the tomatoes to within ½ inch of the rim (be sure to leave the ½ inch of head space).

6. Add 1 teaspoon of salt for each quart of tomatoes. If avail-able, add a small sprig or a leaf of fresh basil to each jar.

7. Wipe the top of each jar and add a lid and screw top. Seal tightly.

8. Arrange the jars in the rack of a canner in hot but not boiling water. The canner should be at least half full of water before the jars are added. When the jars on the rack are lowered into the water, they should be covered by 1 or 2 inches.

9. Cover the canner and bring the water to the boil. After it boils, process pint jars 35 minutes, quart jars 45 minutes. During processing, the water should remain at a gentle but steady boil.

10. Lift the rack from the canner and let it rest on its supports. Remove the jars from the water and let stand at room temperature for 12 hours. If desired, screw bands may now be removed from the jars. To test for sealing, press down the center of the lid. If the dome is already down or remains down when pressed, the jar is properly sealed.

Note: One bushel of tomatoes weighs approximately 50 pounds and makes about 18 quarts of home-processed tomatoes.

Making Sauerkraut

50 *pounds white cabbage*
1 *pound pure granulated salt*
  (noniodized)

1. Remove and discard the outer leaves and any other bruised or otherwise blemished leaves of the cabbage.

2. Cut the cabbage into halves, then into quarters. Cut away the white tough center cores.

3. Using a shredder or sharp slicer, cut the cabbage into fine shreds about the thickness of a penny.

4. In a kettle combine 5 pounds of the shreds with 3 tablespoons of salt. Blend well and let stand 15 minutes or so, until the cabbage wilts and gives up part of its liquid. Transfer this to a large sterilized crock. Add alternate layers of cabbage and salt, pressing down gently but firmly after each layer is added until juice comes to the surface. Continue until the crock is filled to within 3 or 4 inches of the top.

5. Cover the cabbage with a clean white cloth such as a double layer of cheesecloth, tucking in the sides against the inside of the container. Add a free-floating lid that will fit inside the crock and rest on the cabbage. Failing this (perhaps even preferably), add a clean, heavy plastic bag containing water to rest on top of the cabbage. Whatever method is used, the lid or covering should extend over the cabbage to prevent exposure to the air. Air will cause the growth of film yeast or molds. The lid will also act as a weight and should offer enough weight to keep the fermenting cabbage covered with brine. Store the crock at room temperature. The ideal temperature is from 68 to 72 degrees.

6. When fermentation occurs, gas bubbles will be visible in the crock. Total time of fermentation is approximately 5 to 6 weeks.

Yield: Enough for about 18 quarts.

How to preserve fresh sauerkraut

When the sauerkraut has fermented sufficiently, empty it into a large kettle and bring it just to the simmer. Do not boil. The correct simmering temperature is from 185 to 210 degrees. Remove the sauerkraut from the heat and pack it into hot sterilized jars. Cover with hot juice to about ½ inch from the top of the rim. Close and seal the jars with a lid and screw top. Put in a water bath and boil pint jars for 15 minutes, quart jars for 20 minutes. The sauerkraut is now ready to be stored. It will keep on the shelf for months.

Jerry Komarek's End-of-Summer Relish

1	2½- to 3-pound head of new cabbage
8	to 12 onions, peeled
10	to 12 green tomatoes, cored
12	sweet green peppers
6	sweet red peppers
½	cup pure granulated salt
1	tablespoon celery seeds
6	cups sugar
2	tablespoons mustard seeds
1½	teaspoons turmeric
4	cups cider vinegar
2	cups water

1. Remove and discard the tough outer leaves from the cabbage. Halve and quarter the cabbage and cut away the core.

2. Separately, put the vegetables through the medium blade of a food grinder. There should be about 4 cups each of onions, green tomatoes, and cabbage. There should be about 5½ cups of green peppers and 3 cups of ground sweet red pepper.

3. Combine the ground vegetables and salt in a large mixing bowl. Cover with plastic and refrigerate overnight. Rinse the vegetables and drain well.

4. Empty the vegetables into a stainless steel or enamel pot. Combine the remaining ingredients and add them. Blend thoroughly. Bring to the boil and simmer about 3 minutes.

5. Pour the relish into sterilized jars and seal tightly with a lid and screw top. Put in a water bath and process for 3 minutes.

Yield: 8 pints.

Blender Pesto
(Basil and nut sauce for pasta)

We've never been all that keen on home gardening, basically because of a lazy nature and a life-long abhorrence for weeding. There is a small herb garden outside the kitchen door and it has kept us supplied through the hot months with parsley (both curly and flat leaf), rosemary, sage, chives, thyme, tarragon, and fresh coriander. None of these has been as self-assertive as our basil. We have been asked many times this summer how to make and freeze pesto, and we can think of no better formula and technique than the one outlined by our friend, Marcella Hazan, in her *Classic Italian Cook Book*, (Harper's Magazine Press, 1973, $12.50).

2 *cups fresh basil*
½ *cup olive oil*
2 *tablespoons pine nuts (pignoli)*
2 *cloves garlic, peeled Salt to taste*
½ *cup freshly grated Parmesan cheese*
2 *tablespoons grated Romano pecorino cheese (or increase the quantity of Parmesan by this amount)*
3 *tablespoons butter at room temperature*

1. Remove all tough stems from the basil. To measure, pack the leaves gently but somewhat firmly in a measuring cup without crushing the leaves.

2. Empty the basil into the container of an electric blender. Add the olive oil, pine nuts, garlic, and salt and blend on high speed. Using a rubber spatula, scrape the sides down occasionally so that it blends evenly. Pour the mixture into a bowl and beat in the grated cheeses by hand. Beat in the softened butter.

3. When ready to serve, the pesto should be emptied into a bowl and left to stand until it is room temperature. When the pasta is cooked and before draining, quickly add and stir 1 or 2 tablespoons of the hot pasta water into the pesto. Toss with the hot drained pasta and serve.

Yield: Enough for 6 servings.

How to freeze pesto

Prepare the above recipe for pesto but do not add either cheese or butter to the blended basil mixture. Spoon it into a plastic container or freezer jar, filling the container almost to the brim. Seal and freeze. When ready to serve, defrost overnight in the refrigerator. When completely thawed, proceed with the above recipe.

More Chickens

Over the years we've observed that in times of dolorous economics and depressed finances, chicken is the food likeliest to grace the tables of rich and poor alike. In the sixteenth century, it was not idle semantics that Henry IV wished no subject in his realm so poor as to not have a chicken in his pot every Sunday. One of the latest expositions to pinpoint the relation of chickens to parlous times appeared in *The New York Times*. It was a chart that showed percentage changes in the cost of 16 commonly accepted items in the United States over the last 30 years. Both a ticket to a Broadway show and a Nathan's hot dog had increased 150 per cent. A pounds of round steak had increased 100 per cent and a pair of men's shoes 120 per cent. But a pound of chicken had decreased 9 per cent during the same three decades.

To explore the reasons for this phenomenon we went to our favorite source for poultry, Salvadore Iacono, a "custom" poultryman whose farm is just a mile or two outside of town. The Iacono farm has been a source of chickens for, among other notables, Robert Montgomery (before he moved), Phyllis Newman, Adolph Green, and Richard Benjamin. Jacob Javits has reputedly eaten his poultry and so has Henry Kissinger.

Mr. Iacono stated that the reason chicken is historically and universally a good food is because of "efficiency."

"The amount of feed necessary to produce a pound of flesh," he added, "is relatively small." And there is a relatively short feeding period from the time of incubation to the time a chicken is ready for the table. A small squab chicken that weighs about two pounds is ready to eat in five weeks. A three-pound chicken is ready for frying or broiling at the end of six or eight weeks. Roasters and capons, which are among the best buys, require four to five months to mature. At the Iacono market, both roasters, now selling for 59 cents a pound, and capons, now selling for 75 cents a pound, are excellent buys. Each bird, properly cooked, will serve six to eight people.

The cost of chicken is by no means the least of its virtues. Chicken is easily conceivable as the most versatile of foods, adapting itself as it does to countless herbs and spices and scores of ways to cook it including roasting, broiling, frying, grilling, stewing, and barbecuing. Or as prepared in the following recipes.

Cuisses de Volaille aux Herbes

(Baked chicken legs with herbs)

---

16 *chicken legs with thighs attached, about 1 pound each*
   Salt and freshly ground pepper to taste
8 *tablespoons butter*
1½ *cups fresh bread crumbs*
2 *tablespoons finely chopped shallots*
2 *teaspoons finely chopped garlic*
4 *tablespoons chopped parsley*
1 *teaspoon chopped thyme*
2 *teaspoons chopped fresh rosemary*
½ *cup dry white wine*

1. Preheat oven to 425 degrees.

2. Sprinkle chicken pieces with salt and pepper.

3. Melt the butter in a baking dish large enough to hold the legs in one layer. Add the chicken legs and turn them in the butter until well coated. Arrange the pieces skin side down in one layer.

4. Place the chicken legs in the oven and bake 30 minutes.

5. Meanwhile, combine the bread crumbs, shallots, garlic, parsley, thyme, and rosemary.

6. Turn the chicken pieces skin side up and sprinkle with the bread crumb mixture. Bake 30 minutes longer. Pour the wine around (not over) the chicken pieces. Bake 5 minutes longer and serve.

Yield: 8 to 16 servings.

Paupiettes de Volaille Florentine

(Chicken rolls stuffed with spinach)

---

1 *pound fresh spinach*
¼ *pound fresh mushrooms*
8 *very thin slices prosciutto or boiled ham*
3 *tablespoons butter*
1 *cup finely chopped onion*
2 *small cloves garlic, finely minced*
1 *cup cold cooked rice*

Salt and freshly ground
pepper to taste
3   *whole, skinless, boneless*
    chicken breasts, about
    1½ pounds
    Flour for dredging
⅜   *cup finely diced carrot*
¼   *cup finely diced celery*
2   *tablespoons flour*
½   *cup dry white wine*
1   *cup chicken broth*
1   *tablespoon tomato paste*
1   *sprig fresh thyme or ½*
    teaspoon dried
½   *bay leaf*

1. Preheat oven to 375 degrees.

2. Pick over the spinach. Pull off and discard any tough stems. Rinse the leaves thoroughly to remove any trace of sand. Drop the spinach into boiling salted water and cook about 1 minute, stirring. Drain immediately in a colander.

3. When the spinach is cool enough to handle, press it between the hands to extract excess liquid. Put the spinach on a board and chop it finely with a knife. Set aside.

4. Slice the mushrooms and chop them. Set aside. There should be about 1¾ cups.

5. Cut 2 of the prosciutto slices into thin strips. Chop finely. Set aside.

6. Heat 1 tablespoon of butter in a skillet and add ½ onion, 1 small clove of garlic, and ½ cup of diced mushrooms. Cook about 3 minutes and add the chopped prosciutto. Stir in the spinach and rice. Sprinkle with salt and pepper and stir until blended. Set aside to cool.

7. Split each chicken breast in half. Trim away and discard the cartilage and nerve tissues. Place the chicken breast halves skinned side down on a flat surface and pound lightly with a flat mallet or the bottom of a clean skillet. Center a slice of prosciutto on each chicken breast. Spoon equal amounts of filling down the center of each chicken breast half. Roll the end of the chicken over to enclose the filling and tuck in the bottom and top. Tie each bundle in 2 places with string.

8. Dredge each bundle in flour seasoned with salt and pepper.

9. Heat the remaining 2 tablespoons of butter in a skillet large enough to hold the pieces and brown them all over, about 10 minutes.

10. Remove the chicken pieces and add the remaining onion, mushrooms, and garlic. Cook briefly and add the carrots and celery, stirring. Sprinkle with 2 tablespoons flour and add the wine, stirring with a wire whisk. Cook 5 minutes and add the broth and tomato paste. Stir to blend and add the thyme and bay leaf. Return the chicken rolls to the skillet. Cover with a round of wax paper and place in the oven. Bake 30 to 40 minutes or until chicken is tender.

11. Remove chicken rolls and discard the strings. Serve hot with the sauce spooned over. The leftover chicken rolls are good cold.

Yield: 6 servings

Stuffed Chicken Thighs Esterhazy

12 large chicken thighs
¾ pound ground pork
¾ cup finely chopped onion
1 clove garlic, finely minced
1 teaspoon finely chopped rosemary
½ teaspoon sage
2 tablespoons chopped parsley
1 egg yolk
½ cup fine bread crumbs
   Salt and freshly ground pepper to taste
4 tablespoons butter
2 green peppers, about ½ pound
½ pound onions
½ pound mushrooms
1 teaspoon finely chopped garlic
2 tablespoons flour
2 tablespoons paprika
½ cup dry white wine
2 cups rich chicken broth

1. Bone the chicken thighs or have them boned by the butcher. Save the bones. Do not remove the skin. Set aside.

2. Cook the ground pork in a skillet, stirring to break up any lumps, until the meat loses its pink color. Add the onion, garlic, rosemary, sage, parsley, egg yolk, bread crumbs, salt and pepper.

3. Place the chicken thighs skin side down on a flat surface and flatten them lightly with the flat side of a mallet or the bottom of a clean skillet. Sprinkle with salt and pepper.

4. Add about 2 tablespoons of filling to the center of each thigh and bring up the edges to enclose the filling, envelope-fashion. Tie with string.

5. Heat the butter in a large skillet and add the stuffed thighs skin side down. Brown them about 8 minutes and scatter the reserved bones around the thighs. Turn the chicken in order to brown on all sides.

6. Meanwhile, core and seed the green peppers. Cut the peppers into ½-inch strips. There should be about 3 cups. Set aside.

7. Peel the onions and cut them in half. Cut them into thin slices. There should be about 3 cups. Set aside.

8. Slice the mushrooms. There should be about 3 cups. Set aside.

9. When the chicken thighs are browned on all sides, remove them from the skillet. Add the peppers, onions, mushrooms, and garlic. Sprinkle with flour and paprika and stir in the wine, stirring constantly. Cook about 2 minutes and add the chicken broth. Cook about 5 minutes and return the thighs to the skillet, skin side up. Cover and simmer about 30 minutes. Remove the chicken to a serving platter and discard the strings and bones. Cover with foil to keep warm.

10. Tilt the pan in which the chicken cooked and skim off the surface fat. Return the sauce to the heat and pour it over the thighs.

Yield: 6 to 12 servings.

Chicken Breasts with Mushrooms

3 *whole, skinless, boneless chicken breasts, halved (6 pieces)*
¼ *pound mushrooms*
2 *teaspoons lemon juice*
6 *tablespoons butter*
2 *teaspoons finely chopped shallots*
   Salt and freshly ground pepper to taste
2¼ *cups fresh bread crumbs*
1 *tablespoon finely chopped parsley*
6 *thin slices ham, preferably prosciutto*
2 *eggs*
1 *teaspoon peanut oil, plus oil for deep frying*
   Flour for dredging
¼ *cup finely chopped chives, optional*

1. Preheat oven to 400 degrees.

2. Place each of the chicken pieces between pieces of plastic wrap and pound to flatten lightly without breaking the meat.

3. Slice, then chop the mushrooms finely or slice and blend until coarse-fine in an electric blender. Add the lemon juice.

4. Heat 2 tablespoons butter in a skillet and add the shallots. Cook briefly and add the mushrooms. Sprinkle with salt and pepper and cook about 3 minutes. Add ¼ cup bread crumbs and parsley.

5. Remove plastic and sprinkle the chicken pieces with salt and pepper, and center a piece of ham on each. Spoon equal portions of the mushroom mixture in the center and roll to enclose the filling. Place on a tray and chill.

6. Beat the eggs with the teaspoon of oil and salt and pepper to taste.

7. Dip the chicken rolls first in flour, then in beaten egg, and finally coat them all over with remaining bread crumbs.

8. Heat the oil and cook the chicken roolls until golden brown all over. Drain.

9. Place the chicken rolls on a baking dish and dot with remaining butter. Bake, basting frequently, about 15 minutes. Serve sprinkled with chopped chives.

Yield: 6 servings.

Northern Indian Cookery

Over the years it has seemed that through one default or another Manhattan has rarely boasted an Indian restaurant of almost unfailing distinction. In traditional places where the food is passably cooked, the ventilation is often execrable. If both the food and ventilation pass muster, the service is more often than not something of Olympic indifference. Thus, it is a source of comfort to discover an Indian establishment that has, over a recent period of time, spurred in us both abundant and continuing enthusiasm. It is the Gaylord Restaurant at 50 East 58th Street in the Blackstone Hotel. It is modestly but impressively designed, well-staffed and—as New York restaurants go—relatively inexpensive.

In addition to such virtues, it is, to the best of our knowledge, the only Indian restaurant in the city with genuine tandoors or tandoori, the authentic Indian hot-fired clay ovens. We find these ovens an enormous plus, for without them an authentic "tandoori chicken"—and that of the Gaylord is equal to the best we've eaten in New Delhi or London—cannot really be made. The ovens are also used to excellent purpose for "baking" several delectable Indian breads including nan (a puffed egg bread made with milk, cream, and yogurt) and paratha, made with whole wheat flour.

A tandoor is a deep, wood- or charcoal-fired receptacle, generally made of clay and resembling an urn. At the Gaylord the tandoors are visible to the public and they offer one of the more interesting food preparation spectacles in town. The foods include not only the chicken (baked on skewers) and breads (dampened and applied by hand to the walls of the tandoor) but a laudable sheekh-kabab, cumin-flavored ground meat also cooked on long metal skewers.

There are numerous dishes at Gaylord's of the "curry" type and the assortment of desserts is quite special. The principal chef of the restaurant is a tall, muscular, steel-faced gentleman named Daulat Ram Sharma, a native of Old Delhi and for a long period a chef in New Delhi's world-famed Moti Mahal Restaurant. The chef in charge of the incredible desserts is Ram Dass, also of Old Delhi and former chef of the Bengal Sweet House in the capital city.

They spent a recent morning and part of an afternoon in our kitchen in East Hampton along with Jati Hoon, one of the restaurant's owners, who acted as translator. The chefs, in the kindest of spirits, offered us a cornucopia of instruction in Northern Indian cookery. We were regaled with recipes for two fine appetizers the sheekh-kabab—and a wondrous

Ram Dass, left, is dessert chef at the Gaylord Restaurant, and Daulat Ram Sharma is the principal chef.

boneless chicken dish called murghi tikka, the meat marinated in spiced yogurt. There were three dishes that would be given the catch-all name of "curry" in this country—one chicken, one shrimp, and one lamb—one eggplant dish, and two desserts.

Gaylord's is open seven days a week. Main courses are priced from about $2.75 to $5.75. One of the best bargains in town is the mixed tandoor platter priced at $6.95. The telephone number is 212-759-1710.

Note: Recipes for other Indian dishes can be found on pages 155–158.

Murghi Tikka
(Skewered chicken)

1   *2½- to 3-pound chicken, cut into serving pieces*
1   *cup yogurt*
   Salt to taste
¼   *teaspoon turmeric*
1   *clove garlic, finely minced*
1   *teaspoon freshly grated ginger or ½ teaspoon powdered*
6   *drops yellow food color*

1. Pull off and discard the skin of the chicken or use the skin for soup. It is easy to skin the chicken, using the fingers and a dry clean towel for tugging when necessary. Using a paring or boning knife, cut the meat of the chicken from the bones in as large portions as possible. Save the bones for soup. Cut the meat into 2-inch cubes and set aside.

2. Combine the remaining ingredients and stir to blend. Add the chicken chunks and stir to coat. Cover and let stand several hours or overnight.

3. Skewer the chunks on a spit and grill over hot charcoal (see note) just until cooked through and still moist inside. Do not overcook or the chunks will become dry. Cooking time will vary, but 10 minutes is about average.

Yield: 4 to 6 servings.

Note: The skewered chicken is preferably cooked by turning it on the spits over direct charcoal heat without using a grill. If necessary, however, the chicken may be cooked on the grill, turning frequently so that it cooks evenly.

Sheekh-Kabab

(Ground lamb on skewers)

1   *pound finely ground lamb(see note)*
1   *egg yolk*
    Salt to taste
2   *teaspoons sweet paprika Cayenne, finely chopped hot peppers, or hot red pepper flakes to taste*
⅓   *cup coarsely grated onion*
1   *teaspoon finely chopped garlic*
¾   *teaspoon powdered ginger*
1   *teaspoon grated fresh ginger*
1½ *teaspoons ground coriander*
2   *teaspoons ground cumin*

1. Combine all the ingredients in a mixing bowl and mix well with the hands.

2. Divide the mixture into 6 or 8 approximately equal portions. Shape each portion onto a spit (preferably with square rather than round sides) and, using fingers dampened in cold water, press the mixture closely into thin oval shapes around the spit. Continue adding the portions, ends touching, up and down 1 or 2 spits.

3. Cook, turning the spit or spits frequently, over a very hot charcoal fire. It is best if the spits are turned over the heat without using a grill. Or, if you prefer, do not use spits and shape the meat into small oval patties about the size of frankfurters. Cook on a hot grill over charcoal, turning the pieces frequently.

Yield: 6 to 8 portions.

Note: The lamb should be ground 3 times or blended in a food processor.

Jingha Tarhi

(Prawn curry)

2¼ *pounds large shrimp*
½   *cup peanut, vegetable, or corn oil*
1   *large onion, coarsely chopped, about 1½ cups*
½   *teaspoon celery seed*
1   *tablespoon finely minced garlic*
½   *cup water*
    Salt to taste
1   *teaspoon turmeric*
2   *teaspoons ground coriander*
1   *teaspoon ground cumin*

2 *teaspoons paprika*
½ *cup yogurt*
2 *tablespoons chopped fresh coriander leaves, optional*
   Juice of ½ lemon

1. Shell and devein the shrimp. Rinse and drain well and set aside.

2. Heat the oil in a deep saucepan and add the onion. Cook about 10 minutes, stirring often. When the onions start to turn a golden brown, add the celery seed, garlic, and half the water. Cook about 3 minutes and add the salt, turmeric, ground coriander, cumin, and paprika. Cook, stirring, about 3 minutes, and add the yogurt and remaining water.

3. Cook about 4 minutes and add the shrimp. Cook 8 to 10 minutes, stirring frequently. Cover and cook about 10 minutes. Sprinkle with fresh coriander and lemon juice. Serve hot.

Yield: 6 or more servings.

Murghi Massala
(Chicken curry)

---

1 *3-pound chicken, cut into serving pieces*
⅔ *cup peanut, vegetable, or corn oil*
1 *large onion, coarsely grated, about 1½ cups*
1 *4-inch piece cinnamon stick*
2 *whole, unhusked cardamom seeds or ½ teaspoon ground*

1 *tablespoon finely minced garlic*
2¼ *cups water*
1 *cup yogurt*
⅓ *cup fresh ginger, cut into pieces the size of paper match sticks or 1 tablespoon grated*
1 *teaspoon turmeric*
2 *teaspoons sweet paprika*
1 *teaspoon powdered ginger*
½ *teaspoon ground cumin*
1 *teaspoon ground coriander*
   Salt to taste
½ *cup heavy cream*

1. Pull off and discard the skin of the chicken or use the skin for soup. It is easy to skin the chicken, using the fingers and a dry clean towel for tugging.

2. Heat the oil in a large, heavy kettle and add the onion. Cook, stirring, about 5 minutes until the onion is dry but not brown. Add the cinnamon and cardamom seeds and continue cooking, stirring, until onion is golden brown. Add the garlic and ¼ cup water.

3. Add the yogurt and cook briskly, stirring, about 5 minutes. Add the chopped ginger, turmeric, paprika, powdered ginger, cumin, coriander, and 1 cup of water.

4. Cook, stirring, about 5 minutes and add the chicken pieces. Add salt to taste. Cook 20 minutes, stirring frequently.

5. Add the remaining cup of water and cook about 10 minutes, stirring often. Add the cream and bring to the boil. Cook about 2 minutes.

Yield: 4 to 6 servings.

Bakhara Pasanda
(Curried lamb)

½ cup peanut, vegetable, or
corn oil
1 large onion, coarsely
grated, about 1½ cups
2 whole, unhusked
cardamom seeds or
½ teaspoon ground
½ teaspoon ground ginger
1 2-inch piece cinnamon
stick
2 whole cloves
1 tablespoon finely minced
garlic
2⅔ cups water
½ cup yogurt
2 pounds lean lamb, cut into
2-inch cubes
Salt to taste, about
3 teaspoons
½ cup heavy cream

1. Heat the oil in a large, heavy kettle and add the onion. Cook, stirring, about 5 minutes and add the cardamom seeds, ground ginger, cinnamon, and cloves. Cook, stirring frequently, about 10 minutes longer.

2. When onion starts to brown, add the garlic and ⅔ cup of water. Simmer briefly and add the yogurt and lamb, stirring to coat the pieces. Sprinkle with salt and cook over brisk heat, stirring often, about 5 minutes. Cover.

3. Cook about 30 minutes until the sauce is quite dry. Stir often as the stew cooks. Add the remaining 2 cups of water and cover again. Cook 30 minutes longer, stirring to prevent sticking.

4. Add the heavy cream. Cook, uncovered, about 15 minutes longer.

Yield: 4 to 6 servings.

Bangan Bartha
(Spiced eggplant)

2 eggplants, about 1 pound
each or slightly less
8 tablespoons butter
2 cups finely chopped onion
Salt to taste
1 cup red, ripe tomatoes,
cored and cut into thin
wedges
½ cup fresh ginger, cut into
small cubes or thin sticks
the size of match sticks
¾ cup sliced hot green
peppers or use hot red
pepper flakes to taste
1 teaspoon sweet paprika
3 tablespoons chopped fresh
coriander leaves, optional

1. Place the eggplants on a hot charcoal grill or wrap them in heavy-duty aluminum foil and bake in a very hot (500-degree) oven about 20 minutes. If the eggplants are to be grilled, turn them often over the hot coals. Cook until the eggplants are capsized and thoroughly tender throughout. Remove and let stand until cool enough to handle.

2. Melt the butter in a saucepan.

3. When the eggplants are cool, pull away the skin, scraping off and saving the tender inside pulp. Scoop the tender pulp into the saucepan with the butter. Discard the skins.

4. Add the onion to the eggplant and cook 10 minutes, stirring often and taking care that the mixture does not stick to the bottom and burn.

5. Add salt to taste and the tomatoes. Add the ginger, peppers, and paprika and cook, stirring often while scraping the bottom to prevent scorching. Cook about 15 minutes and remove from the heat. Add the chopped coriander. Serve hot, lukewarm or at room temperature.

Yield: 4 to 8 servings.

Ras Malahyee

(A sweet cheese dessert)

Let would-be cooks be advised that this is one of the most delectable of Indian sweets. It also requires several separate steps to prepare, including an hour to stir and boil a quart of milk until reduced to 1 cup.

    3 quarts milk
    6 tablespoons mild white
       vinegar
    6 quarts cold water,
       approximately
    8 cups granulated sugar
    1 tablespoon flour
    ⅓ cup blanced pistachio nuts
       for garnish

1. Place 1 quart of milk in a flat bottom skillet and cook it, stirring with the flat end of a pancake turner. Stir almost constantly until the milk is slightly thickened and reduced to about 1 cup. Let cool, then chill.

2. Meanwhile, place remaining 2 quarts of milk in a casserole and bring to the boil, stirring constantly, about 15 minutes. Strain the milk into a deep flat dish and add the vinegar, stirring. The milk will curdle.

3. Place the dish in a basin and add 6 cups cold water and cover the surface with a thin cloth or triple layer of cheesecloth. Using a ladle, scoop out much of the liquid or "whey," leaving the "cheese" solids beneath the cloth.

4. Add 6 cups cold water and let stand briefly. Ladle out more liquid. Empty the cheese into the cloth, bring up the 4 edges of the cloth. Let drain, then twist the cloth to extract most of the liquid from the cheese. When ready, the cheese will seem quite dry but pliable.

5. Turn the cheese out into a flat clean pan and knead it well. Shape it into a ball.

6. Bring 2 quarts of water to the boil in a wide casserole and add 8 cups of sugar. Boil briskly about 10 minutes.

7. Blend the flour with about 3 tablespoons of cold water and stir two-thirds of it into the syrup.

8. Pull off a small handful of the cheese and work it with the hands into a sausage shape about 1 inch thick. Break off pieces and roll the pieces into 1-inch balls. Flatten them into small round pillows, using the hands. Continue until all the cheese is used.

9. Drop the cheese rounds into the boiling syrup and cook about 5 minutes, stirring with a slotted spoon while ladling the syrup over and around the rounds. Stir in the remaining water-flour mixture. When not stirring, keep the slotted spoon in a cup of cold water.

10. Carefully ladle out 2 cups of the syrup, letting the cheese rounds continue to simmer. Set the 2 cups of syrup aside to cool. When cool, add about 1½ cups of cold water.

11. Meanwhile, continue cooking the cheese rounds for 20 minutes. As the cheese rounds cook, have 2 cups of cold water standing by. About every 2 minutes dribble a little of the cold water into the simmering syrup. This will help control the temperature of the syrup.

12. Lift the cheese rounds from the syrup and drop them into the cold syrup that was set aside earlier. Let stand until cool. Drain and discard or use the syrup for another purpose. Chill the rounds. Arrange the rounds in one layer in a serving dish and pour over them the cold reduced milk. Garnish with pistachios.

Yield: 20 cheese rounds.

Jalabi

(Indian sourdough fritters in syrup)

4¼ *cups plus 6 tablespoons water*
6 *cups granulated sugar*
1 *cup sourdough starter (use any standard formula; there is one on page 83)*
6 *tablespoons flour*
1 *teaspoon stem saffron*
Oil or fat for frying

1. Prepare a simple syrup by combining 4 cups of water with the granulated sugar. Let simmer about 30 minutes until a light syrup forms. On a candy thermometer the syrup should register about 200 degrees. Let cool.

2. To 1 cup of sourdough starter stir in about 6 tablespoons each flour and water. Add more flour or water as necessary to make a batter like a pancake batter.

3. Put 1 teaspoon of loosely packed stem saffron into a mortar and add about ¼ cup cold water. Mash and grind until well blended. Add this to the starter mixture.

4. Heat liquid fat to a depth of about 1 inch in a skillet until quite hot.

5. Ladle the batter into a pastry bag fitted with a number 5 pastry tube (the one with a small round opening at the tip). Quickly squirt the batter into the hot fat, making various patterns—rounds with every increasing circles, zig-zag shapes, and so on. Cook until crisp, turning once.

6. Remove and drop into the hot syrup. Let stand briefly and transfer to a serving dish. Serve at room temperature. These may be refrigerated.

Sublime Meat Loaves

WITH PIERRE FRANEY

"Gourmet" is one of the most embarrassing and overworked words in the English language. When anyone asks us, "Do you cook gourmet dishes?" it reminds us of the telegram allegedly sent to Samuel Goldwyn in which an author asked, "Would you like to buy a 100,000-word manuscript?" To which Goldwyn replied, "I don't know. How long are the words?" So-called gourmet cooking does not of necessity imply truffles and foie gras. Any dish that is soaringly good to the senses—an expertly cooked hamburger, a platter of sauerkraut, or a well-made meat loaf—can fall into the sublime category. The meat loaves in this column, in addition to a basic goodness, have one thing in common: They all contain vegetables.

Meat and Spinach Loaf

1 *pound loose fresh spinach or 1 10-ounce package*
1¼ *pounds ground veal, pork, or beef or a combination of all*
½ *cup fresh bread crumbs*
Salt to taste
1½ *teaspoons freshly ground pepper*
¼ *teaspoon grated nutmeg*
½ *cup coarsely chopped celery*
½ *cup loosely packed parsley*
¼ *cup milk*
1 *clove garlic, finely minced*
1 *tablespoon butter*
½ *cup finely chopped onion*
2 *eggs, lightly beaten*
3 *slices bacon*

1. Preheat oven to 350 degrees.

2. If the spinach is in bulk, pick it over to remove any tough stems. Rinse the spinach well in cold water, drain, place in a saucepan, and cover. It is not necessary to add liquid; the spinach will cook in the water clinging to the leaves. Cook about 2 minutes, stirring once or twice. Transfer to a colander and douse with cold water to chill. Drain and press with the hands to extract most of the moisture. Chop the spinach.

3. Put the meat in a mixing bowl and add the chopped spinach. Add the bread crumbs, salt to taste, pepper, and nutmeg.

4. Put the celery, parsley, and milk in the container of an electric blender. Blend well and add to the meat mixture. Add the garlic.

5. Heat the butter in a small skillet and add the onion. Cook until wilted and add it to the meat mixture.

6. Add the eggs and blend well with the hands. Shape and fit into an oval or round baking dish, or place in a loaf pan. Cover with the bacon and bake 1¼ to 1½ hours. Pour off the fat and let the loaf stand for 20 minutes before slicing. Serve, if desired, with tomato sauce.

Yield: 6 to 8 servings.

Veal and Mushroom Loaf

⅔ pound mushrooms
1 tablespoon butter
½ teaspoon thyme
8 tablespoons finely chopped onion
1 teaspoon finely chopped garlic
¼ bay leaf or ⅛ teaspoon powdered
2 pounds ground veal
1½ cups fresh bread crumbs
⅓ cup milk
3 eggs
  Salt and freshly ground pepper to taste
3 tablespoons finely chopped parsley
  Sauce Alexandre (see recipe)

1. Preheat oven to 350 degrees.

2. Chop the mushrooms into pieces slightly smaller than ½-inch cubes. There should be about 3 cups.

3. Heat the butter in a heavy skillet. Add the mushrooms and thyme.

4. Chop onions, garlic, and bay leaf together. Add to the mushrooms. Cook until the mushrooms have given up most of their liquid, then scrape mixture into a mixing bowl and let cool.

5. Add the veal and bread crumbs.

6. Combine the milk and eggs and beat until well blended. Add this to the meat mixture. Add salt and pepper to taste and parsley and work the mixture with the hands until thoroughly blended.

7. Pack the mixture into a 9-by-5-by-3-inch loaf pan. Wet the hands and smooth the top. Bake 1¼ hours. Let stand about 15 minutes. Serve sliced with sauce Alexandre. (For a fillip, add a tablespoon of grated horseradish to the sauce.)

Yield: 8 or more servings.

Sauce Alexandre
(Mushroom and cream sauce)

4   *tablespoons butter*
4   *tablespoons flour*
1   *cup chicken broth*
    Salt and freshly ground
    pepper to taste
½   *pound mushrooms*
1   *tablespoon finely chopped*
    shallots
¼   *cup dry white wine*
1½ *cups heavy cream*

1. Melt 3 tablespoons of butter in a saucepan and add the flour, stirring with a wire whisk. When blended and smooth, add the chicken broth, stirring vigorously with the whisk. When blended and smooth, season with salt and pepper to taste and let simmer, stirring occasionally, about 10 minutes. This is called a velouté.

2. Slice the mushrooms thin. There should be about 3½ cups.

3. Melt remaining 1 tablespoon of butter in a saucepan and add the mushroom slices. Sprinkle with salt and pepper to taste and cook, stirring occasionally, until the mushrooms give up their liquid. Add the shallots and stir. Cook until most of the liquid in the saucepan has evaporated.

4. Add the wine and cook until almost all the wine is re-duced. Add the velouté and cream. Stir to blend well. Bring to the boil and season to taste with salt and pepper.

Yield: About 2½ cups.

Note: This sauce goes well with poached fish or chicken.

Chicken Loaf with Watercress Sauce

2   *pounds skinless, boneless*
    chicken breasts
1   *cup finely chopped onions*
2   *egg yolks*
2   *cups fine, fresh bread*
    crumbs
⅔   *cup heavy cream*
1   *cup finely chopped*
    watercress
¼   *teaspoon grated nutmeg*
    Salt and freshly ground
    pepper to taste
    Watercress sauce (see
    recipe)

1. Preheat oven to 400 degrees.

2. Cut the chicken into cubes, place it in an electric blender or food processor and blend, stirring down as necessary. This may have to be done in two or more steps.

3. Scrape the mixture into a mixing bowl and add the remaining ingredients, except for sauce. Blend well, pour into a 6-cup loaf pan and cover with wax paper. Add a close-fitting-lid.

4. Set the mold inside a larger heat-proof utensil and pour boiling water around it. Bake 1½ hours or until set and cooked through. Serve sliced and hot with watercress sauce.

Yield: 6 to 8 servings.

Watercress sauce

6   *tablespoons butter*
6   *tablespoons flour*
3   *cups chicken broth*
1   *bunch watercress*
1   *cup heavy cream*
    Salt and freshly ground pepper to taste
¼   *teaspoon grated nutmeg*

1. Melt 4 tablespoons butter in a saucepan and add the flour, stirring with a wire whisk. When blended, add the broth, stirring rapidly with the whisk. Cook about 20 minutes, stirring often.

2. Meanwhile, cut off and discard the tough bottom stems of the watercress. Drop the cress into a small saucepan of boiling water and simmer about 30 seconds. Drain, squeeze to extract most of the liquid and chop. There should be about ⅓ cup. Set aside.

3. Add the cream to the sauce. Add the salt and pepper to taste and nutmeg. Simmer about 15 minutes. Strain the sauce through a very fine sieve. Return it to a saucepan and stir in the watercress. Swirl in the remaining 2 tablespoons of butter and serve piping hot.

Yield: About 3 cups.

October 1974

I N OCTOBER we wrote about a friend of long standing, an extraordinary dessert cook named Maida Heatter, the daughter of the late Gabriel Heatter, in his day a titan among news commentators. Maida is married to a man named Ralph Daniels, who for many years owned a cozy little restaurant in Miami Beach for which Maida supplied all the desserts. We are absolute foils for corny jokes pertaining to food, and one of the things we remember most about meeting Maida and Ralph is the following story he told us about omelets.

A man walked into a restaurant, sat down and began to read the menu. He noticed listed among the entrees "an elephant omelet." The waitress came to his table and asked, "What would you like, sir?" "The elephant omelet," he said. "How many?" she asked. "Just one," he replied. And the waitress, alarmed, said, "You don't think the chef is going to go out and kill an elephant just to serve you one omelet?" (See what we mean? Corny.)

On one occasion we were pleased to offer Maida a recipe for a cheesecake which she considers one of the best in the world. It is included in her book, as are the other recipes outlined on pages 285–287.

O Splendid Callinectes Sapidus!

WITH PIERRE FRANEY

One of the great (and none too abundant) prizes of American waters is known in unusually informed circles as *Callinectes sapidus*. This is the blue or hard-shell crab of the Atlantic, found from Cape Cod to the Florida Keys. For some reason crab meat is rarely listed among the hors-d'oeuvre riches (caviar, foie gras, smoked salmon, lobster) in classic culinary literature, which seems odd, for it certainly ranks with lobster as one of the treasures of the sea. Crab meat is a versatile delicacy. It makes a splendid key ingredient for curried soup; Maryland crab cakes are a delight and so are crab fritters.

Curried Crab Soup

4 *tablespoons butter*
½ *cup finely chopped onion*
1 *clove garlic, finely minced*
½ *cup peeled, cored, and finely diced apple*
1 *tablespoon curry powder*
3 *tablespoons flour*
½ *cup peeled, chopped, fresh ripe tomato*
3 *cups chicken broth*
 Salt and freshly ground pepper to taste
½ *pound lump or backfin crab meat, picked over*
½ *cup heavy cream*
 Tabasco
 Chopped parsley for garnish

1. Melt the butter in a saucepan and add the onion. Cook, stirring, until wilted and add the garlic and apple. Stir briefly and sprinkle with the curry powder and flour.

2. Add the tomato and chicken broth, stirring rapidly with a wire whisk. When thickened and smooth, add the salt and pepper to taste and crab meat and simmer 10 minutes. Add the cream and bring to the boil. Add a touch of Tabasco. Serve piping hot with chopped parsley garnish.

Yield: 6 servings.

Maryland Crab Cakes

1 *pound backfin or lump crab meat*
¼ *cup finely chopped parsley*
1 *cup chopped scallions*
1¾ *cups fresh bread crumbs*
2 *eggs*
¼ *cup milk* 2 tbs mayo
 Tabasco

1   *teaspoon worcestershire
    sauce
    Salt and freshly ground
    pepper to taste*
1½–2 *tablespoons prepared
    mustard, preferably Dijon
    or Düsseldorf
    Oil for deep frying
    Tartar sauce*

1. If necessary, pick over the crab meat to remove any traces of shell or cartilage.

2. Empty the crab into a mixing bowl and add the parsley, scallions, and ¾ cup of the bread crumbs.

3. In another bowl, beat the eggs and add the milk, Tabasco to taste, worcestershire sauce, salt and pepper to taste, and mustard.

— Mayo

4. Blend well and pour this over the crab mixture. Stir gently to blend, leaving the crab as whole as possible. The mixture will seem rather wet and loose, but it is manageable when the cakes are finally coated with bread crumbs.

5. Shape the crab into oval or round cakes and dredge them in the remaining crumbs. Press between the hands to make the crumbs adhere and the cakes hold together.

6. Heat the oil for deep frying to 325 degrees and cook the cakes in a basket until golden brown all over. Drain and serve hot with tartar sauce.

Yield: 6 crab cakes.

Beignets de Crabe
(Crab fritters)

1½ *cups flour
    Salt and freshly ground
    pepper to taste*
2   *tablespoons olive oil*
¼   *teaspoon grated nutmeg
    Tabasco*
2   *eggs, separated*
1   *cup milk*
1   *cup finely chopped
    scallions*
1   *pound crab meat, lump, or
    backfin, picked over well*
½   *cup corn, vegetable, or
    peanut oil
    Sauce tomate aux herbes
    (see recipe)*

1. Put the flour in a mixing bowl and add salt and pepper to taste, olive oil, nutmeg, and Tabasco to taste. Add the yolks of the eggs and gradually add the milk, stirring constantly with a whisk.

2. Add the scallions and fold in the crab meat.

3. Beat the egg whites until stiff and fold them in.

4. Heat the ½ cup of oil in a heavy skillet and add spoonfuls of the crab mixture. The quantity of each spoonful is optional. The fritters may be very small, only a tablespoon or so, or rather large, 4 tablespoons. Cook until brown on one side, turn and cook until brown on the other. Drain on paper towels. Serve with tomato sauce.

Yield: 20 to 40 fritters.

Sauce tomate aux herbes

4 *tablespoons butter*
1 *medium onion, chopped*
   (about ⅔ cup)
1 *teaspoon finely chopped*
   garlic
2 *tablespoons flour*
1 *1-pound-1-ounce can*
   imported tomatoes with
   tomato paste
1¼ *cups fresh or canned*
   chicken or beef broth
4 *leaves fresh basil, chopped,*
   or ½ tablespoon dried
¼ *cup finely chopped parsley*
   Salt and freshly ground
   pepper to taste

1 *teaspoon dried oregano,*
   crushed

1. Heat half the butter in a saucepan and add the onion and garlic. Cook until onion is wilted.

2. Sprinkle with flour and stir to distribute it evenly. Add the tomatoes and broth, stirring with a whisk until blended and smooth. Add the basil, parsley, salt and pepper to taste, and oregano. Bring to the boil and simmer, stirring frequently, about 30 minutes. Swirl in the remaining butter and serve.

Yield: About 3 cups.

Recipes for crab cakes are as controversial as those for Indian pudding, Boston baked beans, and clam chowder. We have yet to print a recipe for Maryland crab cakes without receiving letters of protest from dyed-in-the-wool Marylanders expressing outrage over one ingredient or another. Most Maryland crab cake recipes insist on a large quantity of mayonnaise. The recipe printed here is our version of what Maryland crab cakes should taste like if they were properly made.

To produce the crab meat mentioned in these recipes (unless you buy it out of the shell which is the convenient and sensible thing to do, particularly if you do not have a great deal of patience), the crabs have to be steamed. Place the crabs in a steamer and steam, covered, over boiling water for about 20 minutes. Let the crabs cool, then remove the pointed "apron" on the underside of each crab by lifting up with a small knife and pulling. Pry the top shell off by holding it in one hand and the body of the crab in the other. Female crabs have a lot of roe (eggs) tucked in the corner points of the top shell. This is quite edible and easy to extract. You should pull away and discard the gray, spongy lungs on either side of the opened up crab body. Crack the crab with the fingers and using a fork, chop sticks, or whatever, extract the white and delicate flesh that fills up the body of the crab, saving the yellow roe from the females. Use the crab roe along with the crab meat. It is a great delicacy.

A Terrific Dessert Cook

For Freudian reasons all our own, we've been haunted through the years by two characters in fact and fiction. One of them was the mythological old king named Sisyphus, who was condemned to roll a boulder up a hill in Hades only to have it tumble back unvaryingly just as he reached the top. Yet, we've always thought his woes small compared to those of Thomas Carlyle, who began a history of the French Revolution in 1835. After months of labor on Volume I, he sent the original and only handwritten copy to a friend to have the work annotated. By grievous mischance the volume was tossed into a fire. Carlyle took up his pen again and at the end of round two commented understandably that not for a hundred years has any book come "more direct and flamingly from the heart."

We mention this to celebrate the publication this month of Maida Heatter's estimable new *Book of Great Desserts* (Alfred A. Knopf, 1974, $10). We visited Miss Heatter in her Miami Beach home about three years ago, and she showed us the original manuscript. We say manuscript in the original sense of the word from the medieval Latin, manuscriptus, meaning "written by hand." It was a lengthy, impressive, well-organized work, and a short while later she shipped the book to a publisher in Manhattan. The book was accepted for publication almost on sight. That would have made for a happy ending except for one thing: Shortly after receiving a letter of acceptance from her publisher, a stove-repair man arrived at Maida's home and discovered that the oven tem-

Maida Heatter, in her kitchen. Clockwise from the top are her prune-pecan cake, the flan, and the pepper poundcake.

perature was almost 25 degrees awry. With singular dedication and patience she returned to the kitchen and started from Chapter 1. Tortes.

We have always thought that Miss Heatter (she is the daughter of the late Gabriel Heatter, the newscaster, and the wife of Ralph Daniels, a retired restaurateur), is one of the world's best home dessert makers and her book reflects her taste. There is lots of chocolate, and we requote her line that it is "the sexiest flavor on earth." There are cakes and meringues and cookies and sauces and garnishes.

In the beginning, there is also a valuable introduction explaining such things as "The Kinds of Chocolate," "How to Clarify Butter," "How to Decorate with Pistachios" and so on. Here is a small sampling of recipes from the *Book of Great Desserts*.

Pepper Poundcake

Fine, dry bread crumbs
3   *ounces cream cheese*
½   *pound (1 cup) butter*
¼   *teaspoon salt*
½   *teaspoon allspice*
¾   *teaspoon black pepper,
     finely ground (freshly
     ground is best)*
1   *tablespoon vanilla extract*
1   *cup dark brown sugar,
     firmly packed*
1   *cup granulated white sugar*
7   *eggs*
3   *cups sifted cake flour*

1. Adjust rack one-third up from bottom of oven. Preheat oven to 350 degrees. Butter a 9-by-3½-inch tube pan. Line the bottom with paper. Butter the paper and dust it all lightly with bread crumbs.

2. In large bowl of electric mixer, cream the cheese and ½ pound butter with the salt, allspice, pepper, and vanilla. Add both sugars and beat for 2 or 3 minutes, scraping the bowl occasionally with a rubber spatula.

3. Increase speed to high and add the eggs one at a time, scraping the bowl with the spatula and beating until each is thoroughly incorporated. The mixture will look curdled. Reduce the speed to low and gradually add the flour, continuing to scrape the bowl with the spatula and beating only until smooth.

4. Turn the batter into the prepared pan. Level batter by briskly rotating the pan in opposite directions. Let stand for 10 minutes before baking.

5. Bake for 80 to 85 minutes or until a cake tester comes out dry. (The top of this cake frequently cracks deeply. It is to be expected and doesn't matter.) Remove from oven and let stand on a rack for 10 to 15 minutes. Cover with a rack or cooky sheet. Invert. Remove pan and paper, cover with a rack and invert again to cool right side up. Let stand 8 to 10 hours or overnight before serving.

Yield: 12 to 16 portions.

Tropical Flan

This tropical custard, flavored with lime, is baked in one large caramelized dish. It has an exquisite flavor and texture. Best made a day ahead.

1⅓ *cups sugar*
  4 *cups light cream*
     Finely grated rind of 1 large lime
  3 *tablespoons lime juice*
 12 *egg yolks*
  2 *10-ounce packages frozen raspberries, optional*

1. Adjust the rack to the center of the oven and preheat oven to 350 degrees.

2. Caramelize 1 cup of the sugar (reserve remaining ⅓ cup) by placing it in a heavy skillet over moderately high heat. Stir occasionally with a wooden spatula until the sugar starts to melt, and then stir constantly until it has all melted to a smooth caramel. It should be a rich brown but do not let it become too dark, or it will have a bitter burnt taste. If it is not cooked long enough, it will be tasteless.

3. Immediately pour the caramelized sugar into a 2-quart soufflé dish or other round ovenproof dish. Using potholders, quickly tilt and turn the dish to coat the bottom and almost all the way up on the sides. Continue to tilt and turn the dish until the caramel stops running. Set aside.

4. Scald the cream, uncovered, in a heavy saucepan or in the top of a large double boiler over boiling water. Meanwhile, mix the lime rind and juice together and set aside. In a large mixing bowl, stir the yolks just to mix. When the cream forms tiny bubbles around the edge and a slight wrinkled skin on top, remove it from the heat. Add the remaining ⅓ cup of sugar and stir to dissolve. Very gradually, just a bit at a time at first, add it to the yolks, stirring constantly. Strain and then gradually stir in the lime rind and juice.

5. Pour into the caramelized dish. Place in a large pan; the pan must not touch the sides of the dish and must not be deeper than the dish. Pour hot water into the large pan to about two-thirds of the way up the sides of the custard dish. Cover loosely with a cooky sheet or large piece of aluminum foil.

6. Bake for 1¼ hours, or until a small knife inserted into the center comes out clean. Do not make any more knife tests than necessary. Do not insert the knife all the way to the bottom of the custard or it will spoil the appearance when inverted. Remove from hot water and place on a rack. Cool uncovered to room temperature. Refrigerate 10 to 24 hours. Do not stint on the chilling time (see note).

7. If necessary, cut around the upper edge of the custard to release. Choose a dessert platter with a flat bottom and enough rim to hold the caramel, which will have melted to a sauce. Place the platter upside down over the custard. Carefully invert. Remove the dish. Refrigerate. Serve very cold.

Yield: 6 to 8 portions.

Optional: Serve with a side dish of thawed and partly drained frozen raspberries.

Note: If flan is underbaked or if it is not refrigerated long enough, it will collapse when cut. It is best not to invert it too long before serving. The shiny coating will become dull as it stands. To remove hardened caramel from utensils, place them in the sink and let hot water run over them until the caramel disappears.

Prune-Pecan Cake

Fine, dry bread crumbs
1½ *cups sifted all-purpose flour*
½ *teaspoon baking soda*
¼ *teaspoon salt*
1½ *teaspoons grated nutmeg*
1¼ *cups pitted, stewed prunes (about 15 extra-large prunes)*
Finely grated rind of 1 lemon
1½ *tablespoons lemon juice*
¼ *pound (½ cup) butter*
1½ *cups sugar*
2 *eggs*
⅔ *cup buttermilk*
½ *pound (2¼ cups) pecans, cut or broken into large pieces*
Confectioners' sugar, optional

1. Adjust rack one-third up from the bottom of the oven. Preheat oven to 400 degrees. Butter a 9-by-3½-inch tube pan and line the bottom with paper. Butter the paper. Dust all over lightly with crumbs.

2. Sift together the flour, baking soda, salt, and nutmeg. Set aside. Cut prunes in quarters. (If they are very small, just cut them in halves.) Spread out on paper toweling to drain. Mix lemon rind and juice and set aside.

3. In small bowl of electric mixer, cream the butter. Add the sugar and beat well. Add eggs one at a time. Beat for 2 to 3 minutes. On lowest speed add about half of the dry ingredients, then all of the buttermilk, and finally the remaining half of the dry ingredients, scraping the bowl as necessary with a rubber spatula and beating only until smooth after each addition.

4. Remove from mixer. Turn into a large bowl. Stir in lemon rind and juice, then prunes and nuts. Turn batter into the prepared pan. Rotate pan briskly to level batter.

5. Bake 1 hour or until cake tester comes out dry and top springs back when lightly touched. Remove from oven and cool in pan on a rack for about 20 minutes. Cover with a rack and invert. Remove pan and paper. Finish cooling on rack, either side up—the top will be flat. Cooled cake may be covered with confectioners' sugar applied through a fine strainer.

Yield: 10 portions.

Hamburger Aristocracy

WITH PIERRE FRANEY

We were about to state that ground beef has more uses than plastic. We will revise that to say it has more uses than filet mignon or sirloin. A hamburger, perfectly made, can be one of the glories of a grill, and a meat loaf is, as we've noted often, only one version of pâté. Ground beef is given an uncommon stature in the recipes here. There are hamburgers à la russe, ground-meat patties with a cream sauce (flavored with a trace of cognac), and beef balls Stroganoff.

Boulettes of Beef Stroganoff

1   pound ground round steak
1   egg, lightly beaten
⅓   cup fine fresh bread crumbs
¼   cup milk
¼   teaspoon grated nutmeg
     Salt and freshly ground pepper to taste
3   tablespoons paprika
4   tablespoons butter
¼   pound mushrooms, thinly sliced

⅓   cup finely chopped onion
¼   cup dry sherry
2   tablespoons brown sauce or canned beef gravy
¼   cup heavy cream
1   cup sour cream
¼   cup finely chopped parsley

1. Place the meat in a mixing bowl and add the egg.

2. Soak the crumbs in milk and add this to the meat. Add the nutmeg, salt and pepper to taste and mix well with the hands. Shape the mixture into balls about 1½ inches in diameter. There should be about 38 to 40 meat balls.

3. Sprinkle a pan with the paprika and roll the meat balls in it.

4. Heat the butter in a heavy skillet and cook the meat balls, turning gently, until they are nicely browned, about 5 minutes. Sprinkle the mushrooms and onions between and around the meat balls and shake the skillet to distribute the ingredients evenly. Cook about 1 minute and partially cover. Simmer about 5 minutes and add the wine and brown sauce.

5. Stir in the heavy cream. Partially cover and cook over low heat about 15 minutes. Stir in the sour cream and bring just to the boil without cooking. Sprinkle with parsley and serve piping hot with fine buttered noodles as an accompaniment.

Yield: 4 to 6 servings

Biftocks à la Russe

(Russian hamburgers)

2 *pounds ground beef,*
  preferably ground round
16 *tablespoons butter*
¼ *teaspoon grated nutmeg*
  Salt and freshly ground
  pepper to taste
2 *cups bread crumbs,*
  approximately
½ *cup finely chopped onion*
1 *tablespoon flour*
¼ *cup dry white wine*
1 *cup sour cream*
½ *cup heavy cream*

1. Put the meat in a bowl and add 12 tablespoons of butter. Add nutmeg, salt and pepper to taste. Mix well and shape the mixture into 16 balls of approximately the same size.

2. Roll the balls, one at a time, in bread crumbs to coat lightly. Flatten each ball into a neat hamburger shape about 1 inch high and 2½ inches in diameter. Score the tops of each patty with the back of a knife, making a crisscross pattern.

3. Heat the remaining butter in a large skillet and add the patties. Cook about 3 minutes until browned on one side, then turn and cook 3 to 5 minutes or longer until done to one's satisfaction. Transfer the patties to a warm platter.

4. Add the chopped onion to the skillet and cook until wilted. Sprinkle with flour and stir to blend. Add the wine, stirring, and when it boils, add the sour cream. When heated thoroughly, remove the skillet and stir the sauce off heat about 1 minute. Add salt and pepper to taste and the heavy cream. Bring just to the boil. If desired, strain the sauce. Serve the sauce, piping hot, over the patties.

Yield: 8 servings.

Ground Meat Patties with Cognac and Cream Sauce

1 *pound ground veal or*
  ground sirloin

¼ pound prosciutto (see
    note), sliced as thin as
    possible
    Salt and freshly ground
    pepper to taste
¼ teaspoon grated nutmeg
¼ cup flour
2 tablespoons butter
¾ cup heavy cream
    Juice of ½ lemon
1 tablespoon cognac

1. Put the veal in a mixing bowl.

2. Cut prosciutto slices into very thin strips, then cut the strips into very fine dice. There should be about ¾ cup. Add the prosciutto to the beef.

3. Add very little salt (the prosciutto is salty), pepper, and the nutmeg. Stir the mixture to blend well and shape it into 4 patties.

Dust the patties on all sides with flour.

4. Melt the butter in a skillet and when it is quite hot, add the meat patties. Cook until golden brown and turn. Reduce the heat and cook the patties until done to the desired degree.

5. Transfer the patties to hot plates and keep warm. Pour off most of the fat from the skillet.

6. Add the cream to the skillet and cook over high heat until it is reduced almost by half. Add the lemon, cognac, and salt and pepper to taste. Stir and serve piping hot on the patties.

Yield: 4 servings.

Note: If prosciutto is not available, substitute thinly sliced boiled ham.

It is probably the 2,000th time to say that hamburger, to our taste, can be infinitely superior to a dull steak. If anyone gave us a slab of filet mignon we would probably put it through a meat grinder and create one of the dishes above. For more ground beef recipes, see pages 274–276.

Ah, Lemon Soufflé

WITH PIERRE FRANEY

Sydney Smith, the English essayist, once described how far distant he was from civilization by noting he was "12 miles from a lemon." We feel similarly. The lemon, like the raspberry and the lime, is one of God's finest creations. Without it some of the world's greatest sauces would be impoverished. There would be no such thing as a cold lemon soufflé, which makes a pleasant ending to a dinner. Happily, lemons are in good supply 12 months a year.

Frozen Lemon Soufflé

12 *egg yolks*
1¾ *cups plus 2 teaspoons*
    sugar
¾ *cup lemon juice (from*
    approximately 4 lemons)
    Grated rind of 1 lemon
½ *cup heavy cream*
6 *egg whites*
    Whipped cream for
    garnish, optional
    Candied flowers for
    garnish, optional

1. Select a skillet with deep sides into which a 2-quart bowl will fit comfortably. Add enough water to come up around the sides of the bowl without overflowing. Remove the bowl and start heating water in skillet.

2. Drop yolks and 1½ cups of the sugar into bowl and beat with a whisk or portable electric mixer until light and lemon colored. Add the lemon juice and, when water is boiling, set the bowl in the skillet and continue beating about 10 minutes or until the egg mix-ture is like a very thick, smooth, and creamy custard. The tempera-ture of the egg mixture at this point should be about 120 to 140 degrees.

3. Scrape the mixture into an-other mixing bowl and stir in the lemon rind. Let cool and chill thoroughly.

4. Prepare a 5-cup soufflé dish. Tear off a length of wax paper that will fit around the out-side of the soufflé dish, adding 1 or 2 inches for overlap.

5. Fold the wax paper length-wise into thirds. Wrap it around the outside of the soufflé dish about 2 inches above the rim, making sure that it overlaps itself at the ends by at least 1 inch. Se-cure it with string or paper clips.

6. Beat the ½ cup heavy cream and when it starts to thicken, add 2 teaspoons sugar. Continue beating until stiff. Fold this into the egg mixture.

7. In a separate bowl beat the whites. When they start to mound, add the remaining ¼ cup of sugar, beating constantly. Continue beating until whites are stiff. Fold them into the soufflé mixture.

8. Pour the mixture into the prepared dish and place in the freezer. Let stand several hours—or overnight—until frozen.

9. Remove the wax paper. Decorate if desired with whipped cream, piped out of a pastry tube, and candied flowers.

Yield: 8 servings.

An Elegant First Course

WITH PIERRE FRANEY

In the days when quenelles de brochet were a rarity outside of grande luxe restaurants, Claude Terrail, patron of Paris's celebrated Tour d'Argent, paid a visit to Manhattan. On two successive evenings he was served quenelles in fine homes on Fifth Avenue. On the third he was taken to the late Henri Soulé's famous Pavillon Restaurant. Extending a menu, Martin Decre, the maître d'hôtel, whispered, "M. Terrail, I recommend quenelles." Terrail looked up. "Tell me, Martin," he said, "are quenelles beginning to replace hamburgers in America?" Terrail's previous dinners, it seems, had been catered by Le Pavillon's kitchen. Quenelles (kuh-*nell*) are made with a forcemeat of fish or seafood and make an elegant first course.

Quenelles de Crevettes

(Shrimp quenelles)

1½ *pounds raw shrimp in the shell*
¾ *pound sole or flounder fillets*
2 *eggs*
Salt and freshly ground pepper to taste
2 *cups heavy cream*
⅛ *teaspoon cayenne*
¼ *teaspoon grated nutmeg*
Shrimp sauce (see recipe)
Finely chopped parsley

1. Peel the shrimp and rinse under cold water to remove the dark vein down the back. Drain well.

2. Place the sole or flounder on a flat surface and run a sharp knife on either side of the thin bone line that runs down the center. Discard the bone. Cut the fish into 1-inch cubes.

3. Place the shrimp and fish into the container of an electric blender or preferably an electric food processor (see note). It may be necessary to do this in two stages if the container is too small to accommodate all the ingredients.

4. Add all the remaining ingredients except the sauce aux crevettes and chopped parsley and blend until thoroughly smooth. Spoon the mousse into a mixing bowl.

5. Butter one or two flameproof cooking utensils large enough to accommodate the quenelles when they are shaped (we used an oval copper baking dish that measured 10 by 16 by 2 inches).

6. To shape the quenelles, have ready two large soup spoons as well as a bowl filled with boiling or very hot water.

7. If you are right-handed, hold one spoon in the left hand and scoop up a heaping amount of the mousse.

8. Dip the other spoon—in the right hand—into the hot water and deftly smooth the top of the mousse held in the left-hand spoon. Dip the right-hand spoon once more into the hot water and scoop the rounded mixture out of the left-hand spoon to make a neat, egg-shaped quenelle. Place it in the buttered cooking utensil. Continue making quenelles, arranging them close together, barely touching.

9. Meanwhile, bring a large quantity of water to the boil in a kettle. Add salt to taste. Ladle enough of the boiling water over the quenelles to barely cover them. Cover closely with a piece of wax paper cut to fit the inside of the cooking utensil. Bring to the boil and simmer gently about 3 minutes. Do not boil. Lift paper and carefully turn each quenelle with a rubber spatula. Remove the cooking utensil from the heat and let stand a couple of minutes. The quenelles are now ready to be finished.

10. Drain the hot quenelles on paper towels, arrange them on a serving dish and spoon enough shrimp sauce over each one to cover it neatly. Serve more sauce on the side. Garnish the center of each quenelle with a small pinch of chopped parsley.

Yield: 26 to 30 quenelles.

Note: For more information about the food processor, see page 69.

Sauce aux crevettes

8 *raw shrimp*
3 *tablespoons butter*
¼ *cup chopped shallots*
¼ *teaspoon finely chopped garlic*
3 *tablespoons cognac*
¾ *cup dry white wine*
6 *tablespoons tomato paste*
1½ *cups fish velouté (see recipe)*
1½ *cups heavy cream*
   Salt and freshly ground pepper to taste
   Cayenne

1. Shell and devein the shrimp, but reserve the shells with the shrimp. Cut the shrimp into ½-inch cubes and refrigerate.

2. Melt ½ tablespoon of butter in a saucepan and add the shells. Cook, stirring, about 1 minute and add the shallots and garlic. Cook, stirring, about 1 minute and pour in 1 tablespoon of cognac.

3. Add the wine and tomato paste and stir to blend. Add the velouté and cream and stir to blend. Add salt and pepper and cayenne to taste. Simmer 20 minutes, stirring occasionally.

4. Put the sauce through the finest sieve available. The ideal sieve is conical, and is known as a chinois in French kitchens. Chinois sieves are available in fine kitchen-supply outlets.

5. As the sauce is sieved, press the solid ingredients with the back of a wooden spoon to extract as much of the liquid as possible. Discard the solid ingredients. Bring the sauce to the boil.

6. In another saucepan, melt ½ tablespoon of butter and add the cubed shrimp. Sprinkle with salt and pepper to taste and cook, stirring, about 1 minute. Add 1 tablespoon of cognac and stir.

7. Pour the sieved sauce over the shrimp. The sauce up to this point can be made in advance and refrigerated.

8. When ready to serve, bring the sauce to the boil and swirl in the remaining 2 tablespoons of butter. Stir in the remaining tablespoon of cognac and serve piping hot.

Yield: 4 to 5 cups.

Fish velouté

4 *tablespoons butter*
5 *tablespoons flour*
2 *cups fish stock (see recipe, page 67, omit tomato)*

1. Melt the butter in a 1½-quart saucepan and when it is melted, add the flour, stirring with a wire whisk.

2. When blended and smooth, add the fish stock, stirring vigorously with the whisk. Cook, stirring frequently, about ½ hour. The velouté must be thoroughly chilled and kept chilled before using.

Yield: About 2 cups.

Fine Dining in Tokyo

If misery loves company, we have garnered some measure of consolation in that food and lodging in the major cities of Japan are only occasionally a shade more costly than in New York. Actually this comes as a pleasant surprise, because we had been warned before leaving Manhattan that the cost of all things large and small in Japan is stratospheric. The cost of a Scotch and soda, we were told, would be in excess of $7; the cost of a modest taxi ride unreckonable. It is happily untrue—the fabrications of alarmists.

Chivas Regal's elixir called Royal Salute does cost $7 a drink, but after all! The most popular brands, including J & B, Cutty Sark, and Black and White, cost about $1.50 for a generous drink. On other costs, a typical taxi ride will cost about $1.50, with the long ride from the Tokyo airport to the center of town perhaps $6. A modest but thoroughly comfortable room with bath at the Okura cost about $29 a night.

Though Tokyo might well claim some of the most expensive restaurants in the world (we are told there are numerous popular and conspicuously costly ones where a $100-a-person tab is not uncommon, but that would also include the attentions of a geisha), it is consoling to know that for every feverishly expensive Japanese restaurant there are scores of yakitori houses, tempura bars, and so on where excellent food may be obtained for as little as $2.

During the course of our stay, we have dined on sushi at midday for about $60 a person, but then we feasted, at the insistence of a host, on luxury fish and fish roe in stunning volume. We have also dined with great pleasure on meals that cost less than $5 a person including sake or beer.

There are numerous reasons for the elevated cost of dining in Japan, including the fact that a strictly limited number of clients are accepted each evening. Each room is served by one or more nakai depending on the number of guests in a party. The nakai attends to pouring sake, serving the numerous individual courses, removing the dishes after each course, and attending to the well-being of each guest.

One thing to remember is that very few if any first-rank restaurants in Japan will accept a customer, Japanese or otherwise, without a reasonable introduction. Westerners generally gain admission through a hotel's vouchsafe or a Japanese business associate or friend. It is advisable, particularly when visiting a fairly formal restaurant, to go with someone who speaks Japanese, preferably someone who is Japanese. Otherwise, you will almost indubitably wind up in the linguistic soup.

If you are planning to visit Japan and are appalled at the thought of eating raw fish (or oysters that come from Hiroshima waters, where some of the best originate), or if soup made with a seaweed base leaves you totally cold, be assured there remain thousands of places almost guaranteed to please the most quarrelsome palate. Among other things, for better or worse, the city has an enormous McDonald's hamburger outlet near the Tennoji railroad station. It is said to have the largest volume in sales of any branch throughout the world. New York may boast that it enjoys the greatest diversity in international restaurants in the world, but Tokyo is almost certainly its peer.

One of the comforts in receiving a dinner or service check in Japan is the knowledge that a service charge has been included in the total, and there is no need to add so much as one yen, not even a sen, as a gratuity. A tip is to many minds here demeaning and at least in questionable taste. Even taxi drivers do not encourage tipping.

When we arrived in Tokyo late one afternoon, our young Japanese host grinned amiably, then expressed his chagrin and dismay that most of the city's best restaurants were closed that evening (it was Sunday). With an air of apology he stated that he would like to invite us to a small, nondescript and crowded yakitori house in the Ginza. We soon arrived in that bustling district and were led into the well-confined entrance of the three-story Torigin Restaurant at 5-5 Ginza. It is a wholly engaging place with jostling room only. To our Western minds, it seemed reminiscent of nothing so much as a Sunday night in the better, popular restaurants of the student quarters in Paris.

Yaki means broil; tori means birds. But the general term yakitori seems to cover almost any skewered grilled dish, and the yakitori in which we reveled included partly boned chicken wings (the best we've ever encountered); cubed chicken livers; umbrellalike black mushroom caps; cubed, medium-rare duck pieces; chicken with black mushrooms; gingko nuts; and quail eggs. All of it served with traditional freshly made pickles, including turnip, cucumber, and baby eggplant. The cost of the various grilled dishes ranges from about 15 cents for the quail eggs to 40 cents for skewered boneless chicken and mushrooms. Rice dishes cost in the vicinity of $1 each. The telephone number of the Torigin is 571-3333, but it won't be of much value because tables are occupied on a first-come first-served basis. It is open seven days a week.

Yakitori could be observed as more or less the Japanese equivalent of hamburger, but in its variety and nature it is infinitely more sophisticated. There seems to be almost universal sides-taking in Tokyo as to the superiority of one fin bec's choice over that of another, and this creates the rather pleasant predicament of having to sample as many yakitori places as time permits. So it was with this challenge that we arrived, at one enthusiast's insistence, at the estimable Kushihachi yakitori house, a comfortable, primitive looking place of contrasting styles— modest modern woodblock prints in league with antiques, a wall air-conditioner, and characteristic wooden benches and barewood tables. Plus a touch of smoke and the pleasant odor of foods being grilled near at hand.

We regaled ourselves there with an appetizing assortment of skewered, grilled dishes including chicken, peppers, ground chicken balls, chicken with mushrooms, scallions, and gizzards.

At the Kushihachi the cost of an elaborate series of yakitori dishes with numerous cups of warm sake was approximately $8 per person. The restaurant is in the Seishido Building, 9-10-3 Roppongi, Minatoku. The restaurant is open from 5 P.M. and is closed Sunday.

It doesn't require an educated guess to speculate that the sushi and sashimi of Tokyo can at its best rival that of almost any place on earth. Some of the best sushi—and, incidentally, some of the most expensive food—we've ever had the good fortune to sample, we found at the Kyubei Restaurant in the Ginza district. It is a tiny restaurant with 11 seats arranged around a neat, polished counter behind which four chefs perform their miracles with a series of well-honed boning knives.

One of the components of sushi is seaweed, which is heated briefly and becomes crisp. Our guide for that meal informed us that the only proper way to eat sushi for a genuine shoku tsu (the Japanese words for connoisseur) is at a counter, otherwise the crispness of the heated seaweed disappears in the seconds a dish is transported from the rice area to the table.

Our sushi feast began with three plump, luscious Japanese oysters on the half shell taken with lemon juice. These were followed by tender, small bite-size slivers of sea ears, a delicacy we had heretofore not sampled; sea urchin roe of remarkable and delicate taste and texture; and pink pickled ginger as a side relish throughout. It cleanses the taste.

We munched on abalone, thinly sliced and available both raw and cooked (we preferred the texture of the cooked abalone), as well as on fresh bay scallops on rice wrapped in seaweed. Among the more than 20 kinds of fish available at Kyubei we also ate sea eel, steamed, grilled and brushed lightly with a savory sauce.

The cost of a traditional series of sushi foods at Kyubei would be in the vicinity of $33 to $66 a person. The address is 5-23, Ginza 8-Chome, Chuo-ku. It is closed Sunday. The telephone number is 571-0523.

It would seem apparent that the chief hallmarks of a fine tempura are two. One is an absence of any apparent oiliness in the various foods when they are served; another is the crisp and fragile nature of the tempura coating as it comes from the wok. One of the best tempuras we've sampled here is that of the Hige-no-Tenpei at 6-1 Chome, Kyobashi, Chuo Ku in Tokyo. It is a series of foods to be marveled at on several counts.

The ingredients are served direct from the wok at a stylish, scrubbed-to-a-polish counter and include shrimp; a fine-fleshed small fish called sillago; small bundles of shimeji, long-stemmed, small-capped, white-fleshed mushrooms; snow white squid; small, mild-flavored green chilies; baby eggplants the size of a midget's index finger; and sea-eel, smooth textured and rich in flavor.

The meal was superior and cost about $17 a person for the complete tempura with fruit for dessert. The Hige-no-Tenpei has "private" dining rooms as well as the tempura bar.

A short while later we were taken to another tempura house, the Inagiku at Ichiba-Dori near Nihonbashi. This is the original of the Japanese restaurant recently opened in the Waldorf-Astoria in New York. It is in a handsome but modest old mansion with the main dining room on the second floor.

The tempura was prepared in a tender batter and cooked in fresh oil. The series included 18 different foods, including small prawns, sea-eel, something translated as kiss fish, white bait, scallops, squid, lotus root, wild mushrooms, eggplant, Japanese celery, and asparagus. All in all, to our taste, it was only a few cuts above what we are accustomed to at tempura bars in New York. The cost, with sake, is about $22 a person.

There are certain restaurants in Japan, we are told, that Japanese men have patronized for a couple of centuries to sip sake and settle those personal animosities that come about in the course of an ordinary day. Arguments of a personal or business nature, our informant told us, are settled in these bistros in a most amicable fashion, for sake has a way of soothing bad tempers and hurt feelings. The prototypes of these places were establishments where working-class people came to solve their frustrations, then the upper class came and agreed that such places were too good for the average man so they opened their own.

These establishments are known as oden restaurants. As the popularity of the sake houses increased, certain foods, known as oden, contrived expressly to complement the drinking of sake, came into being. Oden dishes are rather substantial in contrast to otzumami which are small things, tidbits, appetizers, and the like to be taken with the fingers and eaten with sake.

Our experience (we didn't feel antagonistic toward anything) with oden came about at a small hole-in-the-wall known as Otomi in the New Ginza Daiichi Building, 11-10, Ginza 7-Chome, Chuo-ku. The meal began with appetizers, including cold braised scallops that had been notably cooked in a mixture of soy sauce, sugar, and ginger, followed by a full-bodied clear soup containing slivers of fish, chicken, gingko nuts cooked in various ways(gingko nuts are very big in Japan at this time of year), and matsutake, the meat-flavored wild mushrooms.

Choices were made from a large variety of boiled or steamed foods, including a Japanese version of steamed cabbage, vegetables in consommé, steamed chicken balls, and deep-fried bean curd patties (ganmodoki) made with chopped vegetables. One of the most unusual dishes was a small bowl of cold baked but still rare bonito served like sashimi with a soy and garlic sauce.

The cost of a meal, including six or seven pieces of oden, is about $5. Sake costs about $1 a small bottle.

As you may have noted, most of the restaurants in Japan are specialty places that offer numerous variations on one specific food or method of cooking. Thus, there are sushi and sashimi restaurants; those that serve nothing but dishes made of turtle, for example, or globe fish or noodles. There are places primarily for drinking sake that serve foods designed to go especially well with that notably convivial drink, and there are yakitori restaurants that deal solely (or almost) in grilled chicken pieces on skewers. There are still others where tempura is the main thing.

There are also, however, numerous, perhaps more traditional places, where foods are served in sequence in somewhat formal settings, with guests seated on the floor and served by a hostess in traditional kimono.

We spent a pleasant two hours recently at one such place, the highly acclaimed Ginsaryo Restaurant, Ginza, San-chome, Sanbanchi 3. It is a small, more or less formal restaurant (men may properly remove their jackets) with only seven rooms, and the meal began with the usual steaming face cloth to cleanse the hands and face and a cup of green tea, the national beverage of welcome and cordiality.

The first course consisted of hors d'oeuvres, not so much arranged as designed on various plates. There was fresh salmon and salmon roe; a sweet chestnut; small fish pickled in a sweet soy syrup; and deep-fried shrimp.

Sashimi was served, small slices of fresh-caught Japanese sole and tuna, followed by a bowl of steaming turtle soup containing a small snapper egg. In sequence came an exceptionally good teriyaki dish made with more small fish fillets interlarded with sliced mushrooms, sandwiched between small wooden cedar squares to give flavor and garnished with roasted gingko nuts in the shell.

A chef's fantasy, something dubbed flying dragon's head, appeared. It was a blend of bean curd and fresh lily buds, among other things, deep fried and served in a broth with sliced fish roe and aromatic poached chrysanthemum leaves.

The cost of dinner at Ginsaryo's is about $30 a person and reservations are essential. The telephone number is 561-0355.

If you are in Japan and have never sampled a traditional Japanese breakfast—cho-shoku—you haven't begun to plumb the depths of Japanese dining. There are many Westerners, of course, who would view such a meal—early morning or otherwise—with jaundiced eye, and there are those to whom the thought of eating raw fish—which may or may not figure in a Japanese breakfast—is gastronomic anathema.

One of the most agreeable sources for a cho-shoku in Tokyo is the Japanese dining room of the Okura Hotel. The components of the meal—of which there are several—are served in china or lacquered dishes on a lacquered tray and the principal entry is perhaps shioyaki, a neatly portioned, briefly salted wedge of fresh salmon broiled without a trace of added fat. It is a tantalizing centerpoint complemented in no small way by a piping hot bowl of miso or bean soup containing small squares of bean curd and midget-size brown wild mushroom caps; by a modest portioned and delectable hot side dish of chicken pieces and small-cut vegetables (or whole finger-size eggplant); a wedge of rolled omelet served lukewarm with grated daikon or Japanese radish; a bowl of perfectly cooked rice, unseasoned so as to accentuate the other flavors; and, invariably, assorted fresh pickles, prepared overnight from numerous vegetables, including eggplant, cauliflower, cucumbers, radish, and lotus root.

The meal is served with a never-ending supply of hot green tea, with the cost of a complete meal about $3.35, service included.

Japanese Tempura

Someone here observed recently that all the world's cuisines can be categorized according to their most characteristic cooking medium: Chinese cooking is based on oil, French on butter—and Japanese on water. It has long been a source of fascination—puzzlement even—that where the Japanese kitchen is concerned, there is one outstanding exception to that thought: tempura. Whereas dishes such as muzutaki or mizudaki made with chicken or fish cooked in water with vegetables, or shabu shabu with liquids, seem so much part of a pattern, tempura, consisting of a variety of food all deep fried in oil has always seemed a welcome intruder. Enormously appealing but nonetheless foreign. On this visit we discovered why.

"It is well documented," our friend, Shizuo Tsuji, told us, "that tempura was brought into Japan by Portuguese priests who came to this country by way of Nagasaki in the sixteenth century." Mr. Tauji is the distinguished head of the Ecole Technique Hôtelier here, the largest hotel school in Japan. He is a scholar and an author (his books include *The Life of Escoffier* and annual travel guides to the restaurants of Europe for the Japanese public).

Kaneyoshi Goto's tempura techniques transcend the usual batter-fried shrimp and vegetables.

The word tempura, or tenpura as it is sometimes spelled, is derived from a Portuguese word, tempero, that has to do with cooking. Tempura's original form in Japan was probably as what the French call beignets and the English call fritters. The most important ingredient in tempura—indeed, the essential ingredient—is batter-fried shrimp, with other foods such as batter-fried vegetables used only as a complement to the meal.

Mr. Tauji, who ranks as one of the nation's best-known gastronomes, is in the process of assembling a history of French cooking since its inception. He interrupted his labors long enough to let us come into his school's hotel kitchen to learn various facets of the art of Japanese cooking, of course, the preparation of tempura.We had as our instructor a jovial gentleman named Kaneyoshi Goto, a superb technician who demonstrated techniques that transcended the usual batter-fried shrimp, vegetables, and fish. His repertory for tempura includes multi-colored and appetizing tidbits such as shrimp sheathed in crushed almonds; fish fillets coated with broken noodles and deep fried to resemble porcupines; bite-size miniature hard shell crabs, deep fried; deep-fried gingko nuts stuffed with shrimp paste; and deep-fried shrimp toast.

Tempura

2 egg yolks
2 cups ice water
2 cups plus about 3
   tablespoons flour, sifted
   Oil for deep frying
   Foods to be deep fried (see
   below)
   Salt to taste
   Lemon wedges for garnish
   A tempura dip (see recipe)

1. Place yolks in a mixing bowl and beat well, preferably with chopsticks.

2. Add the ice water, stirring constantly. When well blended add 2 cups of flour all at once, stirring, preferably with thick chopsticks. Do not overblend.

The batter, when ready, should be fairly lumpy.

3. Heat oil to the depth of about 2 inches in a utensil suitable for deep frying. When it is very hot but not smoking, add any combination of the ingredients listed below and prepared as indicated. Cook batter-coated foods until golden but not browned.

4. Lift from the fat and drain on absorbent tissues. As the foods are added and cooked, it is important to skim the surface of the fat to remove any loose bits of batter and particles of food that rise to the top. If the batter seems too thin at any point, sprinkle the surface with a tablespoon of flour and stir briefly leaving it lumpy.

5. Continue cooking until all the foods are deep fried. Sprinkle

the tempura lightly with salt and garnish with lemon wedges. Serve with the tempura dip.

Yield: Any number of servings, depending on quantity of foods cooked.

The single essential ingredient of any tempura is shrimp. All the other batter-fried foods are, to use a phrase, side dishes. Here are some of the ingredients that may be dipped in batter and deep fried for the tempura in the recipe above:

Shrimp: Peel the shrimp tails but leave the last tail segment intact. Make slight gashes in the shrimp at ½-inch intervals on the underside. When ready to cook, dip lightly in flour, then in batter and deep fry. Drain and serve hot.

Squid: Clean the squid thoroughly or buy them cleaned. All the inner digestive tract should be eliminated as well as all bone or cartilage-type parts of the body. The outer mottled skin, as well as the very fine, transparent under skin, should be pulled away and discarded. Rinse the flesh and pat it dry. Cut the squid into strips measuring about 4 inches by 1 inch. Score on the underside. When ready to cook, coat lightly in flour and dip in batter. Deep fry, drain, and serve hot.

Fresh mushrooms: In Japan there are numerous varieties of wild mushrooms included in an elaborate tempura. They include matsutake or pine tree mushrooms; enikodake, delicate, long-stemmed, white-fleshed mushrooms with a tiny cap, generally fried in bundles; and shiitake, the large black mushroom caps common in Japanese and Chinese cookery and which, if not available fresh, may be soaked from the dried state, squeezed, and patted dry. They may then be floured, dipped in batter, and deep fried. Drain and serve hot.

Fish: Almost any white-fleshed, non-oily fish may be cut into bite-size pieces and used. Conger eel, which is quite fatty, is, on the other hand, a frequent addition to a tempura. Sometimes the skinless, boneless eel is used, sometimes whole small fillets. Very small fish are frequently used whole while some small fish are sometimes butterflied, boned, and used. All these are dipped in flour, then in batter and deep fried, drained and served hot.

Onions: Cut onions into ½-inch-thick slices, skewer with toothpicks to keep the rings intact, flour, and batterfry. Drain and serve hot.

There are also special and banquet type foods—deep fried without batter—that may be added to an elaborate tempura:

Shrimp: Peel the shrimp tails, leaving the last tail segment intact. Dip peeled portion in flour, then in egg white, then liberally in a choice of crushed almonds, fine cracker crumbs, white sesame seeds, or finely chopped bean thread (cellophane noodles). Deep fry, drain, and serve hot.

Small fish fillets with green noodles: Break enough Japanese green noodles (green soba) into fine pieces to make ½ cup. Dip fillets in flour, then egg white, then coat with noodles. Deep fry. This gives a porcupine effect. Serve hot.

Small fish fillets with egg noodles: Break enough Japanese egg noodles (udon) into fine pieces to make ½ cup. Dip fillets in flour, then in egg white, then coat with noodles. Deep fry. This gives a porcupine effect. Serve hot.

Miniature eggplant: The eggplant must be very small (no more than 3 inches in length). Leave the eggplant whole and with stems on. Slice them from bottom to center, about half way up, at ¼-inch intervals. Deep fry until cooked through.

Miniature hard-shell crab (very small soft-shell crabs could be substituted): If the miniature crabs are available, break off and discard the tiny "apron" on the front of each. Drop the crab into very hot fat. Cook about 30 seconds or less and drain. Serve as is.

Scallops: Use bay scallops or cut ocean scallops into bite-size pieces. Skewer or not, as desired. Dip in flour, then in egg white, then liberally in a choice of crushed almonds, fine cracker crumbs, white sesame seeds or finely chopped bean thread (cellophane noodles). Deep fry, drain, and serve hot.

Shrimp "toast" sandwiches: Blend enough raw shrimp to make ½ cup of purée. Stir in half an egg yolk, salt to taste, and dash of monosodium glutamate (optional). Cut trimmed white bread slices in half or into quarters. Spread one piece with the shrimp mixture, cover with another slice, sandwich fashion, and cook in very hot oil until brown on one side. Turn and brown on the other. Drain, cut into small squares and serve hot.

Japanese cooks also prepare deep fried gingko nut meats stuffed with the same shrimp mixture as for toast. The gingko nuts are sliced down the center without cutting through. The opening is sprinkled lightly with flour and filled with a small portion of the shrimp mixture. The gingko nut meats are skewered and deep fried.

Tempura Dip

2½ cups dashi (see recipe)
½ cup dark soy sauce, available in oriental markets

½ cup mirin (sweet sake), available in wine and spirit shops near oriental communities
1 cup well-packed katsuobushi, shaved bonito flakes, available in most

*Japanese grocery stores
Monosodium glutamate,
optional
Grated Japanese white
radish (available in
oriental markets)*

1. Combine the dashi, dark soy sauce, and mirin and bring to the boil. Add the katsuobushi and stir. Remove from the heat immediately. Let stand about 30 seconds, skimming the surface as necessary. Add a dash of monosodium glutamate and strain. Serve with grated radish on the side so that guests may add their own.

Yield: About 3½ cups.

Dashi
(Japanese soup stock)

Dashi is one of the basic and broadest foundations of the Japanese kitchen. With very few (if any) exceptions, it is the basis for all Japanese soups that fall into two categories, clear soup or consommé and bean soup. The most basic ingredient for dashi are very thin shavings of dried bonito.

The bonito is a tunalike fish. The fish, skinned and boned, is frequently dried for 2 or 3 years before it is turned into the shavings to make soup. Most restaurants and homes use commercially shaved dried bonito. The finest soup stocks, however, are made with dried bonito freshly shaved before using. The dried bonito and the shavings are known as katsuobushi. Katsuobushi is widely available in packaged form where Japanese foods are sold.

Another ingredient almost invariably employed in preparing dashi is dried seaweed called kombu. The English translation is kelp.

5 *cups cold water*
1 *large square or rectangle of kombu (kelp) measuring about 7 by 7 inches (see note)*
3 *cups loosely packed packaged katsuobushi, or dried bonito, shavings (see note)*

1. Place 5 cups of water in a saucepan and add the kombu. Bring to the boil and immediately remove the seaweed. Do not let the seaweed cook. Add the dried bonito shavings and stir. Remove from the heat immediately. Strain immediately through flannel.

Yield: About 5 cups.

Note: Both kombu and katsuobushi can be mail-ordered from such Japanese markets in New York as Katagiri & Co., 224 East 59th Street.

November 1974

I N THE SMALL town in Mississippi where we grew up, the menu
served in our home at Thanksgiving was not something we discussed with the neighbors. It was not invariable, but it was often
enough that we celebrated the holiday with a large kettle of spaghetti.
None of the children in the family relished roast turkey; somehow it
seemed so ordinary. We lived in a boarding house which our mother ran,
and turkey being plentiful and cheap, it appeared numerous times a
year. At Thanksgiving time the boarders would depart to visit kin, and
we were left alone to indulge ourselves in spaghetti.

Nostalgia plays funny tricks on adults. In retrospect we remember
those meals of roast turkey and corn bread stuffing with considerable affection. It has now become our traditional Thanksgiving fare. The corn
bread stuffing on page 321 is the same stuffing our mother served us, and
though we know it is a throwback to childhood, we still maintain that, to
our palates, no stuffing has ever tasted as good.

Fine Dining in Osaka

There are several complexities involved in writing about the flavors and gastronomic amenities of Japan. First, although most Japanese are almost painfully generous, kind, and hospitable, there are many fine and interesting restaurants here where no one speaks a word of English, and printed menus are all but unknown outside tourist establishments. As a consequence it is almost imperative that such restaurants be visited in the company of someone who speaks Japanese.

Secondly, there are scores of Japanese dishes which, orally described, come off as passing strange to the Western ear. Who can persuade John Doe that there is much to be said in a positive sense for cooked chrysanthemum leaves (similar to, but not identical with, the garden variety) and pickled petals of the chrysanthemum flower? And if John Doe has mastered the art of eating raw fish in sashimi and sushi, who can persuade him that one of the greatest palatable pleasures in that category is chilled raw lobster tail? Who can persuade him that a lunch of nothing but buckwheat noodles served in their natural water bath with a soy sauce soup stock added can make a laudably appetizing and gratifying main course at mid-day?

One of the nicest lunches we recall was at the Izuma Soba House at Sakai-Suzi, Nippon-Bashi, Kitazume, Higashi-Iru in Osaka. Soba is the word for buckwheat noodles and that is the focal point of all the foods served. It is available hot in the broth or icy cold with a highly flavorful grated wild potato and raw egg base dip on the side, sharpened with grated Japanese radish, a touch of cayenne, and chopped scallions. You might well find it irresistible.

And the surroundings are a joy: one small room with walls lined, left to right and top to bottom, with sobachoko, traditional cups for serving noodle broth. The maximum seating capacity is seven. The cost of a complete noodle lunch, sake extra, is from about $1.75.

The word restaurant with its French connotations seems an unhappy choice to describe most of the dining establishments in Japan. In contrast to local manners and ways of dining the word restaurant sounds Western, bare-faced and businesslike. Even the places that specialize in foods cooked over charcoal seem best served by the appellation house: i.e., yakitori house and so on.

The most serious of the eating places here are frequently housed in old mansions with meals served in sparsely furnished, formally arranged rooms, more often than not few in number. If the setting is formal and the food served in an almost ritualistic manner, the meal is by no means all that sobersided and without laughter. On a recent evening the nakai or waitress (what a demeaning ring that word has!) spilled a few drops of sake down the shirtfront of a Western lady guest and no one took it amiss; the nakai cupped her hand over her mouth and giggled and everyone at the table laughed with great and continuing spirit.

There are many full-fledged food enthusiasts in Japan who declare that the Kitcho Restaurant may be the finest restaurant in the nation. It is housed in a splendid old mansion that was once a place for dealing in antique Japanese porcelain. An evening there recently began with a brief gathering in a reception room where a beverage that would seem odd to Western minds—small toasted rice nuggets in hot water—is served to cleanse the palate. The meal is served in any one of seven spacious rooms, Japanese style, of course, with guests seated at low tables on cushions on the floor. First course to last, it is a theatrical experience that gratifies in depth the sense of sight as well as taste.

Our initial course, a great specialty of the Kitcho, was a splashy series of appetizers including an oval shrimp "paste mixture" wrapped in broken noodles and deep fried to resemble a nest. It was filled with a whole sweetened chestnut resembling an egg and surrounded by egg-shaped ginkgo nuts to heighten the illusion of a nest. All these things are illusions of course. Someone said it wasn't a "nest" at all but a "sea urchin."

There was salmon roe and, at various points during the course of a meal, a sashimi of raw tai (known as a "celebration" fish), plus strips of squid, and that great delicacy, cubes of raw lobster tail.

One of the great triumphs of that meal at the Kitcho was a dish of full-fleshed crab halves wrapped in leaves and deep fried. It was served with that incomparable combination of vinegar, soy, ginger, and a trace of sugar. Crab meat in that sauce is a liaison for the gods.

At the Kitcho there is almost invariably one dish served at the table with individual braziers holding small pieces of foods that guests cook themselves. On that recent evening it was thin slices of Kobe beef plus matsutake, the subtly flavored pine tree mushrooms that are rare and expensive and now in season. Soup appeared twice in the meal, both turtle, one clear and meaty and delectably laden with ginger flavor; another with rice and poached egg.

There was a fascinating and appealing custardlike dish made with broiled eel, grated Japanese turnip, and steamed shrimp. Hot house musk melon served as dessert. The cost of a meal per person at the Kitcho is about $68. The Kitcho does not include the presence of a geisha although there are two nakai or waitresses in constant attendance.

We learned during the course of this visit the folk etymology of the word sukiyaki. A suki, we are told, is an ancient long-handled gardening tool with a flat metal plate at the end. Yaki means grilled or broiled. In the olden days a cooking utensil containing various meats and vegetables was balanced on the end of the suki and extended over a fire grate where, by some stretch of a word's meaning, the food was "grilled." We came by this lore while dining on a highly creditable sukiyaki dish called udon-suki made with white noodles known as udon. The Mimiu, where we were eating, is a relatively new and immensely successful place with foods cooked at table (Western seating) with each guest helping himself. The foods were cooked in a simmering pot in a clear well-seasoned soup broth and the various foods included in addition to the tender, long, hand-made noodles, clams, chicken, shrimp, Japanese cabbage, turnips, and shiitake, the large black mushroom caps. An excellent meal. The cost was about $6 per person. Some noodle specialties at the Mimiu cost 75 cents. The Mimiu is at Mido-Kaikan-Ura.

We are among those rare American birds who are not all that enthusiastic about beef unless it is ground into hamburgers, and we therefore probably don't relish sukiyaki as keenly as the next man.

One of the finest we've ever dipped our chopsticks into however—particularly where the quality of the beef was concerned—was at the Harijou. The meat was splendidly marbled and wildly rich in flavor. It was cooked with other traditional ingredients including bean curd, scallions, and wild black mushroom caps all to be dipped in beaten egg before eating.

We had one small reservation about the Harijou's sukiyaki. The cooking liquid was, to our taste, a bit sweet. The Harijou has several tatami rooms—seating is Japanese style—and it is located at Doton-Bori, Minami. The cost per person is about $14.

One of the most interesting of the small restaurants of Osaka, and one where at most meals there is standing room only, is one least likely to appeal to the average Western tourist, American or otherwise. It is the Takoume, an oden restaurant. We have mentioned before that oden establishments—almost always of intimate size and crowds—originated several hundred years ago as places where Japanese men gathered to drink sake. As time progressed foods cooked in a single constantly simmering pot and highly complementary to the drinks came to be very much part of the scene.

The present-day oden house—consisting mostly of men although women are welcome—is a place where hungry customers stop, frequently with eating rather than drinking as the foremost incentive. The clientele changes constantly through the course of a meal hour. Customers sit on bareback stools at a counter devouring numerous and various skewered dishes from the constantly replenished kettle.

The foods include hard-boiled eggs, wild mealy potatoes in their jackets, squid, octopus, shrimp, deep-fried stuffed bean curd, and stuffed fish paste. The most coveted of the foods and the real specialty of the house is long-simmered cubes of whale's tongue on skewers. You chew and chew and all that happens is that the food just shifts about between your teeth like some very interesting, very porous bubble gum. When you get bored chewing you swallow and go on to the next bite. Sake helps. The cost of the skewered foods varies but prices range from about 50 cents to $1. The Takoume is at Nihon-Bashi, Doton-Bori, Asahi-za-mae.

Prunes and Pork:
a Swedish Triumph

WITH PIERRE FRANEY

Certain dishes have a special appeal not only because of their inherent excellence, but because of a certain novelty in presentation. The Swedish pork roast with the jawbreaking name of plommonspäckad fläskkarré is a delectable example. In English, it is a pork loin stuffed with pitted prunes. The technique of stuffing the meat is simple enough, although it may seem a trifle tedious to some. Like most roast pork dishes, this one goes admirably with puréed potatoes or a puréed blend of potatoes and celery root.

Roast Loin of Pork with Prunes

16 *dried prunes*
 1 *3½-pound boneless loin of pork, bones reserved*
1¾ *pounds bones from the loin of pork*
     Salt and freshly ground pepper to taste
 ½ *teaspoon ground ginger*
 ½ *cup water*

1. Pit the prunes and place them in a mixing bowl. Add boiling water to cover and let stand 1 hour.

2. Preheat oven to 375 degrees.

3. Using a knife with a long, thin blade, run it directly through the center of the pork loin to make a pocket for the prunes. It may be necessary to insert the knife from both ends of the meat.

4. Drain the prunes. Insert the prunes throughout the pocket of the pork. Tie the pork with string so that it retains its shape.

5. Sprinkle all over with salt and pepper to taste and ginger.

6. Line a shallow baking dish or roasting pan with a few bones and place the meat fat side up on top. Surround with remaining bones.

7. Place the meat in the oven. Turn the meat as it roasts every 15 minutes. Bake 2 hours.

8. Pour off the fat from the pan and add the water, stirring to dissolve the brown particles that cling to the bottom and sides of the pan. Continue to roast the meat 30 minutes longer. Remove the meat, cover loosely with foil and let stand 15 minutes. Serve sliced with the pan gravy.

Yield: 6 to 10 servings.

Puréed Potatoes

2 *pounds potatoes*
    Salt to taste
1 *cup milk*
4 *tablespoons butter at room temperature*
¼ *teaspoon grated nutmeg*

1. Peel the potatoes and quarter them or cut them into 2-inch cubes.

2. Place the potatoes in a saucepan and add cold water to cover and salt to taste. Bring to the boil and simmer 20 minutes or until potatoes are tender.

3. Drain the potatoes and put them through a food mill or potato ricer. Return them to the saucepan.

4. Meanwhile, bring the milk to the boil.

5. While the milk is being heated use a wooden spoon and add the butter to the potatoes while beating. Add salt and nutmeg and beat in the hot milk.

Yield: About 6 servings.

Purée of Knob Celery

1½ pounds potatoes
¾ pound firm knob celery
  Salt to taste
1 cup milk
4 tablespoons butter
1 cup milk
¼ teaspoon grated nutmeg

1. Peel the potatoes and rinse well. Quarter the potatoes and drop into a kettle or deep saucepan.

2. Peel the knob celery, removing and discarding all the brown exterior. Rinse well and cut into large slices or cubes. Add to the potatoes. Add water to cover and salt to taste and bring to the boil. Simmer 20 to 30 minutes until vegetables are tender.

3. Meanwhile, bring the milk to the boil.

4. Put the potatoes and knob celery through a fine food mill or a potato ricer. Add the butter and beat it in with a wooden spoon. Add the nutmeg and gradually add the hot milk, beating with the spoon. Serve immediately or place the dish in a basin of simmering water and keep warm.

Yield: 6 to 8 servings.

It is evident there is considerable confusion in the minds of many Americans as to precisely what knob celery is. And that confusion is compounded by the fact that knob celery also goes by the names celeriac and celery root. Knob celery is not simply the base or root of stalk celery, the common variety of celery used in almost all American kitchens. It is another, separate vegetable. It tastes like stalk celery, but it has a totally different texture and is a bit more flavorful. It is a root vegetable like turnips and potatoes. It looks like a brownish globe and ranges in size from a goose egg to a cantaloup. To use it, the brown outside skin must be pared away. When combined with potatoes and turned into a purée, it is one of the glories of good eating.

From Bali: One of the Great Soups of the World

It is somewhat astonishing that despite early exposure to European tastes and techniques, hardly anything but the smallest mark of Western influence has been left on Balinese kitchen culture. After all, Marco Polo, an Italian ambassador to the Great Khan of Mongolia, landed in Bali in 1292. And a group of Dutch sailors led by a man named Cornelius Houtman touched shore here nearly 400 years ago. But neither they nor their ancestors seem to have left any imprint on the cuisine.

We explored the subject with Wija Wawo-Runtu, the tall, energetic, and affluent proprietor of the small but esteemed Tandjung Sari compound-type hotel here that may very well have the best Indonesian cooking in Bali. Mr. Wawo-Runtu, dressed in his usual business attire—busily-patterned, snug-fitting swim trunks—was sitting on the splendid thatched roof patio, lined with Indonesian objets d'art, in his home a half-mile from the hotel. As his wife, Tatie, an uncompromisingly good cook in the native tradition, listened, the gentleman told us that the minimal mark on cooking left by the Dutch colonials might very well be a commentary on Dutch cooking in Holland.

"My father was from Celebes, but my mother was Dutch," he told us, and Dutch cooking has never been known for its distinction and imagination. The Dutch, it seems, were all too content to let the natives tend their wajans, the Indonesian round-bottom cooking utensils, duplicates of Chinese woks. If the French had been here for several hundred years, he indicated, it might have changed the flavor of things.

By contrast, Mr. Wawo-Runtu continued, there are numerous strong elements in the Indonesian kitchen suggestive of other cultures, including the Chinese and Indian. The Chinese, with their soy bean culture (soy sauce, bean curd, and so on) arrived in the region during the seventh century. Indian influences, of undated origin, are apparent in many curry-type dishes.

On several evenings in the stylishly-primitive bamboo and rattan dining room of the Tandjung Sari—sometimes with moonlight, sometimes with rain on the ocean a few feet away—we dined on the best rijstaffel we've ever eaten—fine satays with sambals (skewered grilled meat dishes with hot condiments or relishes), curry-type dishes, fresh stews, vegetable salads such as gado-gado, with a spicy peanut sauce and rice.

We had the good fortune of pursuing the foods of Indonesia by watching Mrs. Wawo-Runtu as she prepared food for a private feast in her own kitchen. She is a slender, stunningly-handsome woman (her mother is Sumatran, her father Javanese) and the mother of five children (together the couple are the parents of 10 children, one by their own union).

The pair have a staff of 16 people in their palatial estate or "compound," three of whom are called on at times for such kitchen chores as slicing, chopping, grinding, cleaning up, and fetching various herbs and vegetables from outside. The kitchen is of admirable size and equipped with a standard-size four-burner gas range, a refrigerator-freezer combination, and the universal electric blender, which is seldom used, it being empirically true that an ancient stone mortar and pestle does a better job of grinding and blending.

As we spoke, Mrs. Wawo-Runtu was in the process of preparing one of the consummately great soups of the world, an Indonesian soto ajam.

Rice, she noted as she rinsed out the good blend of spices into simmering broth, is the omnipresent food on all Indonesian tables. In fact, all of the country's traditional foods seem designed to complement or be complemented by rice—i.e., they are spicy, salty, or otherwise flavor-assertive and are frequently of a stewlike nature.

The basic cooking liquid for most dishes, she added, is coconut milk, made by kneading and sieving freshly grated coconut blended with water. One of its virtues is that, unlike milk, it tends to thicken and become saucelike as it cooks without the addition of a starch such as flour or cornstarch.

Various seasonings, almost unknown in the United States but which play an enormous role in Indonesian flavors, are lemon grass (it vaguely resembles a green onion although not in flavor), laos (a root that vaguely resembles ginger but not in flavor), and scented leaves such as kunir, lemon, and salam.

Bean curd plays many roles here and so does a nonsweet soya bean "cake" that looks like a flat, dry white seeded nougat candy. Macadamia nuts are frequently ground to give richness and body to main courses and sauces. Sauces made with ground peanuts are a staple, particularly for satays and saladlike dishes made with cooked vegetables at room temperature. Bean sprouts are essential to many dishes.

To someone fairly well-schooled in the Western kitchen, one of the most intriguing discoveries here is the free-wheeling use to which shallots are put. Shallots, the most delicate member of the onion family, have long been a hallmark of fine French cooking and, though elevated in price, are gradually becoming part of the American repertory. But in Bali they are as common as coconuts and are given about as much currency in cooking. They go into almost every soup or stew or sauce and the large white or yellow onions are relegated to occasional salads.

After two hours of grating, grinding, and stewing we sat down to a feast for 14 people that included pork satays grilled over charcoal, fish stew, numerous salads, and Mrs. Wawo-Runtu's remarkable soto ajam, which means chicken soup but is far more than that with its blend of shredded chicken, bean sprouts, scallions, hard-cooked eggs, touch of lime, and so on. A fine idea to feed many guests on one dish (the other dishes at the feast were elegant and good, but the soto alone could serve admirably).

Wija Wawo-Runtu, proprietor of the esteemed Tandjung Sari restaurant in Bali, with his wife, Tatie.

Soto Ajam

(An elaborate soup with chicken)

Soup

5   *pounds meaty beef bones*
2   *3- to 3½-pound chickens
    left whole*
8   *macadamia nuts*
2   *teaspoons coriander seeds*
⅓   *cup chopped shallots*
3   *cloves garlic*
1½ *teaspoons turmeric (see
    note)*
    Salt to taste
3   *tablespoons peanut or corn
    oil*
1   *stalk of lemon grass (see
    note) or ½ teaspoon grated
    lemon rind*
¼   *teaspoon monosodium
    glutamate, optional*

The garnishes

3   *small, red, waxy "new"
     potatoes*
     Fat for deep frying
2½   *cups peeled shallots*
2   *ounces bean thread (also
     known as Chinese
     vermicelli, cellophane
     noodles, and so on, see
     note)*
3   *cups bean sprouts (see
     note)*
3   *cups finely shredded white
     cabbage*
6   *hard-cooked eggs, peeled*
½   *cup chopped celery leaves
     Sambal soto (see recipe)
     Lime wedges*

1. Place the beef bones in a kettle and add cold water to cover. Bring to the boil and drain immediately. Chill bones under cold water. Return the bones to the kettle and add enough cold water to cover both the bones and the chickens when they are added. Bring to the boil.

2. When the water boils, add the chickens. If the chickens are not covered with water, add enough boiling water to cover them.

3. Blend or, using a mortar and pestle, grind together the macadamia nuts, coriander seeds, ⅓ cup of shallots, garlic, turmeric, and salt.

4. Heat the 3 tablespoons of oil in a small skillet and add the spice mixture. Rinse out the blender or mortar with a little water and add it to the skillet. Cook, stirring about 1 minute, and add the lemon grass. Continue cooking about 3 minutes, stirring. Add this to the soup. Add salt to taste and the monosodium glutamate.

5. Cook the soup, uncovered, about 1 hour or until the chickens are thoroughly tender. Remove the chickens and let cool. Discard the beef bones. Let the soup simmer slowly.

6. Meanwhile, prepare the garnishes.

7. Peel the potatoes and cut them as for potato chips into very thin slices, ⅛ inch thick or less. Drop immediately into cold water.

8. Drain the potatoes and pat them dry. Heat fat for deep frying in a skillet and when it is quite hot, add the potatoes to the fat and cook, stirring frequently, until the potatoes are quite crisp, 20 to 30 minutes. Drain well on absorbent paper toweling. Set aside.

9. Cut the shallots into very thin slices and cook them in hot fat until nicely browned like fried onion rings. Drain well on absorbent paper toweling. Set aside.

10. Place the bean thread in a mixing bowl and pour boiling water over it. Let stand 2 minutes. Drain. Set aside.

11. Drop the bean sprouts into a pan of boiling water and let simmer about 30 seconds. Drain immediately. Set aside.

12. Place the cabbage in a bowl and pour boiling water over it. Let stand 5 minutes and drain. Set aside.

13. Cut the eggs as neatly as possible into ¼-inch slices.

14. Skin and bone the chickens. Shred the meat finely and arrange it in the center of one or two large platters.

15. Arrange the garnishes around it in neat piles. Serve the sambal soto separately in a small bowl with lime wedges around it. Caution guests that the sambal is powerfully hot and optional. By all means use the lime wedges.

16. Serve the boiling hot soup in one or two hot tureens, letting guests help themselves. If desired, half of the garnishes except the sambal and the lime wedges may be added to the soup before serving.

Yield: 12 to 20 servings.

Note: In Indonesia fresh turmeric, a yellow root that resembles a small carrot, is used in cookery. As far as we know, fresh turmeric is not available in the United States, although powdered turmeric is commonplace. Lemon grass is also not available in American markets. Its flavor and taste are only vaguely reminiscent of lemon. Lemon grass may be omitted or a touch of grated lemon rind may be substituted without cooking. Both bean thread and bean sprouts are widely available in Chinese and other oriental markets.

Sambal soto

Remove the stems from 2 or 3 long hot or mild red peppers or several small very hot red or green peppers, available in oriental and Spanish markets. Chop the peppers until they are coarse-fine, seeds and all. Spoon into a serving dish. Use sparingly in other foods.

A Traditional Thanksgiving

WITH PIERRE FRANEY

If there is one menu that most Americans tend—and with reason—to be sentimental about, it is that for Thanksgiving. We know of homes where that particular holiday's menu has remained more or less stable for the past quarter century. On these pages we offer a Thanksgiving menu based partly on a long-remembered Southern recipe—roast turkey filled with corn bread stuffing—plus a few trimmings of European inspiration. These include Brussels sprouts in cream, braised red cabbage with chestnuts, and gratinéed potatoes. A slight departure from tradition, this menu may be yet another reason for giving thanks.

Roast Turkey

1 *16-to-20-pound turkey*
  Corn bread stuffing (see recipe)
4 *tablespoons peanut, vegetable, or corn oil*
  Salt
  Giblet gravy (see recipe)

1. Preheat oven to 450 degrees.

2. Stuff and truss the turkey. Place it in a shallow roasting pan (ours measured 1½ by 12 by 21½ inches).

3. Brush the turkey with oil and sprinkle with salt.

4. Roast the turkey about 50 minutes until it is nicely browned. Turn the pan in the oven occasionally to brown evenly. When browned, cover loosely with a sheet of aluminum foil.

5. Continue roasting, basting at intervals. After 2 hours, reduce the oven heat to 375 degrees.

6. Continue roasting about 2 hours longer or until the turkey is done (a thermometer inserted in the dressing should register about 160 degrees).

7. Remove the turkey and pour off any fat that may have accumulated. Add about ½ cup of water to the roasting pan and stir to dissolve the brown particles clinging to the bottom and sides of the pan. Add this to the giblet gravy. Carve the turkey and serve with dressing and gravy.

Yield: 12 to 20 servings.

Corn Bread Stuffing

12 *tablespoons butter*
2 *cups finely chopped onion*

1   *cup finely chopped green pepper*
1½ *cups finely chopped heart of celery*
4   *cups finely crumbled Southern corn bread (see recipe)*
3   *cups crumbled toast*
2   *hard-cooked eggs, coarsely chopped*
    Freshly ground pepper to taste
½   *cup chicken broth*
3   *raw eggs*
    Salt to taste

1. Melt 4 tablespoons butter and add the onion, green pepper, and celery. Cook, stirring, until vegetables are crisp-tender. Set aside.

2. Place the corn bread and toast in a mixing bowl and add the hard-cooked eggs and the celery mixture. Add a generous amount of pepper and the remaining ingredients. Stir to blend well.

Southern corn bread

⅓   *cup sifted flour*
1½ *cups sifted corn meal*
1   *teaspoon baking soda*
½   *teaspoon salt*
2   *eggs*
1   *cup buttermilk*
1½ *cups milk*
1½ *tablespoons butter*

1. Preheat oven to 350 degrees.

2. Sift the flour, corn meal, baking soda, and salt into a mixing bowl. Beat the eggs until foamy and stir them into the dry mixture. Stir in the buttermilk and 1 cup of milk.

3. Heat the butter in a 9-by-2-inch black skillet and when it is very hot but not brown, pour in the batter. Carefully pour the remaining milk on top of the batter without stirring. Place the dish in the oven and bake 50 minutes or until set and baked through. If this is to be used as a stuffing, it is best if it is a day or so old.

Yield: 8 servings.

Giblet gravy

1   *turkey neck*
1   *turkey gizzard*
1   *turkey heart*
1   *turkey liver*
    Salt to taste
1   *tablespoon peanut, vegetable, or corn oil*
    Freshly ground pepper to taste
1¼ *cups finely chopped onion*
½   *cup finely chopped carrot*
¾   *cup finely chopped celery*
1   *clove garlic, coarsely chopped*
3   *tablespoons flour*
1   *bay leaf*
2   *sprigs fresh thyme or 1 teaspoon dried*
3   *cups chicken broth*
2   *sprigs parsley*
1   *tablespoon tomato paste*
1   *tablespoon butter*

1. Cut the neck into 1 inch lengths and set aside.

2. Cut away and discard the tough casing from the tender part of the gizzard. Place the gizzard pieces in a saucepan. Cut the heart in half and add it. Add the

liver and cold water to cover. Add salt to taste and bring to the boil. Simmer 30 minutes. Remove from the heat and drain. Set aside.

3. Meanwhile, heat the 1 tablespoon oil in a saucepan and add the neck, salt and pepper to taste. Cook, stirring frequently, over medium heat until the neck is golden brown, about 20 minutes. Add ¾ cup onion, the carrot, celery, and garlic and stir. Sprinkle with flour and stir until neck pieces are evenly coated. Add the bay leaf, thyme, broth, parsley, and tomato paste. Stir until the sauce reaches the boil. Continue cooking about 1½ hours. Strain the sauce. Discard all solids.

4. Slice the giblets and cut them into slivers. Cut the slivers into fine dice.

5. In a saucepan, heat the 1 tablespoon of butter and add the remaining ½ cup of chopped onion. Add the chopped giblet mixture and cook, stirring occasionally, about 5 minutes. Add the strained sauce and bring to the boil. Simmer about 5 minutes and add salt and pepper to taste.

Yield: About 3 cups.

Gratinéed Potatoes

4 baking potatoes, about 1½ pounds
  Salt to taste
4 tablespoons butter, at room temperature
  Nutmeg
¾ cup milk
  Freshly ground pepper to taste
¼ cup grated Gruyère cheese

1. Preheat oven to 400 degrees.

2. Peel the potatoes and quarter them. Place them in a saucepan and add cold water to cover and salt to taste. Bring to the boil and simmer approximately 20 minutes or until the potatoes are tender.

3. Drain the potatoes and put them through a food mill.

4. Using a wooden spoon, beat in the butter. Add nutmeg to taste.

5. Meanwhile, bring the milk to the boil. Beat it into the potatoes and add salt and pepper to taste. Turn the potatoes into a baking dish (ours measured 8½ by 1½ inches). Smooth the surface of the potatoes and sprinkle with cheese. Bake about 10 minutes or until the potatoes are piping hot and the cheese is melted. If desired, run the dish under the broiler to brown the cheese lightly.

Yield: 6 servings.

Brussels Sprouts in Cream

2 10-ounce packages fresh
   Brussels sprouts
   Salt to taste
3 tablespoons butter
3 tablespoons flour
1 cup cream or milk
1 egg yolk
¼ cup grated Parmesan
   cheese

1. Preheat oven to 375 degrees.

2. Pull off and discard any tough outer leaves from the sprouts. Trim the bottom of the sprouts and make a shallow incision in the form of a cross on the stem end. Place the sprouts in a skillet and add cold water to cover and salt to taste. Bring to the boil and simmer 10 to 15 minutes or until the sprouts are crisp-tender. Drain.

3. Melt 2 tablespoons of butter in a saucepan and add the flour, stirring with a whisk. When blended and smooth, add the cream, stirring vigorously with the whisk. When thickened and smooth, remove from the heat and add the egg yolk, stirring. Add salt to taste.

4. Select a casserole large enough to hold the sprouts in one layer. Melt the remaining tablespoon of butter in the casserole and add the sprouts. Carefully spoon the sauce over each sprout until they are all coated. Sprinkle with cheese and bake 10 to 12 minutes. Run the dish under the broiler briefly until nicely glazed.

Yield: 6 to 8 servings.

Buttered Whole Chestnuts

2 pounds chestnuts
3 tablespoons butter
   Salt to taste
¾ cup chicken broth
1 tablespoon sugar

1. Preheat oven to 400 degrees.

2. Using a sharp paring knife, make an incision around the perimeter of each chestnut, starting and ending on either side of the "topknot" or stem end. Place the chestnuts in one layer in a baking dish just large enough to hold them. Place them in the oven and bake about 10 minutes or until they open. Let the chestnuts cool just until they can be handled. Peel them while they are hot.

3. Place the chestnuts in a saucepan and add the butter, salt to taste, broth, and sugar. Cover and cook over low heat, stirring frequently, 10 to 15 minutes. Place them in the oven and bake, stirring occasionally, 25 to 30 minutes or until thoroughly tender. Serve as a vegetable.

Yield: 6 to 8 servings.

Braised Red Cabbage with Chestnuts

1	3-pound red cabbage
12	chestnuts
¼	pound salt pork, cut into small cubes
¼	cup finely chopped onion
3	cooking apples, about 1 pound
1	cup dry white wine
	Salt and freshly ground pepper to taste
2	tablespoons dark brown sugar
2	tablespoons butter
1	tablespoon red wine vinegar

1. Preheat oven to 450 degrees.

2. Pull off and discard any blemished outer leaves from the cabbage. Quarter the cabbage and shred it finely.

3. Using a sharp paring knife, make an incision around the perimeter of each chestnut, starting and ending on either side of the "topknot" or stem end. Place the chestnuts in one layer in a baking dish just large enough to hold them. Place them in the oven and bake about 10 minutes or until they open. Let the chestnuts cool just until they can be handled. Peel them while they are hot.

4. Heat the salt pork in a heavy saucepan large enough to hold the cabbage. When the salt pork is rendered of its fat, add the onion and cook briefly.

5. Meanwhile, peel and core the apples and cut them into quarters. Thinly slice the apple quarters. There should be about 4 cups. Add the apples to the saucepan.

6. Add the wine and bring it to the boil. Add the cabbage, salt and pepper to taste. Add the brown sugar and chestnuts and cover. Simmer 10 minutes, stirring occasionally. Make sure that the bottom does not stick and burn.

7. Place the saucepan in the oven and bake 30 minutes. Reduce the oven heat to 375 degrees and bake 1 to 1¼ hours or until cabbage is thoroughly tender. Stir occasionally as it cooks. Stir in the butter and vinegar and blend well. Serve piping hot.

Yield: 8 to 12 servings.

From the Strait of Malacca: The Wedding of Two Cuisines

The older one gets in the pursuit of national and ethnic tastes, the more solid the thought that man is indeed what he eats. Among the most intriguing aspects of exploring the foods of this lusty, proud, and immaculately clean self-governed territory are the categories into which the island dishes fall—Chinese, Malayan, Indian, and Eurasian. And, yes, Virginia, they do sell hamburgers.

Out of the Chinese and Malayan kitchens has evolved a fifth category, referred to as Straits Chinese (the name deriving from the Strait of Malacca) or nonya cooking, which has a cultural history all its own.

Chinese food here is of the traditional sort found around the world— generally a blend of subtle, spiced muted harmonies. Malayan cooking is characterized by pronounced, pungent flavors, more often than not made hot with peppers that excite or "enrage" the tongue and appetite. Straits Chinese, scorned by many a pure Chinese, is a long-time marriage of the two.

One of the great cooks of Singapore and the island's best-known authority on Straits cookery is Mrs. Lee Chin Koon, the mother of Singapore's Prime Minister, Lee Kuan Yew.

"The Straits Chinese," she said one recent morning in her home, "are those families who have lived in Singapore for many generations and whose marriage lines are interlinked with Malaysians. This is as opposed to the Chinese Chinese who obviously are those who have married only within Chinese families. Sixty or seventy years ago," she continued, "the food differences between the two groups were a real barrier. But, then again, at that time so was the language."

Mrs. Lee is a gray-haired, effusive, marvelously articulate, and agile woman with a well-honed sense of humor. She views such cultural patterns with amusement and adds, a bit dotingly, "My son says I shouldn't speak of 'Straits Chinese' and 'Chinese Chinese.' After all, he says, we're all Singaporeans."

Mrs. Lee, now approaching her 70th year (she will celebrate her birthday next year, as is customary, on the Chinese New Year rather than her actual birthdate), states blithely that she is afflicted with all the ailments of the aged—arthritis, bursitis, and elevated blood pressure—but cooking, eating well, and feeding her family and friends remain the chief pleasures of her life. She lives in a modest, somewhat spacious, red-tiled home, about a 15-minute taxi ride from the center of Singapore. She has a large kitchen with four gas burners, a movable table that serves as a chopping island and, of course, a refrigerator and freezer. In the Lee home there are frequent family celebrations, and on almost any Saturday she can count on a sizable number of her 14 grandchildren to come over for a feast. Mrs. Lee is a cunningly warm and hospitable woman who boasts that she can stretch a modest soup for two into a dinner for 12 or more, given a moment's notice.

Mrs. Lee has for years conducted cooking classes in her home, many of her students being American or European women, and her great specialties include a fine pork and prawn ball soup called pong tauhu. Another is garam assam, a full-bodied fish soup with a tart flavor derived from water in which tamarind is soaked until soft (tamarind is available in this country). The soup, she states, has been a traditional dish in her family and on the island for more than 150 years. She is also noted for her "curries," and here the word curry is used loosely as a point of reference to denote foods in a sauce flavored with spices. Like the Indians, the Singaporeans give specific names to such dishes and only use the word curry when communicating a kind of dish to Westerners.

As in other parts of Asia, much of the cooking here uses coconut milk as a basic liquid, as well as certain herbs and spices all but unknown in Western kitchens. These include fresh turmeric root, candlenuts (macadamia nuts are a good substitute), lemon leaves, and lemon grass. With a few adjustments, however, all of Mrs. Lee's recipes may be duplicated with commendable success in American kitchens.

She has recently completed the manuscript for a book on her family's cooking, which is predominately nonya or Straits Chinese. It will be published privately in Singapore this month and promises to be the definitive word on the amalgam of Malayan and Chinese gastronomy. Mrs. Lee finds justifiable pleasure in the thought that she is the last and only person who could have written such a volume, in that she is the last of a generation that knows such cooking in painstaking detail.

Pong Tauhu

(Pork and shrimp balls in soup)

½ pound fresh shrimp, the smaller the better and preferably fresh, with heads left on

5 to 10 cloves garlic
2 ounces belly pork (fresh bacon), trimmed of rind, available in pork stores and Chinese meat markets
2 cups bamboo shoots cut into thin, matchlike strips
½ pound ground pork

½ cup lean and fat pork cut
   into ¼-inch cubes
½ cup chopped scallions
4 pads fresh but fairly firm
   bean curd, not the very soft
   variety, available in
   Chinese markets
10 tablespoons corn oil
2 teaspoons bean paste,
   widely available in
   Chinese groceries
1 teaspoon freshly ground
   black pepper
¼ teaspoon monosodium
   glutamate, optional
1 egg
½ teaspoon dark soy sauce,
   available in Chinese
   groceries
   Salt to taste

1. Peel and devein the shrimp
and save both the tail meat and
the shells. Set aside.

2. Chop the garlic, put it in
cheesecloth and rinse under cold
water. Squeeze to extract much of
the moisture. Set aside.

3. Prepare the belly pork,
bamboo shoots, ground pork, lean
and fat pork, and scallions and set
aside.

4. Put the bean curd in a bowl
and mash it to a smooth pulp. Put
it in a flannel cloth and squeeze to
extract most of the moisture. Set
aside.

5. Heat the oil in a wok and
when very hot, add the garlic,
stirring and draining quickly. Do
not burn the garlic, or it will be
bitter. Reserve both oil and garlic.
Set aside.

6. Grind the shrimp tails to a
paste and set aside.

7. Grind the lean and fat pork
to a paste and set aside.

8. Return 2 tablespoons of oil
to the wok and add 2 tablespoons
of garlic and the bean paste. Add
the pork belly and cook, stirring,
until pork starts to become brown.
Add the bamboo shoots. Add 4 tablespoons of water and stir. Spoon
the mixture into a kettle.

9. Add about ½ cup more
water to the wok and stir to collect
pan juices remaining. Add this to
the bamboo shoot mixture.

10. Wipe out the wok and reheat it. Add 4 tablespoons of oil to
the wok and when hot, add the
shrimp shells. Cook, stirring,
about 30 seconds and scoop out.
Grind, using a mortar and pestle,
or put the shells through a meat
grinder, using the coarse blade.
Save all juices.

11. Put 7 cups of water in a
kettle and add the shrimp shells
and juices. Blend well. Squeeze
the mixture through flannel into
the bamboo shoot mixture. Discard shells. Bring to the boil.

12. In a bowl combine the
ground pork, ground shrimp, fat
and lean pork. Blend well and add
the ground bean curd. Blend and
add the pepper, monosodium glutamate, egg, dark soy sauce, and
remaining browned garlic. Add
salt and chopped scallions and
shape into 2-inch balls, using
lightly oiled fingers. There should
be about 3 dozen meat and shrimp
balls.

13. Bring the soup to a full
boil and drop in the balls. Reduce
heat and simmer 10 minutes, stirring occasionally. Add salt to taste.
Serve piping hot.

Yield: 8 to 12 servings.

Mrs. Lee Chin Koon, mother of Singapore's Prime Minister, specializes in Straits Chinese dishes. They are a blend of Malay and Chinese tradition.

Garam Assam

(A tart-flavored fish soup)

5 *to 10 ¼-inch slices fresh*
  ginger or 1 teaspoon dried
  (see note)
4 *candlenuts or macadamia*
  nuts
2 *teaspoons ground turmeric*
  (see note)
4 *small hot peppers, seeded*
  or not according to taste

¾ *cup quartered or halved*
  shallots or small onions
1½ *tablespoons shrimp paste*
  (see note)
1 *teaspoon grated lemon rind*
⅓ *cup tamarind (available in*
  Oriental, Spanish, and
  Puerto Rican markets)
1 *1-pound unboned whole*
  fish, cleaned but with skin
  and head left on
10 *large prawns or shrimp in*
  the shell
8 *tablespoons corn oil*
2 *tablespoons sugar*
2 *teaspoons salt*

1. Grind or blend together the ginger, nuts, turmeric, hot peppers, shallots, shrimp paste, and lemon rind.

2. Put the tamarind in a bowl and add 3½ cups water. Let stand, stirring occasionally, until tamarind softens. Massage the mixture with the hands until seeds start to come clean.

3. Split the fish in half widthwise. Set aside. Set the shrimp aside.

4. Heat the oil in a wok or kettle and add the spices which should be pastelike. Cook, stirring, until well blended. Cook very briefly or they will darken. Sprinkle with a teaspoon of water to lower the temperature. Cook over very low heat about 2 minutes, stirring.

5. Meanwhile, stir and work the tamarind mixture with the hands and pour off but reserve the liquid plus as much tamarind flesh as possible. Discard the seeds.

6. Add the tamarind liquid to

the wok, stirring. Add the sugar and salt. When simmering add the fish and cook, gently and carefully turning the fish in the liquid. Add the prawns and stir gently. Cook about 5 minutes and remove from the heat. Serve piping hot.

Yield: 6 or more servings.

Note: Actually, Mrs. Lee uses a form of ginger, unavailable in America, known as blue ginger. It is a bit milder than regular fresh ginger. Fresh turmeric, a small root that looks like a carrot, is also used in Singapore. Shrimp paste gives a definite flavor to this recipe, but many Westerners may find the odor and flavor a bit too strong and "fishy."

Throughout our lives, we have always assumed "important" people to have lofty, imperious attitudes. When we met Mrs. Lee Chin Koon, the mother of Singapore's Prime Minister, we expected her to be formidable. As it turned out, she was the kindest, warmest, and most down-to-earth individual you could have imagined. She was a grand old dame who lived quite simply, and her entire life really revolved around her kitchen. She was not in the best health, but she laughed a lot and told us that if she couldn't cook well and eat well, life would no longer be worth living.

Fine Dining in Singapore

Most legends die hard. Singapore is a place of such beauty and good will it is difficult to reconcile it with that yeasty, adolescent, long-fancied image of a city with dark alleys and dark shadows, opium, silk brocade, heavy breathing, and a lusty traffic in human bodies. Singapore (the name, we discovered, derives from the Malay "singa" meaning lion and "pura" meaning city) is almost ostentatiously pure and prosperous looking. The only mean pollution here seems that of the island's automobiles.

There are nearly a dozen new hotels, most of them less than four years old and most of them maintained—despite their sharply modern surroundings—with old-fashioned dignity, efficiency, and civility—qualities frequently presumed to have fled the earth. Several of the new hotels have very good restaurants—particularly those that serve dem sem, which include steamed dumplings plus other appetizers. After a few days here it becomes difficult to believe you will be served a bad meal anywhere.

By far the largest category of restaurants in Singapore is Chinese, and the vast majority of these eating places are highly reminiscent of some of the best Chinese restaurants in Manhattan. At times they may be conventional, but those that put forth their best talents can be uncommonly good. The kitchens represent many regions of China and, as in Manhattan, very spicy Szechwan cooking is popular and very much in evidence.

It would require months to pretend any comprehensive coverage of all (or even of most) of Singapore's restaurants. They exist at every turn and on every level. All we can hope to achieve here is a capsule resumé of several places that we visited.

We've never collected anything in our life unless you speak, sentimentally, perhaps, of memories of hotels that have become or became legends in their time. We take comfort in remembering the nights we spent at the old, now-demolished Frank Lloyd Wright masterpiece in Tokyo, the original Imperial Hotel, the Peninsula in Hong Kong, the Ritz in Paris, the Ritz in Madrid, and so on. We will regret the rest of our days we did not make it to the original Shepherds in Cairo before it burned and may never see the inside of the Manila Hotel in the Philippines, now scheduled for demolition.

It was thus with some awe and quiet joy that we made it on this visit to the old Raffles Hotel that Somerset Maugham called a monument to all the fables of the exotic East. It is regrettable that during Singapore's feverish four-year period of construction no one stepped in to bring Raffles into the present century with air-conditioning throughout. To our minds it could easily have thus become one of the most stylish, stunning, and coveted places to stay in the world.

Despite warnings by several local acquaintances that the food at Raffles might be disappointing, we were immensely pleased not only with the bill of fare but with its preparation. The service borders on the impeccable and in this day and age that alone would almost make a visit worthwhile. We dined in the hotel's only air-conditioned dining room, the Elizabethan Grill. The former main dining room is now a vast, humid place with a nightly floor show under ceiling fans. There is also an outdoor Palm Court that specializes in Italian cooking, including pizza.

The very comfortable grill is a modest-size, rectangular room, a bit too well lighted, perhaps, and little that is grand in the upholstery although it is neat and the napery snow white. The silver plate is genuine and bears the hallmarks of bygone days when Britannia ruled the nearby waves and then some. There are orchids on each table and the menu is extensive. So much so we ordered cautiously and in retrospect suspect we underestimated the kitchen.

The menu is international—piccata of veal, beef Stroganoff, tournedos Rossini, fritto misto, sole Provençale, veal Florentine, and so on. We dined very well on a gratin of crab with mushrooms baked in the shell ($2.75) and properly cooked, very tender sirloin steak ($5) of excellent flavor. The beef was from New Zealand and was first rate. We ended the meal with Stilton cheese, admirably scooped from a whole wheel ($1.10).

Most main courses are priced from about $2.25 to $2.75. Wines fetch from about $10 for a California wine to $20 for a French. In our book, Raffles is chief among the very few tourist attractions Singapore offers. If you haven't dined at Raffles, you haven't been to Singapore.

On the other hand, we were recently charged with another kind of emotion at one of the world's great nocturnal street spectacles—the raffish, ingenuous, and captivating bazaar for dining that happens in a half-acre lot close by all the major hotels. It serves as a car park by day. It is a food extravaganza of irresistible vigor and charm, and the food is excellent. So are the beverages (the freshly squeezed sugar cane juice over ice is a remarkably refreshing thirst quencher).

Much of the cooking at Car Park is of a sort wholly dependent on quick cooking and immediate consumption. Most of it is done in woks fired over portable but sizeable charcoal braziers, and the dishes include Asian omelets; a multitude of soups, simmering in cauldrons, some with chicken or pork, some with fish and seafood; fried rice; stir-fried noodle dishes; and various foods on skewers. There is Indonesian cooking and Indian as well as Chinese and Malayan. There are steamed and fried dumplings, great vats with the porridge known as a congee, and so on, plus scores of fruits served whole or by the slice. You can dine very well for a single United States dollar; elaborately for the likes of $2.

In Singapore if you mention an evening at Car Park, someone will almost reflexively ask if you've been to Albert Street as well. It is a similar exercise in dining but a bit sober-sided and not nearly as much fun. There, too, are food stalls but they are not wholly impromptu. These are set up each evening outside established restaurants on one side of the street and serve more or less as open air extensions of indoor dining areas. The foods include not only those cooked immediately on the streets—satays, crab dishes, dem sem, soups, noodles, and so on—but selections may be made from complete menus, mostly Chinese or Indian. The quality is high. This might accurately be pegged as snap judgment but whereas Car Park seems more an integral part of the throbbing night activity of Singapore, Albert Street seems like the last-stop-but-one for tourist buses. The cost of dining there will range from about $1 for a wholly adequate meal to $5 for crabs.

There are rare circumstances when a certain dish will have such an immediate and unqualified appeal it is instantly apparent the food will probably remain in memory forever. That was the psychic response to the platter of chili crabs around which one meal centered recently at the Golden Lion Restaurant about half an hour's drive from the center of Singapore Town. Chili crabs are perhaps the most indigenous dish of the island, an original creation, but believed to be of Cantonese derivation. In any event, the crabs in some degree bear a resemblance to what is listed as Cantonese lobster (or crab) on many Chinese menus in the Occident. Chili crabs consist of a similar ground pork sauce but one that is well spiced with hot or mild red chilies. The crabs at the Golden Lion were in all respects an exceptional creation—a superb, extraordinary blend of meat and juices and remarkably balanced spices, all as a coating for tender, sweet, and stir-fried flesh-filled crabs.

Almost anything else on the menu might have seemed commonplace, anticlimactic. But that was not the case. Masterfully cooked fresh abalone with spinach arrived, and notable fresh water fish (Western counterpart unknown but with a moist, flaky texture like scrod) plus good prawns.

The atmosphere of the Golden Lion is clean, bright, and undistinguished—a very plain rectangular room with tables functionally placed. The prices are modest. A superb meal for four cost less than $15 total. The Golden Lion is at 496 Upper East Coast Road, Singapore, 16; telephone 46-39-55.

If we were joyously dazzled by the food with which we regaled ourselves at the Golden Lion, we were almost equally elated by Hugo's Restaurant, somewhere aloft by elevator in the Singapore Hyatt Hotel. Rarely have we spent a more interesting evening, and if we seemed to stare and seem awestruck, it was our wonder that there is not a restaurant interior in Manhattan (nor Chicago, San Francisco, or New Orleans, in our purview) more cunningly executed. The restaurant is in shades of antique brown and gold with carved-back chairs and handsome, plush, overstuffed banquettes, ochre-colored napery, and carefully contrived lighting. A joy to the senses.

What's more, the menu is interesting and the food, Western-style, admirable. The oysters, flown in from Australia, are delectable; and a fish called karau was more than competently prepared with a light cream sauce. The roast beef from New Zealand, while not strikingly well marbled, was of good texture and served laudably rare from the center of the roast.

To be negative, the Yorkshire pudding with the beef was leaden, an order of steak au poivre was woefully overcooked, and the wine—a reasonably priced bottle of Pommard—a bit too warm. The chef's Sachertorte was edible but a travesty on the original. A real heavyweight.

A scoop of cheese from a wheel of Stilton was good and complemented by a glass of port wine. It is always a pleasure to find that curiously compatible combination, port and Stilton. The meal ended with a nice conceit: small balls of vanilla ice cream in a frozen chocolate coating.

Main courses at Hugo's are priced from about $4 to $6. The cost of that Pommard was $15. At the time of our visit there were strolling Philippine musicians playing mariachi-style music with great panache.

Another memorable dining experience here was a luncheon for six at the Sea View Hotel overlooking the bay, with its hundreds of ships at anchor. The meal began with an excellent assortment of appetizers—a blend of steamed shrimp, cold spinach, sliced sea cucumber, and boned duck feet with a light sesame seed sauce; a quite special dish of deep-fried foods, including seaweed, fresh bamboo shoots, mushrooms, and bits of fresh fish; a beggar's chicken, the chicken cooked in clay with its inner wrapping of lotus leaves and a savory filling of pork and onions; shark's fin soup; fried dumplings; and chili prawns (which is to say large shrimp in the shell in a spicy sauce). We found the Sea View version a bit too sweet.

The foods are all priced at about $2.50 to $3 or $4 a portion. It is at Amber Close.

If you are keen on Indian cooking, one of the grandest Indian meals you're apt to experience in Singapore (or elsewhere, for that matter) is at Omar Khayyam's on Hill Street, just opposite the American Embassy. It is a handsome restaurant with conservative, well-executed Indian art on the walls, and the food is said to be Northern in general, Kashmiri in particular. It is quite exceptional, starting with the chicken tikka, small bits of masterfully seasoned chicken breasts on skewers; and the shish kebabs, a coriander and onion flavored ground lamb specialty, also cooked in a tandoor on skewers. Among the main courses sampled, the "curried" dishes are well spiced and the management takes the caution when an order is taken of asking if a guest likes foods hot to the taste or mild in seasoning. The spicy hot dishes can be vouched for as authentically spirited, foods like shrimp in brown sauce and beef in a very thick yogurt creation. Both are interesting and good, first bite to last, as are the breads at Khayyam's, particularly the nan stuffed with a touch of chopped scallions and coriander.

Omar Khayyam's menu notes that its clientele on past occasions has included such dignitaries as the king and queen of Nepal, the president of Guyana, the prime ministers of Mauritius, Sri Lanka, and India, and Ravi Shankar. The cost of main courses is from about $2.50 to $3. The restaurant is at 55 Hill Street and the telephone number is 36-15-05.

Neither the Majestic nor the Peking restaurants, visited recently, seem nearly as worth visiting as their adherents claim them to be. They are mentioned in passing because both have a doting clientele. The Majestic's squab in lettuce and deep-fried batter-dipped crab claws were both so-so.

An extensive menu at the Peking started with assorted cold appetizers including prawns. In a mayonnaise sauce, of all things. There was Peking duck in which only the crisp and admirable skin was served (to our dismay, we will never know what happened to the rest of that fowl; when we asked, we were greeted with a curious stare); ginger beef with bamboo shoots and pea pods; and steamed breads. The Peking is very big with gaudy food garnishes including illuminated plastic fruits centered on most dishes and a plethora of maraschino cherries. Main courses at both the Majestic and Peking cost from about $2 to $8.

Another restaurant visited at the behest of Singaporeans is the Golden Phoenix of the Hotel Equatorial, a busily decorated room with the inevitable hanging lanterns, skeletonlike carvings of Phoenix birds, and little to distinguish it in atmosphere from a dozen other restaurants. The food is Szechwan and good. The dishes we dined on, with the exception of frogs' legs deep fried and garnished with ginger, were very much like similar fare we've admired in the Szechwan kitchens of New

York—hot and sour soup, stir-fried chicken with bean sauce and hot peppers, plus bean curd with ground meat and scallions in hot sauce. Superior but less than devastating. Main courses are priced from about $3.50 to $8; small portions from about $2.50 to $6.

At lunch the Chinese dining room of Shangri-La, Singapore's most distinguished hotel and least available because of its popularity, is cordially recommended, particularly the dem sem or "appetizers." Young women pass each table with a vast array of hot, freshly cooked, and vari-shaped dumplings in individual steamers, deep-fried foods such as shrimp, roast meats, and so on. These alone are enough to comprise a complete meal, but there is an à la carte menu as well with main courses priced from about $2 to $2.50.

The Jade Room here is well known and much touted. It, too, has well-made dem sem at midday. It is a vast barnlike structure with a large bandstand that juts from one room into the dining room. Even when there is no band, someone sits, or did recently, and played "Chopsticks," with or without a sense of humor for a good half hour. The main courses are, or were recently, mediocre, with the exception of fish in wine sauce with tree ears. Main courses from about $2 to $3.50.

December 1974

A S DECEMBER, the end of the year, is the universal time for summing up, we thought we would review the highlights of the year's food experiences. If we were to name the one kitchen happening that came about most forcefully since our return to *The Times,* it would be the fact of breadmaking. It came about through an interview with a friend in Washington, D.C., Clyde Brooks. We had rarely made bread until we met this gentleman, who is not only a great breadmaker but a fabricator of molds for shaping French loaves. Since that interview (pages 80–81) we have made dozens of loaves of French bread, and we now have a rather curious reaction to any store-bought loaf. We never put so much as half a teaspoon of sugar in our homemade bread; consequently, the store-bought variety tastes like cake.

Simultaneously, we were given a batch of sourdough starter and were told by the donor that the original batch from which ours was an offspring was more than 20 years old. It is alive and thriving, and with luck we will be writing about it for the next couple of decades.

Counting our blessings, we also remember in vivid detail some great fish soups (pages 65–67), some wonderful fruit ices (page 16), and two unforgettable meals at the restaurant Taillevent in Paris (pages 173–174). We remember with warmth the good food of Vietnam, that endlessly troubled land (pages 339–343). We remember learning, at long last, the difference between lox and nova (pages 165–166). And, numbered high among our blessings, we remember the kindness and generosity of all the chefs who came to our kitchen to cook and who have contributed so much to the readers of my cookbooks and of *The New York Times.*

P.S. As for our woes, we remember a lot of dreadful food served on airplanes on international flights; three successive land-based dinners where filet mignon was served (we prefer hamburger); and one meal where beef Wellington, the most pretentious of foods, was a principal dish.

Vietnamese Cookery

If any dish was ultimately responsible for a visit that entailed several thousand miles of travel to South Vietnam, it was cha gio, considered by many to be the national dish of the country. It is pronounced zhah-zhaw, and we first sampled it several years ago in a few of the flourishing Vietnamese restaurants of Paris.

Cha gio is a bit curious, perhaps a trifle exotic, by Western standards. It consists basically of morsels of ground meat, sometimes with chopped crab, shrimp, or chicken, wrapped in pastry and deep fried. These morsels, cooked to a golden brown, crisp without, tender within, are served hot at table with an assortment of fresh herbs including mint, basil, and fresh coriander; cold (Boston) lettuce leaves; and that ubiquitous Vietnamese sauce, nuoc mam. The pastries, glorified with fresh herbs, are wrapped in lettuce, dipped in the sauce, and eaten. Cha gio is as irresistible, in sum, as peanuts, popcorn, new radishes, fresh cider, and caviar. And cha gio is but one small savory fragment from the Vietnamese kitchen, which is among the most outstanding on earth.

Comparisons between the Vietnamese and Chinese tables are inevitable, and the relationships are wholly absorbing in that many of the raw materials are basically the same, while the techniques for using them are, more often than not, radically different. Both cuisines employ, among seasoning, fresh garlic, scallions, and fresh coriander; among vegetables, green peppers, bamboo shoots, pea pods, tree ear mushrooms, hot peppers, and the numerous derivatives of soy bean including cellophane noodles (or bean thread), bean curd, and bean sauce. Both use monosodium glutamate.

Whereas the Chinese employ vast quantities of cornstarch and soy sauce, neither is much used in Vietnam—North or South. Very few thickening agents are used, and the principal seasoning is nuoc mam (pronounced nook-mahm), a kind of fish essence used both as a flavoring ingredient and as a sauce into which foods are dipped at table.

There is much deep frying in Chinese cookery, and foods are also stir fried in oil. Foods such as cha gio are sometimes deep fried in Vietnam, but fats as a rule play a very small role in Vietnamese cookery. Shallots are rarely used in Chinese cookery; in Vietnam they are used abundantly.

One of the predominant characteristics of the Vietnamese kitchen is the broad use of fresh herbs and seasonings that include—in addition to mint—basil and coriander, scallions, and citronella, a lemon scented

In the bustling, flourishing food market in Saigon, Mrs. Doan Thi Hon selects shellfish and other provisions for dinner.

stalk that resembles a scallion in appearance and is sometimes called lemon grass. Two other herbs, widely employed, are tia to, known as melissa in English but little known in Western cookery; and rau diep ca, a fishy-smelling and much employed herb known in French as hou-theynie.

Vietnamese pork from carefully nurtured pigs is notable, some of the best in the world. The native chickens make an excellent broth and base for soups, but they tend to be a bit stringy. Dairy cattle are a rare commodity and, therefore, butter is almost unknown. Fish and shellfish in the regions where they are available are superlative. The crab and eel are exceptional in quality.

½ cup loosely packed fresh
   basil leaves
½ cup loosely packed fresh
   coriander leaves
40 Boston lettuce leaves
   Nuoc mam sauce (see
   recipe)

1. Place the tree ears in a bowl and add water to cover. Let stand to soften.

2. Place half the bean thread in another bowl and add warm water to cover. Let stand to soften. Reserve the remaining bean thread for future use.

3. Place the pork in a bowl and add the crab meat, monosodium glutamate, 1 teaspoon fish sauce, salt, pepper, garlic, onion, and chives.

4. Drain the tree ears and pat dry. Finely chop and add them to the pork mixture.

5. Drain the bean thread well. Chop coarsely. There should be about 1 cup loosely packed. Add this to the pork mixture.

6. Blend all the ingredients, kneading with the hands. Set aside.

7. Cut the rice paper rounds in half. Or cut the phyllo pastry in half widthwise. If the rice paper is available, brush each half generously with beer before using. If phyllo pastry is used, brush lightly with oil before using.

8. To prepare the cha gio, place about 3 or 4 teaspoons of filling toward the bottom half of the rice paper, phyllo pastry, or won ton skins. Roll, tucking the flaps as necessary. Brush the edges of the won ton skins, if used, with a little beaten egg or a cornstarch and water paste to help seal. Continue adding filling and rolling until all the filling is used.

9. Heat oil for deep frying in a deep fryer. It must not be too hot when the cha gio is added or the skins may break. Cook about a dozen at a time, turning them in the oil to brown evenly. Drain as they are cooked.

10. Serve the cha gio on a platter. Serve separately a combination of mint, basil, and coriander. Serve the lettuce leaves on a third platter. Let guests help themselves, filling one leaf at a time with mint, coriander, and basil leaves and one pastry. Dip into nuoc mam sauce before eating.

Yield: 35 to 40 cha gio. In Vietnam this is reckoned as 6 dinner servings or 10 or 12 appetizer servings.

Note: Rice paper is a very thin, white, translucent round sheet quite common in Vietnam. It is not generally available, if at all, in Western markets. Phyllo pastry is available in Greek grocery stores and in many other stores that specialize in delicacies. Won ton skins are widely available in Chinese groceries in Chinatown. The nuoc mam in Vietnam is generally stronger than the fish sauce easily found in Chinese groceries but the latter is a highly acceptable substitute.

Other garnishes commonly used in Vietnam for the cha gio include carambola, a sour-flavored, star-shaped vegetable resembling a cucumber with 5 pointed sides, and small, green

The Vietnamese are quick to advise that the native cookery is vided into three regions: that of Hanoi in the north; Hué in the cen and Saigon in the south. Of the three, the Northern is said to be the m delicate and refined; the foods are less salty and less spicy in taste. It said that North Vietnamese cookery uses more Chinese-related tec niques than the other regions.

On the other hand, the people of Hué, the old capital of kings, an the people of the central region in general enjoy highly spiced, very ho foods of a sort associated with curries. Hot peppers are much employed.

The Saigonese and South Vietnamese in general have more natural resources in foods including fish, both fresh- and salt-water, and game, including boar, deer, and roebuck. Sugar is also more frequently used as a limited seasoning in the South.

During our visit here we spent many hours in the market in Saigon and in the kitchen of a private home watching the ingenious prestidigitations of Mrs. Doan Thi Hon, a Southerner, and a cook par excellence. It was in her good company that, among other fine dishes, we learned the fine points of making cha gio and chao tom, which is shrimp paste grilled on sugar cane.

Cha Gio

(Deep-fried meat rolls in lettuce leaves)

8 or 9 tree ear mushrooms, available in Chinese grocery stores and supermarkets

1 2-ounce package bean thread (also called cellophane noodles, Chinese vermicelli, and so on), available in Chinese grocery stores and supermarkets

1 pound raw pork, ground or, preferably, chopped fine

½ cup chopped crab meat, raw shrimp, or boneless, skinless, raw chicken breast

¼ teaspoon monosodium glutamate, optional

1 teaspoon fish sauce (available in Chinese groceries and supermarkets) or nuoc mam (see recipe, page 249) Salt and freshly ground pepper to taste

½ teaspoon finely chopped garlic

¼ cup finely chopped red onion

2 tablespoons finely chopped chives

18 to 20 rounds of rice paper (see note), or use phyllo pastry or won ton skins

¼ cup beer Beaten egg or cornstarch and water paste, optional Fat for deep frying

½ cup loosely packed fresh mint leaves

bananas. The carambola is scraped, the banana peeled, and both are thinly sliced. Thinly sliced pineapple quarters may also be used as a garnish.

Chao Tom

(Grilled chopped
shrimp on sugar
cane or other skewers)

4   sugar cane sections, 4½ to
    5 inches in length
2   pounds raw shrimp,
    shelled and deveined
¼   pound unsalted pork fat
1   teaspoon chopped garlic
3   tablespoons finely chopped
    onion
½   teaspoon sugar
    Salt and freshly ground
    pepper to taste
    Nuoc mam sauce (see
    recipe, page 249)

1. Prepare a charcoal fire for grilling.

2. If sugar cane is available, use it; otherwise use wooden skewers. Peel the sugar cane and cut each length into quarters or eighths. There should be about 30 lengths. Using a sharp knife, smooth the sides of each piece. Set aside.

3. Place the shrimp on a flat surface and chop fine or blend to make a not too smooth paste. Chop or blend the pork fat to a smooth paste.

4. In a mixing bowl, combine the shrimp, pork fat, garlic, onion, sugar, and salt and pepper. Blend well with the fingers. The mixture will be very loose. Chill throughout or place briefly in the freezer until manageable. Do not freeze.

5. Scoop up about 3 tablespoons of the mixture at a time. Using lightly oiled fingers, shape each portion into oval shapes around the upper half of each piece of sugar cane. Grill over hot coals, rotating the skewers as often as necessary until cooked through, 6 to 8 minutes. Do not overcook or the shrimp will become too dry.

6. Serve with nuoc mam sauce on the side.

Yield: 6 to 10 servings.

Quiche Alsace

WITH PIERRE FRANEY

To many cooks, a quiche is a quiche Lorraine, that savory concoction of onions, cheese, bacon (or ham), eggs, and cream cooked in a flaky crust. But quiche is really the generic name for a host of non-sweet pies. One of the finest we know—an Alsatian meat pie—is made with ground veal or pork. It is an unusually tasty appetizer or luncheon dish.

Alsatian Meat Pie

Alsatian pastry for 1
10-inch pie (see recipe)
1 *pound lean leg or shoulder of veal, ground, or use an equal quantity of ground lean pork*
⅛ *pound ground lean pork (in addition to the above meat)*
   Salt and freshly ground pepper to taste
⅛ *teaspoon grated nutmeg*
2 *teaspoons butter*
1½ *tablespoons finely chopped shallots*
⅓ *cup finely chopped onion*
¾ *cup finely chopped mushrooms (about ⅛ pound)*
1 *whole egg*
1 *egg yolk*
1 *cup heavy cream*

1. Line a 10-inch tart tin (preferably a black, fluted-edge quiche pan with a removable bottom) with the pastry and chill it.

2. Preheat oven to 375 degrees.

3. Sprinkle the veal and/or pork with salt and pepper to taste and the nutmeg.

4. Heat the butter in a skillet and add the shallots and onion. Cook, stirring, until wilted and add the mushrooms. Cook 5 minutes, stirring frequently. Add the meat, stirring and breaking up lumps of meat with the side of a large metal spoon. Cook until most of the liquid is given up.

5. Beat the egg and yolk with a fork until well blended and add the cream and salt and pepper to taste. Blend well and add the mixture to the meat. Stir well.

6. Pour the mixture into the prepared pie shell and bake 15 minutes. Reduce the oven heat to 350 degrees. Bake 30 to 35 minutes longer or until the custard is set. Remove from the oven and let stand. Serve lukewarm or at room temperature.

Yield: 8 servings.

Alsatian pastry

2½ *cups flour*
¼ *pound butter*
   Salt to taste
6 *tablespoons well-chilled corn oil*

6 *tablespoons cold milk,*
approximately

1. Put the flour in a mixing bowl and place it in the freezer. Place the butter in the freezer and let both stand ½ hour or longer.

2. Remove the flour and cut the butter into bits adding it to the flour. Add salt to taste. Using the fingers or a pastry blender, cut the butter into the flour until the mixture is like coarse cornmeal.

3. Gradually add the oil, stirring with a 2-pronged fork. When blended, add the milk gradually, working the pastry with the hands until it forms a dough. Knead briefly and gather the dough into a ball. Wrap it in wax paper and chill at least 30 minutes.

4. Remove the dough from the refrigerator and place it on a lightly floured surface. Roll it out into a rectangle measuring about 12 by 6 inches.

5. Fold a third of the dough over toward the center. Fold the other side of the dough over toward the center, thus making a three-layer package of dough. Cover and refrigerate about ½ hour.

6. Roll out the dough once more on a lightly floured surface, sprinkling the surface with additional flour as necessary. Roll it into another rectangle. Fold the dough into thirds as before, cover and chill. The dough is now ready to be rolled into a circle for fitting into a 10-inch metal tart tin (preferably a black, fluted-edge quiche pan).

Yield: Enough pastry for a 10-inch pie plus a few trimmings.

Note: Black quiche pans are available at Bridge Kitchenware Corp., 212 East 52d Street, New York.

Pierre Franey, my colleague, had an uncle by marriage named Louis Hirth. By the time I met him, Uncle Louis, as we call him, must have been in his late seventies. He was a kind and gentle spirit whose passionate hobby was baking. He was a native of Alsace and that Alsatian meat pie was one of his great specialties.

A Fruitcake with Christmas Spirit

WITH PIERRE FRANEY

Although fruitcakes seem as American as pumpkin pie, they first came to this country with the early English settlers. Recently, in an attempt to trace the ancestry of a family fruitcake recipe that was given us years ago by a great aunt, we went browsing through *Mrs. Beeton's Book of Household Management*, first published in England in 1859. The dauntless Mrs. Beeton's Christmas Cake bore no resemblance to Nannie Craig's recipe, but then, a few pages later on, there was a recipe for Good Holiday Cake, which did indeed follow Nannie Craig's pattern—to a degree. Mrs. Beeton's recipe calls for two pounds of flour. Perish forbid! We prefer our Mississippi ancestress's version.

Nannie Craig's Fruitcake

½ cup (3½ ounces) chopped glacé cherries
1½ cups (10 to 12 ounces) chopped glacé pineapple
3 cups (15 ounces) seedless black raisins
1½ cups (8 ounces) dried black currants
2 cups (8 ounces) broken pecans
1½ cups (8 ounces) chopped blanched almonds
1 cup bourbon, cognac, or rum
2½ cups flour
½ pound butter
1¾ cups sugar
6 eggs, separated
2 teaspoons baking powder
¾ teaspoon baking soda
1½ teaspoons ground ginger
1½ teaspoons ground mace
1 tablespoon grated nutmeg
1 tablespoon cinnamon
1 cup orange juice
4 cups grated fresh coconut or 2 cups unsweetened dried coconut (available in health food outlets)
1 cup (12 ounces) fig preserves
½ cup quince, apricot, or grape jelly
   Quick fondant icing (see recipe), optional
   Candied fruits such as cherries, angelica, and so on for decorating the cake, optional

1. Combine the glacé cherries, pineapple, raisins, currants, pecans, and almonds in a mixing bowl and add ½ cup of bourbon,

cognac, or rum. Cover with plastic wrap and let stand overnight.

2. Preheat oven to 250 degrees.

3. Empty the fruits onto a flat surface and sprinkle with ½ cup of flour. Toss to coat the fruits and nuts and set aside.

4. Put the butter into the bowl of an electric mixer. Add the sugar and start beating first on low and then on high speed. Cream the mixture well until it is light colored. Beat in the egg yolks one at a time.

5. Meanwhile, combine the remaining 2 cups of flour with the baking powder, soda, ginger, mace, nutmeg, and cinnamon. Sift the dry ingredients together.

6. Gradually beat the flour mixture into the butter and sugar mixture. Gradually beat in the orange juice, remaining ½ cup of bourbon, cognac, or rum, coconut, fig preserves, and quince jelly. Fold in the floured fruit.

7. Beat the egg whites until they stand in stiff peaks. Fold them into the batter. This recipe yields about 4 quarts (16 cups) of batter.

8. Baking pans, of course, should always be prepared before adding the batter. Butter them well. Line them with a double layer of wax paper or one layer of parchment paper and grease the paper. If using Teflon-coated pans, butter the pan and line the bottom with a cutout of wax paper and butter. The batter may be portioned into pans of various sizes, but do not fill any pan full of batter, for it expands as it bakes.

Always leave about 1 inch of space from the top of the pan. This recipe was most recently tested with 2 standard 9-by-5-by-2-inch Teflon loaf pans plus 1 8½-by-4½-by-3-inch (6 cup) loaf pan (a 6 cup round tube pan could also be used).

9. Bake the cakes for 2½ hours and increase the heat to 275 degrees. Bake a total of about 3½ hours for the large loaf pans, a total of about 3¼ for the smaller ones. Cooking times will vary from oven to oven. The correct internal temperature for these cakes is 160 degrees when a meat thermometer is inserted.

10. When the cakes are removed from the oven, cool on a rack for at least 30 minutes, run a knife around the edges and while still warm invert them on a rack. They should not stick on the bottom, but if they do, scrape out the stuck portion and repair the bottom with that. Frost with icing and decorate, if desired, with candied fruit.

Yield: 1 2¼-pound loaf or 6-cup tube pan and 2 3-pound cakes.

Note: These cakes may be kept for days, weeks, and months before they are frosted. To keep them, store closely covered in a dry place. Douse them occasionally with a ¼ cup or so of bourbon, rum, or cognac.

Quick fondant icing

½   cup granulated sugar
2½ tablespoons white corn syrup

¼   *cup water*
1½ *cups confectioners' sugar*
1   *teaspoon egg white*
1   *teaspoon butter at room*
      temperature
      Bourbon, rum, or cognac

1. Combine the granulated sugar, corn syrup, and water in a saucepan and gradually bring to the boil, stirring until sugar is dissolved. Cook over moderate heat until mixture registers 236 to 238 degrees on a candy thermometer.

2. Have ready a pastry brush in a cup of cold water. As the syrup cooks, run the brush around the inside of the saucepan, wiping away sugar crystals that may form above the syrup. If not removed, these will cause crystals throughout the syrup. When the syrup is ready, pour it into another saucepan and let cool.

3. Place the saucepan into a skillet or larger saucepan with water. Bring the water to the boil. Stir the syrup until it is fluid.

4. Gradually add the confectioners' sugar into the syrup, stirring constantly. Stir until well blended and lukewarm. Do not overheat.

5. Beat in the egg white and butter and add enough bourbon, rum, or cognac to bring the icing to a spreadable consistency.

Yield: Sufficient icing for 1 fruitcake.

Mississippi Delta Eggnog

8 large eggs, separated
¾ cup granulated sugar
1 cup bourbon
½ cup heavy cream
   Nutmeg

1. Put the egg yolks and sugar into the bowl of an electric mixer and beat until light and lemon colored.

2. Gradually add the whisky, beating on low speed.

3. Whip the cream until stiff and fold it into the egg yolk mixture.

4. Whip the egg whites until stiff peaks form and fold them into the eggnog. Serve in goblets or mugs with a sprinkling of nutmeg on top.

Yield: 8 servings.

We grew up in a home where alcohol was permitted only once a year and that was at Christmas time. Mother was famous for her eggnog and no wonder—it was heavily spiked with bourbon. A dedicated Southerner, no other whiskey or anything as alien as rum or cognac would do. We remember Christmas as a very special time when everyone in the house, including children, got giddy.

A Real Christmas Pudding

By far the best-known English cookbook is Hannah Glasse's modestly titled *The Art of Cookery, Made Plain and Easy: Which far exceeds any Thing of the Kind ever published*. It is best known as the source—erroneous—of the phrase "First catch your hare." What Mrs. Glasse really indicated in her recipe was "Take your hare when it is cased, and make a pudding," the word in that "case" meaning to skin. Recently, in the midst of this glad and festive Yuletide season, we thumbed through the volume once more to reread Mrs. Glasse's recipe for A Yorkshire Christmas Pie, and reprint it forthwith. We hasten to add that it requires a very large oven.

"First," the author tells us, "make a good standing crust, let the wall and bottom be very thick; bone a turkey, a goose, a fowl, a partridge, and a pigeon. Season them all very well, take half an ounce of mace, half an ounce of nutmeg, a quarter of an ounce of cloves, and half an ounce of black pepper, all beat fine together, two large tablespoons of fat, and then mix them together.

"Open the fowls all down the back, and bone them; first the pigeon, then the partridge, cover them; then the fowl, then the goose, and then the turkey, which must be large; season them all well first, and lay them in the crust, so as it will look like a whole turkey; then have a hare ready cased, and wiped with a clean cloth.

"Cut it to pieces, that is, joint it; season it, and lay it as close as you can on one side; and on the other side woodcocks, moor-game, and what sort of wild fowl you can get. Season them well, and lay them close; put at least four pounds of butter into the pie, then lay on your lid, which must be a very thick one, and let it be well-baked. It must have a very hot oven and will take at least four hours.

"This crust will take a bushel of flour. In this chapter you will see how to make it. These pies are often sent to London in a box as presents; therefore the walls must be well built."

Much more practical, to our thinking, is a sober-minded rum-soaked and excellent plum pudding attributed to a cook of King George V of England.

We came by this recipe from Mrs. Sam S. Emison of Houston, who told us she has been using it each Christmas for the last 40 years, served with a hard sauce of her own creation. Mrs. Emison prepared enough of these puddings to serve 200 assembled guests at a special pre-Christmas celebration attended last evening by Friends of Fondren Library at Rice University in Houston. The pudding, she notes, is best flamed with 151-proof rum, in that lower-proof rums do not burn readily.

The pudding is good if made only a few days before Christmas. It freezes well and is an elegant dessert for any special occasion throughout the winter.

Christmas Plum Pudding King George V

1½ teaspoons salt
1 teaspoon baking powder
1 tablespoon allspice
4 teaspoons ground ginger
½ teaspoon grated nutmeg
½ pound (2 cups) all-purpose flour
1 pound seeded raisins
4 ounces mixed candied peel, cut-up
1 pound currants
1 pound sultanas (golden seedless raisins)
6 ounces whole raw almonds, blanched and chopped or sliced
1 pound dry bread crumbs
1 pound ground suet
1 pound brown sugar
1 pound winesap apples, peeled, cored and finely cubed (weigh apples after peeled and cored)
Grated rind of 1 lemon
½ cup dark rum
6 to 8 eggs (1⅓ cups) well beaten
¾ cup (approximately) 151-proof rum
Hard sauce (see recipe)

Mrs. Sam S. Emison surveys her George V Christmas plum pudding and hard sauce.

1. In mixing bowl, combine the salt, baking powder, allspice, ginger, nutmeg, and flour. Sift 7 times.

2. Separate the seeded raisins and drop them one by one into the flour. Add candied peel and mix well, working with fingers until separated and well coated with flour.

3. Put the currants, sultanas, almonds, bread crumbs, suet, brown sugar, cubed apples, lemon rind, and flour mixture in a large container, approximately 4 gallons capacity. Mix thoroughly with hands, reaching to bottom of pot and lifting up. Then add ½ cup dark rum and mix thoroughly. Add beaten eggs and again mix thoroughly. Mixture will be damp and crumbly. Let stand overnight. Makes about 9¼ pounds.

4. Divide into 3 greased bowls. If necessary, contents may be rounded above top of bowl. Cover tightly with foil. Do not mash down. Pudding will shrink in volume as cooked.

5. Place each bowl on a high trivet in a heavy pot containing 1 inch of water. The bottom of bowl should be above water. Cover the pot closely. Use high heat first, then as steam begins to escape, lower heat just enough so steam will not escape. Steam 8 hours, adding more water if required.

6. After steaming, set aside at room temperature overnight to cool. Remove from bowl. Wrap in foil with double-lock seal. Age in refrigerator. The pudding will keep several months in refriger-ator, or may be frozen and stored indefinitely.

7. To serve, turn each pudding out on a flat plate. Pour approximately ¼ cup 151-proof rum on each plate around the pudding. Light and ladle flaming rum over pudding. When burned away, serve with hard sauce. The rum should burn about 1 minute, as it slightly toasts the surface of the pudding. Use 151-proof rum. Lower proofs do not burn readily.

Yield: 3 puddings serve 50 people.

Hard sauce

½   *pound (1 cup) butter*
1   *pound (4 cups sifted) confectioners' sugar*
1   *(2 tablespoons) egg white*
1½ *tablespoons dark rum*
2½ *tablespoons cognac*
1   *teaspoon vanilla*

1. Cream butter and add 2 cups sugar and egg white alternately. Beat well after each addition.

2. Beat in remaining sugar and rum and cognac alternately, beating well after each addition. Add the vanilla. Store in a screw-top jar. Serve at room temperature.

Yield: 4 cups or 16 servings.

Hot Spiced Cider

New York is famous for its apple cider, produced throughout the state wherever apples are grown. We buy cider at a friendly stand, the immaculate Milk Pail, by the side of the road near Water Mill out on the Montauk Highway. Recently the owners provided us with their recipe for hot spiced cider, delicious by itself late in the afternoon on a cold winter's day. A jigger of rum makes it more like Christmas or New Year's Eve.

2 *quarts fresh apple cider*
3 *slices fresh lemon*
2 *tablespoons honey*
1 *2-inch piece of stick cinnamon*
6 *whole cloves*

1. Combine all the ingredients in a saucepan and bring to the boil. Cover and simmer 10 minutes.

2. Strain into hot mugs. Add jigger of rum to each serving if desired.

Yield: 8 servings.

Sources for Foreign Ingredients

The stores listed below accept mail orders; some of them make catalogues available for that purpose. When making inquiries, find out if there is a minimum mail order charge. Order by mail only if the ingredients you need are unavailable in your community. In urban areas, ethnic foods are usually not hard to find.

Caribbean, South American, and Mexican

District of Columbia
Pena's Spanish Store
1636 17th Street, N.W.
Washington 20009

Illinois
La Preferida, Inc.
177–181 West South Water Market
Chicago 60608

Louisiana
Central Grocery Company
923 Decatur Street
New Orleans 70116

Massachusetts
Cardullo's Gourmet Shop
6 Brattle Street
Cambridge 02138

Michigan
La Paloma-Tenorio and Company
2620 Bagley Street
Detroit 48216

New York
Casa Moneo Spanish Imports
210 West 14th Street
New York 10011

Ohio
Spanish and American Food Market
7001 Wade Park Avenue
Cleveland 44103

Chinese

California
Wing Chong Lung Co.
922 South San Pedro Street
Los Angeles 90015

District of Columbia
Tuck Cheong Company
617 H Street, N.W.
Washington 20001

Illinois
Star Market
3349 North Clark Street
Chicago 60657

Massachusetts
Wing Wing Imported Groceries
79 Harrison Avenue
Boston 02111

New York
Yuet Hing Market, Inc.
23 Pell Street
New York 10013

Texas
Oriental Import-Export Company
2009 Polk Street
Houston 77003

Indian

California
Haig's
441 Clement Street
San Francisco 94119

Michigan
   Delmar and Company
   501 Monroe Avenue
   Detroit 48226
New York
   Kalustyan Orient Export
   Trading Corporation
   123 Lexington Avenue
   New York 10016
Texas
   Antone's
   Box 3352
   Houston 77001
Washington
   House of Rice
   4112 University Way
   Northeast
   Seattle 98105

Indonesian

California
   Holland American Market
   10343 East Artesia Boulevard
   Bellflower 90706
District of Columbia
   Tuck Cheong
   617 H Street, N.W.
   Washington 20001
Illinois
   Mee Jun Emporium
   2223 Wentworth Avenue
   Chicago 60616
New York
   Toko Garuda
   997 First Avenue
   New York 10022
Ohio
   Sun Lee Yuen
   1726 Payne Avenue
   Cleveland 44114
Pennsylvania
   Yick Fung Imports
   210 North 9th Street
   Philadelphia 19107

Italian

California
   R. Fazzi and Co.
   225 South Spring Street
   Los Angeles 90027
Florida
   Joseph Assi's Imported Foods
   3316 Beach Boulevard
   Jacksonville 32207
Indiana
   Guy Montani Fine Foods
   12 West 27th Street
   Indianapolis 46208
New York
   Manganaro Brothers
   488 Ninth Avenue
   New York 10018
Tennessee
   Barzizza Bros. Inc.
   351 South Front Street
   Memphis 38103
Texas
   Cappello's
   5328 Lemmon Avenue
   Dallas 75209

Japanese

California
   Enbun Company
   248 East First Street
   Los Angeles 90012
Colorado
   Pacific Mercantile Company
   1946 Larimer Street
   Denver 80202
Illinois
   Diamond Trading Company
   1108 North Clark Street
   Chicago 60610
Louisiana
   Oriental Trading Company
   2636 Edenborn Avenue
   Metairie 70002

Massachusetts
   Yoshinoya
   36 Prospect Street
   Cambridge 02139

Missouri
   Maruyama's
   100 North 18th Street
   St. Louis 63103

New York
   Katagiri Company
   224 East 59th Street
   New York 10022

Ohio
   Soya Food Products
   2356 Wyoming Avenue
   Cincinnati 45214

Middle Eastern

California
   Mediterranean and Middle
   East Import Company
   233 Valencia Street
   San Francisco 94103

Louisiana
   Progress Grocery Company
   915 Decatur Street
   New Orleans 70116

Massachusetts
   Cardullo's Gourmet Shop
   6 Brattle Street
   Cambridge 02138

Michigan
   American Oriental Grocery
   20736 Lahser Road
   Southfield 48075

Missouri
   Demmas Shish-Ke-Bab
   5806 Hampton Avenue
   St. Louis 63109

New York
   Malko Brothers
   197 Atlantic Avenue
   Brooklyn 11201

Tennessee
   Barzizza Brothers, Inc.
   351 South Front Street
   Memphis 38103

Washington
   Angelo Merlino and Sons
   816 Sixth Avenue South
   Seattle 98134

Vietnamese

Virginia
   Viet Nam Center, Inc.
   3133 Wilson Boulevard
   Arlington 22201

Specialty Shops

New York
   H. Roth and Son
   1577 First Avenue
   New York 10028

   Paprikas Weiss
   1546 Second Avenue
   New York 10028

Kitchenware

New York
   The Bridge Kitchenware
   Corp.
   212 East 52nd Street
   New York 10022

California
   Williams–Sonoma
   576 Sutter Street
   San Francisco 94102

Index